Counting Matters

Counting Matters
Policy, Practice, and the Limits of Gender Equality Measurement in Canada

Edited by Christina Gabriel and L. Pauline Rankin

UBCPress · Vancouver

Printed in Canada on FSC-certified ancient-forest-free paper (100% post-consumer recycled) that is processed chlorine- and acid-free.

UBC Press is a Benetech Global Certified Accessible™ publisher. The epub version of this book meets stringent accessibility standards, ensuring it is available to people with diverse needs.

Library and Archives Canada Cataloguing in Publication

Title: Counting matters : policy, practice, and the limits of gender equality measurement in Canada / edited by Christina Gabriel and L. Pauline Rankin.
Names: Gabriel, Christina, editor. | Rankin, L. Pauline, editor.
Description: Includes bibliographical references and index.
Identifiers: Canadiana (print) 20230577245 | Canadiana (ebook) 20230577318 | ISBN 9780774870160 (hardcover) | ISBN 9780774870177 (softcover) | ISBN 9780774870191 (EPUB) | ISBN 9780774870184 (PDF)
Subjects: LCSH: Sex discrimination against women – Research – Canada. | LCSH: Sex role – Research – Canada. | LCSH: Equality – Research – Canada. | LCSH: Women – Social conditions – Research – Canada.
Classification: LCC HQ1075.5.C3 C68 2024 | DDC 305.3072—dc23

UBC Press gratefully acknowledges the financial support for our publishing program of the Government of Canada, the Canada Council for the Arts, and the British Columbia Arts Council.

This book has been published with the help of a grant from the Canadian Federation for the Humanities and Social Sciences, through the Scholarly Book Awards, using funds provided by the Social Sciences and Humanities Research Council of Canada.

UBC Press is situated on the traditional, ancestral, and unceded territory of the xʷməθkʷəy̓əm (Musqueam) people. This land has always been a place of learning for the xʷməθkʷəy̓əm, who have passed on their culture, history, and traditions for millennia, from one generation to the next.

UBC Press
The University of British Columbia
www.ubcpress.ca

We dedicate this book to Kate McInturff

Contents

Acknowledgments

This volume is dedicated to the memory of Dr. Kate McInturff, who sadly passed away in 2018. An Ottawa-based feminist activist, she fought ceaselessly for gender equality and women's rights. She understood the power and politics of measurement: she wielded numbers and statistics to address gendered wage gaps, occupational segregation, violence against women, and the need for financial support of women's organizations. As a policy analyst at the Canadian Centre for Policy Alternatives, she developed the initiative "Making Women Count." In *The Best and Worst Places to Be a Woman in Canada 2017,* she presciently wrote, "Statistics will never be a substitute for the full experience of lives lived. But as signposts they mark the spot where more attention is needed from our leaders, our policy-makers, and our communities. They point the way toward progress – down paths as unique as the cities in this report" (McInturff 2017, 7). Our thinking on gender equality measurement was influenced by Kate's insightful analyses, and it is our hope that this volume continues the important research agenda she pursued with such conviction.

The impetus for this project derived from our participation in a Carleton-based research group that explored questions related to gender equality measurement. We benefited greatly from its activities and the conversations and collaborations with our inspiring (and fun) cluster colleagues Doris Buss, Diana Majury, Lisa Mills, and Susan Philips. Our cluster was funded by the Carleton Research Excellence Fund, an opportunity generously supported by the Office of the Vice-President (Research and International) at Carleton University.

This volume took much longer to complete than either of us anticipated, as life and work intervened in many unanticipated ways. We would like to thank each of the contributors for their patience. We are so grateful to them for sticking with this project over the years and for their willingness to update their contributions as timelines stretched far beyond our original goals.

Thanks to our UBC editor Randy Schmidt for guiding the manuscript through the approval process and to former UBC editor Emily Andrew for her encouragement in the very early stages of the proposal. Sincere thanks to the anonymous reviewers as well for their detailed assessments and rigorous critical insights; their comments and suggestions improved the final draft. We also acknowledge the excellent and capable research assistance of Veronica Överlid and the tireless administrative support of Cheryl Murphy. Additionally, we are grateful for the Research Completion Grant supplied by the Office of the Dean, Faculty of Public Affairs, which facilitated the completion of the project.

Lastly, we thank our friends, family, and colleagues who supported us over the course of the project. In particular, Christina would like to thank William Walters for his patience, constant support, and love. Pauline thanks Patrizia Gentile, who, as always, offered an endless supply of love and encouragement.

Work Cited

McInturff, Kate. 2017. *The Best and Worst Places to Be a Woman in Canada 2017: The Gender Gap in Canada's 25 Biggest Cities.* Ottawa: Canadian Centre for Policy Alternatives, 2017. https://policyalternatives.ca/sites/default/files/uploads/publications/National%20Office/2017/10/Best%20and%20Worst%20Places%20to%20Be%20a%20Woman%202017.pdf.

Abbreviations

CEDAW	Convention on the Elimination of All Forms of Discrimination against Women
CGE	computable general equilibrium
CIDA	Canadian International Development Agency
CIHI	Canadian Institute of Health Information
CIHR	Canadian Institutes of Health Research
CIRI	Cingranelli-Richards Human Rights Dataset
CSPS	Canada School of Public Service
CUSMA	Canada–United States–Mexico Agreement
CVI	community vitality index
DAC	Development Assistance Committee
DFATD	Department of Foreign Affairs, Trade and Development
ETUC	European Trade Union Confederation
EU	European Union
FTA	free trade agreement
GAC	Global Affairs Canada
GBA	gender-based analysis
GBA+	gender-based analysis plus
GDI	Gender-Related Development Index
GE	gender equality
GEI	Gender Equity Index
GEM	Gender Empowerment Measure
GGI	Global Gender Gap Index
GII	Gender Inequality Index
GRF	Gender Results Framework

HCA	health care aide
HV-GB	Happy Valley–Goose Bay, NL
ILO	International Labour Organization
IPU	Inter-Parliamentary Union
LEAF	Women's Legal Education and Action Fund
LPN	licensed practical nurse
LTRC	long-term residential care
MDGs	millennium development goals
Mercosur	Mercado Común del Sur
MIPEX	Migrant Integration Policy Index
MNCH	maternal, newborn, and child health
MP	Member of Parliament
NAC	National Action Committee on the Status of Women
NAFTA	North American Free Trade Agreement
OECD	Organisation for Economic Co-operation and Development
RAI-MDS	Resident Assessment Instrument–Minimum Data Set
RN	registered nurse
SCSW	Standing Committee on the Status of Women
SDGs	sustainable development goals
SGBA	sex- and gender-based analysis
SGMG	Sex/Gender Methods Group
SIGI	Social Institutions and Gender Index
SMEs	small- and medium-sized enterprises
SRHR	sexual and reproductive health and rights
SWC	Status of Women Canada
TUC	Trades Union Congress
UN	United Nations
UNCTAD	United Nations Conference on Trade and Development
UNDP	United Nations Development Programme
VAW	violence against women
WAGE	Women and Gender Equality Canada
WEF	World Economic Forum
WP	Women's Program
WTO	World Trade Organization

Counting Matters

Introduction

Maggie FitzGerald, Christina Gabriel,
and L. Pauline Rankin

INTRODUCED IN 2010, the United Nations Gender Inequality Index (GII), which encompasses measures on reproductive health, empowerment, and economic inclusion, is often used as a way to gauge a country's progress toward gender equality (UNDP n.d.). Although Canada occupied first place in the Human Development Index of 1995, its GII rating had dropped dramatically to twenty-fifth out of 155 countries by 2016.[1] This decline prompted Canadian women's groups to call upon the newly elected Liberal government of self-described feminist Justin Trudeau to make good on its promises to address gender equality (Glenza 2016). The GII, however, is only one of many gender equality reports. Others include the World Economic Forum's Global Gender Gap Report, Social Watch's Gender Equity Index, and the United Nations (UN) Committee on the Elimination of Discrimination against Women review. In short, as many scholars have noted, mechanisms that track, measure, and report on gender equality have proliferated enormously, giving women's movements a dizzying array of indices on which to focus.

However, a paradox has arisen here: on the one hand, this turn to measurement can be seen as speaking to a broader trend of support for gender equality issues (see, for example, Pew Research Center 2020); on the other hand, it is also "representative of the kind of quantitative policy world to which gender equality politics has been reduced" (Runyan and Peterson 2014, 127). Feminists have problematized this paradox at the global scale (Liebowitz and Zwingel 2014; Merry 2016). The rise of gender equality measurement, and the certainty with which equality is assumed to be quantifiable, prompts complex questions about epistemology, political change, policy innovation, and feminist research. Ironically, though gender equality measurement has become a vibrant field for gender consultants, scholars have paid little attention to gender measurement as a distinct policy and social phenomenon.

In this volume, we approach this development through an examination of the turn to measurement in gender policy, practice, and politics in Canada. We consider the ways in which measurement culture is implicated in a variety of domains and scales, from formal politics to care work. The chapters in this collection provide a snapshot of how gender equality measurement has unfolded in Canada: How is gender equality measured in differing policy areas? How can we attempt to improve practices? What is revealed by examining and critiquing the "technical turn" in policies that promote gender equality? What are the practical and theoretical limitations of measurement?

The Rise of Indicator Culture: Measurement, Knowledge, and Governance

The ubiquitousness of measurement in policy and practice is part of a broader international trend that a number of scholars have flagged. In the 1990s, Michael Power (1994) used the term "audit explosion" in referring to the growth of auditing practices in the United Kingdom. Power (2000, 111) linked their emergence to three imperatives: "the rise of the 'new public management'; increased demands for accountability and transparency; [and] the rise of quality assurance models of organizational control." A few years later, Cris Shore and Susan Wright (2015) advanced the analytic concept of an "audit culture" as a rationality of governance (see also Strathern 2000). As Shore and Wright (2015, 422) explain, "audit culture refers to contexts where auditing has become a central organizing principle of society." The authors note that techniques and instruments – be they quantitative indicators or performance measures associated with actuarial science and the corporate realm – have multiplied to the extent that "institutions are reshaped according to the criteria and methods used to measure them; and organizations and people are transformed into 'auditable' entities that focus their energies on doing 'what counts'" (423). To put it differently, the arrival of an audit culture has affected how governance occurs and is also implicated in the growth of international agencies that specialize in various forms of measurement expertise (Shore and Wright 2015, 426–27).

In a similar vein, Sally Engle Merry (2011, 2016) has written about the spread of indicators and indicator culture as a key dimension of a broader measurement regime. Merry (2011, S86) defines indicators as "statistical measures that are used to consolidate complex data into a simple number or rank that is meaningful to policy makers and the public. They tend to ignore individual specificity and context in favor of superficial but standardized knowledge." Kevin Davis, Benedict Kingsbury, and Sally Engle Merry (2012, 73–74) elaborate:

An indicator is a named collection of rank-ordered data that purports to represent the past or projected performance of different units. The data are generated through a process that simplifies raw data about a complex social phenomenon. The data, in this simplified and processed form, are capable of being used to compare particular units of analysis (such as countries, institutions, or corporations), synchronically or over time, and to evaluate their performance by reference to one or more standards.

Merry (2011) further points out how indicators are implicated in global reform initiatives and global governance. In particular, she makes two critical observations. First, in relation to the production of knowledge, she notes that indicators provide numerical measures without the specifics of context or history that can be ranked and compared. Merry (2011, S84) argues, "This knowledge is presented as objective and often as scientific. The interpretations lurk behind the numbers but are rarely presented explicitly." Second, and importantly, she highlights the role that indicators play in governance, as the knowledge they produce plays a part in decision making: "They influence the allocation of resources, the nature of political decisions ... They facilitate governance by self-management rather than command. Individuals and countries are made responsible for their own behavior as they seek to comply with the measures of performance articulated in an indicator" (S85). In other words, much like various auditing practices, indicator culture involves the abstraction of information from context and the mobilization of this information in a way that has generative effects in terms of behaviours and knowledge production. The terms "audit culture" and "indicator culture" speak to and emphasize the ways in which these measurement techniques have proliferated globally and have become enmeshed in knowledge production and governance.

This rapid increase in the development, circulation, and valorization of measurement is linked in part to the embrace of neo-liberal governing paradigms by many states in the global North. Indeed, as Shore and Wright (2015, 430) state, though regimes of audit are not unique to neo-liberalism, there is an affinity between the two: "the characteristics of this new order include all of neo-liberalism's key ingredients – including 'governing at a distance'; a relentless pursuit of economic efficiency; deregulation, outsourcing, and privatization; marketization and the privileging of competition over cooperation." The turn to measurement and the broader rise of audit and indicator culture, then, are neither neutral, technical, nor apolitical. As many have noted, neo-liberal paradigms are now treated as common sense. Judy Brown (2015, 432) writes, "As neoliberal logic has become increasingly sedimented ... it is perhaps unsurprising that many people cannot see how things could be different ... People are understandably hesitant to look as though they are *against* accountability, efficiency, and good governance, albeit that the real issue is arguably the need to contest the meanings ascribed to these concepts under neoliberalism and the related marginalization of other values (e.g., social justice, democratic participation, ecological sustainability)."

This volume, therefore, responds to this call to contest and problematize the meanings ascribed to measurement and, specifically, the measurement of gender equality in Canada.

Measuring Gender Equality: The International Context

Although it has long been acknowledged that measurement and quantification processes – regarding who and what to measure and determining "what counts" (Waring 1999) – are gendered, the upsurge of audit and indicator culture involves a further *explicit* gender component in that there is now a global push to measure gender (in)equality. The impetus for this can perhaps be traced to the Convention on the Elimination of All Forms of Discrimination against Women (CEDAW). Adopted in 1979 by the UN General Assembly, CEDAW is often described as "an international bill of rights for women" (UN Women 2009) in that it defines what constitutes discrimination against women and provides an agenda for ending it. Thus, as Debra Liebowitz and Susanne Zwingel (2014, 362) summarize, CEDAW "articulates a set of norms that prohibit all forms of discrimination, against all groups of women, in all spheres of life ... and 'achieving gender equality' is on the agenda of all major international institutions." To date, 187 countries – the vast majority of the 194 UN member nations – have ratified CEDAW (UN Treaty Collection 2019). Following CEDAW, the report from the UN Third World Conference on Women, held in Nairobi in 1986, noted explicitly that "a lack of reliable data prevents the assessment of relative improvement in women's status" and called for greater cooperation among UN institutions in the "collection, analysis, utilization and dissemination of statistical data on the question of women" (United Nations 1986, 84).

Corresponding to this commitment to addressing gender inequality at the international level is the need to measure and evaluate progress toward gender equality; to this end, international organizations have established various gender (in)equality indicators. Gender inequality indices are typically intended to quantify aspects of gender-based inequality, thereby painting a portrait of inequality in differing countries and contexts, with the goal of supplying a means to compare, contrast, and rank countries and their level of gender-based inequality. Table I.1 provides examples of some prominent indices.

Table I.1

Quantitative measures of gender (in)equality

Publisher	Name of measure	Number of indicators or indices
United Nations	Millennium development goal 3: Promote gender equality and empower women	3
United Nations	Sustainable development goal 5: Achieve gender equality and empower all women and girls	14
UN Development Programme	Gender Inequality Index (GII)	5
Organisation for Economic Co-operation and Development	Social Institutions and Gender Index	12
World Economic Forum	Global Gender Gap Index (GGI)	14
Social Watch	Gender Equity Index (GEI)	11
Cingranelli-Richards	Cingranelli-Richards Human Rights Data Project (CIRI)	27
WomanStats	WomanStats	55
European Institute for Gender Equality	Gender Equality Index	8
World Bank	Women, Business and the Law	24
Economist Intelligence Unit	Women's Economic Opportunity Index	29

Sources: Adapted from Liebowitz and Zwingel (2014), using European Institute for Gender Equality (2015); UN Statistics Division (2016)

Although such indicators are useful because they can assist in the identification of broad trends and can give visibility to a range of issues that exacerbate gender inequality (see, for example, Johnson 2015; Walby 2005), "the limits of the information produced by quantitative measures must be made transparent" (Liebowitz and Zwingel 2014, 364). These limits, importantly, entail more than the literal accuracy of indicators; rather, they refer to the ways in which quantification is always-already a political and social process, steeped in and shaped by relations of power. As Merry (2016, 5) writes,

indicators are part of a regime of power based on the collection and analysis of data and their representation. It is important to see who is creating the indicators, where these people come from, and what forms of expertise they have. Rather than revealing truth, indicators create it. However, the result is not simply a fiction but a particular way of dividing up and making known one reality among many possibilities.

The epistemic consequences of the political and social nature of quantification point toward numerous limitations. Although dominant discourses construct indicators, quantification processes, and counting as objective (Liebowitz and Zwingel 2014, 364),[2] they are not apolitical representations of reality. Instead, they come to produce and construct that which they purport to measure. Furthermore, value becomes ascribed to that which is easy to measure. Key issues and complex social relations are rendered invisible while simplified and decontextualized information gains currency as it circulates in the indicator ecology. In this process, the gap between what is measured and the complex realities that comprise our lives is also obfuscated (Parisi 2009), as are the political and social aspects of the measurement process itself. In this way, measurement regimes serve as important epistemic frames in that they determine, to some degree, "*what* can be known at any given time, as well as *how* this knowledge can be used" (Poovey 1998, 7, emphasis in original). Consequently, "measurement is never an innocent act" (Buss 2015, 381, quoting Mohr and Ghaziani 2014, 237), although this fact becomes lost in the authority of the final numbers (Buss 2015).

The Canadian Case

In Canada, the advancement of gender equality has been on the federal state's policy agenda for several decades, largely in response to pressure from women's groups and feminist organizations. In 1967, for instance, Ottawa acknowledged women's claims of inequality by creating the Royal Commission on the Status of Women, which ultimately produced 167 recommendations for government action in its 1970 report (Canada 1970). Although the commission did not call for the adoption of indicators, its report did note the limitations of the available economic indicators such as the gross national product, particularly with respect to women's role in the economy (Canada 1970, 19).

In 1971, in the aftermath of the commission report, a coordinator on the status of women was appointed in the Privy Council Office to oversee cabinet's response to the commission, and an Office of Equal Opportunity was also established (Bergqvist and Findlay 1999). The following year, women's groups banded together and founded the National Action Committee on the Status of Women (NAC), whose purpose was to monitor Ottawa's implementation of the report's recommendations (Gabriel and Macdonald 2005, 74–75; Vickers, Rankin, and

Appelle 1993). This gender-based infrastructure (Brodie 2008) expanded with the establishment of a variety of women's policy mechanisms that were mandated to monitor gender equality, including the Canadian Advisory Council on the Status of Women, an arm's-length organization formed in 1973 and designed to liaise between the federal government and women's groups, and Ottawa's interdepartmental coordinating agency, Status of Women Canada (SWC), created in 1976 (Brodie 2008, 153). Although SWC finally became a federal government department in 2018 when it was renamed Women and Gender Equality Canada, it still serves as the "national machinery for gender equality" (Hankivsky 2013, 634). Taken together, these various institutional structures – sometimes deemed the "Women's State" (Paterson 2010) – allowed Canada to emerge "as a leader among Western welfare states with respect to the development of policies and agendas designed to promote women's equality and to open spaces for equality-seeking groups in the policy process" (Brodie 2008, 153).

Throughout the decades, lobbying by women's groups for gender equality and the equity-seeking agenda pursued by the women's policy machinery were bolstered by data from other quarters of the Canadian government. Monitoring women's participation in the paid workforce, for example, had been undertaken much earlier by the Women's Bureau, which was established in 1954 in the Department of Labour. During the early 1970s, Statistics Canada began to estimate the "volume and value of unpaid household work" in response to a need for "more accurate measures of economic activity and well-being" (Zukewich 2003, 9). By 1985, Statistics Canada had adopted the General Social Survey on Time Use to estimate the value of unpaid household work. That same year, it also released the first edition of *Women in Canada: A Statistical Report* "to aid the continuing discussion and evaluation of the changing roles and social characteristics of Canadian women as well as contribute to the development of policies concerning the status of women in Canada" (Statistics Canada 1985, iii).

Despite advances in the availability of data and, indeed, the reputation of Statistics Canada as an international leader in the field of gender statistics, Ottawa's efforts to address gender equality were subject to various limitations. As Christina Gabriel and Laura Macdonald (2005, 76) argue, for instance, SWC's original efficacy was limited given its designation as a stand-alone agency that did not occupy an influential position in the state's institutional matrix. Whenever a new party wins an election, this change can render strategies and infrastructures designed to address gender equality more or less effective. As Olena Hankivsky (2013, 639) maintains, whether gender equality initiatives succeed in gaining traction is "so often dependent on the political commitment of governments of the day." Several scholars demonstrate that this held true for SWC and other departments and agencies whose purpose was to advance gender equality; when governments changed, so too did the prioritization and funding of certain issues (see, for example, Brodie 2008; Gabriel and Macdonald 2005; Tiessen and Carrier 2015).

A renewed interest in and commitment to addressing gender inequality was catalyzed by Canada's participation in the UN's Fourth World Conference on Women, the Beijing Conference, in 1995 (Paterson 2010). In particular, the Beijing Conference cemented the policy strategy of gender mainstreaming as a crucial avenue for addressing gender inequality at the international level. Although the approaches to gender mainstreaming vary from state to state (see, for example, Hankivsky 2013), it is generally understood to be "a globally accepted policy strategy that promotes the assessment of institutions, legislation, policies, and programs to determine their potential or real gendered impacts with the ultimate goal of advancing gender equality" (Hankivsky 2013, 631). As a result, it requires a commitment to measurement: measuring and evaluating how policies, political processes, and institutions contribute to or alleviate gender inequality; measuring and evaluating the efficacy of initiatives implemented to address the inequality; and measuring and evaluating the overall situation of unequal gender relations in a given context.

In Canada, gender mainstreaming at the government level first took the form of gender-based analysis (GBA), which stems from the idea that "social impact analysis, including gender analysis, is not just an add-on, to be considered after costs and benefits have been assessed, but an integral part of good policy analysis. GBA identifies how public policies differentially affect women and men" (SWC 1995, 16). In 1995, Ottawa pledged to implement GBA in all its departments and agencies – with SWC playing a key part in the roll out and monitoring of its success. SWC pursued several avenues of gender mainstreaming work, including on economic gender equality indicators (SWC 1997). The initial implementation strategies were varied and mixed, as individual units attempted to develop their own approaches to gender mainstreaming and GBA (Rankin and Wilcox 2004, 55). As L. Pauline Rankin and Krista Wilcox (2004) explain, this was unsurprising given that the capacity of SWC to monitor developments was compromised by both insufficient resources and a lack of clout within the state infrastructure.

In 1999, a more centralized approach to GBA emerged as SWC and the newly established GBA Directorate developed a six-point strategy – encompassing training, tool development, policy case studies, research and education, evaluation and accountability, and coordination – for the widespread application of GBA (Brodie 2008, 157). As Francesca Scala and Stephanie Paterson (2017) suggest, GBA in this form consisted of an expert-bureaucratic approach – that is, an integrationist approach that introduced gender issues to policy processes and paradigms without questioning either the paradigms or their founding assumptions (Lombardo 2005, 415). It was organized around a hub-and-spoke model, with authority extending from the hub to various spokes. Despite this effort, however, a 2005 report released by the House of Commons Standing Committee on the Status of Women (2005) found that GBA remained at the margins of most departmental activities.

Many feminists were not surprised by these findings, as feminist activists and scholars had criticized the implementation of gender mainstreaming, including GBA, on a number of fronts. Christina Gabriel (2017, 183) notes that the "disjuncture between theoretical conceptualizations of policy analysis and how gender analysis is actually practiced" limits the potential for gender mainstreaming strategies such as GBA to address gender inequality, as the expert-bureaucratic approach fails to alter policy paradigms, raising questions about the "ability of the model to promote wider social transformation." Stephanie Paterson (2010), on the other hand, emphasizes the fact that the lack of a compliance mechanism resulted in uneven applications of GBA. Petra Meier and Karen Celis (2011) point to more conceptual issues, arguing that because there is no consensus on the meaning of "equality" in the context of gender mainstreaming, the ultimate goal of gender mainstreaming tools remains unclear. Rankin and Wilcox (2004, 55–57) highlight this problem by noting that the application of GBA focused on internal and procedural aspects of gender analysis, at the expense of critically examining government outcomes. As a result, the women's movement – and its visions for gender equality – was further marginalized from the politics involved in government initiatives to address gender inequality. At the same time, the views of so-called gender experts were valorized, obfuscating the ways in which they themselves were constituted by the impetus to evaluate gender equality and ensuring that their biases remained unscrutinized (Paterson 2010, 409).

Paterson (2010, 402–3) also criticizes the GBA model for the very way in which it frames the problem of gender inequality. In particular, the GBA approach assumes that the problem arises from limited information, rather than from patriarchal institutions, social relations, or even measurement frameworks and analysis. According to this logic, the problem becomes addressable once there is simply more, better, and sex-disaggregated data to allow policy-makers to reach informed decisions. Similarly, Carol Bacchi (2010, 26) emphasizes the ways in which gender mainstreaming conceptualizations are based on the notion that policy needs to respond to gender difference, as opposed to uncovering and interrogating the ways in which policy itself serves as a gendering process, functioning through institutions that are gendered. The GBA approach, as Paterson (2010, 400) observes, thus involves a failure to recognize that "policies have a creative or productive force; that is, they also play a role in ensuring the reproduction of the necessary social conditions, norms, values, relations of ruling, etc., that allow for (present and future) action."

Lastly, gender mainstreaming approaches, and GBA specifically, have been extensively criticized for relying on sex-disaggregated statistics, premised on a simplistic dichotomy between women and men, coded according to "sex" (Bacchi 2010; Gabriel 2017; Hankivsky 2005, 2013; Paterson 2010). Although the conflation of sex and gender permeates measurement processes more generally (see, for example, Bittner and Goodyear-Grant 2017), the perpetuation of the female/male or woman/man binary does not reflect the reality of gender experience today. Nor does it acknowledge feminist theorizing, which has complicated and challenged binary notions of gender and sex. Further, in focusing on sex-disaggregated data, gender mainstreaming and GBA have prioritized gender relations over other social relations and axes of oppression, including race, class, disability, and age (Gabriel 2017; Hankivsky 2005, 2013; Siltanen 2006). Again, this fails to capture adequately the lived realities that result from multiple forms of oppression and ignores the feminist literature and feminist activism that have asserted the importance of the intersectionality of social relations (Crenshaw 1989).

Over time, Ottawa sought to address some of these concerns through various changes to the GBA model and approach. Since 2007, GBA has been required for all cabinet submissions, and though SWC (and later Women and Gender Equality Canada) remained a key authority on GBA, its implementation shifted somewhat, as *all* public service employees are now expected to train in and use gender analysis (Scala and Paterson 2017, 432). Further, in 2011, a new iteration of the GBA framework, GBA+, was developed. Significantly, "GBA Plus is an intersectional analysis that goes beyond biological (sex) and socio-cultural (gender) differences to consider other factors, such as age, disability, education, ethnicity, economic status, geography (including rurality), language, race, religion, and sexual orientation" (Women and Gender Equality Canada n.d.). This reorientation was designed to more substantially incorporate the concept of intersectionality and to address the problem of privileging gender relations at the expense of other intersecting axes of oppression.

Despite these strides, the Office of the Auditor General of Canada (2016) found that gender mainstreaming in the form of GBA+ was either absent or incomplete in most federal agencies. On the other hand, the findings of Scala and Paterson (2017) are somewhat more encouraging. When the authors interviewed a small sample of public servants to gauge whether GBA+ was living up to the transformative potential claimed by its proponents, they discovered that despite bureaucratic obstacles and institutional challenges, key actors had used GBA+ to make small discursive and relational gains in terms of gender equality that could potentially prove fruitful. Post-2015, the embrace of an overtly feminist orientation by the new Liberal government, including, for example, the adoption of a Gender Results Framework as part of the 2018 federal budget, now requires gender measurement indicators that align with the UN sustainable development goals. In fact, the ambitious goals of the Trudeau government around gender equality have ushered in an even more robust indicator culture. Clearly, the drive toward enhanced gender measurement persists; whether it will yield substantive gender equality, however, remains the question with which the contributors to this volume engage.

Outline of the Volume

Although gender mainstreaming and GBA/GBA+ have garnered particular attention in terms of the numerous tensions and potentials for addressing gender inequality via technologies of measurement and evaluation, the literature has not focused on the actual measurement techniques, processes, and indicators that are inherent in the GBA/GBA+ framework. Research on other sites of gender equality measurement in Canada is similarly lacking. In this volume, our contributors begin to address these gaps, to critically consider the various manifestations of measurement culture as related to gender equality, and to explore the questions mentioned previously: How is gender equality measured in differing policy areas? How can we improve current practices? What is revealed by examining and critiquing the technical turn in policies that promote gender equality? What are the practical and theoretical limitations of measurement?

Counting Matters begins with four chapters that discuss gender equality measurement at various locales in the federal government. In Chapter 1, Marika Morris examines how the government responded to the 1995 United Nations call, made during the Beijing Conference, to develop indicators measuring gender equality. She outlines the latest effort of Women and Gender Equality Canada, the Gender Results Framework (GRF), and compares it to its immediate predecessor, the performance measures of SWC. Morris details how the GRF links gender equality measures to progress on the sustainable development goals of the United Nations and to the new role of Statistics Canada in tracking these measures. She suggests that though the GRF constitutes an improvement over its predecessor, it nonetheless falls short because it does not adopt an intersectional frame. The chapter illustrates the manner in which gender equity measurement is inherently political, reminding us to ask how gender equity data are collected, who is engaged in the task, and what questions are used.

In Chapter 2, Joan Grace focuses on the House of Commons and argues that gender equality indicators must be developed to counter its masculinist norms. She notes that though some research has assessed the gender dimensions of the House, much more is needed. An important step here would be the creation of gender equality indicators that take stock of the gendered dynamics in the House. Grace foregrounds the linkages between the House, political parties and electoral processes, and other government agencies, noting that gender equality can be achieved only when a gender lens is applied to both the administrative state and political institutions. She advocates for a holistic approach to gender equality indicators, in which all levels, sectors, and agencies of government are assessed in a systematic and ongoing manner.

Stephanie M. Redden's contribution, Chapter 3, uses an autoethnographic approach to reflect on the process of developing GBA/GBA+ infrastructure in the Canada School of Public Service (CSPS), where she was employed for a time. Specifically, Redden argues that though numerous resources are available to government units *about* GBA+, almost none explain how to go about constructing it. Yet, this is the very task set before many departments as Ottawa prioritizes GBA+. This lack of information, Redden posits, reflects a failure in knowledge transfer between units and departments regarding GBA+ and its implementation. Given that Canada's auditor general has continually noted the disappointing application of GBA+, Redden uses her personal experience as a key actor in the development of GBA+ infrastructure in the CSPS to argue that more readily engaging in cross-departmental knowledge sharing may improve the situation.

Chapter 4, by Rebecca Tiessen, Liam Swiss, and Krystel Carrier, provides a case study of gender measurement in the Government of Canada's official development assistance through a discussion of the Muskoka Initiative, one of the largest Canadian development programs to target women. Introduced by the Stephen Harper Conservatives in June 2010, it aimed to improve maternal and child health in developing countries, and as the authors argue, it provides an excellent case study to examine the measurement of gender equality in the context of programs that inherently should have gendered effects. By interrogating the ways in which small changes to coding definitions, processes, and language can result in vastly different pictures of the performance of the program in terms of gender equality, the authors show that the Muskoka Initiative was not used to directly promote gender equality through its maternal health work; instead, gender equality was simply a *result* of the initiative. In this way, Tiessen, Swiss, and Carrier underscore the highly political nature of gender equality coding as a measurement device. They conclude with suggestions for what an approach to maternal health that meaningfully incorporates gender equality would look like.

The volume then turns to non-governmental sites of gender equality measurement. Chapter 5, by Pat Armstrong, Hugh Armstrong, and Jacqueline Choiniere, analyzes measurement in long-term residential care (LTRC), focusing specifically on a tool called the Resident Assessment Instrument–Minimum Data Set (RAI-MDS). The authors distinguish between medical and social care, noting that LTRC is both medical, as residents often have complicated health conditions that require medical responses and treatments, and social because their conditions are typically chronic and are thus treated via the provision of comfort, respect, and maintenance, as opposed to cure. However, measurement regimes such as RAI-MDS tend to focus on the medical aspects of care, as these are often easiest to quantify. The authors reveal what is lost through such a focus: aspects of care that are relational and difficult to quantify, such as autonomy, quality of life, and social engagement. The related types of care work that support these aspects, typically performed by women and racialized individuals, are omitted and devalued. Although the authors do not reject measurement, they insist that evidence informed by measurement alone is insufficient in the context of care, and they warn against the resulting hierarchies of differing aspects of care – and the people who need and provide them – that often arise through measurement processes.

In Chapter 6, Sari Tudiver and her colleagues, members of the Sex/Gender Methods Group, describe their nearly two-decade-long research project that sought to develop and mobilize sex- and gender-sensitive methodologies and measurement devices in the design and reporting of health research. The authors focus on how to foster consideration for sex and gender in systematic health reviews – high-level metasyntheses that critically analyze, assess, and summarize evidence from primary research studies on a given topic. As governments and research organizations increasingly called for such systematic reviews, the scholars of the Sex/Gender Methods Group realized that without robust sex and gender methodologies, these reviews would fail to identify important aspects of various health research topics. This was a particularly worrisome omission, given that reviews are increasingly used by researchers, clinicians, policy-makers, and consumers to provide evidence-based assessments of the state of a field of research. Noting that the exclusion of women from health studies has compromised the quality of health evidence in the past, the authors trace the history of their project, providing a breadth of strategies for incorporating sex/gender analysis into disciplines that have historically failed to adopt a gender lens. The chapter foregrounds the challenge of measuring variables, such as sex and gender, that are not simply static identity categories but are themselves dynamic processes in various research endeavours.

In Chapter 7, Lee Lakeman and her colleagues draw upon their various experiences as feminist legal scholars, social science researchers, and front-line workers to reflect upon measurement in the context of the fight to end violence against women (VAW). They contend that VAW is the lynchpin of women's inequality and that gender equality is therefore necessary for its eradication. They argue that data and measurement have an important part to play in the movement to end VAW, although they note that the current mobilization of data and measurement – as an end in itself – is insufficient. Instead, the authors call for new ways of thinking about data so that measurement can serve as a tool to tie together individual stories of VAW, thereby demonstrating more fully its force, scope, and persistence. In other words, this chapter ultimately asks us to consider the relationship between gender equality and VAW, and to ponder how data and measurement might be enhanced or reconceptualized to illuminate and demonstrate this relationship. In the end, it leaves us with a call for new global statistics, data, theories, methodologies, and strategies to help us better identify and understand the connection between gender equality and VAW.

The final chapters in this volume foreground how measurement operates in and across various scales – from the local to the international. In Chapter 8, Maggie FitzGerald continues, in some ways, the discussion of the previous chapter by summarizing recent developments and practices related to the measurement of, and subsequent creation of indicators for, VAW at a variety of scales. Specifically, she reviews how VAW has been counted internationally, particularly by the United Nations system, and at the supranational level, demonstrated via the case of the European Union and the Council of Europe. She then explores how VAW has been measured at the national level in Canada, before reviewing some of the challenges pertaining to the measurement of VAW at the local level or for subpopulations. For the latter, FitzGerald reviews the Royal Canadian Mounted Police's initiative to develop statistics and indicators related to the crisis of missing and murdered Indigenous women and girls. She points to numerous issues and challenges that are involved in these processes. Finally, the chapter illustrates the ways in which quantification methodologies, data, and indicators come to circulate and gain currency (or not) across scales.

Linda Briskin similarly turns a critical eye on international indicators and data in Chapter 9, noting that they largely pivot around measuring the gender gap, the discrepancy between women and men in terms of achievements and access to resources. However, as Briskin argues, the gender gap is often a poor proxy for women's equality and empowerment, as it is premised on the idea that the conditions of men are the standard against which women's experience and status should be evaluated. As she reveals, the indices consistently show that the greatest, and most persistent, gender gap relates to women's empowerment through political participation and representation. The indicators typically link the problem to a lack of political representation, as opposed to economic representation. To counter this, Briskin calls for a new focus on "collective agency," as fostered through union membership and organization; this shift to economic representation and empowerment may be fruitful, given the evidence that political representation does not (necessarily) translate to gender equality. Additionally, a plenitude of sex-disaggregated data on union membership is available internationally, and such data could be collected in Canada. They could be mobilized to form other indicators that capture collective agency and its relationship with gender equality.

In Chapter 10, Laura Macdonald and Nadia Ibrahim discuss Canadian trade policy, flagging the importance of trade agreements to gender equality. They contend that "trade agreements and policies themselves have been used as a form of measurement – to quantify trading relationships and the flow of goods and services, and to establish tariffs, quotas, and penalties" (page 228). In seeking to problematize this development, they highlight and analyze the widespread use of computer-based modelling to assess the impact of trade liberalization. The authors show that this modelling is itself often premised on narrow gender assumptions, which limits its ability to identify gender impacts. Unlike in other policy areas, attempts to measure and evaluate gender equality in trade agreements are in their very early stages. Macdonald and Ibrahim use the case of Canada's inclusive trade policy to examine the efficacy of including gender chapters in trade agreements and the redesign of evaluation measures to take gender and trade more seriously. They conclude that the development of new evaluation models must involve the active participation of civil society organizations.

In the final chapter, Leah Levac and her colleagues present a rare case study of the development of an indicator at the local level, specifically in Happy Valley–Goose Bay, Labrador. Using a feminist intersectional participatory research process, they created a women's well-being framework and index called a community vitality index (CVI). Created through a community-grounded process, it was designed to capture a localized picture of women's well-being that simultaneously reflected participant understandings of the subject. During the research process that generated the CVI, the authors were able to imbue it with conceptual clarity and relevance for the community, to maintain equitable collaboration with participants, and to facilitate leadership development for them. Importantly, the authors assert that their approach can push back against the risks of indicator development – the fact that indicators are often developed by "experts" who are removed from the contexts that the indicators will ultimately come to represent, and that indicators measure standardized definitions that do not reflect local understandings. As the authors demonstrate, the process and resulting CVI point to new possibilities for approaches to gender equality measurement that better capture the realities of the experiences being measured and that may better inform policy initiatives that seek to address gender inequality in Canada.

Together, the chapters in this collection contextualize, query, and assess both the potential and the challenges of gender equality measurement in Canada. In so doing, they offer critical perspectives on the nexus of gender equality and measurement as it has manifested, and continues to manifest, in Canada, and provide us with directions for future research.

Notes

1 Canada ranked nineteenth in the 2020 GII.
2 As feminist scholars have long pointed out, objectivity is a myth.

Works Cited

Bacchi, Carol. 2010. "Gender/ing Impact Assessment: Can It Be Made to Work?" In *Mainstreaming Politics: Gendering Practice and Feminist Theory,* ed. Carol Bacchi and Joan Eveline, 17–38. Adelaide: University of Adelaide Press.

Bergqvist, Christina, and Sue Findlay. 1999. "Representing Women's Interests in the Policy Process: Women's Organizing and State Initiatives in Sweden and Canada, 1960s–1990s." In *Women's Organizing and Public Policy in Canada and Sweden,* ed. Linda Briskin and Mona Eliasson, 119–46. Montreal and Kingston: McGill-Queen's University Press.

Bittner, Amanda, and Elizabeth Goodyear-Grant. 2017. "Sex Isn't Gender: Reforming Concepts and Measurements in the Study of Public Opinion." *Political Behavior* 39, 4: 1019–41.

Brodie, Janine. 2008. "We Are All Equal Now: Contemporary Gender Politics in Canada." *Feminist Theory* 9, 2: 145–64. http://doi.org/10.1177/1464700108090408.

Brown, Judy. 2015. "Problematizing Audit Culture – A Comment on Shore and Wright." *Current Anthropology* 56, 3: 432–33.

Buss, Doris. 2015. "Measurement Imperatives and Gender Politics: An Introduction." *Social Politics* 22, 3: 381–89. http://doi.org/10.1093/sp/jxv030.

Canada. 1970. *Report of the Royal Commission on the Status of Women.* Ottawa: Government of Canada.

Crenshaw, Kimberlé. 1989. "Demarginalizing the Intersection of Race and Sex: A Black Feminist Critique of Antidiscrimination Doctrine, Feminist Theory and Antiracist Politics." *University of Chicago Legal Forum* 140: 139–67.

Davis, Kevin, Benedict Kingsbury, and Sally Engle Merry. 2012. "Indicators as a Technology of Global Governance." *Law and Society Review* 46, 1: 71–104.

European Institute for Gender Equality. 2015. *Gender Equality Index 2015.* Vilnius, Lithuania: European Institute for Gender Equality. http://eige.europa.eu/sites/default/files/documents/mh0215616enn.pdf.

Gabriel, Christina. 2017. "Framing Families: Neo-Liberalism and the Family Class within Canadian Immigration Policy." *Atlantis* 38, 1: 179–94.

Gabriel, Christina, and Laura Macdonald. 2005. "Managing Trade Engagements? Mapping the Contours of State Feminism and Women's Political Activism." *Canadian Foreign Policy Journal* 12, 1: 71–88. http://doi.org/10.1080/11926422.2005.9673389.

Glenza, Jessica. 2016. "Canada Urged to Quell Discrimination against Women after Fall in UN Ranking." *Guardian*, October 26, 2016. https://www.theguardian.com/world/2016/oct/26/canada-women-un-ranking-discrimination-justin-trudeau.

Hankivsky, Olena. 2005. "Gender vs. Diversity Mainstreaming: A Preliminary Examination of the Role and Transformative Potential of Feminist Theory." *Canadian Journal of Political Science* 38, 4: 977–1001.

–. 2013. "Gender Mainstreaming: A Five-Country Examination." *Politics and Policy* 41, 5: 629–55. https://doi.org/10.1111/polp.12037.

House of Commons Standing Committee on the Status of Women. 2005. *Gender-Based Analysis: Building Blocks for Success.* Ottawa: House of Commons. https://www.ourcommons.ca/Content/Committee/381/FEWO/Reports/RP1778246/feworp02/feworp02-e.pdf.

Johnson, Holly. 2015. "Degendering Violence." *Social Politics* 22, 3: 390–410. https://doi.org/10.1093/sp/jxv021.

Liebowitz, Debra, and Susanne Zwingel. 2014. "Gender Equality Oversimplified: Using CEDAW to Counter the Measurement Obsession." *International Studies Review* 16: 362–89. https://doi.org/10.1111/misr.12139.

Lombardo, Emanuela. 2005. "Integrating or Setting the Agenda: Gender Mainstreaming in the European Constitution-Making Process." *Social Politics* 12, 3: 412–32.

Meier, Petra, and Karen Celis. 2011. "Sowing the Seeds of Its Own Failure: Implementing the Concept of Gender Mainstreaming." *Social Politics* 18, 4: 469–89.

Merry, Sally Engle. 2011. "Measuring the World: Indicators, Human Rights, and Global Governance." *Current Anthropology* 52, S3: S83–S95. https://doi.org/10.1086/657241.

–. 2016. *The Seductions of Quantification: Measuring Human Rights, Gender Violence, and Sex Trafficking.* Chicago: University of Chicago Press.

Mohr, John, and Amin Ghaziani. 2014. "Problems and Prospects of Measurement in the Study of Culture." *Theory and Society* 43: 225–46. https://doi.org/10.1007/s11186-014-9227-2.

Office of the Auditor General of Canada. 2016. "Report 1 – I, Implementing Gender-Based Analysis: Fall 2015 Reports of the Auditor General of Canada." https://www.oag-bvg.gc.ca/internet/english/parl_oag_201602_01_e_41058.html.

Parisi, Laura. 2009. "The Numbers Do(n't) Always Add Up: Dilemmas in Using Quantitative Research Methods in Feminist IR Scholarship." *Politics and Gender* 5, 3: 410–19. https://doi.org/10.1017/S1743923X09990201.

Paterson, Stephanie. 2010. "What's the Problem with Gender-Based Analysis? Gender Mainstreaming Policy and Practice in Canada." *Canadian Public Administration* 53, 3: 395–416.

Pew Research Center. 2020. *Worldwide Optimism about the Future of Gender Equality, Even as Many See Advantages for Men.* https://www.pewresearch.org/global/wp-content/uploads/sites/2/2020/04/PG_2020.04.30_Global-Gender-Equality_FINAL.pdf.

Poovey, Mary. 1998. *A History of the Modern Fact: Problems of Knowledge in the Science of Wealth and Society.* Chicago: University of Chicago Press.

Power, Michael. 1994. "The Audit Explosion." Demos. https://www.demos.co.uk/files/theauditexplosion.pdf.

–. 2000. "The Audit Society – Second Thoughts." *International Journal of Auditing* 4, 1: 111–19. https://doi.org/10.1111/1099-1123.00306.

Rankin, L. Pauline, and Krista Wilcox. 2004. "De-gendering Engagement? Gender Mainstreaming, Women's Movements and the Canadian Federal State." *Atlantis* 29, 1: 52–58.

Runyan, Anne Sisson, and V. Spike Peterson. 2014. *Global Gender Issues in the New Millennium.* 4th ed. Boulder: Westview Press.

Scala, Francesca, and Stephanie Paterson. 2017. "Gendering Public Policy or Rationalizing Gender? Strategic Interventions and GBA+ Practice in Canada." *Canadian Journal of Political Science* 50, 2: 427–42.

Shore, Cris, and Susan Wright. 2015. "Audit Culture Revisited: Rankings, Ratings, and the Reassembling of Society." *Current Anthropology* 56, 3: 421–44. https://doi.org/10.1086/681534.

Siltanen, Janet. 2006. "Gender, Diversity and the Shaping of Public Policy: Recent Aspects of the Canadian Experience." *Scottish Affairs* 56: 88–104.

Statistics Canada. 1985. *Women in Canada: A Statistical Report.* Ottawa: Government of Canada.

Strathern, Marilyn, ed. 2000. *Audit Cultures: Anthropological Studies in Accountability, Ethics, and the Academy.* London: Routledge.

SWC (Status of Women Canada). 1995. *Setting the Stage for the Next Century: The Federal Plan for Gender Equality.* Ottawa: Status of Women Canada. https://publications.gc.ca/collections/Collection/SW21-15-1995E.pdf.

–. 1997. *Economic Gender Equality Indicators.* Ottawa: Government of Canada.

–. 2018. "What Is GBA+?" Government of Canada. https://cfc-swc.gc.ca/gba-acs/index-en.html.

Tiessen, Rebecca, and Krystel Carrier. 2015. "The Erasure of 'Gender' in Canadian Foreign Policy under the Harper Conservatives: The Significance of the Discursive Shift from 'Gender Equality' to 'Equality between Women and Men.'" *Canadian Foreign Policy Journal* 21, 2: 95–111. https://doi.org/10.1080/11926422.2014.977310.

United Nations (UN). 1986. *Report of the World Conference to Review and Appraise the Achievements of the United Nations Decade for Women: Equality, Development and Peace.* New York: UN.

United Nations Development Programme (UNDP). n.d. "Gender Inequality Index (GII)." UN. http://hdr.undp.org/en/content/gender-inequality-index-gii.

UN Statistics Division. 2016. "SDG Indicators: Global Database." UN. http://unstats.un.org/sdgs/indicators/database/.

UN Treaty Collection. 2019. "Convention on the Elimination of All Forms of Discrimination against Women." UN. Accessed February 2, 2019. https://treaties.un.org/Pages/ViewDetails.aspx?src=TREATY&mtdsg_no=IV-8&chapter=4&lang=en#top.

UN Women. 2009. "Convention on the Elimination of All Forms of Discrimination against Women." UN. Accessed February 1, 2019. http://www.un.org/womenwatch/daw/cedaw/cedaw.htm.

Vickers, Jill, Pauline Rankin, and Christine Appelle. 1993. *Politics as If Women Mattered: A Political Analysis of the National Action Committee on the Status of Women.* Toronto: University of Toronto Press.

Walby, Sylvia. 2005. "Measuring Women's Progress in a Global Era." *International Social Science Journal* 57, 184: 371–87. https://doi.org/10.1111/j.1468-2451.2005.00556.x.

Waring, Marilyn. 1999. *Counting for Nothing: What Men Value and What Women Are Worth.* Toronto: University of Toronto Press.

Women and Gender Equality Canada. n.d. "About Gender-Based Analysis Plus (GBA Plus)." https://women-gender-equality.canada.ca/en/gender-based-analysis-plus/what -gender-based-analysis-plus.html.

World Economic Forum. 2018. *The Global Gender Gap Report.* Geneva: WEF. http:// www3.weforum.org/docs/WEF_GGGR_2018.pdf.

Zukewich, Nancy. 2002. "Using Time Use Data to Measure and Value Unpaid Caregiving Work." Master's thesis, Carleton University.

1

The Government of Canada's Gender Results Framework: A Tool in the Construction of Equity for All

Marika Morris

RENOWNED FEMINIST ECONOMIST and former member of the New Zealand parliament Marilyn Waring (1988) wrote extensively about whether and how women are counted. One of her main arguments was that what can be measured and what is measured are not necessarily of most value to human well-being. Her conclusion was not that everyone should stop measuring everything, but rather that we need to change our views about what we value and what and how we count. Like qualitative research, quantitative research measures what the research participant thinks is being asked and reflects the perspectives, interests, and knowledge of the researcher. The quantitative versus qualitative debate, however, illustrates that many people do not understand the role of statistics. Those who dismiss anything that is not quantitative are entrenched in the false view that statistics provide a perfectly unbiased measure of everything. Those who dismiss the quantitative outright may not be aware that any source of data, including qualitative, historical, archaeological, and other forms of research, is also open to many of the same problems as quantitative research: asking the wrong questions, looking in the wrong places, misinterpreting the results. Both qualitative and quantitative data, however, are tools that can be used for or against equity for all. When they are created or shaped with the participation of the people whose issues are being measured, both qualitative and quantitative research can be valuable and can provide social justice organizations with an additional tool for progress, including in the drive to create gender equality.

One quantitative tool for potential progress is the Government of Canada's Gender Results Framework (GRF). This chapter offers a descriptive and analytical discussion of the GRF, which was introduced in 2018. It explains how the GRF improves on the Status of Women Canada (SWC) performance measures that it replaced but also notes what indicators are missing from it, particularly in intersectional data.[1] This relatively brief essay cannot fully chronicle the development of gender equality indicators in Canada, but it does offer a short overview of what the GRF replaced. My purpose is to show that the GRF represents a significant advance over previous government efforts, or non-efforts, to measure progress on gender equality. Because human rights, including women's rights, can be cut back as well as expanded, this chapter also warns against the potential actions of future governments. As Donald Moynihan and colleagues (2011, i141) observe,

> Much of the appeal of performance measurement is explained by its image as a simple and value-neutral way to monitor and improve government. But contemporary governance is characterized by complexity. Few public officials have the luxury of directly providing relatively simple services, the context in which performance regimes work best. Instead, they must work in the context of a disarticulated state, with policy problems that cross national boundaries and demand a multi-actor response.

SWC Performance Measures and Gender Equality

Following the United Nations Fourth World Conference on Women, in 1995, the Canadian government promised to develop indicators to assess progress made toward gender equality as a part of its commitment to gender-based analysis published in *Setting the Stage for the Next Century* (SWC 1995). In 1997, the Federal-Provincial/Territorial Ministers Responsible for the Status of Women released *Economic Gender Equality Indicators,* and Ottawa held an interesting and successful symposium the following year on gender equality indicators. Nothing came of these indicators, however. Instead, in some government circles, SWC departmental performance indicators were cited as a replacement for the national gender equality indicators that had been promised and piloted earlier in the decade.

Every year, all federal government departments and agencies must submit their planning and priorities documents to parliament (see SWC 2012b, 2013b, 2014). These documents describe what they plan to do with their budget in the coming year, and at the end of that year, account for how that money was spent. Departmental performance indicators are a key component of these submissions. They are used to show parliament and the public whether the department met its targets and are a cornerstone of accountability and transparency in a democracy. The rationale for using performance measurement in the public sector, apart from simply copying private sector methods, comes from a concern about the level of taxation and value for money. In the private sector, performance measures are used internally to look for areas of improvement. In the public sector, they often serve as a tool for both communication and legitimacy (de Bruijn 2002, 4).

Each federal department and agency must have a "strategic outcome," which is a "long-term and enduring benefit to Canadians that stems from a department or agency's mandate, vision and efforts. It represents what a department or agency wants to do for Canadians and should be a clear measurable outcome that is within the department or agency's sphere of influence" (Treasury Board Secretariat 2012). The department's performance is measured against its strategic outcome. However, its strategic outcome is not the same as its legislated mandate. For example, the 1976 legislation that created SWC mandated it "to coordinate policy with respect to the status of women and administer related programs" (SWC 2013c). Prior to 2013, SWC's (2013a, 4) strategic outcome was "equality for women and their full participation in the economic, social and democratic life of Canada" (SWC 2014, 4).

The departmental performance report is issued at the end of the fiscal year, recording the performance indicators, targets, and actual results for that year. I systematically examined SWC performance reports (now called departmental results reports) for three years of the Harper Conservative government (SWC 2011, 2012c, 2013a) to determine whether these performance indicators could indeed be used as a stand-in for national gender equality indicators, as the government claimed. I discovered that many of the SWC performance indicators were inconsistent over time, which meant that they could not be used to measure progress on gender equality. The few indicators that were consistent in the 2010–11, 2011–12, and 2012–13 reports included representation of women in senior decision-making positions in the public and private sectors, their representation in the labour market, and their participation in political processes. Noticeably absent was any indicator concerning income, wealth, earnings, or the wage gap. Also absent, rather oddly given that "addressing violence against women and girls" was the first priority listed in all the analyzed documents, was any indicator that dealt with gendered violence.

The problem with SWC using such broad indicators, therefore, regardless of their lack of comprehensiveness in terms of reflecting some key aspects of gender inequality, is that women's equality is a multi-faceted outcome that is influenced by many factors and actors, not just by SWC. In other words, SWC was measuring progress toward a goal that it could not control and for which it was not solely responsible. This may explain why the indicators shifted after 2012–13 to become much more focused on agency activity (such as numbers of public servants to receive SWC gender-based analysis plus [GBA+] training) rather than women's equality writ large.

The Introduction to this volume notes the criticism of performance measures in the public sector as trying to quantify everything. Paradoxically, my research on SWC documents found that SWC did not employ quantitative data to prove the effectiveness of its women's equality measures. Instead, brief narratives alluding to progress but providing no evidence for it appeared in lieu of quantitative measures. For example, in reference to the strategic outcome of "equality for women and their full participation in the economic, social and democratic life of Canada," the 2011 report stated, "The 2010-2011 performance analysis shows steady progress toward this strategic outcome, as demonstrated by the gains made in women's representation in the labour market, workforce and women's participation in leadership and decision making roles" (SWC 2011, 8). Exactly what constituted this progress was never mentioned.

Clearly, SWC performance measures could not substitute for gender equality indicators, as no actual numbers were used for the strategic outcome. Instead of furnishing numbers for gender-based violence, for example, SWC reported its funding for various small projects and events. To be fair, Statistics Canada counts gender-based violence in numerous ways, but it gathers only one of these measures (police-reported violence) every year. However, because women commonly do not report being assaulted, relying on this measure is not a good way of determining the extent of the problem (Moreau, Jaffray, and Armstrong 2020), and increases or decreases in the number of incidents reported to police tend to reflect broader societal events and awareness rather than an upsurge or a diminishment of the violence itself. Statistics Canada's General Social Survey, which measures intimate partner violence, along with a few other crimes, as experienced and identified privately to Statistics Canada by women (and others), takes place once every five years. Government departments and agencies, on the other hand, must report on their progress every year.

SWC's task was also to measure "increased policy effectiveness in addressing women's issues and gender equality" as part of its own performance along with the "capacity of the federal government to apply GBA [gender-based analysis]" and the "increased integration of women's issues in the formulation of policies and programs" (SWC 2013a, 13). Not surprisingly, the indicator of "number of new and improved policies" was dropped in 2014–15. The only expected result that can actually be measured indirectly in quantitative terms is the GBA capacity of other departments. SWC can measure the inputs – the GBA training given, tools used, and advice requested. Outcomes, however, are much harder to measure. This led SWC simply to report any government initiative or workshop that involved a consideration of gender or equality, rather than any results.

Another item listed in the 2013–14 SWC report as proof of "new and improved policies and programs" was a national roundtable on gender and economic development. No doubt, this was very useful, but instigating a national childcare program or changing employment insurance regulations and benefit levels to provide low-paid workers with a parental leave income on which they could actually live would have been more meaningful contributions to women's equality. Also listed was interdepartmental work on the Family Violence Initiative and in the Federal-Provincial/Territorial Ministers Responsible for the Status of Women, neither of which were new. All of this confirms a point made by Hans de Bruijn (2002), a public sector performance indicator specialist: although the reports were meant to be an accountability tool, and they did describe activities, they were also shaped by the pressure for departments and agencies to look good and to justify their existence and level of funding.

Part of the SWC mandate included managing the Women's Program (WP), a grants and contributions program that funds non-governmental and private sector activities that meet the eligibility criteria and are aligned with SWC priorities. The evaluations of the WP (SWC 2006, 2012a) noted that according to some "stakeholders," such as women's organizations that received WP funds, SWC priorities were often out of sync with the women's movement. Although SWC activities in encouraging equality, particularly in ending violence against women and girls and promoting women's economic well-being, are in keeping with feminist activism and on-the-ground-work, SWC is not a part of the women's movement. Rather, it is a government agency staffed by public servants and headed by a minister who is elected by the men and women of a riding somewhere in Canada on her political party's platform. She is accountable to her constituents, to the public through parliament, and to the prime minister and her cabinet colleagues. In its reporting documents, SWC must state how its priorities align with those of the government, not those of the women's movement, and gender equality was never a priority for the Harper government.

SWC used its funding of activities through the WP to measure "increased participation of women in their communities." Not surprisingly, SWC (2011) reported that all the targets had been met, using the logic that since women participated in these WP-funded projects, their community involvement was greater than it would have been had the projects not existed.

The 2013–14 departmental performance report made a significant shift, with major changes in expected results and indicators. The broader measures of equality were dropped completely in favour of agency-specific indicators, such as percentage of SWC initiatives covered by the media. None of the original or subsequent measures were intersectional, and by 2014, the reports themselves had become difficult for people to locate. Although hosted on the SWC website, there was no link to the reports, so you had to know exactly what you were looking for to find them. As a result of this shift to bean-counting the agency's tasks, Canada had no official measures of progress toward women's equality at all between 2013 and 2016, even hidden ones of questionable value.

Pietro Micheli and Jean-François Manzoni (2010) warn that strategic performance measurement systems can be distorted and can lead to perverse outcomes, depending on whether they are used primarily for control or for learning purposes. In the case of SWC, a performance management framework and indicators based on Treasury Board requirements were used primarily for reporting and accountability, not to identify gaps and opportunities for improvement. Year after year, targets were set low enough so that they could easily be met. Although useful as a report to parliament, the SWC performance framework (including strategic outcomes, expected results, indicators, targets, and actual results) did not identify gaps and areas for improvement, did not identify how the organization could be doing better, and did not identify where things were at with gender equality or how to achieve it. Both public and private sector divisions or organizations want to present themselves in the best possible light to get their bonuses and legitimize their expenditures or to justify their continued existence and the resources and employment that go with it. As de Bruijn (2002) explains, there is a huge incentive to ensure that any numbers reported by the organization make it look good.

Enter the Gender Results Framework

In September 2015, the United Nations sustainable development goals were adopted by world leaders and came into force in January 2016. Their emergence coincided with the November 2015 federal election of the Liberal Party under Justin Trudeau, which committed to advancing a gender equality agenda. In December 2018, SWC was transformed into Women and Gender Equality Canada (WAGE) as part of Trudeau's prioritization of gender equality.

Earlier that year, the Gender Results Framework (GRF) was introduced in the federal budget. As WAGE (2023c) explained, it represented

> the Government of Canada's vision for gender equality, highlighting the key issues that matter most. It is a whole-of-government tool designed to:
> - Track how Canada is currently performing
> - Define what is needed to achieve greater equality
> - Determine how progress will be measured going forward.

Progress on the GRF indicators was achieved in collaboration with Statistics Canada, the Department of Finance, and Global Affairs Canada. Responsibility for tracking the process was given, in part, to Statistics Canada, the national data collection agency, and its newly formed Gender, Diversity and Inclusion Statistics Hub, which was launched to better capture gendered intersectionality. Statistics Canada too had been making significant progress on its understanding and collection of data on gender identities, and by 2018 it had adopted standards for cisgender and transgender data.

By creating the GRF (see WAGE 2023c), the government tied measurement of gender equality to Canada's progress on the United Nations sustainable development goals (SDGs), which were "to create more sustainable and inclusive societies." Particularly germane were SDG 1, no poverty; SDG 3, good health and well-being; SDG 4, quality education; SDG 5, gender equality; SDG 8, decent work and economic growth; SDG 16, peace, justice, and strong institutions; and SDG 17, partnerships for the goals (WAGE 2023c). Particular attention was afforded SDG 5, to "achieve gender equality and empower all women and girls," which contains several specific objectives.[2] Countries are asked to report on their progress, using both quantitative and qualitative indicators of their choice. Statistics Canada has identified quantitative indicators related to most of these objectives and is exploring data sources for the rest (Statistics Canada 2020). The GRF also enumerated six goals:

1 Education and skills development: Equal opportunities and diversified paths in education and skills development.
2 Economic participation and prosperity: Equal and full participation in the economy.
3 Leadership and democratic participation: Gender equality in leadership roles and at all levels of decision-making.
4 Gender-based violence and access to justice: Eliminating gender-based violence and harassment and promoting security of the person and access to justice.
5 Poverty reduction, health and well-being: Reduced poverty and improved outcomes.
6 Gender equality around the world: Promoting gender equality to build a more peaceful, inclusive, rules-based and prosperous world. (WAGE 2023c)

Each goal is accompanied by a set of objectives and indicators, which suggests that Ottawa believes that SDG 5 can be implemented through progress on its GRF goals.[3] A closer examination of the objectives and indicators, however, reveals systemic shortcomings, particularly the absence of consistent attention to intersectionality. Some select examples illustrate this point.

The first GRF goal, education and skills development, has an objective of "more diversified paths and career choices for women," which is measured by five indicators:

1 Proportion of post-secondary qualification holders who are women, by field of study and qualification type;
2 Proportion of post-secondary students who are women, by field of study and credential type;
3 High school completion rate;
4 High school reading and mathematics test scores; and
5 Adults' literacy and numeracy test scores. (WAGE 2023c)

A tenet of second-wave feminism held that the wage gap between women and men would narrow as women entered "non-traditional occupations," such as engineering, with the same qualifications as men. However, Anthony Jehn, David Walters, and Stephanie Howells (2019) use Statistics Canada data to show that, in fact, the wage gap between recent male and female graduates in Canada remains highest for those whose qualifications are in trades, math, computer science, and engineering. Their analysis exposes ongoing discrimination against women in male-dominated workplaces and confirms that simply educating more women to work in male-dominated fields will not achieve economic equality by itself. Whatever the field, women are more likely than men to work part-time due to caring for children, and their careers are interrupted more frequently and for longer periods. Consequently, they still suffer an earnings gap (Zhang 2009). Perhaps the starkest proof that education alone is insufficient arises when we compare "visible minority" women with other Canadian women.[3] The former are more likely than the latter to have a university degree (30.0 percent versus 19.5 percent), which is more likely to be in a non-traditional field. Yet, they have a higher unemployment rate and lower average earnings than women who are not visible minorities (Hudon 2016). Education is a great step, but it is not enough to overcome structural and overt discrimination based on race, sex, and gender. Quantitative data that include attention to intersectionality can show people who use a deficiency model ("racialized women are poorly educated") that they are wrong – racialized women are doing everything they can to succeed, but they are caught in a system that hinders them from doing so.

GRF goal 2, economic participation and prosperity, is measured by twelve indicators, four of which are gender wage and employment income gaps. There is also a measure of subsidized childcare and part-time work. Importantly, one measure is the proportion of the day spent on unpaid domestic work and care work by sex, which ties directly to one of the SDG 5 objectives, "recognize and value unpaid care and domestic work" (UN 2020). As Melissa Moyser and Amanda Burlock (2018) point out, "Knowing how women and men allocate their time to various activities during a typical day is essential to understanding gender inequality in society, as one's activities in the private sphere (i.e., housework and caregiving) have implications for the extent and nature of their participation in the public sphere (i.e., paid employment), and vice versa."

Unpaid work indicators are also important for countering the widespread erroneous belief that men and women now do an equal amount of the caring work in the family. The Economic Participation and Prosperity section of the GRF (WAGE 2023a) lists one indicator of unpaid work, "Proportion of time spent on unpaid domestic and care work," which links to a Statistics Canada table (Statistics Canada 2019). Neither the Economic and Prosperity section (WAGE 2023a) nor the Statistics Canada table, which has a section underneath entitled "Related Products," offer any links to any explanatory materials or research on the history of gendered unpaid work or on how and why it persists. The fact that Statistics Canada operates at arm's length from the rest of government is a good thing, as its data are not manipulated to suit the party in power. However, because it has no desire to be seen as political or as promoting any particular position, its website does not provide links to explanatory material. Nevertheless, it would be an improvement if below the table under "Related Products," Statistics Canada could at least list Moyser and Burlock (2018), which it published itself, and not just a table about transport to activities and time spent on various activities. Moyser and Burlock put the unpaid and paid work ("total work burden") into international context. It turns out that Canadian women, followed by Canadian men, have the highest total work burden in the G7 countries, plus Sweden. In addition, collecting this quantitative data over time shows that time spent caring for children has become increasingly intensive, a trend that affects primarily middle-class mothers. These issues are not captured by the GRF's single table of unpaid work indicators (see Statistics Canada 2019). A 2009 Statistics Canada study examined the earnings of women who had children and those who did not. It quantitatively documented the earnings gap that the presence of children created for women, providing evidence for the widespread "motherhood penalty" that feminists had criticized. As there is no fatherhood penalty when it comes to earnings, eliminating the motherhood penalty would be a good indicator for gender equality (see Zhang 2009).

All of the economic participation and prosperity measures are useful for measuring progress on gender equality, but I would also add the wealth gap between women and men, which is possibly much greater than the wages and earnings gap. An intersectional approach to economic participation and prosperity is also extremely important, as much is hidden in the averages for all women and all men. In Chapter 9 of this volume, Linda Briskin addresses an aspect of measuring economic participation relating to trade unions.

GRF goal 4 is to eliminate gender-based violence and harassment and to promote security of the person and access to justice. The eight indicators for this goal are proportion of employees who self-report being harassed in the workplace; proportion of women and girls aged fifteen and over who are subjected to physical, sexual, or psychological violence by a current or former intimate partner; proportion of population who self-report being sexually assaulted since the age of fifteen; proportion of population who self-report "childhood maltreatment" occurring before the age of fifteen by type of maltreatment; homicide rate by relationship to the perpetrator; proportion of self-reported incidents of violent crime that were also reported to police; proportion of Indigenous women and girls subject to physical, sexual, or psychological violence, by Indigenous identity; and, as a measure of whether the accountability and responsiveness of the Canadian criminal justice system are increasing or decreasing, proportion of sexual assaults reported to police that are deemed "unfounded." Although looking specifically at violence against Indigenous women and girls is a step forward, other groups are also at heightened risk of violence, such as women with disabilities and racialized women. Data for them would be useful, but they are absent from these indicators.

The fifth GRF goal is poverty reduction, health, and well-being, measured by ten indicators. Among them are prevalence of low income by family type, proportion of food-insecure households, core housing need, and enforcement of child and spousal support measured by collection rate by type of beneficiary. The health indicators are leading causes of death, health-adjusted life expectancy at birth, proportion of population that participates regularly in sport, and proportion of adults with high self-rated psychological health. There are also two measures of access to contraception – adolescent birth rate and the proportion of the population aged fifteen to forty-nine who were sexually active and not trying to conceive but who did not use birth control. All of these are issues with enormous intersectional differences, but they are not measured intersectionally in the GRF. For example, the Inuit Health Survey found that 69 percent of Inuit households in Nunavut were food insecure and that substantial food insecurity rates of between 24 and 46 percent occurred in the other Inuit regions in Canada (Pauktuutit Inuit Women of Canada 2021). As Inuit make up less than 1 percent of the population, however, this issue is invisible because the indicator lacks an intersectional lens.

The final GRF goal is to promote gender equality to build a more peaceful, inclusive, rules-based, and prosperous world. When this chapter was being written, objectives had been set out for this goal, but there were no links to indicators to measure them. The objectives are a feminist international approach to all policies and programs, including diplomacy, trade, security, and development; increased and meaningful participation of women in peace and security efforts; more women in leadership and decision-making roles, and stronger women's rights organizations; more women and girls with access to sexual and reproductive health services, and more promotion of their rights; more of Canada's trade agreements are to include gender-related provisions; more women with equitable access and control over the resources they need to build their own economic success and that of their communities; fewer people as victims of sexual and gender-based violence and sexual exploitation, including in conflict settings and online; and more girls and women (in the world) with access to quality education and skills training. It will be interesting to see if and how these objectives can be measured, particularly whether an action constitutes a feminist approach, and how worldwide sexual exploitation is to be quantified, given that most of it occurs behind closed doors and is uncounted.

These critiques notwithstanding, the GRF represents a vast improvement on what it replaced. It provides greater opportunities for activists, scholars, and the public to use Statistics Canada data to effect social change. Although the gender equality measures could potentially be altered by a future government, they are no longer incomplete moving targets buried in obscure departmental reports and subject to manipulation by bureaucrats who are worried about making the department look good. Additionally, the indicators are related directly to gender equality and other SDGs fixed by the UN, which have been subject to criticism by some feminist scholars (Esquivel 2016). Finally, by moving the indicators to an arm's-length agency, Statistics Canada, and tying the GRF to the unchanging SDGs, Canada now really does have official gender equality indicators that may be useful.

The GRF in Context

Existing international indices give an indication of where Canada stands on gender equality, as compared to other countries, and demonstrate the value of alternative forms of measurement. The World Economic Forum (2019), for example, benchmarks gender data on economic participation and opportunity, political empowerment, educational attainment, and health for 153 countries. In its "Global Gender Gap Report 2020," Canada ranked 19th of the 153, having sunk to that level from a high of 14th in 2006, when the reports were first issued. Canada is tied for 1st place in educational attainment, but is 25th in political empowerment, 30th in economic participation and opportunity, and a surprising 105th in health. This index can give direction on what area of gender equality needs more work, as well as the depth of what needs to be done. The World

Economic Forum (2019) suggests that at the current rate, gender equality will be achieved only in a hundred years and only if no gains are rolled back. International comparisons also bring out national competition and establish that more equality can be attained. For instance, Canada ranks behind Iceland, Norway, Sweden, New Zealand, and Denmark, each of which may have policies affecting gender equality that Canada could emulate. The World Economic Forum (2019) also provides fodder for the skeptical, as it ranks Canada behind France, Switzerland, Namibia, and Spain, none of which have a particularly sterling reputation for gender equality. The report ranks countries by the gap *between* women and men on various measures; for example, Canada trails Syria in the Global Gender Gap Index on Health and Survival, a measure that reflects the discrepancy between women and men's health, not the health or life expectancy of women. Syria's ranking rose, not because Syrian women enjoy exemplary health, but because the conflict in Syria has damaged everyone's health, and life expectancy for both women and men has diminished.

The European Institute for Gender Equality (2021), a European Union (EU) agency, builds an index that is currently based on six "core" indicators (work, money, knowledge, time, power, and health) and two "additional" domains – violence and intersecting inequalities. The intersections are limited to disability, age, level of education, country of birth, and family type. The index produces a number for each EU country, and for the EU as a whole, a model that is adaptable for Canadian provinces, territories, and the federal level. The institute has determined that at the current rate, the EU is at least sixty years away from reaching gender equality. Interestingly, an "Index Game" has been added, so that you can enter a gender and country of birth "to see how your life could have turned out." This could be a tool to raise awareness about how our lives are influenced by matters beyond our control.

Another option for Canada could be to increase the effort to produce gender-disaggregated and intersectional data for the Canadian Index of Wellbeing, a project based at the University of Waterloo. It mines various data sources to create an index in eight domain areas: community vitality, democratic engagement, education, environment, healthy populations, leisure and culture, living standards, and time use. These eight areas are themselves crunched into the overall Index of Wellbeing (see CIW 2021). Typically, mainstream well-being measures do not include elements that are important to Indigenous communities, such as spiritual health and connection to language and culture (Rountree and Smith 2016). In Chapter 11 of this volume, Leah Levac and her colleagues explore intersectional gender considerations in the participatory development of a community vitality index.

A possible model that could address some of the problems in measuring the *impact* of GBA+ implementation, rather than just the *inputs* (such as GBA+ training), is the Migrant Integration Policy Index (MIPEX). MIPEX is produced by the Barcelona Centre for International Affairs and the Migration Policy Group, co-funded by the EU, with the participation of a large network of expert collaborators. It looks at fifty-eight policy indicators for countries such as EU member states, Norway, Australia, Japan, Canada, and the United States (see MIPEX 2020). It looks specifically at policy (including legislation and regulations), comparing the policies of various countries regarding immigration and migrants, and is capable of tracking change over time. A handy feature that makes MIPEX accessible to the public is the invitation to "play with the data" and create custom charts on its website (MIPEX 2020). MIPEX is based on its own definitions of what the integration of migrants looks like. It measures the gap between its vision of full migrant integration and the realities. So to adapt MIPEX to a Canadian gender equality context, a vision of what equality would look like would be necessary with which to compare current policy.

Canada's GRF differs from the equality measures discussed above in that it is a set of many indicators rather than an index of one number representing progress toward gender equality that can be directly compared year over year. Making an index out of the GRF could be problematic, as indicators such as "high school completion rate," which in Canada is common and does not reflect gender inequality, would be on par with the gender wage gap or the burden of unpaid work. The upshot here is that progress toward gender equality can be measured in many ways and that using such measures is complementary to qualitative data and feminist social justice actions. The major criticism of all the measures is that they are not intersectional, with the result that they hide disparities within the category of "women." However, they could be made intersectional.

Conclusion

This chapter describes Canada's new Gender Results Framework and the frustrating years that led up to it, with wholly inadequate SWC performance indicators used as a stand-in for national gender equality indicators. In this sense, it is also a warning of what gender equality indicators could revert to. Although the GRF is an improvement, it would be greatly enhanced if it were intersectional in nature and if it included a measurement of the motherhood penalty in income and earnings, as well as the gender wealth gap. The indicators are based on Statistics Canada data, and unlike WAGE, Statistics Canada is not prey to political or bureaucratic manipulation of results. The objectives and indicators are also tied to the SDGs of the United Nations, which further anchor them, unlike the fluctuating performance indicators of the former SWC.

Whether activists will avail themselves of the GRF or Statistics Canada's Gender, Diversity and Inclusion Statistics Hub remains to be seen. At the time of writing, they did not seem to be widely familiar with these resources. Statistics Canada is now attempting to better communicate its data, such as by creating infographics that can be circulated on social media to counter misinformation, though the success of this effort remains unclear. As a government agency, Statistics Canada cannot use sensationalism or policy hooks to capture attention. In addition, people tend to discount data with which they disagree, taking their lead from Donald Trump by attacking the data source as lacking in credibility. Thus, any data that make a case for gender equality may be dismissed as having been manipulated by the Trudeau government.

Canadians need to understand how Statistics Canada collects its data, what shapes the questions it asks, how the data are interpreted, how they can be used, and how people can participate in Statistics Canada consultations about what information to collect. Given the increasing role of quantitative data and the level of confusion and misinformation about them, the elementary and secondary school curriculums should cover how they are gathered, how they can be manipulated, what they mean and do not mean, and where people can find reliable sources of them. The value of qualitative data, including oral history, should also be taught and explored. Such data can provide the human stories, the depth, and the explanations for why things are as they are. They are also a starting point for further quantitative, qualitative, and documentary investigation.

Throughout my lifetime, feminist activists have used Statistics Canada data on violence against women and the gap between women and men's earnings to support their advocacy. Much of these data were written up in a Statistics Canada publication titled *Women in Canada: A Gender-Based Statistical Report* (2013), which is issued about every five years. However, each chapter was written by a different author or authors, who chose to highlight differing statistical tables, which meant that there was no comparable way to list, for example, total average income of Canadian men as a whole, Canadian women as a whole, women and men living with a disability, Indigenous women and men, and racialized women and men. One chapter could examine earnings (which are just one form of income), another might even narrow that down to earnings of the core working-age population (twenty-five to fifty-four), and another could use after-tax income. Different measures cannot be compared. With greater access to actual data tables, equality-seeking Canadians could potentially locate comparable data for various groups, although truly intersectional data are still hard to come by. There is still room to grow on intersectional data and to compare the economic and political power of gendered groups in society, which remains a hierarchy topped by white men. These data are important in an era of misinformation in which some white men feel threatened, marginalized, and powerless. I am not arguing that Statistics Canada or the GRF are perfect, but I do suggest that progress has been made on developing national gender equality indicators for Canada and that they provide some useful, albeit quite imperfect, tools for change.

A recent example illustrates this point: For several years, I have delivered presentations both in Japan and online for Japanese public officials and academics on how Canada collects quantitative data that can be used for policy development. The focus has been on gendered data for disaster management planning, but when the COVID-19 pandemic arose, it changed to the gendered and intersectional effects of the pandemic in Canada. Statistics Canada pivoted to produce mainly gender-disaggregated data about the effects of COVID-19 on various groups, including parents, persons with disabilities, seniors, children, Indigenous people, racialized Canadians, lesbian, gay, bisexual, transgender, queer, questioning, and two-spirit Canadians, and female and racialized small-business owners.[4] In addition, activists, the media, and local and provincial/territorial public health bodies provided qualitative and quantitative data about the effects of the pandemic. Although COVID-19 is the most wide-reaching pandemic in a hundred years, it will not be the last. If policy is not changed, the next pandemic is likely to hit the same groups in the same ways. The effects of any policy changes will be directly measurable by comparing the gendered intersectional effects of the next pandemic to this one. Measuring policy change is incredibly difficult because there are so many local, regional, national, and international variables. In the case of pandemics, the collection of gendered intersectional data can show whether a country, region, or local area has made progress or has regressed on equity policy issues.

In short, we need to remain vigilant about how quantitative data are collected and by whom, and about what questions are asked. We need also to learn how best to use quantitative data to measure and contribute to social change. The GRF is an imperfect but nonetheless useful tool, but unless voters know and care about it and its implications, it will not be enough. I argue that social movements can effect real and lasting change by moving the population, not simply the government, toward their goals. This requires outreach that connects with people where they live. Quantitative tools such as the GRF and international reports can be used in conjunction with personal stories, qualitative data, and an articulated vision of how a better world would work.

Notes

1 In the interest of full disclosure and to ground my perspective, I will briefly outline how my knowledge of the subject matter of this chapter was constructed over time, the relationships I have had with some of the entities named in this chapter, and what my affiliations were which may have shaped my perspective. I worked as a public servant for the Canadian government at two points in my career, including at Status of Women Canada. My work as a senior policy research adviser in Research and Academic Relations at Public Safety Canada involved developing and using qualitative and quantitative research, including working closely with Statistics Canada. I remain a member of Statistics Canada's Advisory Committee on Social Conditions. I was a researcher/legislative assistant to two New Democratic Party of Canada members of parliament and used quantitative indicators to criticize government performance on gender equality and health. I also worked as research coordinator in a women's organization, where the most popular products I created were quantitative factsheets with feminist, contextual interpretations for use by activists and the public. Currently a consultant, I develop indicators and qualitative and quantitative research for intersectional feminist organizations, Inuit groups, federal and provincial governments, and the United Nations Development Programme. I developed an equity-based analysis and process for Library and Archives Canada, and I conducted research for the Interdepartmental Circles on Indigenous Representation in the Public Service on the recruitment and retention of First Nations, Inuit, and Métis public servants.

2 SDG 5 has the following objectives: End all forms of discrimination against all women and girls everywhere; eliminate all forms of violence against all women and girls in the public and private spheres, including trafficking and sexual and other types of exploitation; eliminate all harmful practices, such as child, early, and forced marriage and female genital mutilation; recognize and value unpaid care and domestic work through the provision of public services, infrastructure, and social protection policies and the promotion of shared responsibility within the household and family as nationally appropriate; ensure women's full and effective participation and equal opportunities for leadership at all levels of decision making in political, economic, and public life; ensure universal access to sexual and reproductive rights as agreed in accordance with the Programme of Action of the International Conference on Population and Development and the Beijing Platform for Action and the outcome documents of their review conferences; undertake reforms to give women equal rights to economic resources, as well as access to ownership and control over land and other forms of prosperity, financial services, inheritance, and natural resources, in accordance with national laws; enhance the use of enabling technology, in particular information, communications technology, to promote the empowerment of women; adopt and strengthen sound policies and enforceable legislation for the promotion of gender equality and the empowerment of all women and girls at all levels (UN 2020).

3 Statistics Canada uses the term "visible minority," which also appears in the Employment Equity Act, to refer to persons who do not describe themselves as white or Indigenous.

4 The smaller the sample size, the harder it is to be truly intersectional; for example, there are no Statistics Canada data about Black lesbians living with mobility impairments.

Works Cited

CIW (Canadian Index of Wellbeing). 2021. "Domains and Indicators." https://uwaterloo. ca/canadian-index-wellbeing/what-we-do/domains-and-indicators.

de Bruijn, Hans. 2002. *Managing Performance in the Public Sector.* London: Routledge.

Esquivel, Valeria. 2016. "Power and the Sustainable Development Goals: A Feminist Analysis." *Gender and Development* 24, 1: 9–23.

European Institute for Gender Equality. 2021. "Gender Equality Index." https://eige.europa. eu/gender-equality-index/about.

Federal-Provincial/Territorial Ministers Responsible for the Status of Women. 1997. *Economic Gender Equality Indicators.* Ottawa: Status of Women Canada.

Hudon, Tamara. 2016. "Visible Minority Women." Statistics Canada. https://www150. statcan.gc.ca/n1/pub/89-503-x/2015001/article/14315-eng.htm.

Jehn, Anthony, David Walters, and Stephanie Howells. 2019. "Employment and Wage Gaps among Recent Canadian Male and Female Postsecondary Graduates." *Higher Education Policy* 34: 724–46. https://link.springer.com/article/10.1057/s41307-019-00162-0.

Micheli, Pietro, and Jean-François Manzoni. 2010. "Strategic Performance Measurement: Benefits, Limitations and Paradoxes." *Long Range Planning* 43, 4: 465–76. http://dx.doi. org/10.1016/j.lrp.2009.12.004.

MIPEX (Migrant Integration Policy Index). 2020. "Migrant Integration Policy Index." Accessed January 12, 2021. http://www.mipex.eu.

Moreau, Greg, Brianna Jaffray, and Amelia Armstrong. 2020. "Police-Reported Crime Statistics in Canada, 2019." Juristat, October 29. https://www150.statcan.gc.ca/n1/pub/ 85-002-x/2020001/article/00010-eng.htm#a10.

Moynihan, Donald, Sergio Fernandez, Soonhee Kim, Kelly LeRoux, Suzanne Piotrowski, Bradley Wright, and Kaifeng Yang. 2011. "Performance Regimes amidst Governance Complexity." *Journal of Public Administration Research and Theory* 21, suppl. 1: i141–55. https://doi.org/10.1093/jopart/muq059.

Moyser, Melissa, and Amanda Burlock. 2018. "Time Use: Total Work Burden, Unpaid Work, and Leisure." Statistics Canada. https://www150.statcan.gc.ca/n1/pub/89-503-x/ 2015001/article/54931-eng.htm.

Pauktuutit Inuit Women of Canada. 2021. "Food Security." https://www.pauktuutit.ca/ social-and-economic-development/food-security/.

Rountree, Jennifer, and Addie Smith. 2016. "Strength-Based Well-Being Indicators for Indigenous Children and Families: A Literature Review of Indigenous Communities' Identified Well-Being Indicators." *American Indian and Alaska Native Mental Health Research* 23, 3: 206–20. https://doi.org/10.5820/aian.2303.2016.206.

Statistics Canada. 2013. *Women in Canada: A Gender-Based Statistical Report.* 6th ed. Ottawa: Statistics Canada.

–. 2020. "Goal 5 – Gender Equality." Accessed December 15, 2020. https://www144.statcan. gc.ca/sdg-odd/goal-objectif05-eng.htm.

SWC (Status of Women Canada). 1995. *Setting the Stage for the Next Century: The Federal Plan for Gender Equality.* Ottawa: SWC.

–. 2006. *Women's Program Evaluation Report and Management Response.* Ottawa: SWC.

–. 2011. *2010–2011 Departmental Performance Report.* Ottawa: SWC.

–. 2012a. "Summative Evaluation of the Women's Program Final Report – 2012." Accessed June 25, 2018. http://www.swc-cfc.gc.ca/trans/account-resp/pr/sewp-espf/sewp-espf -eng.html.

–. 2012b. *2011–12 Report on Plans and Priorities.* Ottawa: SWC.

–. 2012c. *2011–2012 Departmental Performance Report.* Ottawa: SWC.

–. 2013a. *2012–2013 Departmental Performance Report.* Ottawa: SWC.

–. 2013b. *2012–13 Report on Plans and Priorities.* Ottawa: SWC.

–. 2013c. "Who We Are." Accessed June 25, 2018. http://www.swc-cfc.gc.ca/abu-ans/who -qui/index-eng.html.

–. 2014. *2013–14 Report on Plans and Priorities.* Ottawa: SWC.

–. 2019. "Daily Average Time in Hours and Proportion of Day Spent on Unpaid Domestic Work and Care Work by Sex." Table 45-10-0014-02. Accessed November 16, 2023. https://www150.statcan.gc.ca/t1/tbl1/en/tv.action?pid=4510001402.

Treasury Board Secretariat. 2012. "Results-Based Management Lexicon." Accessed June 25, 2018. http://www.tbs-sct.gc.ca/cee/pubs/lex-eng.asp.

UN (United Nations). 2020. "Goal 5: Achieve Gender Equality and Empower All Women and Girls." Accessed December 10, 2020. https://www.un.org/sustainabledevelopment/gender-equality/.

Waring, Marilyn. 1988. *If Women Counted: A New Feminist Economics.* New York: Harper and Row.

Women and Gender Equality Canada (WAGE). 2023a. "Economic Participation and Prosperity." Accessed November 16, 2023. https://women-gender-equality.canada.ca/en/gender-results-framework/economic-participation-prosperity.html.

–. 2023b. "Education and Skills Development." https://women-gender-equality.canada.ca/en/gender-results-framework/education-skills-development.html.

–. 2023c. "Gender Results Framework." Ottawa, WAGE. https://women-gender-equality.canada.ca/en/gender-results-framework.html.

World Economic Forum. 2019. *The Global Gender Gap Report 2020.* Geneva: World Economic Forum. http://www3.weforum.org/docs/WEF_GGGR_2020.pdf.

Zhang, Xuelin. 2009. "Earnings of Women with and without Children." *Perspectives.* Statistics Canada Catalogue no. 75-001-X. https://www150.statcan.gc.ca/n1/en/pub/75-001-x/2009103/pdf/10823-eng.pdf?st=LV9ovwAf.

2

Working toward a Gender-Sensitive Canadian Parliament: The Politics of Gender Equality Measurement

Joan Grace

A PARADOXICAL SITUATION has arisen in many legislatures around the world: as legislators debate the issues that profoundly shape socio-economic conditions and women's inequalities, parliaments have simultaneously "become the public face of political disengagement" (Leston-Bandeira 2012, 265). In response, the Inter-Parliamentary Union (IPU), an international organization dedicated to promoting democracy, has encouraged state authorities to develop "gender-sensitive" parliaments to improve the participation of women and to ensure that policy and legislative debates employ a gender lens (Palmieri 2011). The IPU (2017, 7) defines a gender-sensitive parliament as one that strives for and achieves an equal number of male and female legislators; devises a gender equality policy framework that is implemented within its own legislative context; and mainstreams gender equality and facilitates an "internal culture that respects women's rights, promotes gender equality and responds to the needs and realities of MPs [members of parliament] – men and women – to balance work and family responsibilities," ensuring too that parliamentary staff are provided the capacity and resources to further gender equality. In research and practice – and in this chapter – gender sensitivity describes gender mainstreaming processes and internal, contextual policies "that take into account the different impacts that they have on men and women, boys and girls" (IPU 2016, 38).

With its atmosphere of an "old-fashioned men's club in which women are interlopers," the Canadian House of Commons is considered by many feminists one of the "last bastions of male culture in Canadian institutions" (Steele 2002, 14). In this chapter, I focus on this aspect of the House, arguing that applying certain indicators to its inner workings could increase the gender sensitivity of its practices and processes. I use the term "gender sensitivity" to align with the definition of the IPU, noting that if the institutional and organizational practices of parliaments take gender and diversity into account, they may well become responsive. That is, they will promote women's equality and will address discrimination that is embodied in legislative debates and parliamentary outputs. Three fundamental interrelated components are required to create a gender-sensitive parliament that is capable of addressing women's place in politics and society: the presence of women in legislative bodies, gender mainstreaming legislative practices and debates, and the promotion of women's empowerment. In effect, I suggest that these elements can feminize a parliamentary system by infusing alternative ideas, practices, and discourses that recognize women's voices and experiences and can instill a measure of gender balance between men and women in parliamentary work and outputs.

My approach, inspired by the work of Karen Celis and Sarah Childs (2018, 314), focuses on processes and institutional arrangements rather than on the role of critical actors and the "content" of substantive representation in terms of outcomes. I suggest that integrating gender mainstreaming with a series of interconnected indicators will produce a measurement and analytical approach that can generate data and highlight areas of improvement in the House of Commons. This approach will track implementation of gender mainstreaming and will create an empirical accountability method to facilitate the continuous improvement of the organization and promote a gender-sensitive House.

I look to amalgamating historical institutionalism with gender and organization theory into a feminist-institutional approach to capture a nuanced understanding of the House as a gendered social structure. A historical institutional approach is instructive, given its theoretical focus on explaining "how and why institutions lock the expectations and behaviour of individuals into relatively predictable, self-reinforcing patterns," even when confronted by major sociocultural changes such as the rise of feminism and gender equality discourses (Krook and Mackay 2011, 12).

From a feminist institutional perspective, formal and informal practices and rules of behaviour, along with the interplay between institutional sites and actors within the organization, are conceptualized as deeply embedded in and mediated by male norms, gendered power relations, and the "institutionalization of sexism," which too often structures and informs politics (Lovenduski 2014). The representational system and legislative practices in the House of Commons are the products of history, significantly influenced by Westminster parliamentary culture and conventions. Like other formal bodies, the House is structured along a command-and-control delineation in the division of work and privilege (Acker 2006; Itzin and Newman 1995; Mills and Tancred 1992). It is a gendered organization that, in the absence of transformative reforms to feminize institutional processes and practices, will continue to perpetuate complex inequalities between men and women, both within and outside of the legislative chamber.

The approach advanced in this chapter has been explored in other contexts. The IPU has produced several extensively researched studies on how to weave gender mainstreaming into legislative practices, agreeing to a Plan of Action at its 127th assembly held in Quebec City in October 2012 (IPU 2006, 2009, 2012, 2017; Palmieri 2011). And many legislators have heeded the call. Across the global North and South, there are currently over a hundred gender-focused entities in legislative assemblies, ranging from parliamentary standing committees to cross-party women's caucuses and issue-based parliamentary groups (Celis, Childs, and Curtin 2016; Freidenvall and Erikson 2020; Sawer 2020). Other measures to gender a parliament include passing electoral quota laws to promote the election of women, gender mainstreaming, and initiatives that balance work and life, such as on-site childcare, family-friendly legislative sitting hours, and proxy voting (Palmieri 2010; Sawer, Freidenvall, and Palmieri 2013). In varying ways and in combination, these measures are examples of reform instruments that can construct a gender-sensitive parliament. The first democratic parliament to undergo a systematic audit, via a working partnership with the IPU, was that of the United Kingdom (Childs and Challender 2019). In 2018, the Commission of the House of Commons and the Commission of the House of Lords agreed to a gender-sensitive parliament audit (UK Parliament 2018). Reported in 2018, its findings were comprehensive, identifying a parliamentary culture of bullying and sexual harassment, as well as the ongoing challenge of balancing work and family life for female MPs, who were also the targets of online threats to their physical security (UK Parliament 2018, 27). Whether plans resulting from the audit will actually be implemented remains unclear. From June to December 2019, the UK House of Commons Women and Equalities Committee inquired into gender sensitivity, but its queries were discontinued due to the dissolution of parliament (Erikson and Verge 2022, 12).

Except for the work of Cheryl Collier and Tracey Raney (2018) and, more recently, Jeanette Ashe (2020), there has been limited attention to analyzing formal policies and organizational practices in the Canadian House of Commons that influence the work of female MPs or how institutional practices frame policy and legislative debates to the detriment of women in society. Although some tenacious women have penned memoirs in which they recount their difficult experiences as MPs (Campbell 1996; Carstairs 1993; Copps 1986; Fairclough 1995), only a few studies in the Canadian political science literature refer specifically to women in parliament (Arscott and Trimble 1997; Trimble and Arscott 2003). And, except for the work of Manon Tremblay (1998, 2003), there are negligible substantive studies of female parliamentarians' influence on gendering legislative debates in national politics. In American, Australian, British, European, and Latin American jurisdictions, however, rigorous empirical analyses discuss the array of opportunities and barriers that shape women's power and authority in legislatures, with a notable focus on substantive representation, the role of female parliamentarians, and parliamentary committees (Allen and Childs 2019; Celis and Childs 2020; Erikson and Verge 2022; Heath, Schwindt-Bayer, and Taylor-Robinson 2005; Holli 2012; Lovenduski and Norris 2003; O'Brien 2012; Rosenthal 2000).

In the Canadian House of Commons, attempts are being made to gender legislative deliberations. Established in 2004, the Standing Committee on the Status of Women (SCSW) was struck as a dedicated gender-focused legislative committee in the House. It has produced an impressive number of studies on a wide array of policy issues that affect the lives of women, as well as their families and communities. The SCSW has also argued strongly for the application of gender mainstreaming in policy development and for the implementation of gender-responsive budgets (House of Commons 2005, 2008). The Library of Parliament has produced two concise reports reflecting on arguments presented by the IPU about the importance of women in elected office and the gender dimensions of the Canadian House (Barnes and Munn-Rivard 2013; Munn-Rivard 2013). That said, there is much work to be done in enhancing the organizational capacity of the House to attend to troublesome issues that sustain women's inequalities.

Gender, Institutions, and Inequalities

I begin the analysis in terms of how our everyday lives are structured and ordered within institutions to complicate our ideas and expectations of the House of Commons. Here I see the House not simply as a chamber of legislative debate, but as a place of work and a public organization of gendered social relations. My analysis is guided by the following questions:

- How and where do gender norms emanate within an institution?
- How do institutions perpetuate women's inequality?
- How is "gendering" identified in an organization or institution?
- What gender equality indicators can be used to identify gender processes in an institution?
- How is change instigated and how is it measured?
- How do we know when gendering processes have been disrupted in the promotion of women's equality?
- How does an institution become feminized?

In the IPU literature, gender is defined as "the social attributes associated with being male and female and the relations between women, men, girls and boys" (Palmieri 2011, 5). Although this definition is well accepted and quite valid, it does not encompass the role of institutions in both sustaining and re-creating appropriate *and* expected behaviours of masculine and feminine. Nor does it attend to the way that women in organizations often struggle with institutionally developed gender systems, where their positions and decision-making roles are typically less powerful than those of men. I contend that this is a stubborn truism found in both the private and public sectors. In the construction of power relations in organizations, "everyone has a sex and performs a gender," but masculine forms of gendering generally dominate (Chappell 2006, 226). From this perspective, organizations evolve into institutional instruments of social control that "exercise power over a number of generations" (Vickers, Rankin, and Appelle 1993, 133–34).

Organizations become gendered through four interrelated processes (Acker 1992, 2006):

- the production of gender divisions and the recruitment and the organization of work
- the production of symbols, images, and other forms of consciousness that explicate and justify
- interactions between individuals in the organization
- the internal mental work of individuals in the institution.

Joan Acker (2006, 443) further argues that all organizations, in effect, are "inequality regimes," which she defines as "loosely interrelated practices, processes, actions, and meanings that result in and maintain class, gender, and racial inequalities within particular organizations." Inequality regimes mirror women's inequality in society; all organizations are embedded in a particular socio-political gender regime of power relations that are intimately structured by age, race, ethnicity, Indigeneity, class, sexual orientation, and sex/gender identification, along with the intersectionalities of those preferences, attributes, and identities. Acker (2006, 443) understands inequality as "systematic disparities" between actors in the organization regarding control over resources and how and where they participate in decision making, along with career opportunities such as promotions, financial rewards, or informal incentives that influence their behaviour in the work environment. An inequality regime is open to change when relationships shift; it is not static or always permanent (Acker 2006). The steepness of hierarchy, however, certainly structures the depth of inequalities and determines the regime's resilience. In steeply hierarchical systems such as bureaucracies or legislatures, the inequality regime is fixed and more difficult to modify than in a flatter structure that *potentially* provides more opportunities for women to engage in decision making (Acker 2006, 445).

The House of Commons is decidedly a steep hierarchal system made operational through traditional offices and clearly delineated lines of communication. The executive, though having to retain the confidence of the chamber, is at the apex of the legislative system, which has been made all the more powerful over the last few decades due to the centralization of authority in the Office of the Prime Minister. A Speaker presides over debate in the House and holds the privilege of identifying who will express their views and that of their constituents. Which MPs are permitted to speak in the chamber is determined solely by party leaders and party whips. The chamber is divided into two sides, one officially designated as the "Opposition," with institutional focus on the leaders of political parties who command the loyalty and discipline of the caucus. The allocation of work is further underpinned by the production of gender divisions and images. The chamber's "winner take all" culture, coupled with militaristic ceremonial practices such as the sergeant-at-arms' placement of the mace as a symbol of the authority of the Speaker, reminds everyone that men fought men in the pursuit of what's best for the nation and the Commonwealth. Westminster parliaments were founded when men alone held the franchise and were the only legal persons and property owners: they were the nation builders of yesterday and are the leaders of today. The parliamentary arena in Canada, as elsewhere, is one in which men dominate decision making, choose what issues are for public attention, frame political discourse, and determine the standards of evaluation (Childs and Challender 2019; Erikson and Verge 2022).

Gender Critiques of the House of Commons

Although the House of Commons is linked to an upper house, the Senate, from a political and representation standpoint, it is a relatively stand-alone institution. In its functioning, however, layers of institutions are at work in sustaining continuities and shaping gendered inequalities. The House exists because of the presence of *other* organizations. Political parties, each quite diverse in terms of their cultures and objectives, merge into inherited parliamentary practices. Indeed, the House produces and reproduces complex inequalities (Acker 2006, 442), all the more sharply due to institutional dynamics. As Kareen Jabre (2009, 55) reminds us, "Parliaments are in essence a platform where conflicts are channelled into politically negotiated solutions, and where diverging or conflicting interests are transformed into policies and legislation that is applicable to all." Yet, some organizations in the House of Commons have a value-driven notion of what constitutes "applicable to all," being able to justify women's place in society, the economy, and the family through ideological lenses. Women in the current Conservative Party of Canada, for example, may well support the party's position on "choice in childcare" but know that it is women who are the primary caregivers and who disproportionately comprise the economically disadvantaged. They are also probably aware that for immigrant and Indigenous women, these situations are often much more desperate. Complex inequalities are overshadowed, however, by the priorities of the party and Westminster parliamentary conventions.

A member of parliament, a position still largely based on the white male breadwinner citizen, is desexed and degendered. Indeed, the "structuring of physical space" and the conditions of work in the chamber "assume that parliament representatives are not at the same time primary carers for family members," a role that typically falls to women (Sawer 2000, 370). In the House of Commons, a "logic of appropriateness" is clearly at work (Chappell 2006, 225). As Louise Chappell (2006, 225–26) notes, all institutions construct and justify certain types of conduct while discouraging others, often in terms of acceptable masculine and feminine traits and behaviours. In the House, behaviours are sometimes obviously gendered, such as the accepted dress of MPs based on male business attire, or the issue of women MPs bringing their children to the chamber or onto the floor of the House. More often, gendering processes are subtle, resulting from unconscious actions such as perceptions about appropriate leadership traits. In either form, the logic of appropriateness upholds traditional practices that reinforce the archetype of a masculine/male parliamentarian, who is expected to wear a suit to work, assume a particular leadership persona, and evidently have no worries about balancing work and family. Childcare services have been in place for over thirty years, and many House washrooms are equipped with change tables, with two installed in 2012 (Barnes and Munn-Rivard 2013). Unlike in some other jurisdictions, however, until recently, there has been no financial assistance to cover childcare expenses, and the benefits received by parliamentarians do not specifically cover parental leave (Barnes and Munn-Rivard 2013, 3–4). However, some promising reforms have occurred. During the first session of the forty-second parliament (2015–19), the House passed a Members' Sessional Allowance Regulation, which stipulates that members who miss a day of attendance due to pregnancy or because of a caring responsibility will nonetheless be recorded as in attendance (Equal Voice 2020; Montpetit 2020). And since 2015, codes of conduct addressing sexual harassment have been implemented in the House and Senate (Collier and Raney 2018; Montpetit 2020).

Still, the culture of the House remains problematic for female members. Parliamentary privilege upholds that MPs have the "right to carry out their parliamentary duties without being assaulted, menaced, intimidated or insulted," yet there are no stated objectives prohibiting sexist language (Barnes and Munn-Rivard 2013, 4). House decorum undergirds an uneasy, sometimes hostile gendered environment for female legislators. In a survey of MPs in the forty-second parliament (2015 to 2019), 67 percent of women reported gendered heckling (as opposed to 20 percent of men) that disrupted and affected their legislative performance (Equal Voice 2020, 9). One female MP reported being called "bossy, loud, abrasive, a know it all, and too big for my boots" (Equal Voice 2020, 9).

Although change is difficult to instigate in hierarchical, consolidated institutions such as the House of Commons, inequality regimes can be disrupted, especially if one organization within the operation of the legislature influences other actors. The idea of an electoral contagion has been used to explain why hesitant political parties such as the federal Conservatives have become more sensitive to criticism about the lack of women in their ranks (Goodyear-Grant 2013, 125–26). Currently an Opposition party, the New Democratic Party has had a long-standing commitment to parity in the nomination of men and women as candidates, and the Liberal Party supports the nomination and election of women through the National Women's Commission. Although the motives of the Conservative Party are about expanding its electoral base rather than furthering women's equality, the actions of its main competitors probably influenced its attention to women as voters. This may in part explain why, after the May 2011 election, a record 76 women were elected, representing 24.7 percent of the seats in the House – an encouraging increase from the previous 22.1 percent (Cool 2013, 1). The record election of women to the House continued in two subsequent elections, with 98 women elected in 2019, representing 29 percent of the legislature (Montpetit 2020). That percentage grew marginally in the 2021 election, in which 103 women MPs won their seats, thus advancing women's representation in the House to 30.0 percent.

Some commentators argue that increasing the number of female MPs in the House until their presence reaches a "critical mass" can instigate changes in its culture and can facilitate legislation that benefits women. According to presence theory, when more women enter the chamber, a feminized politics acts as a catalyst, given women's shared experiences in the home, the economy, and public life (Lovenduski and Norris 2003). It has also been suggested that women tend to bring their own style of politics to the chamber, preferring less combative, consensus-based processes – a politics that conflicts with party practices and parliamentary mores (IPU 2009; Palmieri 2011; Steele 2002).

In a study of the British parliament conducted after a number of women were elected in 1997, Joni Lovenduski and Pippa Norris (2003, 87) assessed the proposition that the political values and policy issues of women differed from those of men. Their findings did not support the argument that a higher number of women led to radical change in the culture of Westminster, but nor was the situation one of "politics as usual" (Lovenduski and Norris 2003, 100). The authors found that the values of female politicians across the parties did differ from those of their male counterparts, particularly in debates on equality measures. Although we have less evidence in the Canadian case, in a study of female parliamentarians in the thirty-fifth parliament, which sat from 1993 to 1997, Manon Tremblay (2003, 224–25) found that a majority of respondents tended to hold territorial conceptions of political representation and tangential conceptions of representation in terms of group identity, such as women. In other words, identity was shaped and expressed by where they lived as legislative representatives, not foremost as women representing women. Tremblay (1998, 464) did conclude, however, that during the term of the parliament, female MPs were most likely to accord priority to issues that spoke to and acted for women's betterment in policy areas such as support payments, childcare, and ending violence against women through gun control.

The political aspirations of women vary; in Canada, this is particularly the case due to regionalism and linguistic and ethno-cultural diversities. Contemporary research has questioned gender stereotypes of women as "naturally more principled" and conciliatory than men, complicating the link between the presence of women in legislatures and substantive actions on behalf of women (Mackay 2008; Ross 2002, 190). The focus has now turned to the actions of critical actors, which include men, in the promotion of women's equality initiatives (Childs and Krook 2009). As many feminist scholars have pointed out, there is no one category of woman, and there are no guarantees that a critical mass of women will make a difference (Childs and Krook 2009; Hankivsky 2013; Sawer 2012). As I argue, an institutional environment influences and often transforms behaviours when individuals uphold or internalize its logic of appropriateness. As members of a political party, female MPs have varying identities, cultural backgrounds, and socio-economic experiences. They hold a spectrum of political values and *choose* the party that best reflects their beliefs. Yet, if organizational processes shift, so too will gendered understandings of feminine and masculine, gender, and power.

As a consequence, particular patterns of behaviour emerged in the House of Commons and became institutionalized through party practices and parliamentary custom. Men's access to power "has been reinforced over time through 'constantly repeated processes of exclusion' of women" (Chappell and Waylen 2013, 602). Gendering processes, shaped by historical trajectories and inevitable in all organizations, eventually become normalized. The resultant institutional culture in the House of Commons, especially during Question Period, is an overly oppositional, hierarchical environment that suppresses women's experiences, as well as their expertise, talents, and styles of politics. This has prompted some observers to suggest that female parliamentarians often find the smaller setting of legislative committees more comfortable than the theatre of parliament (Sawer 2000, 370). For example, they can use House committees as "leverage beyond that of individual parliamentarians, who may have conflicting accountabilities" between their personal preferences and party policy (Sawer 2012, 322). The inequality regime, however, still matters. Research indicates that female MPs are typically concentrated in or chair social policy committees rather than finance and industry committees because the former are considered less powerful and status-driven than the latter (Darcy 1996; O'Brien 2012; Palmieri 2011). Gender dynamics persist in committee, with female MPs participating less in discussions and interrupting less often during deliberations than their male counterparts (Kathlene 1994). A 2013 study of all the standing committees in parliament found that only one had a female participation rate of over 75 percent – as expected, this committee was the SCSW. Four of thirty-nine standing committees had 50 percent or more female parliamentarians – all four of them were in the Senate (Barnes and Munn-Rivard 2013, 5). In the House, nine standing committees had female participation rates between 25.0 and 49.9 percent, and in April 2013, only two women chaired a House committee: Health and Status of Women (Barnes and Munn-Rivard 2013, 5–6). More recently, Jeanette Ashe's (2020, 72) research on representation in Canadian parliamentary bodies, however, found that women chaired 17 percent of House standing committees as of 2019 but chaired 50 percent of Senate standing committees. Despite this increased representation, Ashe (2020, 73) notes that "women are still disproportionately chairing standing committees dealing with 'soft' policy issues such as women's issues and social welfare issues rather than 'hard' policy issues such as defence and the economy."

To upend the institutional dominance of masculinity, reforms are required that attend to both the formal and informal aspects of the House. Even with the record number of women who were elected in 2021, and the implementation of a few measures such as the Code of Conduct, if structural changes do not occur in the chamber, gendering processes will continue unabated or will re-emerge, perhaps stealthily, after reforms are put in place. As Fiona Mackay (2008) observes in her analysis of the reconstituted Scottish parliament, which integrated gender equality initiatives into its operations post-devolution, an established institution can overwhelm attempts to introduce new ideas and perspectives. Institutional legacies can revive embedded Westminster norms, leaving power relations intact and requiring gender equity actors to remain vigilant to ensure enforcement (Chappell 2011, 166; Mackay 2008). Indeed, achieving gender equality reforms is a challenge, given that they are subject to the "liability of newness" (Mackay 2014). As Mackay (2014, 551) insightfully explains, because the new is nested within "old rules" (or current rules), innovative ideas and associated practices are difficult to root into environments that are structured by long-standing norms and concomitant political interests.

Gendering Parliaments

Even in the face of daunting reform challenges, change and institutional innovations in the Canadian House of Commons ought to move forward as an expression of Canada's commitment to equality and democratic participation. Gender mainstreaming can provide one path to follow. I acknowledge that except for the few studies published by the IPU, gender mainstreaming initiatives have been developed to analyze public policy processes *within* the administrative state, not the organizational surround of a political institution such as the House of Commons. As Sonia Palmieri (2010, 5) notes in her analysis of the Australian parliament, "in much of the literature on gender mainstreaming, the role of parliament is not emphasised or considered." In Canada, gender-based analysis, later referred to as GBA+ to account for changing diversities in Canada and how gender "interacts" with varied identities of women, based on, for example, ethnicity, age, and ability (Scala and Paterson 2017, 432), was devised specifically to challenge administrative practices and to raise awareness among public administrators that policies and programs have unequal gendered and diversity impacts. Formulating appropriate indicators and evaluation methods to provide empirical insights into how best to work toward a gender-sensitive parliament is still evolving.

Since the mid-1990s, GBA+ has been employed across federal government departments, albeit with varying degrees of success (Hankivsky 2013). Some progress has been achieved, but GBA has suffered from a lack of organizational capacity and political clout on the part of the lead government agency, Status of Women Canada (1996), to compel its application throughout government. As well, GBA is viewed by many analysts (Grace 1997; Paterson 2010) as too narrow in its interpretation and development, given the emphasis on an expert-bureaucratic model that integrates gender into policy development by professional public administrators but does not critique the *need* for GBA and why a critique of gender is required based on the socio-economic lives of women (Grace 1997; Paterson 2010; Scala and Paterson 2017). In reality, gender mainstreaming can be "demanding and challenging" (Hankivsky 2013), not only because of a lack of knowledge as to what it entails, but also due to vague objectives and conceptual ambiguity with terms such as "gender" and "equality" (Grace 1997; Hankivsky 2013; McNutt 2010; Paterson 2010). As a "policy about policy," gender mainstreaming is squarely focused on planned actions, programs, and policy analysis (McNutt 2010, 3). Applying it in the House of Commons will be challenging, given that the GBA+ model does not account for how institutional factors contribute to sustaining women's inequality.

Gender mainstreaming can be effective, however, if it incorporates "systematic identification, collection and analysis of gender data backed by qualitative assessments" (Breitenbach and Galligan 2006, 598). Gender equality indicators are often the subject of criticism, given the delicacy of determining objectives and defining key concepts. Disagreement will surely emerge between actors in the House of Commons in defining what is meant by gender equality and how it should be achieved. One political party will probably prefer reform measures that are voluntary or that support individual responsibility; others will favour legislative intervention. Unlike the formulation of indicators for policy analysis, applying gender equality indicators in a place of public debate will be at the mercy of the various parties working in concert for purposes beyond ideological partisanship. Indicators are criticized already because they can be used for political purposes. Indeed, government officials sometimes invoke indicator-driven data as proof that they are acting in a policy area (Breitenbach and Galligan 2006, 598). In a legislative chamber, these criticisms will surely be more acute. One party may disagree, for example, with what constitutes effectiveness or "good practices" in light of how the indicator impinges on its perspective of an issue or its legislative preferences. As well, parties may baulk at the suggestion of developing indicators that evaluate their performance because they perceive themselves as independent bodies that are free to conduct their business in support of their constituents' objectives and demands. In essence, attempts to establish acceptable measurements through gender mainstreaming may be seen as stifling democratic deliberation and representation.

Moreover, indicators can "suffer from the danger of measuring what is easy to measure, ignoring qualitative concerns, or leaving aside areas of importance less easy to measure" (Breitenbach and Galligan 2006, 600). Gendering processes can be obvious and easy to detect, as in the quantifiable absence of women from the legislative chamber, but they can also be invisible (Acker 2006, 452). This is particularly salient in the House of Commons. Because it is a public institution, its processes are shaped by a confluence of legal requirements to ensure transparent public reporting juxtaposed with cabinet and caucus conventions of secrecy. Indicators to reveal organizational myths, symbols, and attitudes in the House, and the so-called rules of the game, are ambiguous to conceptualize and difficult to measure, particularly in terms of assessing change and discerning shifts in gendering processes.

The application of gender mainstreaming in a legislative arena will also mean that political parties must surrender some of their control over framing deliberations and setting the legislative agenda. This situation will unfold when gender mainstreaming questions conventional ideas about "expert knowledge" and which groups or individuals are seen as legitimate witnesses who are invited to meet with legislative committees. Feminist activists and women's equality organizations who give testimony at committee meetings often struggle against state architectures that tend to view their contributions as non-objective, experiential information rather than evidence-based, empirical data given by "entrenched groups who are already seen as legitimate actors" (Smith 2005, 87). The participation of women through various accessible consultation processes will be critical but will be affected by some of the usual consultation challenges such as low survey response rates or the inability to attend in person due to a lack of financial resources (Culver and Howe 2004). If gender mainstreaming is to have any real effect, a process of "public engagement from the ground up" must be organized to hear from women from across diversities and life experiences, regions, and communities (Levac and Wiebe 2020).

The IPU, and indeed many bodies that support the idea of gendering or feminizing organizations and practices, strongly argues that indicators must be developed through participatory processes. Members of the SCSW are presently well versed in gender analysis and are well placed to consult with Canadians and to promote the importance of gender mainstreaming to their legislative colleagues. The SCSW has already undertaken extensive studies of GBA, recommending a number of measures such as gender framed training prior to each session of parliament, GBA of all committee deliberations, and the establishment of a commissioner for gender equality, who is to be appointed as an officer of parliament to oversee the implementation of GBA (House of Commons 2005, 2008).

In sum, the unique objectives of the House of Commons, along with the practicalities associated with the political, multi-organizational surround of a parliamentary setting, present numerous burdens in building a gender-sensitive parliament both in means and measurement. Gender equality indicators will be questioned and will rely substantially on political will to be implemented. Reform measures need to be realistic, given the political dynamics in the House and the public purpose of the chamber. Some hierarchical dimensions of the House, for example, will have to remain intact to ensure accountability. To inaugurate a gender-sensitive parliament, strategies to persuade legislative actors ought to be cast in terms of enhancing parliamentary responsiveness – common ground upon which all parties can agree. From my reading, Canada has been a relatively active member of the IPU, contributing data in the development of its premiere document on gender-sensitive parliaments (IPU 2011). I suggest that the IPU Action Plan could be a guide for the formation of a gender mainstreaming strategy. The House of Commons could assume a leadership role, making the case that a gender-sensitive parliament is not just about making parliament work better for women: it is about a "modern parliament; one that addresses and reflects the equality demands of a modern society" (IPU 2012, 9).

Gender Mainstreaming toward a Gender-Sensitive Parliament – A Plan of Action

I suggest that the IPU Plan of Action be used in conjunction with indicators that are agreeable to political actors yet substantive enough to target areas requiring reform. I argue for indicators to ensure that a rigorous process is developed and that results can be tracked with trends compared over time. A strategy with indicators may improve the possibility that gender mainstreaming will become a formalized commitment, which is especially important given the expected turnovers in government and Opposition parties in the House. Indicators can act as a "pointer" to highlight "a specific condition or situation," and in pursuit of a gender-sensitive House of Commons, they can put into practice objectives set out in the IPU Plan of Action (CIDA 1997, 5).

I look to the work of the Canadian International Development Agency (CIDA), which generated a broad range of gender equality indicators for women in development initiatives. I suggest that these indicators could highlight an emphasis on institution building and project development. Admittedly, CIDA indicators have been criticized for creating a disjuncture between donor-oriented meanings and their effectiveness for community recipients. As Jamey Essex (2012, 340) observes, development programs that are intended to improve the lives of aid recipients "may not be measureable" or "captured" by "political rubrics and benchmarks." I use CIDA indicators mindfully, however, because of their focus on institution building and because they attend to promoting important dimensions of gender equality. Four indicators are offered as follows.

Risk indicators highlight aspects of the external environment that may impede or facilitate the realignment of gendering processes. *Input indicators* look to the array and type of resources that are available to encourage, for example, the participation of MPs in legislative debates. *Process indicators* are the delivery of resources and how rules and practices support gender mainstreaming. Finally, *output and outcome indicators* measure effectiveness and performance achievements (CIDA 1997, 16–20).

To achieve results, indicators must be realistic, must be based on clearly defined objectives, and must include an array of measurements. The objective of gender mainstreaming is to "achieve gender equality, making institutions more reflective of the needs, aspirations and experiences of all women in society" (IPU 2011, 6–7). The IPU Plan of Action (2012) addresses these objectives, specifically noting the importance of

- increasing the number and diversity of women in parliament, as well as their equitable participation there
- implementing gender equality legislation
- mainstreaming gender equality throughout parliamentary work
- creating a more sensitive gender infrastructure and parliamentary culture
- assuring that gender equality is implemented as a responsibility of men and women
- encouraging political parties to champion gender equality
- enhancing gender sensitivity among parliamentary staff.

To implement a gender mainstreaming strategy, an initial working group of parliamentarians could be struck, collaborating with the SCSW, to establish common ground between the parties, building on existing working relationships among MPs. Fundamentally, ideas generated by this group will become part of a strategy to counter party discipline, facilitate participation of all parliamentary actors, infuse a new standard of legislative discourse, and realign hierarchical methods of control and decision making.

I propose that the strategy should begin with risk factors, discussing why a gender-sensitive parliament can facilitate parliamentary responsiveness, less in terms of devising indicators but as a plea for legislative reforms. Given the politics of devising indicators in a parliamentary setting, the practices of political parties are a key barrier to injecting gender mainstreaming into the House of Commons. The parties must be encouraged to promote women in their ranks, specifically targeting recruitment strategies for candidates and leaders. This encouragement can be made all the more appealing if it is connected to a discussion about support among Canadians who are underwhelmed by the performance of the House. Discussion points may include

- attitudes of Canadians toward public institutions and percent changes over time
- Canadians' satisfaction with democracy and the House
- percentage of Canadians who did not vote compared with those who did in previous elections

- percentage of Canadians possessing socially tolerant attitudes
- percentage of Canadians supporting the advancement of women in non-traditional occupations
- number of women nominated by a party in relation to men
- number of female party leaders in relation to men.

Input indicators will be quite extensive, given the many processes and internal institutional practices involved in the chamber. Of crucial importance here is finding ways to flatten the steepness of the organization to encourage inclusion in decision making and cross-party collaboration for MPs, who generally huddle in their own groups. Procedural and institutional reforms can potentially realign parliamentary practices and hence gendering processes if they question gender neutralities and conventional practices.

As a start, data can be accessed through the PARLINFO search engine on the Parliament of Canada website. PARLINFO does a good job of providing data on the number of women who ran as candidates from 1921 to the present, as well as the current number of women in the Senate and the House. This type of information – called a *participation indicator* – is one of the first steps in building a suite of input indicators. Other input indicators may include

- the presence of a gender- and diversity-focused parliamentary committee and resources allocated to it in relation to other committees
- creation of cross-caucus committees supported by party leadership
- collective caucus decision making in allocation of committee memberships
- GBA across all parliamentary committees
- gender-based training of MPs and parliamentary staff
- production of sex-disaggregated data not available through PARLINFO
- formulation of a gender code of conduct
- creation of a commissioner for gender equality to act as an independent oversight mechanism to ensure consistent application of gender mainstreaming and to track results across all indicators.

An *empowerment indicator* must also be devised to measure the actual involvement of female MPs in decision making and the extent of their control over their work environment (CIDA 1997, 34–39). Empowerment indicators could reveal gender divisions of labour if assessments investigate the committee membership of women *and* track how many times, and to what effect, female parliamentarians participate in other key leadership positions and if male MPs interject an equality discourse. Quantitative and qualitative methods could work together to gauge, for example, how many times female MPs speak during discussions and what kind of language they use to support a policy prescription. Assessments can also be conducted to examine the participation of community and women's groups in committee deliberations to reveal what kind of knowledge and discourse they bring to the table and the degree of knowledge transfer between witnesses and committee reports. Indicators may include

- percentage of women elected to the House in relation to men
- percentage of women on the Speaker's list in relation to men
- percentage of women appointed or elected to leadership roles in the chamber, such as Speaker, committee chairs, House leaders, party whips, and caucus chairs, in relation to men
- code of conduct to promote less aggressive language in the chamber
- autonomy for legislative committees to conduct research and hold public consultations
- percentage of funds dedicated to offset travel expenses of community-based groups and private individuals.

In many ways, output and outcome indicators are some of the most important, given that they track the results of input processes, which are then used to assess change, evaluate capacity building, and identify performance achievements. Indicators may include

- increase in the number of women elected to the House in relation to men
- increase in the diversity of women elected to the House
- percentage of committees that apply a GBA in relation to those that do not
- increase in the number of community-based groups that provide testimony to committees in relation to other types of organizations
- election of women as Speaker (and to other leadership roles)
- reports of cross-caucus committees on discussions with the commissioner for gender equality
- legislation that requires gender analysis
- diminished use of gender-specific language and elimination of sexist language during Question Period
- annual reporting to parliament by the commissioner for gender equality, tracking results and party responses from previous legislative sessions.

If implemented, this strategy may lead to the feminization of the House of Commons, thus derailing its institutionalized male dominance. Existing institutional practices diminish the number of women elected to the chamber, restrict the opportunities available to female parliamentarians for leadership positions, and entrench ideas about acceptable masculine and feminine behaviour, leading to legislative outcomes that too often work against women's diversities. Change can occur, though probably only incrementally, if a gender mainstreaming strategy is carefully devised, persistently monitored, and genuinely motivated by MPs who work toward a gender-sensitive parliament.

Conclusion

A 2003 Library of Parliament study, which interviewed MPs on the issue of legislative performance, found that they were in favour of reforming the House. They called for the modernization of procedures and practices so that they themselves would have "more influence in decision-making and accountability" (Library of Parliament 2003, 1). Many parliamentarians also agree that Canadians are seeking more input into democracy and want their representative institutions to be more meaningful and viable. I am proposing a gender mainstreaming strategy that targets organizational practices, in both the House of Commons and political parties, rebalances gendering processes, and infuses feminized practices and behaviours into the chamber in an effort to achieve those aims. No doubt there are significant challenges ahead in implementing the above indicators in conjunction with gender mainstreaming. Working in diversity via GBA+ as a way to "disrupt the status quo" (Hankivsky and Mussell 2018, 305) is a daunting task, especially when a consolidated institution such as the House of Commons is pushed to implement a new framework (Hankivsky and Mussell 2018, 309). The election of the Trudeau Liberals in 2015, followed by their minority wins in October 2019 and September 2021, offers cautious promise. At a post-election UN women's conference in March 2016, Justin Trudeau publicly proclaimed that he was a feminist (Panetta 2016). Although this remark may have been grounded in at least some political posturing, it was followed by the appointment of gender-balanced cabinets, mandatory GBA+ assessment for all memorandums to cabinet and Treasury Board submissions (House of Commons 2016), the transformation of Status of Women Canada to Women and Gender Equality Canada, and the inclusion in the 2018 budget of a Gender Results Framework as an assessment tool for departments. Nevertheless, moving toward a gender-sensitive parliament will take broad partisan support and clear, determined leadership.

Works Cited

Acker, Joan. 1992. "Gendering Organizational Theory." In *Gendering Organization Analysis*, ed. Albert J. Mills and Peta Tancred, 248–60. Newbury Park: Sage.
–. 2006. "Inequality Regimes: Gender, Class, and Race in Organizations." *Gender and Society* 20, 4: 441–64. https://doi.org/10.1177/0891243206289499.

Allen, P., and Sarah Childs. 2019. "The Grit in the Oyster? Women's Parliamentary Organizations and the Substantive Representation of Women." *Political Studies* 67, 3: 618–38.

Arscott, Jane, and Linda Trimble, eds. 1997. *In the Presence of Women: Representation in Canadian Governments.* Toronto: Harcourt Brace.

Ashe, Jeanette. 2020. "Gender Sensitivity under Trudeau: Facebook Feminism or Real Change?" In *Turbulent Times, Transformational Possibilities? Gender and Politics Today and Tomorrow,* ed. Fiona MacDonald and Alexandra Z. Dobrowolsky, 67–99. Toronto: University of Toronto Press.

Barnes, Andre, and Laura Munn-Rivard. 2013. *Gender-Sensitive Parliaments: Advancements in the Workplace.* Ottawa: Library of Parliament.

Breitenbach, Esther, and Yvonne Galligan. 2006. "Measuring Gender Equality: Reflecting on Experiences and Challenges in the UK and Ireland." *Policy and Politics* 34, 4: 597–614. https://doi.org/10.1332/030557306778553114.

Campbell, Kim. 1996. *Time and Chance.* Toronto: Doubleday.

Carstairs, Sharon. 1993. *Not One of the Boys.* Toronto: Macmillan Canada.

Celis, Karen, and Sarah Childs. 2018. "Good Representatives and Good Representation." *PS: Political Science and Politics* 51, 2: 314–17.

–. 2020. *Feminist Democratic Representation.* Oxford: Oxford University Press.

Celis, Karen, Sarah Childs, and Jane Curtin. 2016. "Specialised Parliamentary Bodies and the Quality of Women's Representation: A Comparative Analysis of Belgium, the United Kingdom and New Zealand." *Parliamentary Affairs* 69: 812–29.

Chappell, Louise. 2006. "Comparing Political Institutions: Revealing the Gendered 'Logic of Appropriateness.'" *Politics and Gender* 2, 2: 223–35. https://doi.org/10.1017/S1743923X06221044.

–. 2011. "Nested Newness and Institutional Innovation: Expanding Gender Justice in the International Criminal Court." In *Gender, Politics and Institutions: Towards a Feminist Institutionalism,* ed. Mona Lena Krook and Fiona Mackay, 163–80. London: Palgrave Macmillan.

Chappell, Louise, and Georgina Waylen. 2013. "Gender and the Hidden Life of Institutions." *Public Administration* 91, 3: 599–615. https://doi.org/10.1111/j.1467-9299.2012.02104.x.

Childs, Sarah, and Chloe Challender. 2019. "Re-gendering the UK House of Commons: The Academic Critical Actor and Her 'Feminist in Residence.'" *Political Studies Review* 17, 4: 428–35.

Childs, Sarah, and Mona Lena Krook. 2009. "Analysing Women's Substantive Representation: From Critical Mass to Critical Actors." *Government and Opposition* 44, 2: 125–45. https://doi.org/10.1111/j.1477-7053.2009.01279.x.

CIDA (Canadian International Development Agency). 1997. *Guide to Gender-Sensitive Indicators.* Ottawa: Minister of Public Works and Government Services Canada.

Collier, Cheryl N., and Tracey Raney. 2018. "Canada's Member-to-Member Code of Conduct on Sexual Harassment in the House of Commons: Progress or Regress?" *Canadian Journal of Political Science* 51, 4: 795–815.

Cool, Julie. 2013. *Women in Parliament.* Ottawa: Parliamentary Information and Research Services.

Copps, Sheila. 1986. *Nobody's Baby: A Survival Guide to Politics.* Toronto: Deneau.

Culver, Keith, and Paul Howe. 2004. "Calling All Citizens: The Challenge of Public Consultations." *Canadian Public Administration* 47, 1: 52–75.

Darcy, Robert. 1996. "Women in State Legislative Power Structures: Committee Chairs." *Social Science Quarterly* 77, 4: 888–98.

Equal Voice. 2020. *Gender-Sensitive Legislatures Report.* Ottawa: Equal Voice.

Erikson, Josefina, and Tania Verge. 2022. "Gender, Power and Privilege in the Parliamentary Workplace." *Parliamentary Affairs* 75, 1: 1–19.

Essex, Jamey. 2012. "The Politics of Canada's Effectiveness in International Development Assistance." *Canadian Journal of Development Studies* 33, 3: 338–55.

Fairclough, Ellen. 1995. *Saturday's Child: Memoirs of Canada's First Female Cabinet Minister.* Toronto: University of Toronto Press.

Freidenvall, Lenita, and Josefina Erikson. 2020. "The Speaker's Gender Equality Group in the Swedish Parliament: A Toothless Tiger?" *Politics, Groups, and Identities* 8, 3: 627–36.

Goodyear-Grant, Elizabeth. 2013. "Women Voters, Candidates, and Legislators: A Gender Perspective on Recent Party and Electoral Politics." In *Parties, Elections, and the Future of Canadian Politics,* ed. Amanda Bittner and Royce Koop, 119–39. Vancouver: UBC Press.

Grace, Joan. 1997. "Sending Mixed Messages: Gender-Based Analysis and the 'Status of Women.'" *Canadian Public Administration* 40, 4: 582–98. https://doi.org/10.1111/j.1754-7121.1997.tb02174.x.

Hankivsky, Olena. 2013. "Gender Mainstreaming: A Five-Country Examination." *Politics and Policy* 41, 5: 629–55. https://doi.org/10.1111/polp.12037.

Hankivsky, Olena, and Linda Mussell. 2018. "Gender-Based Analysis Plus in Canada: Problems and Possibilities of Integrating Intersectionality." *Canadian Public Policy* 44, 4: 303–16.

Heath, Roseanna Michelle, Leslie A. Schwindt-Bayer, and Michelle M. Taylor-Robinson. 2005. "Women on the Sidelines: Women's Representation on Committees in Latin American Legislatures." *American Journal of Political Science* 49, 2: 420–36. https://doi.org/10.2307/3647686.

Holli, Anne Maria. 2012. "Does Gender Have an Effect on the Selection of Experts by Parliamentary Standing Committees? A Critical Test of 'Critical' Concepts." *Politics and Gender* 8, 3: 341–66. https://doi.org/10.1017/S1743923X12000347.

House of Commons. 2005. *Gender-Based Analysis: Building Blocks for Success.* Ottawa: Standing Committee on the Status of Women.

–. 2008. *Towards Gender Responsive Budgeting: Rising to the Challenge of Achieving Gender Equality.* Ottawa: Standing Committee on the Status of Women.

–. 2016. *Interim Report on the Implementation of GBA+.* Ottawa: Standing Committee on Public Accounts.

IPU (Inter-Parliamentary Union). 2006. *The Role of Parliamentary Committees in Mainstreaming Gender and Promoting the Status of Women.* Geneva: IPU.

–, ed. 2009. *Is Parliament Open to Women?* Geneva: IPU.

–. 2011. *Gender-Sensitive Parliaments: A Global Review of Good Practice.* Geneva: IPU.

–. 2012. *Plan of Action for Gender-Sensitive Parliaments.* Geneva: IPU.

–. 2016. *Evaluating the Gender Sensitivity of Parliaments: A Self-Assessment Toolkit.* Geneva: IPU.

–. 2017. *Plan of Action for Gender-Sensitive Parliaments.* Geneva: IPU.

Itzin, Catherine, and Janet Newman, eds. 1995. *Gender, Culture and Organizational Change: Putting Theory into Practice.* London: Routledge.

Jabre, Kareen. 2009. "Challenges Faced by Women in Parliament: An Overview." In *Is Parliament Open to Women? An Appraisal,* ed. Inter-Parliamentary Union, 55–56. Geneva: Inter-Parliamentary Union.

Kathlene, Lyn. 1994. "Power and Influence in State Legislative Policymaking: The Interactions of Gender and Position in Committee Hearing Debates." *American Political Science Review* 88, 3: 560–76. https://doi.org/10.2307/2944795.

Krook, Mona Lena, and Fiona Mackay, eds. 2011. *Gender, Politics, and Institutions: Towards a Feminist Institutionalism.* London: Palgrave Macmillan.

Leston-Bandeira, C. 2012. "Studying the Relationship between Parliament and Citizens." *Journal of Legislative Studies* 18, 3–4: 265–74.

Levac, Leah R.E., and Sarah Marie Wiebe. 2020. *Creating Spaces of Engagement: Policy Justice and the Practical Craft of Deliberative Democracy.* Toronto: University of Toronto Press.

Library of Parliament. 2003. *The Parliament We Want: Parliamentarians' Views on Parliamentary Reform.* Ottawa: Library of Parliament.

Lovenduski, Joni. 2014. "The Institutionalization of Sexism in Politics." *Political Insight* 5, 2: 16–19.

Lovenduski, Joni, and Pippa Norris. 2003. "Westminster Women: The Politics of Presence." *Political Studies* 51, 1: 84–102. https://doi.org/10.1111/1467-9248.00414.

Mackay, Fiona. 2008. "'Thick' Conceptions of Substantive Representation: Women, Gender and Political Institutions." *Representation* 44, 2: 125–39. https://doi.org/10.1080/00344890802079607.

–. 2014. "Nested Newness, Institutional Innovation, and the Gendered Limits of Change." *Politics and Gender* 10: 549–71.

McNutt, Kathleen. 2010. *An Integrated Approach to Gender Equality: From Gender-Based Analysis to Gender Mainstreaming.* JSGS Working Paper Series. Regina: Johnson Shoyama Graduate School of Public Policy.

Mills, Albert J., and Peta Tancred, eds. 1992. *Gendering Organizational Analysis.* Newbury Park: Sage.

Montpetit, Dominique. 2020. "Women in the Parliament of Canada." *HillNotes.* Ottawa: Library of Parliament. https://hillnotes.ca/2020/01/23/women-in-the-parliament-of-canada/.

Munn-Rivard, Laura. 2013. *Gender-Sensitive Parliaments: The Work of Legislators.* Ottawa: Library of Parliament.

O'Brien, Diana Z. 2012. "Gender and Select Committee Elections in the British House of Commons." *Politics and Gender* 8, 2: 178–204. https://doi.org/10.1017/S1743923X12000153.

Palmieri, Sonia. 2010. *Gender Mainstreaming in the Australian Parliament: Achievement with Room for Improvement.* Canberra: Parliamentary Studies Centre, Australian National University.

–. 2011. *Gender-Sensitive Parliaments: A Global Review of Good Practice.* Geneva: Inter-Parliamentary Union.

Panetta, Alexandra. 2016. "'I Am a Feminist,' Trudeau Tells UN Conference." *Toronto Star,* March 16, 2016.

Paterson, Stephanie. 2010. "What's the Problem with Gender-Based Analysis? Gender Mainstreaming Policy and Practice in Canada." *Canadian Public Administration* 53, 3: 395–416. https://doi.org/10.1111/j.1754-7121.2010.00134.x.

Rosenthal, Cindy Simon. 2000. "Gender Styles in State Legislative Committees." *Women and Politics* 21, 2: 21–45. https://doi.org/10.1300/J014v21n02_02.

Ross, Karen. 2002. "Women's Place in 'Male' Space: Gender and Effect in Parliamentary Contexts." *Parliamentary Affairs* 55: 189–201.

Sawer, Marian. 2000. "Parliamentary Representation of Women: From Discourses of Justice to Strategies of Accountability." *International Political Science Review* 21, 4: 361–80. https://doi.org/10.1177/0192512100214003.

–. 2012. "What Makes the Substantive Representation of Women Possible in a Westminster Parliament? The Story of RU486 in Australia." *International Political Science Review* 33, 3: 320–35. https://doi.org/10.1177/0192512111435369.

–. 2020. "Gender Mainstreaming and the Substantive Representation of Women: Where Do Parliamentary Bodies Fit?" *Politics, Groups, Identities* 8, 3: 648–60.

Sawer, Marian, Lenita Freidenvall, and Sonia Palmieri. 2013. "Playing Their Part? Parliamentary Institutions and Gender Mainstreaming." Paper presented at the Third European Conference on Politics and Gender, Universitat Pompeu Fabra, Barcelona.

Scala, Francesca, and Stephanie Paterson. 2017. "Gendering Public Policy or Rationalizing Gender? Strategic Interventions and GBA+ Practice in Canada." *Canadian Journal of Political Science* 50, 2: 427–42.

Smith, Miriam. 2005. *A Civil Society? Collective Actors in Canadian Political Life.* Peterborough: Broadview Press.

Status of Women Canada. 1996. *Gender-Based Analysis: A Guide for Policy-Making.* Ottawa: Status of Women Canada.

Steele, Jackie. 2002. "The Liberal Women's Caucus." *Canadian Parliamentary Review* 25, 2: 13–19.

Tremblay, Manon. 1998. "Do Female MPs Substantively Represent Women? A Study of the Legislative Behaviour in Canada's 35th Parliament." *Canadian Journal of Political Science* 31, 3: 435–65.

–. 2003. "Women's Representational Role in Australia and Canada: The Impact of Political Context." *Australian Journal of Political Science* 38, 2: 215–38. https://doi.org/10.1080/1036114032000092693.

Trimble, Linda, and Jane Arscott. 2003. *Still Counting: Women in Politics across Canada.* Peterborough: Broadview Press.

UK Parliament. 2018. "UK Gender-Sensitive Parliament Audit 2018: Report of the Gender-Sensitive Parliament Audit Panel to the House of Commons Commission and the House of Lords Commission." Accessed February 12, 2019. https://www.parliament.uk/globalassets/documents/lords-information-office/uk-parliament-gender sensitiveparliament.

Vickers, Jill, Pauline Rankin, and Christine Appelle. 1993. *Politics as If Women Mattered: A Political Analysis of the National Action Committee on the Status of Women.* Toronto: University of Toronto Press.

3

Making the Equality Policy Process Visible: Developing a Gender-Based Analysis Plus Framework in the Canada School of Public Service

Stephanie M. Redden

> *Like a cancerous growth in the body-(politic) of justice and democracy, the identification, isolation and removal of gender has been delineated as necessary; both morally and in line with competent and just governance practices. A variety of tools, tactics and techniques have been gathered together over many decades most recognizably under the political and epistemological banner of feminism, with the explicit aim of removing the obdurate vestiges of outdated gender ideas and practices. At the forefront of feminist success in policy, gender mainstreaming has emerged as a significant outcome of this burgeoning corpus of scholarly, activist and governmental work.*
>
> – MARYSIA ZALEWSKI (2010)

IN 1995, THE CANADIAN government committed to utilizing gender-based analysis (GBA) – "an analytical policy assessment process created by the Government of Canada as an attempt to support greater gender equality in Canada" – with its adoption of the Federal Plan for Gender Equality (Canada, Senate 2023). However, efforts to operationalize this approach throughout the public service have encountered difficulties (Government of Canada 2017; Scala and Paterson 2017). As Francesca Scala and Stephanie Paterson (2017, 582) explain, "a 2009 report by Canada's Auditor General noted the absence of a government-wide policy for the use of GBA, which resulted in considerable variance in the existence and depth of GBA frameworks across departments." Undoubtedly, the Conservative government's response to the 2008–09 global financial crisis affected these efforts. Sophie O'Manique (2015, 293) observes, "the Harper government's response ... involved the implementation of both austerity and stimulus measures. The impact of these policies was felt differently along gendered, racialized and class lines, in part because both the stimulus and austerity adhered to the government's preference for neoliberal restructuring of the state." A report issued by the auditor general in 2016 noted that the way in which gender-based analysis plus (GBA+) is being used remains problematic (Scala and Paterson 2017, 582).[1]

However, more recent developments have provided reason to be optimistic that efforts to implement GBA+ across the Government of Canada will improve. In particular, Prime Minister Justin Trudeau made GBA+ one of his Liberal government's top priorities. As stated in the "Gender Results Framework" section of the 2018 federal budget, "from the time the Government took office, it has been working to ensure GBA+ is applied comprehensively to all aspects of policy development and decision-making, and strengthening the quality of GBA+ with better data and the full consideration of impacts across a wide range of intersectional lenses" (Government of Canada 2018a). Following this commitment, federal departments, which had not previously outlined and implemented gender equality policies, began developing and implementing them.

Nevertheless, very few resources, whether government or academic, actually explore the *process* of constructing a departmental gender equality policy or framework. Some GBA+ resources that help with this task, such as copies of government department policies, are available, primarily through Status of Women Canada (SWC).[2] However, there are no documents or materials that offer an in-depth discussion of *how* the departments arrived at these policy end points. I suggest that this lack is a major contributor to the less-than-positive GBA+ results identified in the auditor general's reports for both 2009 and 2016, and that it continues to hinder the implementation of more consistent and substantive GBA+ policies throughout government. Overall, I maintain that engaging in "knowledge transfer" (SWC n.d. "The GBA+ Framework") across federal departments *throughout* the policy development process will lead to better informed and ultimately more effective and consistent gender equality policies. I make this case through a consideration of the Canada School of Public Service (CSPS), which, according to its most recent departmental plan, is engaged in an ongoing project to design its GBA+ framework.[3] My goal is to contribute, at least in some small way, to achieving much-needed GBA+ knowledge transfer and giving public servants facing the same task an idea of where to begin, especially in addressing issues related to the structure of institutional responsibility and the measurement of progress over time.

Gender Equality in Canada: Setting the Scene

It is important to note that "gender equality is a core Canadian value and is enshrined in the *Charter of Rights and Freedoms,* which is part of the Canadian Constitution" (SWC n.d., "An Overview"). In line with the national emphasis on equality, "the Canadian approach to GM (gender mainstreaming) was designed and implemented ... in response to the Beijing Platform for Action that was drafted at the Fourth United Nations Conference on Women" in 1995 (Scala and Paterson 2017, 582). More specifically, the centrepiece of the 1995 Federal Plan for Gender Equality was to "implement gender-based analysis throughout federal departments and agencies" (Government of Canada 2017). In 2011, Canada's GBA approach developed into GBA+, which called for a more intersectional analysis of inequality (Paterson and Scala 2017, 4). As SWC (2017, quoting Bishwakarma, Hunt, and Zajicek 2007) explains,

> GBA+ ensures the inclusion of women, men and gender-diverse people. Moreover, it draws on insights of "intersectionality," a research and policy model that recognizes the complex composition of factors that shape and influence human lives. Intersectional analysis attempts to "examine the consequences of interacting inequalities on people occupying different social locations as well as address the way that specific acts and policies address the inequalities experienced by various groups."

After Ottawa adopted GBA in 1995, significant problems arose with its implementation (Scala and Paterson 2017, 582). As Scala and Paterson (2017, 582–83) state,

> a 2009 report by Canada's Auditor General noted the absence of government-wide policy for the use of GBA, which resulted in considerable variance in the existence and depth of GBA frameworks across departments. Moreover, in the departments and agencies that had implemented GBA, the analyses performed were often incomplete and inconsistent in terms of depth and quality. In addition, the report indicated that there was limited evidence of impact, as departments were unable to demonstrate if and how the results of GBA were being used in policy design.

The auditor general's report made it clear that significant changes were required to improve the way that GBA was being applied and to allow for the realization of more substantive gender equality gains. Thus, in an effort to rectify the issues highlighted by the report, "Status of Women Canada, the Treasury Board of Canada Secretariat and the Privy Council Office created the Departmental Action Plan on Gender-Based Analysis in autumn 2009" (SWC n.d. "An Overview"; see also Scala and Paterson 2017, 583). As SWC explained, "the Action Plan provides the structure for departments and agencies to make GBA+ a sustainable practice. Two main areas for departmental action are included: 1) To build GBA+ organizational capacity by implementing a GBA+ Framework

[and], 2) To routinely apply GBA+ to programs, policies and legislation" (SWC n.d. "An Overview"). A follow-up report from the auditor general in 2016 "revealed persistent issues" with GBA+ in the federal government (Scala and Paterson 2017, 583). A lack of knowledge transfer (SWC n.d. "The GBA+ Framework") has certainly contributed to these disappointing results.

Importantly, though SWC does not provide a precise definition of knowledge transfer, I use the term throughout this chapter to refer to the informal and formal intra- and interdepartmental exchanges of knowledge between government employees who work broadly in the area of GBA+ in some capacity. These exchanges could take place digitally (perhaps through online discussion forums), over the phone (during teleconferences), or face-to-face (during meetings). They could cover a wide range of topics, including, but not limited to, GBA+ best practices, difficulties and roadblocks experienced, or ideas related to the aims, design, and implementation of departmental GBA+ policies and practices, as well as indicators used to measure their success. In this context, knowledge transfer should be understood as a multidirectional process, with knowledge exchanged between practitioners (including those working in Women and Gender Equality Canada [WAGE], as well as those in all other departments).[4]

As Ian D. Graham and colleagues (2006) point out, the term "knowledge transfer" is defined and employed in many ways. The most useful definition for this chapter runs as follows: "a systematic approach to capture, collect and share tacit knowledge in order for it to become explicit knowledge. By doing so, this process allows for individuals and/or organizations to access and utilize essential information, which previously was known intrinsically to only one or a small group of people" (Graham et al. 2006, 15). This definition is particularly germane for the case study presented here, as I argue that valuable GBA+ knowledge gained within departments should be shared widely across departments. María Bustelo, Lucy Ferguson, and Maxine Forest (2016, 3) offer "an analytical framework for exploring the process of feminist knowledge transfer." They assert that

such a process may exhibit some or all of the following characteristics:

1 An understanding that gender inequality is "structural" and "systemic," and a capacity to use gender lenses or feminist lenses or feminist glasses in knowledge transfer scenarios.

2 Transfer of knowledge which aims at being "transformative"; that is, knowledge use should aim not only at better understanding, but also at changing the world, fighting against social injustices, and redressing unequal power relations.

3 Feminist knowledge understood as situated knowledge, filtered through the standpoints of different knowers, in which some ways of knowing are

privileged over others. This implies the acknowledgement of the plurality of feminist "knowledges."

4 An explicit acknowledgement of the inherently "political" nature of the contexts in which such knowledge is transferred, as well as of feminist knowledge transfer as a site for contestation.

5 A key focus on "reflexivity" in order to acknowledge biases and limitations and allow for the recognition of multiple perspectives. (Bustelo, Ferguson, and Forest 2016, 3)

Although the types of knowledge transfer outlined above would not necessarily include all of these characteristics at all times, at least some could be classified as examples of "feminist knowledge transfer" (as defined by Bustelo, Ferguson, and Forest 2016). In an effort to ensure consistency with the language used by SWC/WAGE, however, I continue to use "knowledge transfer" throughout this chapter.

Gender Equality at the Canada School of Public Service

As the CSPS website details,

The Canada School of Public Service was created on April 1, 2004, when the legislative provisions of Part IV of the *Public Service Modernization Act* came into force. The School has been part of the Treasury Board Portfolio since July 2004. It was created from an amalgamation of the following three organizations: the Canadian Centre for Management Development, Training and Development Canada and Language Training Canada. (Canada School of Public Service n.d.)

Overall, the school provides training and educational resources to federal public servants – through both its online learning portal (GCampus) and in-person classroom sessions. As a result, it plays an incredibly important role in the provision of GBA+-related training and education to the public service.[5] It is divided between two primary functions: the learning services branch and the corporate services branch. In a 2015 mandate letter to Scott Brison, president of the Treasury Board of Canada, Prime Minister Trudeau wrote, "you are expected to do your part to fulfill our government's commitment to transparent, merit-based appointments, *to help ensure gender parity* and that Indigenous Canadians and minority groups are better reflected in positions of leadership" (Office of the Prime Minister 2015, emphasis added). Thus, from the beginning of his tenure as president, Brison was expected to make gender equality a key priority.

After Scott Brison resigned from cabinet in January 2019, the position of Treasury Board president saw considerable turnover. Jane Philpott soon replaced him but resigned her cabinet position in March 2019 in response to the SNC-Lavalin affair (Harris 2019). Carla Qualtrough was acting president from March 4 to 18, 2019, with Joyce Murray taking over from her, serving from March 18 to November 2019. In December 2019, following the federal election, Jean-Yves Duclos was appointed to the position, only to be replaced by Mona Fortier after the 2021 election. Throughout these transitions, however, Prime Minister Trudeau's insistence on the importance of gender equality for the Treasury Board operations remained clear. In his December 2019 Treasury Board mandate letter to Jean-Yves Duclos, for example, Trudeau asserted that "we are committed to evidence-based decision-making that takes into consideration the impacts of policies on all Canadians and fully defends the *Canadian Charter of Rights and Freedoms.* You will apply Gender-based Analysis Plus (GBA+) in the decisions that you make" (Office of the Prime Minister 2019).

In January 2018, I was hired as a casual employee with the corporate services branch of the CSPS, and I worked for the school until early September of that year. I was hired as an analyst and in February 2018 was also designated the GBA+ team lead for my unit (Access to Information and Privacy, Parliamentary Affairs, and Government Accountability). This role entailed organizing and hosting meetings and discussions with other units in the school and with external stakeholders, as well as undertaking in-depth research on gender mainstreaming and gender budgeting efforts in Canada and internationally. Along with my manager, I took a lead role in beginning to draft the school's GBA+ policy statement and framework. I had not intended to undertake research on gender equality policy development and implementation in the government – in fact, when I was hired I did not know that I would be assisting my manager (the school's gender focal point [GFP]) with the development of the framework.[6]

In line with the government's strong commitment to gender equality, the school started to develop its GBA+ framework early in 2018, shortly after I began to work there. Although I had researched gender mainstreaming efforts in Canada and beyond, I was less familiar with the gender equality policies that other federal departments had already produced. In my search for useful information, I located examples of their policies and frameworks, but rather frustratingly, I could find no detailed information on how they had arrived at these final products. Their policy development process – including what questions and considerations were of central importance, in addition to what obstacles they had encountered – was rendered invisible. Furthermore, when I discussed the matter with employees from other departments during events and GBA+

training exercises, I learned that the information resources were indeed signifi-cantly deficient and that they too were trying to navigate the GBA+ policy development process without being certain of how to proceed.

Questions, Challenges, and Roadblocks

As noted, implementing GBA+ frameworks throughout government depart-ments has proven difficult. A key reason for this is the lack of knowledge transfer between the departments. Documents or resources that could offer insights simply don't exist, with the result that departments cannot learn from the ex-periences of other departments that have already generated their policies. As a result, gender champions, GFPs, and other GBA+ actors in the government can feel overwhelmed by the daunting task of constructing such a policy from the ground up.

Although some questions, challenges, and roadblocks will be specific to cer-tain departments, given their particular focus, most departments will confront the same issues as they attempt to formulate their GBA+ policy. Thus, to pull back the curtain, so to speak, on the process behind GBA+ policy development, I outline some of the most significant issues that arose while I worked at the CSPS. What follows is in no way exhaustive, but it showcases some of the most pressing concerns and questions.

Determining Institutional Responsibility for GBA+

At the CSPS, discussions around GBA+ often grappled with how to establish its structure of responsibility (and accountability). SWC advises departments to create a "responsibility centre" that will "monitor implementation of the framework and practice of GBA+" (SWC n.d. "The GBA+ Framework"). As it outlines, the "centre's mandate and authority may vary according to the GBA+ statement of intent and the resources accorded to such a centre, but its overall role is to lead, enhance, support, and monitor implementation of a GBA+ framework and the actual practice of GBA+" (SWC n.d. "The GBA+ Frame-work"). SWC notes that the centre could take on one or multiple roles, including that of facilitator, convenor, expert, and/or monitor (SWC n.d. "The GBA+ Framework").

That said, SWC does not provide specific guidance on how to implement the structure of responsibility. In other words, it does not mention the key ques-tions that organizations will be forced to consider in making decisions regard-ing responsibility (including, but not limited to, whether SWC's suggestions fit and make sense given their size or structure). For example, SWC recom-mends "locating the responsibility centre in a strategic setting (e.g., strategic policy branch/directorate)" and adds that "including it in policy and program development, implementation and decision-making can further assist in entrenching GBA+ within the organization's broader machinery" (SWC n.d. "The GBA+ Framework"). However, the CSPS consists of two branches, each with very different roles and responsibilities (and, in turn, foci when it comes to implementing GBA+). Given this fact, much discussion occurred around the question of whether each branch should have its own responsibility centre, which would oversee the implementation of the GBA+ framework, or whether having one centre would best serve the school.

This issue remained unresolved when I left the CSPS. I highlight it here because it is one point in the framework development process where having greater input from other (similarly structured) departments on how they tackled the problem would have proved incredibly useful. Had the CSPS been able to benefit from the knowledge of what worked – and what did not – in other departments, its decisions around responsibility and accountability would have been much more informed.

What Are Our Goals? How Can We Measure Improvement?

Throughout the framework development process, the problem of how to measure improvement and success in implementing GBA+ policies and processes over time was a major consideration. Our discussions often contemplated which indicators *would* be used but also which ones *could* be used (in other words, what data did the school already collect and have access to, and what data could it start collecting to assist in tracking GBA+ goals over time). Everyone understood that progress would need to be tracked and reported through regular departmental procedures and that indicators would therefore need to include aspects that were (or could be) readily measured, given the current capacities of the school. In short, the CSPS would need to be able to show improvement in relation to the application of its GBA+ policies and the positive outcomes related to the use of GBA+. Additionally, it needed to identify ways to track and measure the application of GBA+ over time to identify areas that needed improvement and those where significant gains had been achieved. As a result, our team consulted on several occasions with representatives from both the CSPS Human Resources team and the Learning Evaluations team (who administer evaluations of course material offered by the school) to determine which indicators were possible. Many options were explored during these discussions, and important questions were raised about adding more GBA+-focused questions to forms of data collection that were already in place. Although this was one possible solution to our dilemma, it was not without problems of its own. Sally Engle Merry (2016, 7) writes that the reliance on existing data and measurement tools can lead to "data inertia." As she explains, "it is relatively hard to address new problems without new data collection, [as] the way categories are created and measured often depends on what data are available" (7).

At various stages in the development of the framework, we agreed that a central goal (from both an institutional and service-provider perspective) was to achieve a "taken-for-grantedness" of GBA+ in the school.[7] That is, the application of GBA+ and the important critical questions that it forces employees to ask of policies and programs (and in the case of the CSPS, educational resources) would eventually become a standard part of the job. Whereas everyone agreed that department-wide buy-in and commitment to the principles and goals of GBA+ were important and worthwhile, exactly how this culture shift might be measured was less clear. Using employee surveys was one option, but this type of tool may not be able to accurately capture a substantive shift in culture over time. And though this was seen as a key goal in the school, less consideration was given to how this type of change may be captured (at least during the initial development-stage discussions that I attended). Instead, the focus centred on fleshing out existing measures at the school to include GBA+ elements. Overall, there was an obvious preference for exploring easily quantifiable aspects of the school's work. This is understandable, given that its resources are limited. At the same time, however, this raises questions about what we choose to measure and what impact those choices can have. This is particularly important given that indicators can be become set and difficult to change (Merry 2016, 8), and because they can have a significant effect on "what gets done" (Buchanan, Byers, and Mansveld 2018, 117).

As Stephane Lavertu (2014, 865) explains, "the wave of enthusiasm for 'big data' in public administration is the most recent manifestation of continued efforts to base public decision making on measured quantities and to enhance transparency and accountability." This is representative of a notable "shifting from government by rules to 'governance by numbers'" (Mennicken and Espeland 2019, 224, quoting Supiot 2015).[8] And indeed, as Doris Buss (2015, 381) highlights, "doing gender equality work increasingly involves measurement, whether through the gathering and analysis of data on gender inequality, or the reporting and accounting for gender programming outcomes and outputs." This was very much the case for the CSPS, as discussed above.

Yet, as Buss (2015) points out, the very act of measurement is political and potentially problematic. She notes (2015, 383, emphasis in original) that "increasingly feminist and critical scholars are opening up the black box of measurement, to explore *how* measurement regimes work to reduce social phenomena to specific categories, numbers, or rankings, and the effects these knowledge formats have on official representations." My point here is not that attempting to capture the impacts of the application of GBA+ in the CSPS was inherently negative – in fact, it could potentially shed a great deal of light on which elements of the school's work had been strengthened as a result and which needed further attention. Rather, I wish to suggest that the choices about what gets measured, and how, are important ones, given the weight that data hold. As Merry (2016, 4–5) asserts,

> the way indicators are constructed and used shows that they reflect the social and cultural worlds of the actors and organizations that create them and the regimes of power within which they are formed. This social aspect of indicators is typically ignored in the face of trust in numbers, cultural assumptions about the objectivity of numbers, and the value of technical rationality.[9]

Buss (2015, 384) echoes this point, noting that "once selected, measurement formats take on an authority that belies the power imbalances and highly contested nature of their initial design, as well as the exercise of discretion required for their use. These intensely political contexts are located firmly backstage to the visible performance of indicators as objective, universal, and useful."[10]

Some observers, such as Catherine Powell (2016), have asked whether feminist aims are weakened due to the reliance on quantitative indicators of gender equality to gauge progress, particularly in the development field. Among several other powerful questions, Powell (2016, 781) asks, "when using indicators to measure legal rights in the context of gender equality, what do these quantitative measurements make visible, and what do they obscure? What are the normative and practical implications of quantifying equality for feminism? And what are the implications of economizing gender equality for breaking down gender hierarchy?" Ultimately, Powell (2016, 780, emphasis in original) proposes that the World Bank "has co-opted feminism to advance the Bank's economic *growth* agenda, rather than the other way around to advance feminism's redistributive agenda." More broadly, Powell (2016, 807) states,

> Governance almost certainly has a deradicalizing effect on feminism, even as feminists have come to power in international institutions, in foreign ministries, in parliaments, and as heads of state. As mechanisms of governance, gender indicators seek to institutionalize gender equality and thereby reshape policies, priorities, and laws, in both international and national law and development efforts. But the reach of gender indicators will continue to be limited so long as they are primarily used to mainstream women into existing structures of power, rather than transform those structures.

In an effort to address these issues, Powell (2016, 777) suggests using "the feminist methodology of participatory decision-making (including in the creation of the indicators themselves)."

Although it is unclear if (or how) such an approach could be deployed in the current operating structures of Canadian federal departments, Powell's analysis does support the need to go beyond relying on existing measures, which usually include things that are easily quantifiable. Dependence on easily quantifiable indicators is problematic, given the wealth of critically important information they can render invisible (Connell 2005; Powell 2016). Powell (2016, 787–88) explains, "as a practical matter, the emphasis on indicators 'neglects what cannot be counted' and obscures women's empowerment, voice, and agency." For example, she writes that the United Nations Development Programme Gender Empowerment Measure's "heavy emphasis on representation at the national political level and in the formal economy obscured the important role women play in local institutions and grassroots organizations" (804). In discussing a study of Australian public sector organizations, Raewyn Connell (2005, 16) similarly notes that

> a simple statistical account of the gender division of labour will not tell us what we need to know about gendered authority in an organisation. Resources, networks, cliques, legal powers, coercion, insider knowledge, and capacity to mobilise support, must also be considered ... Nor will the facts about the gender division of labour, by themselves, tell us how the staff of the organisation understand the local gender arrangements, or gender equity policies. Whether these arrangements and policies are thought legitimate or unfair, fixed or fluid, consistent or inconsistent, must be established directly, and not assumed.

Thus, though statistical data may be available on an organization's workforce, they will not necessarily provide the full picture of how power operates within that environment. Instead, when departments are deciding how they will measure progress on particular equality and diversity goals, they must fully consider what the available quantifiable data can reveal but also, importantly, what will not be revealed. Whenever possible, they should build on these data, so that a more representative baseline picture can be presented at the outset and progress (or its lack) can be more accurately captured over time.

Learning from Other Departments' Experiences, Not Just Outcomes

SWC has indicated that departments need to engage in knowledge transfer practices. For example, in "The GBA+ Framework," SWC (n.d.) asserts that "the sharing of information, promotional and educational activities and training opportunities helps to ensure a more profound knowledge of the concepts related to gender equality and the process of GBA+." Further, it highlights that

> dissemination of GBA+ knowledge can be achieved through channels normally used to inform and meet the specific needs of an organization, either on a large or small scale. This can be accomplished, for example, by posting GBA+-related information on your organization's intranet or internet sites, or by holding information sessions for employees. (SWC n.d. "The GBA+ Framework")

Taking this approach "enhances learning and reduces duplication" (SWC n.d. "The GBA+ Framework"). In practice, however, these suggested procedures occur infrequently and are inadequate to prepare GBA+ teams in federal departments (such as the CSPS) to build and develop their own GBA+ frameworks fully. Several departments have made their finished frameworks available online, but they typically do not cover the deliberative process that went into constructing these end policies (including how decisions related to critical issues such as accountability and measurement were made).

Some departments, such as the CSPS, are only just getting started in implementing their gender equality policies, whereas others are much further ahead.[11] Given this, one would expect that those who were starting out could refer to an abundance of resources for guidance. However, most of these come from SWC, which has done a great job of providing general instructional material for departments to follow, as well as examples of various frameworks. All of this is invaluable, but its usefulness would have been greatly enhanced by a discussion of the process that went into creating the frameworks, including the challenges and questions that arose along the way. Equipped with such information, public servants would know what to expect as they formulated their own policies and frameworks. Further, engaging in GBA+ knowledge transfer between departments would allow for more reflection and guidance on which paths and structures work and which are less successful.

Conclusion: What Lessons Can Be Derived?

The aim of this chapter is to contribute to both the academic literature on the gender equality policy development process (and gender mainstreaming more broadly) and the government resources that are available to public servants. In particular, by offering a detailed discussion of some key issues encountered by the CSPS – focusing on those that are applicable across the government – I hope to assist public servants as they develop and advance their own gender equality policies. The 2009 and 2016 auditor general's reports on GBA+ painted a less than positive picture of its implementation and integration in the Canadian public service, but substantial improvement is possible if public servants reach across departmental lines to share their experiences with each other. Taking this step will help to create better informed, and ultimately more effective and consistent, gender equality policies.

Perhaps with the establishment of WAGE (which occurred while I was completing this chapter), this goal will be realized. In a statement announcing the creation of the new department, Minister for Women and Gender Equality Maryam Monsef asserted that

> after 42 years of serving Canadian women, the small but mighty agency known as Status of Women Canada has become a full department under the law. The new Department for Women and Gender Equality (WAGE) continues the work of advancing more equitable economic, political and social outcomes for Canadian women, and has an expanded mandate for gender equality that includes sexual orientation, gender identity and expression. WAGE will maintain and forge new connections to grassroots organizations advancing equality in Canada, *while acting as a coordinating body for gender equality issues within the Government of Canada.* Today, we celebrate this important milestone and honour the advocates, leaders and survivors whose hard work, hope and courage has made our great country even stronger. (Government of Canada 2018b, emphasis added)

Although SWC played an invaluable role in the development and implementation of GBA/GBA+ throughout the federal government, perhaps WAGE will serve an even deeper coordination function, especially in relation to the development of departmental GBA+ frameworks and policies. If this occurs, perhaps the inconsistency noted by the auditor general in 2009 and 2016 could be remedied. In any case, the creation of WAGE offers a positive and hopeful signal for the future of gender equality and diversity efforts in Canada.

Acknowledgments

I wish to thank Andrew Maw, Natasha Parriag, Sunita Gingras, Jarret Anderson, and all my teammates and coworkers at the CSPS who made coming to work every day a pleasure. Also, thank you to Christina Gabriel and Maggie FitzGerald for their incredibly insightful and detailed feedback on earlier versions of this chapter, as well as the anonymous reviewers for their very helpful comments. I presented earlier versions of this chapter at the 2018 Atlantic Provinces Political Science Association Annual Conference, as well as the 2019 International Studies Association Annual Convention, and I wish to express my gratitude to my panel discussants, Elizabeth Goodyear-Grant and Muireann O'Dwyer, for their invaluable feedback. Finally, I received no financial support for the research, authorship, and/or publication of this chapter. However, the experiences mentioned throughout occurred while I was a paid employee of the Canada School of Public Service.

Notes

1 As Scala and Paterson (2017, 583) highlight, "in 2011, to better respond to the realities of diversity, GBA was also reoriented towards GBA+, which acknowledges that 'intersecting identity factors' (such as gender, age, education, ability, sexual orientation, ethnicity, marital status, language, culture, income and geography) shape the ways in which policies are experienced."

2 In 2018, SWC became a full-fledged federal department (Women and Gender Equality Canada, or WAGE) (Government of Canada 2018b). However, throughout the chapter I continue to reference SWC, as many of the documents I cite were published before SWC became WAGE.

3 In "Departmental Plan 2020–2021," the Canada School of Public Service (2020) states that "the School is developing a framework to ensure that GBA+ will be integrated into departmental decision-making processes. Appropriate monitoring and reporting mechanisms for GBA+ will be identified as part of the framework."

4 Ian D. Graham et al. (2006, 16) explain that knowledge transfer "has sometimes been interpreted as, and criticized for, suggesting that the process is unidirectional, from knowledge producers to stakeholders. However, many using the term consider knowledge transfer a two-way process, although this is not always made explicit."

5 In the fall of 2018, the CSPS began a pilot program for an intensive four-day course on GBA+. Aimed at providing detailed instruction for public servants who work on GBA+ throughout various stages of the federal policy cycle, the course represents a strong effort on the part of the CSPS to foreground the importance of GBA+ to the public service. Since then, it has been listed along with other CSPS course offerings (although participants must be nominated to attend). For more information, see https://csps-efpc.gc.ca/Catalogue/courses-eng.aspx?code=P004.

6 According to the UN Women Training Center (2016), a gender focal point's (GFP) "basic functions may include: coordinating the organization/office/program gender mainstreaming strategy; contributing gender information and technical support for inclusion of gender issues; supporting capacity development on gender equality within the organization; knowledge management; and coordination on interagency initiatives, among others." While I worked at the school, the GFP served primarily as a GBA+ coordinator. She organized the necessary discussions and meetings to work toward building and implementing a successful framework and advocated for the importance of this project to senior management. Clearly, the GFP played a crucial role in the school's framework development process and in ensuring that once the framework was in place the necessary leadership roles and responsibilities would have been designated so that it could be sustained over time. I obtained permission from her to write about my experiences as part of the GBA+ framework development team. I also consulted a representative from the school's Office of Values and Ethics to ensure that this was acceptable.

7 Discussions around issues of measurement were focused on how GBA+ progress could (or should) be measured in relation to the school itself (i.e., internally, the CSPS workforce), as well as on the products and services it offered (i.e., externally, the educational and training resources that CSPS provides to public servants across departments).

8 As Andrea Mennicken and Wendy Nelson Espeland (2019, 230) explain, "enthusiasm for quantification is often driven by the desire to hold to account, to counteract despotism and arbitrariness, and to make visible social and economic inequality. Numbers have come to be integral to how democracy is justified and operationalized as a particular set of mechanisms of rule (Rose 1991; see also Alonso and Starr 1989; Desrosières 2014; Didier 2009), and the relation between politics and numbers is mutually constitutive. As

Rose (1991, 675) writes, numbers are always preceded by political judgement of what to measure, and our images of political life are shaped by numbers – by the realities of our society that statistics appear to disclose."

9 For more information, see Berman and Hirschman (2018); Buchanan, Byers, and Mansveld (2018); Erkkilä, Peters, and Piironen (2016); Larsen (2012); Merry (2011); Powell (2016); and Urueña (2015).

10 A 2016 special issue of the *Journal of Comparative Policy Analysis* sought to bring these processes to light. In their contribution to the issue, Tero Erkkilä, B. Guy Peters, and Ossi Piironen (2016, 319, 326) explain, "this issue contributes to comparative policy analysis by analyzing places of politics in and behind the most familiar measurements that feature in many comparativists' work." They conclude by noting that "we find politics in conceptualizations, operationalization, measurement methods and the presentation of results. We see traces of political standpoints not only in the numbers presented and the methodologies that are used, but also when we examine the producers and users of governance data, as well as the motives, networks, and those who benefit and those who lose."

11 This variance actually contributed to the difficulties in obtaining guidance on developing the framework. In some instances, the person (or people) who had played a central role in creating a department's framework – and who could ostensibly have provided key insights – no longer worked there.

Works Cited

Alonso, William, and Paul Starr, eds. 1989. *The Politics of Numbers: Population of the United States in the 1980s.* New York: Russell Sage.

Berman, Elizabeth Popp, and Daniel Hirschman. 2018. "Review Essay: The Sociology of Quantification: Where Are We Now?" *Contemporary Sociology* 47, 3: 257–66.

Bishwakarma, Ramu, Valerie Hunt, and Anna Zajicek. 2007. "Educating Dalit Women: Beyond a One-Dimensional Policy Formulation." *Himalaya* 27, 1–2: 27–39.

Buchanan, Ruth, Kimberley Byers, and Kristina Mansveld. 2018. "'What Gets Measured Gets Done': Exploring the Social Construction of Globalized Knowledge for Development." In *Research Handbook on the Sociology of International Law,* ed. Moshe Hirsch and Andrew Lang, 101–21. Cheltenham: Edward Elgar.

Buss, Doris. 2015. "Measurement Imperatives and Gender Politics: An Introduction." *Social Politics: International Studies in Gender, State and Society* 22, 3: 381–89.

Bustelo, María, Lucy Ferguson, and Maxine Forest. 2016. "Introduction." In *The Politics of Feminist Knowledge Transfer: Gender Training and Gender Expertise,* ed. María Bustelo, Lucy Ferguson, and Maxine Forest, 1–22. New York: Palgrave Macmillan.

Canada, Senate. 2023. *All Together – The Role of Gender-Based Analysis Plus in the Policy Process: Reducing Barriers to an Inclusive Intersectional Policy Analysis.* Report of the Standing Senate Committee on Social Affairs, Science and Technology, March 2023. https://sencanada.ca/content/sen/committee/441/SOCI/Reports/COM_SOCI_GBA -Plus_Report_E.pdf.

Canada School of Public Service. 2020. "Departmental Plan 2020–2021." https://www. csps-efpc.gc.ca/About_Us/currentreport/dp-pm2020-21/index-eng.aspx.

–. n.d. https://www.csps-efpc.gc.ca/index-eng.aspx.

Connell, Raewyn. 2005. "Advancing Gender Reform in Large-Scale Organisations: A New Approach for Practitioners and Researchers." *Policy and Society* 24, 4: 5–24.

Desrosières, Alain. 2014. *Prouver et gouverner. Une analyse politique des statistiques publiques.* Paris: La Découverte.

Didier, Emmanuel. 2009. *En quoi consiste l'Amérique? Les statistiques, le New Deal et la démocratie.* Paris: La Découverte.

Erkkilä, Tero, B. Guy Peters, and Ossi Piironen. 2016. "Politics of Comparative Quantification: The Case of Governance Metrics." *Journal of Comparative Policy Analysis: Research and Practice* 18, 4: 319–28.

Government of Canada. 2017. "Mainstreaming of a Gender Perspective." http://international.gc.ca/world-monde/funding-financement/mainstream-integration.aspx?lang=eng&_ga=2.38609125.774529356.1509411285650188062.1495724982.

–. 2018a. "Budget 2018's Gender Results Framework." https://www.budget.gc.ca/2018/docs/plan/chap-05-en.html.

–. 2018b. "Creation of the Department for Women and Gender Equality: Statement by Minister Monsef on the Creation of the Department for Women and Gender Equality." Accessed December 13, 2018. https://www.canada.ca/en/status-women/news/2018/12/creation-of-the-department-for-women-and-gender-equality.html.

Graham, Ian D., Jo Logan, Margaret B. Harrison, Sharon E. Straus, Jacqueline Tetroe, Wenda Caswell, and Nicole Robinson. 2006. "Lost in Knowledge Translation: Time for a Map?" *Journal of Continuing Education in the Health Professions* 26, 1: 13–24.

Harris, Kathleen. 2019. "Jane Philpott Resigns from Cabinet, Citing Loss of 'Confidence' over Government's Handling of SNC-Lavalin." *CBC News,* March 4. https://www.cbc.ca/news/politics/philpott-resignation-trudeau-snc-lavalin-1.5042411.

Larsen, Tord. 2012. "Introduction: 'Objectification, Measurement and Standardization.'" *Culture Unbound* 4: 579–83.

Lavertu, Stephane. 2014. "We All Need Help: 'Big Data' and the Mismeasure of Public Administration." *Public Administration Review* 76, 6: 864–72.

Mennicken, Andrea, and Wendy Nelson Espeland. 2019. "What's New with Numbers? Sociological Approaches to the Study of Quantification." *Annual Review of Sociology* 45: 223–45.

Merry, Sally Engle. 2011. "Measuring the World: Indicators, Human Rights, and Global Governance." *Current Anthropology* 52, suppl. 3: S83–S95.

–. 2016. *The Seductions of Quantification: Measuring Human Rights, Gender Violence, and Sex Trafficking.* Chicago: University of Chicago Press.

Office of the Prime Minister. 2015. "President of the Treasury Board Mandate Letter." Accessed March 26, 2018. https://pm.gc.ca/eng/president-treasury-board-canada-mandate-letter.

–. 2019. "President of the Treasury Board Mandate Letter." December 13. https://pm.gc.ca/en/mandate-letters/2019/12/13/president-treasury-board-mandate-letter.

O'Manique, Sophie. 2015. "Gender and Austerity in Post-Crisis Canada: How the Government Is Leaving Women Behind." In *The Harper Record 2008–2015,* ed. T. Healy and S. Trew, 293–305. Ottawa: Canadian Centre for Policy Alternatives.

Paterson, Stephanie, and Francesca Scala. 2017. "Gender Mainstreaming and the Discursive Politics of Public Service Values." *Administrative Theory and Praxis* 39: 1–18.

Powell, Catherine. 2016. "Gender Indicators as Global Governance: Not Your Father's World Bank." *Georgetown Journal of Gender and the Law* 17: 777–807.

Rose, Nikolas. 1991. "Governing by Numbers: Figuring Out Democracy." *Accounting, Organizations and Society* 16, 7: 673–92.

Scala, Francesca, and Stephanie Paterson. 2017. "Bureaucratic Role Perceptions and Gender Mainstreaming in Canada." *Gender, Work and Organization* 24, 6: 579–93.

Supiot, Alain. 2015. *La gouvernance par les nombres.* Paris: Fayard.

SWC (Status of Women Canada). 2017. "GBA+ Research Guide." Accessed January 26, 2018. https://cfc-swc.gc.ca/gba-acs/guide-en.html.

–. n.d. "The GBA+ Framework: A Guide to Building Organizational Capacity for Gender-Based Analysis+ (GBA+)." Accessed January 25, 2018. http://www.swc-cfc.gc.ca/gba-acs/guide-eng.pdf.

–. n.d. "An Overview of GBA+ in the Federal Government." Accessed March 26, 2018. http://www.swc-cfc.gc.ca/gba-acs/course-cours-2017/eng/global/resources_ressources.html.

UN Women Training Centre. 2016. "Gender Equality Glossary." https://trainingcentre.unwomen.org/mod/glossary/view.php?id=36&mode=letter&hook=G&sortkey=&sortorder=&fullsearch=0&page=1.

Urueña, Rene. 2015. "Indicators as Political Spaces: Law, International Organizations, and the Quantitative Challenge." *International Organizations Law Review (Special Forum on Indicators)* 12: 1–18.

Zalewski, Marysia. 2010. "'I Don't Even Know What Gender Is': A Discussion of the Connections between Gender, Gender Mainstreaming and Feminist Theory." *Review of International Studies* 36: 3–27.

4

Missing the Mark: Measuring Gender Equality in Maternal Health Programs in the Muskoka Initiative

Rebecca Tiessen and Liam Swiss,
with the assistance of Krystel Carrier

CODING DEVELOPMENT PROGRAMS for their achievements in promoting gender equality (GE) is a strategy for measuring their outcomes and is an important offshoot of gender mainstreaming initiatives. Gender mainstreaming is the strategy employed internationally to ensure that the needs and interests of all individuals, and especially the most marginalized, are integrated into the policy process in all stages (planning, implementation, and evaluation). In this context, "coding for GE" refers to the process by which development agencies and aid donors categorize their projects according to their level of impact or targeting of gender equality. Coding schemes indicate the absence or presence of a GE focus in a project and often demarcate its intensity. Coding supports efforts to ensure accountability for the promotion of gender mainstreaming and has become a widely adopted (but highly manipulated) tool to demonstrate that gender mainstreaming policies and commitments are translated into practice. In this chapter, we present strategies for measuring success in the promotion of GE in maternal health programs funded by Canada under the Muskoka Initiative of 2010. We begin by summarizing Canadian and international commitments to the promotion of GE and maternal, newborn, and child health (MNCH) initiatives in the 2010–15 period, and subsequently present an analysis of coding and measures of GE in these MNCH programs. We also provide the parameters for an alternative approach to measuring GE in maternal health initiatives.

The Canadian government has adopted a number of strategies to integrate gender into its development programs. Its goals were clearly spelled out in the Gender Equality Policy (CIDA 1999) and further highlighted in the commitment to gender-based analysis plus (GBA+) (Status of Women Canada 2017) and in "Gender Equality 2010–2013: CIDA's Gender Equality Action Plan" (CIDA 2010), a document that addresses the implementation gaps identified in the "Evaluation of CIDA's Implementation of Its Policy on Gender Equality:

Executive Report" (Bytown Consulting and CAC International 2008). In "Gender Equality 2010–2013" (CIDA 2010), several actions and implementation steps were spelled out in an effort to better equip development experts in the Department of Foreign Affairs, Trade and Development (DFATD),[1] now Global Affairs Canada. Staff members who were familiar with this action plan and who took part in gender training sessions were better able to formulate, implement, and report on GE results (DFATD 2014). The objectives of the action plan point to the importance of capacity building by working closely with partners, improved accountability to ensure the delivery of GE results, and engagement with partners to achieve better GE results. One of the many strategies and implementation steps to achieve these objectives during the Harper government era was the introduction of a "revised" and "more robust" GE coding process (CIDA 2010) – a direct response to the criticism of CIDA's coding practices as "not entirely reliable" and "arbitrary" (Bytown Consulting and CAC International 2008, 11). The Action Plan on Gender Equality took effect in 2010, and by 2011 Canada had revised its system of coding GE results in projects, building on the coding framework of the Organisation for Economic Co-operation and Development's (OECD) Development Assistance Committee (DAC).

At the same time, Canada made a significant commitment to maternal health at the 2010 Group of Eight (G8) Summit – promising to spend more than $2.85 billion on maternal, newborn, and child health between 2010 and 2015 (DFATD 2014). The program was one of the Conservative government's flagship initiatives in foreign aid and is considered a central component of Harper's legacy (McTeer 2014; Zerbisias 2011). The Muskoka Initiative on MNCH was named after the location of the June 2010 G8 Summit held in Ontario. Prime Minister Stephen Harper championed it to improve child and maternal health in developing countries. Choosing maternal health as a priority for funding was perhaps not surprising given the international community's commitment at the time to address this issue as one of the eight millennium development goals (MDGs) introduced by the United Nations in 2000. Through MDG 5, the international community agreed to reduce maternal mortality by 75 percent by the year 2015. However, by 2010, progress on this front was demonstrably slow, and MDG 5 was considered the least likely of the eight MDGs to be met by 2015, with the worst track record in terms of impact. The Muskoka Initiative on MNCH led to the 2011 Muskoka Initiative Partnership Program, the result of pooled resources from several nations and organizations totalling US $7.3 billion to fund fifty-one Muskoka Initiative projects in twenty-six countries (Government of Canada 2011). Projects included health and nutrition programs for mothers, access to maternal health services, upgraded training for maternal health care providers, and information services to promote improved maternal health practices and access to maternal and newborn health care resources (Government of Canada 2011).

By 2015, though maternal mortality had been reduced, the MDG 5 target had not been achieved. Despite the mandate provided by MDG 5 and commitments to funding projects under the Muskoka Initiative Partnership Program, the Muskoka Initiative was not without controversy (Carrier and Tiessen 2012). Canada was criticized for failing to incorporate a gender lens into it by initially refusing to fund family planning. Eventually, after significant internal and international pressure, the Harper government changed its stance, expanding commitments to family planning but leaving out abortion in a bid to maintain support from the Conservative base (Brown 2018). In 2015, shortly after Justin Trudeau and the Liberal Party came to power, maternal health remained a priority, but programs were widened to encompass sexual and reproductive health and rights (SRHR), including funding for programs that contained information about – or services related to – abortion. The announcement that Canada would devote $650 million to a comprehensive program on SRHR (Government of Canada 2017a) signalled a departure from the previous Conservative government.

The early Muskoka Initiative commitments to MNCH during the 2010–15 period, however, provide an interesting case study of gender measurement in official development assistance, as the Muskoka Initiative is one of the largest Canadian development programs with women as a main beneficiary and is therefore important for considering how gender equality coding was exercised. This expansion of Canadian aid to maternal health and the simultaneous reforms to CIDA's GE coding practices provide a unique case through which to examine how GE is measured in the context of programs that *should* have significant gender results.

International and Canadian Efforts to Measure GE

Important debates over the appropriate measure of GE have occurred at national and international levels since the introduction of the United Nations Development Programme's (UNDP) Gender-Related Development Index (GDI). The GDI and the Gender Empowerment Measure (GEM) suffer from several limitations, most notably that they conflate relative GE with absolute levels of development, which, as a result, yields no information on comparative gender inequality between countries (Dijkstra 2006; Dijkstra and Hanmer 2000). In this respect, the GDI and GEM indicate only how equal/unequal gender relations are in a country at a specific level of development but do little to allow for comparison between countries with differing development levels. Alternative measures of GE have been suggested, such as the Relative Status of Women

Index (Dijkstra and Hanmer 2000), the Multidimensional Gender-Related Development Index (Permanyer 2008), the Multidimensional Gender Equality Index (Permanyer 2008), the Relative Women Disadvantage Index (Bérenger and Verdier-Chouchane 2011), and the Women's Quality-of-Life Index (Bérenger and Verdier-Chouchane 2011). The United Nations has also noted that several challenges remain to the integration and measurement not only of GE, but also of gender mainstreaming approaches since, it argues, not enough gender statistics and sex-disaggregated data are available, and the lack of data remains a major barrier to addressing gender inequalities (UNECE 2009).

A key aspect of Canada's GE measurement in development assistance is the aid marker – a system of coding all aid programming for GE aims and results. Such measurement tools have become ubiquitous among major aid donor countries as a way of tracking and documenting their work across a range of priorities including gender. Coding systems are, however, highly political bureaucratic tools rather than means of objectively documenting donor practices. Systems of coding data and outcomes distill the messiness of aid activities into easily counted and sorted categories and tick boxes. In the case of donor GE coding, the first such system was introduced in 1991 by the DAC of the OECD. Earlier versions of the marker system were employed only by a limited number of DAC members, on a limited portion of total DAC donor aid (O'Neill 2012). The DAC gender equality policy marker was revised in 2007 and is now used by all DAC donor member countries. The stated purpose of the aid marker system is to ensure a uniform ranking of gender impacts for bilateral aid commitments. The ranking has three levels: 0, screened for promoting GE but not a target; 1, significant: GE is important but secondary; 2, principal: GE is an explicit objective of the activity and fundamental to the design. The Canadian government refined its aid marker system in 2011 in response to the 2008 evaluation, reacting to critiques that its earlier system had inaccurately inflated the amount of Canadian aid dedicated to the "principal" category (OECD 2012). In contrast to the DAC marker system, the new Canadian policy marker system includes four categories and focuses on project results rather than objectives. It is characterized as follows: 0: no GE results; 1: results are at the immediate (short-term) outcome; 2: results are at the intermediate (medium-term) outcome; and 3: GE is the principal objective and result of the initiative. When this new coding structure was adopted, CIDA agreed that it should be applied to all CIDA-financed aid activities (Tomlinson 2013).

In adopting GE markers and coding frameworks, as well as other policy commitments, Canada has made some notable achievements, particularly in its efforts to measure results rather than objectives. Indeed, among the donor community, Canada has been viewed as a leader in managing for and measuring

GE results in recent years (OECD 2012). However, in discussing these seemingly outstanding accomplishments, Brian Tomlinson (2013) questions whether the praise is deserved for Canada's efforts to ensure that 43 percent of its bilateral commitments include GE as fundamental to the project's design. In his analysis of Canada's performance in the DAC gender marker, Tomlinson flags a remarkable increase in GE performance from the 2008–09 period to the 2010–11 period, noting that no other donors come close to this level. For example, 16.6 percent of Sweden's programs have GE as a principal objective compared to Canada's 43.0 percent. Tomlinson (2013, 4) argues that Canada's commitment to ensuring that GE is a principal purpose in projects is greatly exaggerated and challenges readers not to take CIDA's report to the DAC on its GE marker for 2010–11 "at face value." This underscores the highly political nature of GE coding as a measurement tool. Tinkering slightly with the coding definitions and processes results in a reported performance level that is viewed as a great success by some but as dubious at best by aid experts such as Tomlinson, who question the validity of current coding practices.

Challenging the reporting on GE markers must also consider other evidence of declining support for the promotion of GE, namely the disappearance of references to GE in policy documents and official statements and a shift to the use of "equality between women and men" (see Carrier and Tiessen 2012; Tiessen and Carrier 2015). Furthermore, since GE was not a central feature of Canada's Muskoka Initiative commitments to promoting maternal health, observers questioned the genuineness of the Conservative government's embrace of GE (Carrier and Tiessen 2012).

Despite its significant emphasis on the needs and health priorities of mothers, the Muskoka Initiative rarely referred to its beneficiaries as women, choosing instead to call them "vulnerable mothers," which limited the potential for understanding maternal health challenges as a result of gender inequality (Keast 2017). Furthermore, the emphasis on easily measured or counted technical solutions, clinic visits, and healthy babies came at the expense of addressing broader challenges that determined whether women could access specialized services, travel to clinics, and exert control over their reproductive lives. It is worth pointing out that not all women with maternal health needs will become mothers. Some may suffer a miscarriage or may choose to have the child adopted or be raised by relatives. The proposed technical solutions fail to get at the heart of why women are in need of improved maternal health options in the first place. The real issues begin with understanding gender dynamics that enable or prevent them from accessing maternal health services. This is why it is essential to measure gender equality in the Muskoka Initiative programming.

Measuring GE in Canada's Maternal Health Initiatives

Given the weaknesses of promoting GE in the Muskoka Initiative, it is increasingly unclear how GE was coded for in its programs. When we commenced this research, we tried to meet with DFATD staff who were responsible for coding GE in various programs, including those for maternal health. However, numerous staff members refused to participate, referring to the state of "flux" that currently characterized anything to do with GE activities in DFATD, which had only recently been created. As the government staff informants noted, it is challenging to document and code maternal health programs because some activities have a gender focus whereas others do not, making it difficult to code accurately.

Despite the reluctance of DFATD staff to discuss the coding of GE in maternal health programing, the projects linked to the Muskoka Initiative are coded for GE results, like all other projects administered by DFATD. By examining how Muskoka-linked programming was coded, we can evaluate whether its impact on GE was being presented as greater than in any other DFATD programming. To this end, we ask: Does Canada's work on maternal, newborn, and child health make a significant impact on the promotion of GE? To answer this question, we analyzed data on Canadian aid for the two fiscal years immediately following the announcement of the Muskoka Initiative: 2010–11 and 2011–12. These data are drawn from the DFATD Historical Project Data Set and made available through the department's open data portal (GAC 2013).

First, we identified projects that could be linked to the Muskoka Initiative. Unfortunately, there is no Muskoka marker in the Historical Project Data Set or in other DFATD open data sources. Thus, we created one, drawing on two separate sources to identify Muskoka-related projects. The first is a list of 74 MNCH projects that was posted on the DFATD website in early February 2014.[2] The second is a list of 688 MNCH projects and imputed Muskoka projects compiled by the North-South Institute.[3] It includes the 74 projects in the first list and the programs and projects that qualify as Muskoka-related based on the imputation methodology given in the G8's Muskoka Initiative.[4]

Once we identified the Muskoka-related projects in the Historical Project Data Set, we could directly compare them against all other DFATD projects in a given fiscal year. We compared the distribution of GE marker coding in each category, using both lists of Muskoka projects. Table 4.1 shows the conditional frequencies for each marker category by Muskoka status. The differences between Muskoka and non-Muskoka projects in each list are statistically significant (at $p < 0.1$ for the DFATD list and $p < 0.001$ for the imputed list).[5] Several differences in coding patterns are notable. First, in both categories of Muskoka projects, the proportion of projects coded as having "no GE results"

Table 4.1

Project-level GE marker coding by Muskoka status, 2010–12

Gender marker	DFATD list		Imputed list		Total
	Non-Muskoka	*Muskoka*	*Non-Muskoka*	*Muskoka*	
No GE results	39.71	22.95	44.29	26.19	39.38
GE results, immediate outcome level	19.03	22.95	19.04	19.29	19.11
GE results, intermediate outcome level	37.57	50.82	33.04	50.71	37.83
GE principal objective and result	3.69	3.28	3.63	3.81	3.68
Total	100.00	100.00	100.00	100.00	100.00
Chi-square statistic	7.55[a]		101.55[b]		

Notes: a = p <0.1; b = p <0.001
Source: DFATD (2013)

is significantly lower than for the other DFATD projects. Likewise, the percentage of projects coded as having GE results at the intermediate level is much higher. Given that the proportion of projects coded as having immediate GE results is relatively consistent between the categories, there appears to be a shift of projects in the Muskoka category from the no results to the intermediate results marker code. The proportion of projects coded as having GE as a principal objective is also very consistent, with less than a 4 percent difference between the two categories.

Figures 4.1 and 4.2 depict these differences, starkly reflecting the shift from coding of no results to intermediate results. More interestingly, they reveal that despite this shift, the proportion of projects coded with the "principal objective" category is nearly identical. The absence of difference in this case is telling. If the maternal health programming linked to the Muskoka Initiative were effectively integrating GE and taking seriously the idea that maternal health is a GE intervention, we would expect to see this reflected in the coding. Instead, what the coding displays is a tacit admission that DFATD's maternal health programming did not address GE as a principal objective or result.

As Figure 4.3 demonstrates, the coding of the GE marker shifted over time at CIDA and DFATD – despite the increased identification of GE results at immediate and intermediate levels, the average proportion of projects that had GE as their principal objective again remained relatively constant. In this respect, the Muskoka Initiative–linked projects confirm the stagnation of GE-focused work at CIDA and DFATD – a particularly troubling fact, given that

Figure 4.1

GE marker coding of Canadian aid projects by Muskoka status (DFATD list), 2010–12

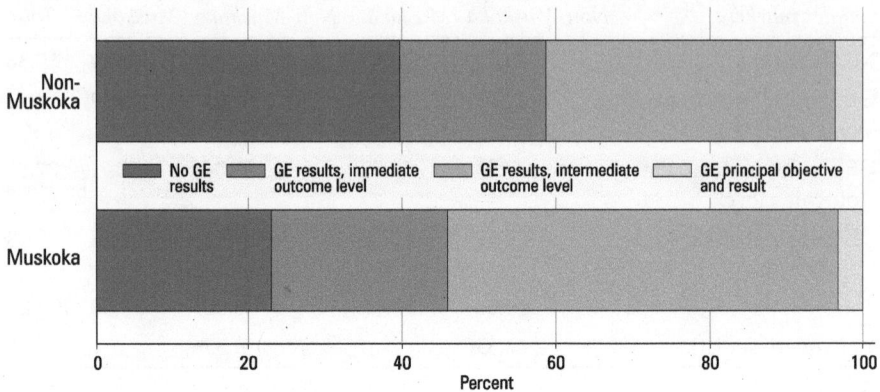

Figure 4.2

GE marker coding of Canadian aid projects by Muskoka status (imputed list), 2010–12

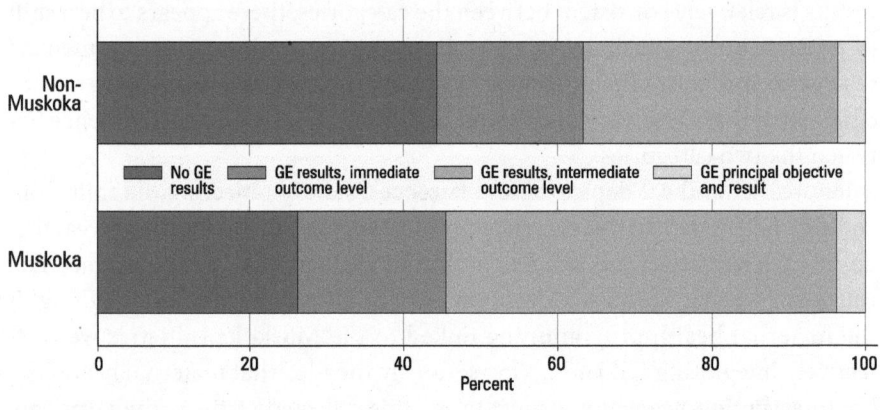

a GE-focused approach to maternal health can both improve women's health outcomes and promote GE in a significant fashion. Canada did not seize the opportunity to directly promote GE as a primary focus of its maternal health work, as the coding reveals that GE was just one of many results. This failure is not surprising given the rhetorical shift away from GE and the significant constraints placed on Canada's Muskoka contribution by the Harper government (Swiss and Barry 2017; Tiessen and Carrier 2015).

Figure 4.3

GE marker coding of Canadian aid projects by fiscal year, 2005–12

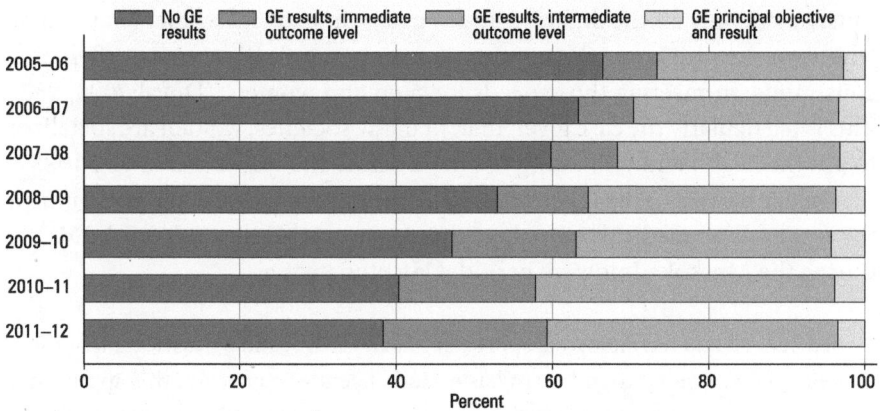

Alternative Ways of Measuring Maternal Health

Our analysis illustrates that, though Canada's Muskoka investments in maternal health did achieve some gender-related results, DFATD did not see GE as a principal objective or result to any greater degree than the rest of its aid programming. Despite the inconsistencies, arbitrariness, and inherent political nature of the GE coding system, we interpret this finding as indicative of the fact that Canada fundamentally failed to take a GE approach to maternal health. Given this failure, and the limitations of the quantitative data for GE coding, it is worth contemplating what an approach to maternal health that incorporates GE would look like and what the prospects for Canada adopting such an approach might be. The focus on hard numbers tracked in the health sector in the coding approach used to measure the success of the Muskoka Initiative does not lend itself well to measuring improvements in attaining GE.

The literature on maternal health is unequivocal in stating that certain factors are key to integrating GE into programming that spans beyond the health sector. Significant improvements in women's health can be achieved only when gender inequality is fully taken into consideration, so that strategies can address the cultural and socio-economic barriers that prevent women from accessing health care, and improving and protecting their health. Lesley Doyal (2000) contends that the first step toward integrating GE in health programming is to achieve a better understanding of what the term actually means. For example, Doyal (2000, 932) argues that the "most obvious goal," which may seem to be equality in health outcomes between men and women, "is clearly unachievable. Because individuals (and groups) begin with very different biological constitutions, any attempt to equalize male and female life expectancy or morbidity rates is doomed to failure." If a gender-integrated approach to health is to be effective, the focus must be not only on the differing health needs of men and women, but also on "the ways in which current modes of social organization place differential constraints on meeting those needs for men and women" (Doyal 2000, 932). This is particularly the case given that, in many societies, women are socialized to put the health and well-being of others before their own (Kandiyoti 1988).

A major barrier to the integration of GE in maternal health programming is the emphasis on medical technology that accompanied the push for the MDGs during the Muskoka Initiative period. Unfortunately, a

> medicalized and technological approach to MDGs 4, 5, and 6 has meant that the political discussion around them has excluded gender equity. Yet this approach marginalizes the analysis of gender equity as a root cause and contributing variable to maternal and child health, and is reflected in the absence of a gender focus in public health policies and programmes. Technological fixes, such as access to services, drugs, and vaccines will not by themselves achieve long lasting change for future generations. (*The Lancet* 2010, 1939)

The medicalized approach to MDG 5 also had implications for the ways in which GE outcomes in projects and programs are measured:

> Integrating gender-sensitive performance indicators in evaluations and monitoring expands the scope of biomedical and technological approaches, but does not necessarily change the targets, standards, and methods. In addition ... the obligation to document and evaluate services lead[s] to a tendency for quick fixes ... Only non-controversial and easy-to-measure areas are evaluated. This means that precisely those dimensions of good care that are emphasized in women-centred caring models are excluded from standardized models of defining and monitoring quality of care. (Kuhlmann 2009, 147; see also Eckman 1998; Grol, Baker, and Moss 2002)

A GE-based approach to maternal health would shift the focus away from medical technologies to the underlying causes that prevent women from accessing and seeking health care.

A central aspect of a GE-based approach to maternal health is the *removal of financial barriers* to health care. This includes both, at the institutional level, the mitigation of the gendered impact of user fees, and, at the household level, greater control over resources and decision making. User fees negatively affect the health of women and girls at a higher rate than for men (Mattson 2010; WHO 2009). Some factors that account for this discrepancy include the tendency for men to control the currency flow of their households, pay inequity, and the preference in certain societies for sons, which results in an allocation of health resources toward male children. Women also tend to have less access to health insurance, particularly when coverage is tied to paid employment (WHO 2009). Enhancing their access to the financial "resources they need to realize their potential for health" improves maternal health outcomes (Doyal 2000, 932; Doyal and Gough 1991; Nussbaum and Glover 1995). Directly linked with the removal of financial barriers is increasing women's autonomy at the household level, which is particularly important for their health behaviours and outcomes (Basu and Basu 1991; Bloom, Wypij, and Das Gupta 2001; Jejeebhoy 2000). Their involvement in decision making at the household level is positively associated with accessing maternal health services, independent of other factors such as education, income, and employment (Allendorf 2007; Becker, Fonseca-Becker, and Schenck-Yglesias 2006; Furuta and Salway 2006; Govindasamy 2000; Matsumura and Gubhaju 2001; Matthews et al. 2005; Odei Boateng et al. 2014). Women's participation in decision making, especially on issues related to family planning, household purchases, and health care, is correlated to an increased likelihood of receiving prenatal care and is more likely to occur when women are employed outside the home (Allendorf 2007; Furuta and Salway 2006; Matthews et al. 2005; Odei Boateng et al. 2014).

A gender-based approach to maternal health would also *address gender-based violence,* which "is the most prevalent and socially tolerated form of gender inequality; this problem results in major costs to the health care system, as well as at the individual and societal level in all countries" (Shaw 2006, 211). Thirty percent of women who experience violence during pregnancy will have maternal complications, as opposed to 23 percent of the larger population (Romero-Gutiérrez et al. 2011). The type of violence also has an impact: compared to the general population of pregnant women, those who experience psychological violence are more likely to have neonatal complications, and those who experience sexual violence are more likely to have maternal complications (Romero-Gutiérrez et al. 2011). Armed conflicts also have a discernable impact on maternal health by sustaining "high fertility levels through increased social insecurity, loss of reproductive health services, and lower female education. Further, war's deteriorating impact on health infrastructure is expected to increase the relative risk that women die from complications associated with pregnancy and childbirth" (Urdal and Che 2013, 489; see also Price and Bohara 2013). As Marian Tankink and Annemiek Richters (2007, 191) write, "Sexual violence during war and other conflict situations is increasingly recognized as a severely traumatic event," yet we know little about the "health strategies women develop in an attempt to overcome their health problems or live with them." Moreover, because women have important cultural motivations to remain silent about their experiences, there is a lack of good information about the nature, extent, and consequences of sexual violence during and after armed conflict. Gender-based violence hence poses many challenges for maternal health. The gendered physical, sexual, and psychological violence that targets women during wartime is directly related to maternal health issues and must therefore be considered in maternal health initiatives. Henrik Urdal and Primus Che Chi (2013) further note that being a refugee can diminish maternal mortality; women are over-represented in refugee camps and are easily accessible to health care providers, rendering maternal health initiatives in these settings highly effective. A number of studies (Orach and De Brouwere 2004; Van Damme et al. 1998) also conclude that refugees tend to have better access to health care services than their host communities, including major obstetric interventions. These studies demonstrate that interventions can effectively address the gendered impact of war on maternal health outcomes.

A gender-based approach to maternal health would also *involve men*. Positive male involvement in maternal health can be defined as "the mental and physical participation of males in maternal and prenatal health and family planning in such a way as to increase maternal and fetal survival rates and improve family planning outcomes" (USAID 2009). It has been recognized as a cornerstone of a successful strategy for achieving women's rights since the 1994 International Conference on Population and Development. Gary Barker and Abhijit Das (2004, 148) describe the conference as "a fundamental moment in the growing international field of promoting men's positive involvement in sexual and reproductive health." Studies have demonstrated that negative or absent male involvement has a detrimental effect on maternal and reproductive health (Agadjanian 2002; Barker and Das 2004; Cohen and Burger 2000; Mufune 2009; Obionu 2001; Odimegwu and Okemgbo 2008; Peacock and Levack 2004; Sternberg and Hubley 2004; United Nations Population Fund 2003; USAID 2000, 2003, 2006). A.V. Camacho, M.D. Castro, and R. Kaufman (2006) further point out that patriarchal social constructs are key to the lack of improvement of women's health. Factors that limit or constrain positive male engagement include local beliefs, traditional customs, and gendered systems of decision making (Barker and Das 2004; Cohen and Burger 2000; Peacock and Levack 2004). Involving men in maternal health programs "free[s] up individuals from the constraints of rigidly defined gender roles" (Doyal 2000, 937) and can actually lead to improved health outcomes for men as well by reducing risk-taking behaviours associated with traditional constructions of masculinity. It also addresses the lack of women's autonomy in sexual and reproductive decision making. Men are increasingly being integrated into gender-based approaches to maternal health (Barker, Ricardo, and Nascimento, 2007; Chattopadhay 2004, 2012).

Lastly, a GE-based approach to maternal health would include a *focus on access to reproductive health care,* including contraception and abortion. Doyal (2000, 937) argues that the largest emphasis of a GE-based approach must be on universal access to this form of health care, followed by the removal of gender inequalities in access to resources. A review of global research on community-level reproductive health initiatives concludes that the majority are inadequate, as they consist of training rather than clinical interventions, and they accommodate gender differences rather than address inequalities (Ravindran and Kelkar-Khambete 2008). This evidence is compounded by the reality that unsafe abortion is one of the three leading causes of maternal mortality (WHO 2011). It is the second leading cause of maternal mortality in the world (Okonofua 2008), with an estimated sixty-eight thousand women dying every year as a result of complications (Grimes et al. 2006, 1913). Ninety-eight percent of these deaths occur in developing countries (Cornwall, Lynch, and Standing 2008, 3). Two strategies have proved effective in reducing maternal mortality associated with unsafe abortions. The first is to improve access to contraceptives, and the second is to improve access to safe and legal abortions (Barot 2011). As Sneha Barot (2011, n.p.) states,

> Extensive research shows that behind almost every abortion is an unintended pregnancy, and the most effective way to prevent unintended pregnancy is through correct and consistent use of contraceptives ... 40% of the 185 million pregnancies in the developing world in 2008 were unintended, and ... about half of them – or almost one in five of all pregnancies – ended in abortion. In addition, four in five unintended pregnancies in the developing world occurred among women with an unmet need for modern contraceptives. And, around the world, abortion rates are lowest in subregions where contraceptive use is high.

However, despite the evidence and the increasing recognition of the importance of reproductive health to maternal health outcomes, "the discussion of unsafe abortion remains limited, and that of safe abortion, decidedly taboo" (Barot 2011, n.p.) among the international community, with few notable exceptions such as the United Kingdom.

These qualitative measures of GE ought to be incorporated into maternal health funding and coded in relation to the promotion of GE. These measures would tell policy-makers if programs are working and what areas of programming need improvement. Evidence-based policy is the *only* type of policy that

Canada should embrace, and for programs to be based on policy, the government must invest in reporting and monitoring tools. However, these program objectives are difficult – if not impossible – to measure using existing coding tools. In the case of measuring GE, policy-makers and programming experts at Global Affairs Canada (GAC) should promote qualitative research and narrative-based studies during the evaluation process to document and analyze the experiences of women, men, children, and health care providers. Such qualitative data collection may be more labour-intensive and may require on-the-ground researchers and evaluators, but it also offers a deeper and more detailed understanding of the experiences of project beneficiaries and the impact of aid programs. This qualitative information can then be numerically coded in relation to the promotion of GE. Though project results were incorporated in DFATD's GE policy marker system, connecting richer qualitative assessments of the GE results of Canada's Muskoka programming to the existing GE coding system would be a positive step toward increasing the perceived validity of existing coding practices. It would also work to better integrate a more nuanced approach to GE into Canada's maternal and child health programming.

The lessons learned from the period 2010–15 on GE coding in maternal and newborn health programming can inform subsequent gender equality evaluations of GAC programming. Under the leadership of the Trudeau Liberal government since 2015, commitments to maternal health continue, though they have been bolstered by increased support for wider programmatic priorities in sexual and reproductive health and rights, as well as abortion-related information and services. Also of significance is a set of commitments to increased funding and programming for gender equality under the 2017 Feminist International Assistance Policy, with 95 percent of Canada's bilateral international development assistance investments earmarked for programs focusing on gender equality and the empowerment of women and girls by 2021–22 (Government of Canada 2017b). Clearer coding schemas and greater transparency are therefore needed to measure the impact of the growing number of programs that are self-defined as promoting gender equality.

Conclusion

The review of the literature makes it clear that very little information is publicly available on the ways in which Canada and other donor countries evaluate the GE impact of their programming. This lack of information makes it difficult for scholars and activists to engage in an informed and meaningful dialogue with policy-makers, politicians, and development workers on the effectiveness of aid programming linked to maternal health. Findings from an analysis of DFATD projects also demonstrate that DFATD's maternal health programming did not ensure GE as a principal objective or result in these projects. This is especially problematic given that the GE focus in maternal health holds much promise for addressing gender inequality. Some key ways that gender inequality can be addressed in maternal health programs include removal of financial barriers, addressing gender-based violence, involving men in reproductive health programs and education campaigns, and increasing the focus on access to reproductive health care programs, including options for abortion when requested. Nonetheless, Canada did not seize its chance to promote GE as a central focus of maternal health in the 2010–15 period, and the evaluation of the coding results shows that GE was just one of many results measured, with the coding system at the time inflating the extent to which Canada's Muskoka programming resulted in GE outcomes. Although these findings are important and instructive, they are not terribly surprising, given that senior policy-makers in the Harper government explicitly stated that sexual and reproductive health would not be the focus of their maternal health strategy and that between 2009 and 2013, official policy statements and speeches typically referred to "equality between women and men" rather than "gender equality," as policy shifted away from the promotion of GE. The net result is that Canada failed to take a GE approach to maternal health in that period, signalling an important missed opportunity.

With Canada's 2017 Feminist International Assistance Policy commitments, new opportunities are emerging for ensuring that GE remains a priority in its foreign aid strategy and that GE coding is designed to reflect the outcomes of these commitments. Future research would benefit from more publicly available information on how Canada and other donor countries evaluate – and code for – GE impacts in their programs to broaden the conversation about aid effectiveness to diverse audiences.

Acknowledgments
We wish to thank the Social Sciences and Humanities Research Council and the Canada Research Chairs program for the funding that facilitated this research.

Notes
1 In March 2013, the Canadian International Development Agency (CIDA) was merged with the Department of Foreign Affairs and International Trade (DFAIT) to form the Department of Foreign Affairs, Trade and Development (DFATD). Following the 2015 election, the new Trudeau government renamed DFATD as Global Affairs Canada (GAC). Throughout this chapter, we refer to work done by CIDA and the reports that it produced before the Trudeau government came to power. In connection with all development and aid-related topics post-2013 and pre-2015, we also refer to DFATD rather than GAC.
2 DFATD, "Project Browser: MNCH Projects," 2014, accessed February 8, 2014, http://www.acdi-cida.gc.ca/cidaweb/cpo.nsf/fWebProjListEn?ReadForm&profile=SMNE-MNCH.

3   See Canadian International Development Platform, "Muskoka-MNCH Tracker: Data and
    Technical Details," http://cidpnsi.ca/blog/muskoka-mnch-tracker-data-technical-details/.
4   Imputation here refers to agreed upon percentages of different DAC spending categories
    attributed to MNCH expenditure. This allows the counting of some MNCH expenditure
    on projects that may not be MNCH-specific. See G7 Research Group, "Methodology for
    Calculating Baselines and Commitments: G8 Member Spending on Maternal, Newborn
    and Child Health," http://www.g8.utoronto.ca/summit/2010muskoka/methodology.html.
5   We ran a parallel analysis using the CIDA imputed list of Muskoka projects and DFATD's
    International Aid Transparency Initiative data file to January 31, 2014. Though the data file
    shows the DAC GE marker rather than the DFATD one, the trend was consistent with the
    result here, except that there is no ability to differentiate between projects that coded within
    the DAC principal objective category and DFATD's two intermediate result/principal
    objective categories. For the sake of simplicity, we elected not to include these alternative
    models in the final analysis.

Works Cited

Agadjanian, Victor. 2002. "Men's Talk about 'Women's Matters': Gender, Communication, and Contraception in Urban Mozambique." *Gender and Society* 16, 2: 194–215. https://doi.org/10.1177/08912430222104903.

Allendorf, Keera. 2007. "Couples' Reports of Women's Autonomy and Health-Care Use in Nepal." *Studies in Family Planning* 38, 1: 35–46. https://doi.org/10.1111/j.1728-4465.2007.00114.x.

Barker, Gary, and Abhijit Das. 2004. "Men and Sexual and Reproductive Health: The Social Revolution." *International Journal of Men's Health* 3, 3: 147–55. DOI:10.3149/jmh.0303.147.

Barker, Gary, Christine Ricardo, and Marcos Nascimento. 2007. *Engaging Men and Boys in Changing Gender-Based Inequity in Health: Evidence from Programme Interventions.* Geneva: World Health Organization. https://apps.who.int/iris/bitstream/handle/10665/43679/9789241595490_eng.pdf.

Barot, Sneha. 2011. "Unsafe Abortion: The Missing Link in Global Efforts to Improve Maternal Health." *Guttmacher Policy Review* 14, 2: n.p.

Basu, Alaka Malwade, and Kaushik Basu. 1991. "Women's Economic Roles and Child Survival: The Case of India." *Health Transition Review* 1, 1: 83–103.

Becker, Stan, Fannie Fonseca-Becker, and Catherine Schenck-Yglesias. 2006. "Husbands' and Wives' Reports of Women's Decision-Making Power in Western Guatemala and Their Effects on Preventive Health Behaviors." *Social Science and Medicine* 62, 9: 2313–26. https://doi.org/10.1016/j.socscimed.2005.10.006.

Bérenger, Valérie, and Audrey Verdier-Chouchane. 2011. "From the Relative Women Disadvantage Index to Women's Quality-of-Life." *Journal of Human Development and Capabilities* 12, 2: 203–33. https://doi.org/10.1080/19452829.2010.520893.

Bloom, Shelah S., David Wypij, and Monica Das Gupta. 2001. "Dimensions of Women's Autonomy and the Influence on Maternal Health Care Utilization in a North Indian City." *Demography* 38, 1: 67–78. https://doi.org/10.2307/3088289.

Brown, Stephen. 2018. "All about That Base? Branding and the Domestic Politics of Canadian Foreign Aid." *Canadian Foreign Policy Journal* 24, 2: 145–64. https://doi.org/10.1080/11926422.2018.1461666.

Bytown Consulting and CAC International. 2008. *Evaluation of CIDA's Implementation of Its Policy on Gender Equality: Executive Report.* Ottawa: Bytown Consulting and CAC International. http://www.oecd.org/derec/canada/42174775.pdf.

Camacho, A.V., M.D. Castro, and R. Kaufman. 2006. "Cultural Aspects Related to the Health of Andean Women in Latin America: A Key Issue for Progress toward the Attainment of the Millennium Development Goals." *International Journal of Gynecology and Obstetrics* 94, 3: 357–63. https://doi.org/10.1016/j.ijgo.2006.04.028.

Carrier, Krystel, and Rebecca Tiessen. 2012. "Women and Children First: Maternal Health and the Silencing of Gender in Canadian Foreign Policy." In *Canada in the World: Perspectives on Canadian Foreign Policy*, ed. Heather A. Smith and Claire Turenne Sjolander, 183–200. Oxford: Oxford University Press.

Chattopadhay, Tamo. 2004. *Role of Men and Boys in Promoting Gender Equality: Advocacy Brief.* Bangkok: UNESCO.

–. 2012. "Men in Maternal Care: Evidence from India." *Journal of Biosocial Science* 44, 2: 129–53. https://doi.org/10.1017/S0021932011000502.

CIDA (Canadian International Development Agency). 1999. *CIDA's Policy on Gender Equality.* Gatineau, QC: CIDA.

–. 2010. *Gender Equality 2010–2013: CIDA's Gender Equality Action Plan.* Gatineau, QC: CIDA. http://publications.gc.ca/collections/collection_2011/acdi-cida/CD4-69-2010-eng.pdf.

Cohen, Sylvie I., and Michèle Burger. 2000. *Partnering: A New Approach to Sexual and Reproductive Health.* Technical Paper 3. New York: United Nations Population Fund.

Cornwall, Andrea, Andrea Lynch, and Hilary Standing. 2008. "Unsafe Abortion: A Development Issue." *IDS Bulletin* 39, 3: 47–54.

DFATD (Department of Foreign Affairs, Trade and Development). 2014. "Maternal, Newborn and Child Health." Accessed February 8, 2014. http://www.acdi-cida.gc.ca/acdi-cida/acdi-cida.nsf/eng/FRA-127113657-MH7.

Dijkstra, A. Geske. 2006. "Towards a Fresh Start in Measuring Gender Equality: A Contribution to the Debate." *Journal of Human Development* 7, 2: 275–83. https://doi.org/10.1080/14649880600768660.

Dijkstra, A. Geske, and Lucia C. Hanmer. 2000. "Measuring Socio-Economic GENDER Inequality: Toward an Alternative to the UNDP Gender-Related Development Index." *Feminist Economics* 6, 2: 41–75. https://doi.org/10.1080/13545700050076106.

Doyal, Len, and Ian Gough. 1991. *A Theory of Human Need.* London: Macmillan.

Doyal, Lesley. 2000. "Gender Equity in Health: Debates and Dilemmas." *Social Science and Medicine* 51, 6: 931–39. https://doi.org/10.1016/S0277-9536(00)00072-1.

Eckman, Anne K. 1998. "Beyond the Yentl Syndrome: Making Women Visible in the Post-1990s Women's Health Discourse." In *The Visible Woman*, ed. Paula Treichler, Lisa Cartwright, and Constance Penley, 130–68. New York: New York University Press.

Furuta, Marie, and Sarah Salway. 2006. "Women's Position within the Household as a Determinant of Maternal Health Care Use in Nepal." *International Family Planning Perspectives* 32, 1: 17–27. https://doi.org/10.1363/ifpp.32.017.06.

GAC (Global Affairs Canada). 2013. "Historical Project Data Set 2012–2013." Accessed February 8, 2014. https://www.international.gc.ca/transparency-transparence/international-assistance-report-stat-rapport-aide-internationale/index.aspx?lang=eng.

Government of Canada. 2011. "Projects under the Muskoka Initiative Partnership Program." News release, September 20. Accessed December 23, 2020. https://www.canada.ca/en/news/archive/2011/09/projects-under-muskoka-initiative-partnership-program.html.

–. 2017a. "Canada Announces Support for Sexual and Reproductive Health and Rights." Global Affairs Canada, March 8. Accessed December 23, 2020. https://www.canada.ca/en/global-affairs/news/2017/03/canada_announcessupportforsexualandreproductivehealthandrights.html.

–. 2017b. "Canada's Feminist International Assistance Policy." https://www.international. gc.ca/world-monde/issues_development-enjeux_developpement/priorities-priorites/ policy-politique.aspx?lang=eng.

Govindasamy, P. 2000. "Poverty, Women's Status, and the Utilization of Health Services in Egypt." In *Women, Poverty, and Demographic Change*, ed. B. García, 263–85. Oxford: Oxford University Press.

Grimes, David A., Janie Benson, Susheela Singh, Mariana Romero, Bela Ganatra, Friday E. Okonofua, and Iqbal H. Shah. 2006. "Unsafe Abortion: The Preventable Pandemic." *The Lancet* 368, 9550: 1908–19. https://doi.org/10.1016/S0140-6736(06)69481-6.

Grol, Richard, Richard W. Baker, and Fiona Moss. 2002. "Quality Improvement Research: Understanding the Science of Change in Health Care." *Quality and Safety in Health Care* 11, 2: 110–11. http://dx.doi.org/10.1136/qhc.11.2.110.

Jejeebhoy, Shireen J. 2000. "Women's Autonomy in Rural India: Its Dimensions, Determinants, and the Influence of Context." In *Women's Empowerment and Demographic Processes: Moving beyond Cairo*, ed. Harriet B. Presser and Gita Sen, 204–38. New York: Oxford University Press.

Kandiyoti, Deniz. 1988. "Bargaining with Patriarchy." *Gender and Society* 2, 3: 274–90.

Keast, Julia. 2017. "Missed Opportunity: A Discursive Analysis of Canada's Commitments to Maternal Health under the Muskoka Initiative." In *Obligations and Omissions: Canada's Ambiguous Actions on Gender Equality*, ed. R. Tiessen and S. Baranyi, 49–69. Montreal and Kingston: McGill-Queen's University Press.

Kuhlmann, Ellen. 2009. "From Women's Health to Gender Mainstreaming and Back Again: Linking Feminist Agendas and New Governance in Healthcare." *Current Sociology* 57, 2: 135–54. https://doi.org/10.1177/0011392108099160.

The Lancet. 2010. "Gender Equity Is the Key to Maternal and Child Health." *The Lancet* 375, 9730: 1939. https://doi.org/10.1016/S0140-6736(10)60905-1.

Matsumura, M., and B. Gubhaju. 2001. "Women's Status, Household Structure and Utilization of Maternal Health Services in Nepal." *Asia-Pacific Population Journal* 16: 23–43.

Matthews, Zoë, Martyn Brookes, R. William Stones, and Mian Bazle Hossain. 2005. "Village in the City: Autonomy and Maternal Health-Seeking among Slum Populations of Mumbai." In *A Focus on Gender: Collected Papers on Gender*, ed. S. Moore, 69–92. Calverton, MD: ORC Macro. https://dhsprogram.com/pubs/pdf/OD32/5.pdf.

Mattson, Susan. 2010. "Millennium Development Goals and Global Women's and Infants' Health." *Journal of Obstetric, Gynecologic and Neonatal Nursing* 39, 5: 573–79. https://doi.org/10.1111/j.1552-6909.2010.01164.x.

McTeer, Maureen. 2014. "How Harper Can Lead on Maternal Health." *Ottawa Citizen*, September 27. http://ottawacitizen.com/news/politics/maureen-mcteer-how-harper -can-lead-on-maternal-health.

Mufune, Pempelani. 2009. "The Male Involvement Programme and Men's Sexual and Reproductive Health in Northern Namibia." *Current Sociology* 57, 2: 231–48. https://doi.org/10.1177/0011392108099164.

Nussbaum, Martha C., and Jonathan Glover. 1995. *Women, Culture and Development: A Study of Human Capabilities*. Oxford: Clarendon Press.

Obionu, Christopher N. 2001. *Primary Health Care for Developing Countries*. Enugu, Nigeria: Delta.

Odei Boateng, Godfred, Daniel Mumba, Yvonne Asare-Bediako, and Mavis Odei Boateng. 2014. "Examining the Correlates of Gender Equality and the Empowerment of Married Women in Zambia." *African Geographical Review* 33, 1: 1–18. https://doi.org/10. 1080/19376812.2013.814188.

Odimegwu, Clifford, and Christian N. Okemgbo. 2008. "Men's Perceptions of Masculinities and Sexual Health Risks in Igboland, Nigeria." *International Journal of Men's Health* 7, 1: 21–39.

OECD (Organisation for Economic Co-operation and Development). 2012. *Canada: Development Assistance Committee (DAC) Peer Review 2012*. https://www.oecd-ilibrary.org/development/oecd-development-assistance-peer-reviews-canada-2012_9789264200784-en.

Okonofua, Friday E. 2008. "Contribution of Anti-Abortion Laws to Maternal Mortality in Developing Countries." *Expert Review of Obstetrics and Gynecology* 3, 2: 147–49. https://doi.org/10.1586/17474108.3.2.147.

O'Neill, Patti. 2012. "Follow the Money – Tracking Financing for Gender Equality." Paper presented at the United Nations Commission on the Status of Women, Fifty-sixth session, February 27–March 9, 2012, New York. http://www.un.org/womenwatch/daw/csw/csw56/panels/panel4-Patti-ONeill.pdf.

Orach, Christopher Garimoi, and Vincent De Brouwere. 2004. "Postemergency Health Services for Refugee and Host Populations in Uganda, 1999–2002." *The Lancet* 364, 9434: 611–12. https://doi.org/10.1016/S0140-6736(04)16854-2.

Peacock, Dean, and Andrew Levack. 2004. "The Men as Partners Programme in South Africa: Reaching Men to End Gender-Based Violence and Promote Sexual and Reproductive Health." *International Journal of Men's Health* 3, 3: 173–88.

Permanyer, Iñaki. 2008. "On the Measurement of Gender Equality and Gender-Related Development Levels." *Journal of Human Development* 9, 1: 87–108. https://doi.org/10.1080/14649880701811427.

Price, James I., and Alok K. Bohara. 2013. "Maternal Health Care amid Political Unrest: The Effect of Armed Conflict on Antenatal Care Utilization in Nepal." *Health Policy and Planning* 28, 3: 309–19. https://doi.org/10.1093/heapol/czs062.

Ravindran, T.K.S., and Aarti Kelkar-Khambete. 2008. "Gender Mainstreaming in Health: Looking Back, Looking Forward." *Global Public Health* 3, suppl. 1: 121–42. https://doi.org/10.1080/17441690801900761.

Romero-Gutiérrez, Gustavo, Victor Hugo, Claudia Areceli Regalado-Cedillo, and Ana Lilia Ponce-Ponce de León. 2011. "Prevalence of Violence against Pregnant Women and Associated Maternal and Neonatal Complications in Leon, Mexico." *Midwifery* 27, 5: 750–53. http://dx.doi.org/10.1016/j.midw.2010.06.015.

Shaw, D. 2006. "Women's Right to Health and the Millennium Development Goals: Promoting Partnerships to Improve Access." *International Journal of Gynecology and Obstetrics* 94, 3: 207–15. https://doi.org/10.1016/j.ijgo.2006.04.029.

Status of Women Canada. 2017. "Gender Based Analysis Plus (GBA Plus)." Government of Canada. https://www.swc-cfc.gc.ca/gba-acs/index-en.html.

Sternberg, Peter, and John Hubley. 2004. "Evaluating Men's Involvement as a Strategy in Sexual and Reproductive Health Promotion." *Health Promotion International* 19, 3: 389–96. https://doi.org/10.1093/heapro/dah312.

Swiss, Liam, and Jessica Barry. 2017. "Did Changes in Official Language Lead to Spending Shifts?" In *Obligations and Omissions: Canada's Ambiguous Actions on Gender Equality*, ed. R. Tiessen and S. Baranyi, 23–48. Montreal and Kingston: McGill-Queen's University Press.

Tankink, Marian, and Annemiek Richters. 2007. "Silence as a Coping Strategy: The Case of Refugee Women in the Netherlands from South-Sudan Who Experienced Sexual Violence in the Context of War." In *Voices of Trauma: Treating Psychological Trauma across Cultures*, ed. Boris Drozdek and John P. Wilson, 191–210. New York: Springer.

Tiessen, Rebecca, and Krystel Carrier. 2015. "The Erasure of 'Gender' in Canadian Foreign Policy under the Harper Conservatives: The Significance of the Discursive Shift from 'Gender Equality' to 'Equality between Women and Men.'" *Canadian Foreign Policy Journal* 21, 2: 95–111. https://doi.org/10.1080/11926422.2014.977310.

Tomlinson, Brian. 2013. *Briefing Note on Canada's Aid Marker for Gender Equality.* Waterville, NS: AidWatch Canada.

UNECE (United Nations Economic Commission for Europe). 2009. *Regional Review of Progress: Regional Synthesis.* Geneva: Economic Commission for Europe.

United Nations Population Fund. 2003. *It Takes 2: Partnering with Men in Reproductive and Sexual Health: Programme Advisory Note.* New York: UNDP.

Urdal, Henrik, and Primus Che Chi. 2013. "War and Gender Inequalities in Health: The Impact of Armed Conflict on Fertility and Maternal Mortality." *International Interactions: Empirical and Theoretical Research in International Relations* 39, 4: 489–510. https://doi.org/10.1080/03050629.2013.805133.

USAID (United States Agency for International Development). 2000. *Involving Men in Sexual and Reproductive Health: An Orientation Guide.* Washington, DC: USAID/Interagency Gender Working Group.

–. 2003. *Reaching Men to Improve Reproductive Health for All Implementation Guide.* Washington, DC: Interagency Gender Working Group.

–. 2006. *SysteMALEtizing: Resources for Engaging Men in Sexual and Reproductive Health.* Washington, DC: USAID/Interagency Gender Working Group.

–. 2009. *Country Health Statistical Report: Nigeria.* Washington, DC: USAID.

Van Damme, Wim, Vincent De Brouwere, Marleen Boelaert, and Wim Van Lerberghe. 1998. "Effects of a Refugee-Assistance Programme on Host Population in Guinea as Measured by Obstetric Interventions." *The Lancet* 351, 9116: 1609–13. https://doi.org/10.1016/S0140-6736(97)10348-8.

WHO (World Health Organization). 2009. *Women and Health: Today's Evidence, Tomorrow's Agenda.* Geneva: WHO.

–. 2011. *Unsafe Abortion: Global and Regional Estimates of the Incidence of Unsafe Abortion and Associated Mortality in 2008.* Geneva: WHO.

Zerbisias, Antonia. 2011. "Tory Legacy Leaves Little to Attract Women Voters." *Toronto Star,* April 1. http://www.thestar.com/news/canada/2011/04/01/tory_legacy_leaves_little_to_attract_women_voters.html.

5

Measuring Care: Neo-liberalism Comes to the Nursing Home

Pat Armstrong, Hugh Armstrong, and Jacqueline Choiniere

AS FEMINISTS KNOW, "measurement, curiously enough, is not an exact science," for the "very act of measurement implies some sort of assessment" (Hancock, Labonte, and Edwards 1999, S23). Making choices about what to measure, and how and when to measure it, means exercising power. So do the decisions about whether, how, and when to act on what is measured, raising questions about who holds power, over whom, and in what circumstances. These choices, and these power relations, are profoundly gendered. The vulnerabilities of those who live in, work in, and visit long-term care facilities have become dramatically visible and intensified by COVID-19, indicating the limitations of our pre-pandemic measurement systems and how they are used.

In this chapter, we take the case of long-term residential care (LTRC) and one means of measuring it – the Resident Assessment Instrument–Minimum Data Set (RAI-MDS) – to explore the gendered nature of measurement. Women make up the vast majority of both LTRC residents and paid and unpaid workers. Yet positions of power in health care are typically occupied by men, who can choose what to measure, how and when to measure it, what to ignore, and what to do with what they find. Developed in the United States, RAI-MDS is now used in several Canadian provinces to regularly assess the needs of residents and to determine the level and type of care required to fulfill these needs. Reflecting neo-liberal or new public management assumptions, it focuses primarily on standardized and measurable process and outcome indicators (Erlandsson et al. 2013), largely ignoring social aspects of care, including residents' histories or other important considerations such as gender, race, or class (Kontos, Miller, and Mitchell 2010). It also usually ignores the knowledge of the women who do the traditional women's work of personal care and structures their labour in standardized, measurable ways. This devaluing of social care has significant implications for residents and for workers.

Long-Term Residential Care and Measurement

In Canada, health care is a provincial/territorial responsibility, and unlike hospitals and doctors, LTRC does not fall clearly under the federal Canada Health Act, which requires that care be universal, accessible, comprehensive, publicly administered, and portable. The result is substantial variation across Canada in regulations and funding, although all jurisdictions provide extensive support for LTRC facilities. The residents are vulnerable in medical, functional, and economic terms. They need twenty-four-hour nursing care, which is not generally available from home care programs or retirement homes; they need help with daily activities such as bathing, toileting, dressing, and eating; and they are seen as economic burdens because they no longer have paid jobs. Over two-thirds (68 percent) of residents are female (Statistics Canada 2021). Women tend to outlive men, have less income to buy care, and are less likely to have a partner at home who can provide it. Although most provinces require a registered nurse (RN) on duty at all times, the majority of paid providers have titles such as health care aide (HCA) or personal support worker. The vast majority are women and over a third of those who do this work at the bottom of the hierarchy are new to Canada (Turcotte and Savage 2020) and/or from racialized groups. Those who are classified as immigrants are five times as likely as their Canadian-born counterparts to have at least a bachelor's degree (Turcotte and Savage 2020). Doing what is traditionally classed as women's work and seldom recognized as skilled, these workers are not seen as health professionals and may not even be counted in the health sector workforce (Armstrong, Armstrong, and Scott-Dixon 2008; CIHI 2020a). In short, both the residents and the individuals who look after them are among the most vulnerable, and least powerful, members of society. This is reflected in the resources, protections, and research attention allocated to hospitals, doctors, and pharmaceuticals, in contrast to nursing homes.

Nursing home care is both medical and social: medical because residents have increasingly complex health conditions and social because their conditions tend to be chronic and incurable. Residents need comfort, dignity, respect, social connections, and maintenance, but support on these non-curative dimensions is seen as far less essential and far more difficult to count than pills and restraints. As feminists (Glenn 2010; Mol 2008) argue, an emphasis on the social entails understanding care as a relationship involving many sources of knowledge and many ways of responding appropriately. It means focusing on support in various forms rather than on medical interventions. And it means taking care providers' working conditions into account, including the physical violence, sexual harassment, and racism they encounter.

Nursing homes are increasingly assessed according to multiple indicators such as number of bedsores and falls, with the findings sometimes consolidated into a single number by which they can be ranked. The Canadian Institute of Health Information (CIHI) collects and publishes reams of statistics on long-term care each year, as do provincial and local health authorities. Often, the results are beneficial, can help keep LTRC accountable to both government and the public, and can promote appropriate care. For example, such data can tell us about differences among municipal, non-profit, and for-profit homes or about the median wait times for those who transfer from hospital versus those who come from home. It can track, as it did during the pandemic, the COVID-related death rates in Canada compared to those of other countries (CIHI 2020b). But the data can also ignore critical aspects of care in ways that not only distort the picture of care but also ignore the knowledge of care providers and result in an inappropriate allocation of resources, as well as a quite hierarchical division of labour.

Facilities measure for administrative purposes (counting beds, workers, deaths), prescriptive purposes (such as protocols, task definitions, and care pathways), workload purposes (how many staff of what types on what schedules), and outcome purposes (changes in health condition, mortality rates). Whatever the purpose, these technologies tend to reflect and reinforce resource inequalities and gender segregation. They typically build on and thus bolster existing patterns of and assumptions about traditional women's work, in the process undervaluing the work that women do. Workload measures are based on assumptions about care and skill, and on assumptions about tasks that any woman can perform. Outcome data routinely ignore the occupational health and safety of health workers, notwithstanding the reality that health care is Canada's most dangerous industry (Armstrong, Armstrong, and Messing 2009), as was especially the case during the COVID-19 pandemic (CIHI 2020b).

Originating in the United States, the most common of all these measurement techniques is RAI-MDS, which is used in many Canadian LTRC facilities and in more than twenty other countries. It is used to assess residents when they enter a nursing home and typically every three months thereafter, barring significant resident change. It is intended for care planning, for inspection purposes, and in many jurisdictions, for decisions about relative funding levels for facilities. According to CIHI (2010, 3), "The RAI-MDS 2.0 is a comprehensive assessment that documents the clinical and functional characteristics of residents, including measures of cognition, communication, vision, mood and behaviour, psychosocial well-being, physical functioning, continence, disease diagnoses, nutritional status, skin condition, medications and special treatments and procedures."

Although the proponents of RAI-MDS set out multiple purposes (Fries and Fahey 2003), our focus is its overlapping effects on accountability mechanisms and on the residents and workers who are directly involved in the caring relationship. We consider both what is measured and what is missing, and what this means for those who provide and those who need care.

Theory and Method

Our feminist political economy approach means attending to the broader political and economic contexts that influence how quality and accountability are understood. Over the past few decades, neo-liberal thinking and action have led to the introduction and intensification of market forces in long-term care, altering how quality is regulated and frequently transforming accountability into exercises in counting (Armstrong 2013). This influence appears in the emphasis on standardized, measurable clinical assessments of quality (Erlandsson et al. 2013) and in the attendant benchmarking and comparisons of quality indicators. It posits that quality can be assessed and compared this way, reproducing market-based notions of consumer choice (Anttonen and Meagher 2013), which assume that families are at liberty to select the nursing home of their choice even as the lack of spaces in care homes prevents choice.

Our approach is particularly well suited to nursing home care analysis. It challenges the belief, prevalent in "evidence-based" medicine, that all genuine knowledge is objective and that the best evidence comes from randomized clinical trials that tightly focus on a specific body part while eliminating all other considerations, ranging from the medical effects on other body parts and the body in all its physical, emotional, cognitive, and spiritual dimensions. This notion also ignores the broader economic, social, historical, and cultural contexts within which the body and its parts are located. By contrast, our approach holds that exploring qualities such as dignity and respect requires the active participation of those who provide and receive care, as well as attention to context. It requires understanding that women as residents and workers have histories and skills that differ from those of men. We do not reject evidence informed by measurement but insist that most measurement does not and cannot tell the whole story. World views, meanings, and preferences of both subjects and measurers are also important, as are the many and nuanced aspects of caring relationships. Appropriate individualized care demands sensitivity to each resident's values and preferences, biography, and body language, as well as to changes in these factors. Such intimate knowledge cannot be obtained solely by means of detached, standardized assessment systems. Indeed, such systems can "undermine quality care by neglecting the importance of the decision making and care practices" undertaken by those who are most familiar with the residents themselves (Kontos, Miller, and Mitchell 2010, 352–53). The nature of the care relationship is transformed as staff are pressured to concentrate on specific tasks, rather than on what they see residents need, resulting in a relational distancing and the undervaluing of women's skills (Colón-Emeric et al. 2010; Woolford and Curran 2011). Important gendered aspects of care and care work are discounted in this environment, which deteriorated with COVID (CIHI 2020a).

The following discussion is based on research from an international project, which sought to identify promising practices for conceptualizing and organizing LTRC, learning from and with other countries to help us reimagine it (Armstrong and Lowndes, 2018). We analyzed documents from Germany, the United Kingdom, the United States, Norway, Sweden, and four Canadian provinces, and conducted rapid site-switching ethnographies in each of them. Our feminist political economy strategy is constantly evolving, as we seek to capture rich complexity. Prepared with background contextual data, an interdisciplinary, international team of twelve faculty and students observed and conducted interviews in a facility over a week, regularly meeting to share insights and analysis. In addition, we included a day-long visit at a second and sometimes a third site. We interviewed residents, volunteers, and families, as well as the full range of paid staff and managers. We share our perspectives while developing detailed portraits from which we all learn. Informed by our work in other countries, we draw here exclusively on our Canadian data.

Accountability

The Health Council of Canada defines "accountability" as the mechanism for assigning responsibilities for activities and decisions, often in connection with finances, health care performance, and the actions of politicians. It asks, "who is being held accountable, to whom, for what, and to what end?" (Health Council of Canada 2012, 6). These are complex and important questions. Behind them lie other, more fundamental contextual issues. In neo-liberal ideology and practice, the state selectively withdraws from service provision, governing from a distance while using information technologies to accumulate, store, and transfer massive databases that impose marketplace logic, create the illusion of consumer choice, and exercise power at multiple levels. We see RAI-MDS as a neo-liberal tool, however much (or little) it measures what is relevant to care (validity) and measures consistently (reliability), attending to how it reflects and reinforces gender inequities.

With goals such as dignity and respect for residents and those who care for them, the absence of RAI-MDS data on issues of quality of life, autonomy, and satisfaction is striking (Sutherland, Repin, and Crump 2013). Instead, RAI-MDS items mirror and support a medical model, with detailed information on such clinical topics as falls, pressure ulcers, restraint use, and antipsychotics. All of these are important to residents, but so too is the missing information. In its "Your Health System" series based on RAI-MDS, CIHI publishes long-term care indicators and links them to whether homes are for-profit, not-for-profit, or public. Indicators on falls and so on are available at the provincial, regional, and facility levels, linked to ownership. But CIHI is not prepared to use RAI-MDS data to generate an indicator for what it and others (Gerritsen et al. 2008) call "social engagement," a recognized major contributor to quality of life. For CIHI in the foreseeable future, social engagement is just a "place holder," and no other social care indicators are planned, confirming both the low value accorded to this traditional female work and the difficulty in attaching numbers to social care. Social engagement relies on care workers having the time and support to know and incorporate residents' histories, contexts, and preferences into care, recognizing how gender and racialization matter. It can be undermined when care is standardized and when staff-resident interaction is focused on specific tasks and problems (Coughlan and Ward 2007).

In connection with reliability, serious concerns have been raised about data accuracy, including some of the "Your Health System" indicators. The indicators for both pain and depression, for example, have been identified as of potentially suspect reliability (Sutherland, Repin, and Crump 2013, 12). One problem is that pain is inconsistently assessed, sometimes before and sometimes after pain medication is given. Perhaps more telling is a comment made at a 2014 conference by a quality manager from a for-profit chain whose target was to *reduce* its inaccuracy rate to 10 percent,[1] thus diminishing a validity problem (the inability to accurately capture and compare levels of pain) to a simple reliability issue (just getting workers to measure properly). Managers from other homes and chains who were also present at the conference did not suggest that this approach was unreasonable. Another problem is the failure to analyze the collected data by gender. In its study of depression using RAI-MDS, for example, CIHI (2010, 3) notes that seven out of ten residents are women, but there is little analysis of the data by gender, even though considerable research demonstrates that women are much more likely than men to suffer from depression, providing another example of how gender is erased (McMullen and Stoppard 2006).

In addition to these basic questions about data quality, we need to ask about who is responsible, to whom, for what, and why. In Ontario and two other provinces, the use of RAI-MDS is mandatory. Held responsible for transmitting accurate and comprehensive data to government, those in charge of homes seldom participate in the design of this standardized tool, although they have some influence on its implementation.[2] Unlike in other sectors, women for many years have accounted for the majority of managers in LTRC (Armstrong, Armstrong, and Scott-Dixon 2008, 53), but they have very limited power over what questions are asked and answered. Nursing homes have a RAI-MDS coordinator who assembles and transmits their data in a timely and comprehensive fashion. Sitting before a computer, she must rely on others to furnish the data, raising questions about both data quality and the division of labour. She is distant from the work and thus has few means of assessing the data she processes.

At CIHI, the data are organized and analyzed into provincial, regional, and individual facility reports. Facility management can view these data directly for care planning, resource allocation, quality improvement, research, and other purposes. In Ontario, the data are also used for allocating some provincial resources among facilities. This opens the data to the distorting possibility of gaming, the practice of manipulating a funding regime in order to secure extra revenue. In the process, the usefulness of RAI-MDS for other purposes can be undermined. Moreover, the usefulness of RAI-MDS data for resource allocation purposes among homes is limited by various other factors. Both issues are further discussed below. Finally, the RAI-MDS data are made available to management and to nurses, social workers, therapists, and other professionals in each home but very seldom to the HCAs who handle most of the actual care. This means that whatever inaccurate information and misinterpretations exist in the standardized data, those who are most familiar with the individual residents are not able to correct them.

Residents and Measurement

RAI-MDS collects data on residents, which is intended to provide a basis for funding, accountability, and resident-focused care, among other purposes. This information comes from two main sources: the staff and the residents, as supported by their families. Although there is some evidence of improvements in resident care as a result of the RAI-MDS data use, our ethnographic research and our more quantitative work suggest that the system fails these mainly female residents and fails to take gender into account.

In Ontario, the detailed data on the multiple health issues and frailties of residents are translated into just three categories that are assumed to reflect levels of need, with more funding attached to those classified in the highest need category. Our research uncovered a number of problems with this approach. One is that restricted LTRC admission means that virtually every new resident has complex care needs. Given this, they should all attract the highest funding level, making the distinction among levels based on RAI-MDS data of little use, especially while funds remain relatively constant. Lack of funding hurts everyone, but given that nearly seven out of ten residents are women, it hurts them more.

A second problem is the way that funding is linked to the data. Ontario divides the funding into four envelopes: nursing and personal care, program support and services (therapy, recreation), raw food, and other accommodation (laundry, housekeeping, buildings). Set amounts are allocated to each envelope, and although some minor adjustments among envelopes are allowed, money not spent in the envelope must generally be returned to the government (Ministry of Health and Long-Term Care 2022). Our research and that of others reveal that the funding for nursing and personal care is inadequate, regardless of how many residents are classified at the highest level of need. Less research has been done on food, housekeeping, and laundry services, where most of the work is also done by women and is largely invisible in the data (Armstrong, Armstrong, and Scott-Dixon 2008; Armstrong and Day 2017). However, residents, their families, and staff referred to problems with each of these areas, blaming them mainly on lack of staff. When problems arise with laundry and food, it is usually female family and friends who take on the resulting unpaid care and advocacy work.

With less than ten dollars a day per resident for raw food in Ontario, it is difficult to provide delicious and nutritious meals, or too often even palatable ones. The funding for therapy is similarly limited, as is also the case in British Columbia. Listen to this BC family member on the inadequate provision of therapy:

> I saw the slow decline [of her mother] ... For example I know that they have physiotherapists and people that come and help her to assess her physically but then they said "If you need to have her to move around, if you need to have therapy, you need to hire your own therapist."
>
> Anyway so I hired somebody for my mom they call companion so she'll come and she'll try to help her, massage, do the exercise with her when I'm not here.

To keep her mother mobile, this woman must pay privately for therapy. The measurement system does indicate that the mother needs such care, but the data do not translate into funding, and fewer women than men have the means to pay for care. According to a BC RN,

> Well, the only thing is that there's not enough working hands, right? I don't know if I'm right or not now because I know that how the government assigns the staff ratio is that they give only one and a half hour care per resident per day. So basically that's not enough. That's not enough. And so I can see the care aides they are rushing all the time. And I think the bowel care that's the main problem. You can

see some of them [residents] they are quite alert. They still know that they need to go to the washroom. They are sitting there, they are asking, but sometimes say they were sitting in the dining room, there's no call bell, they just yell. No one will go and help them.

A family member in Ontario echoed the nurse, reiterating that "there are not enough hands." Women are more likely than men to have incontinence problems, yet there is no indication that this difference is taken into account in the data or the practices (Nitti 2001).

In addition to providing a basis for funding, RAI-MDS is intended to ensure accountability, not only to governments but also to residents and families. Several challenges to this notion emerged in our research. First, the HCAs who provide most of the daily care and who know both the residents and their families are not primarily responsible for developing the care plans. They provide the data to licensed staff, who input these data into the computer system and translate the results into care plans. This means second-hand reporting, with all its attendant possibilities of misrepresentation. Families complained to us that collecting and entering the data takes time away from care, and the ensuing rush leads to additional inaccuracies.

Second, care plans and the data on the residents are developed in mandatory meetings – known as care conferences – with the family and the resident. HCAs are seldom part of the plan development in Ontario, although they are more often in British Columbia. A daughter reported that in the care conference "they were right there to find out all her issues and what she was taking and recording everything in the computer and spent quite a bit of time with me." But, as the daughter of a BC resident explained, the care conference may not produce the appropriate data or provide the required service:

We sit with the staff and they talk about her physical needs and her medicine and different things ... I don't remember the activity staff being there. I know the physio was there. The care aides were there. The doctor was there. But at the time it was such I didn't really express that "She likes this" because ... I feel that it's my responsibility that I should take her to these activities or encourage her. I didn't want to put the blame on the staff when they're already stretched to say. You know, of course we want our own loved ones to be cared for but I can see so many rooms and people that are in need of care so I didn't really demand or ask for "Oh you have to get her out of her room and get her there."

This daughter was confused and not empowered by the care conference, because she was not provided with the information she wanted, did not know the questions to ask, and like many women, felt guilty both for taking scarce resources from others and for not providing the care herself. Her guilt was reinforced rather than relieved by the meeting. What she wanted was more information on her mother's non-medical needs and guidance on how these needs could be addressed. As she explained,

> Maybe there can be some sort of testing or something that can evaluate their mental state and say okay, with this individual these are the activities that will help her. Like the physio. The physio came and said "She can't move this but I think if you do this exercise with her it will help her." Now if somebody would assess her in the sense of her cognitive state and say "This is the test we ran" ... "this is the kind of level she's at and these would be the few things that could help her," so that even if it doesn't increase but it doesn't decrease so much.

In other words, undertake some assessment and provision of social care.

RAI-MDS is intended to furnish the basis for a written, comprehensive, individualized care plan (Stosz and Carpenter 2009). It has contributed to improvements in readily measurable individual outcomes such as bed sores, dehydration, nutrition, and falls (Hawes et al. 1997), but it may also neglect other health issues (Phillips et al. 1997). It can contribute to better medication distribution, although more efforts are needed to reduce resident medications to appropriate levels, and women in particular are likely to be overmedicated (Rochon Ford and Saibil 2010). What RAI-MDS is not good at capturing, let alone translating into action, is the social care that helps make daily life worth living. Moreover, as Pia Kontos, Karen-Lee Miller, and Gail Mitchell (2010, 359) point out, RAI-MDS assumes that standardization improves care and thus "restricts the care plan to standardized interventions."

There are then at least four issues in terms of person-centred care: Are critical aspects of social care captured at all? How does what is captured shape the care that individuals receive? Can standardization contribute to person-centred care? And is gender taken into account? We have heard many stories about how care and personal preferences are not translated into action, especially when it comes to non-medical aspects of care, how social care is not even part of the plan, and how standardization contradicts individualized care.

Food, which is the main event of the day in LTRC facilities, provides one example of how recorded data can undermine resident-centred care or contradict personal choices. A Vancouver resident asked the dietician not to serve him dried sliced pork, which he was having trouble eating. As a result, all pork was removed from his diet, including porkburgers and pasta sauce made with ground pork. Now, he is given "chicken legs, chicken legs. You get sick of chicken legs. How do you explain the hard, dry roast stuff? Whether it's a [pork] patty or something else or it's pasta ... that would be alright." With dietitians only occasionally encountering individual residents, decisions about food are primarily made through a standardized process that limits the input from the staff member who knows the residents and their preferences. If the issue is medically defined, as in the case of a celiac, there is little trouble getting gluten-free food. But where personal preference rather than medical issues drive food options, the choices are too often very restricted. Talking to the resident is replaced by standardized processes, denying person-centred care and the capacity of care providers to decide based on a knowledge of the resident. The Vancouver man chairs the residents' council and is accustomed to exercising authority. Imagine how women, who are often accustomed to taking orders, would fare.

Even if the care plan does allow some choices, they are not necessarily put into action. Asked if the plan and the RAI-MDS paperwork made a difference in terms of his care, a male resident said that staff may not be familiar with the plan or might be unable to apply it, given the time pressures they face:

> In some cases it just causes confusion, I think, if it's not kept up to date and sometimes it isn't. And if a new casual care aide comes on and looks at the guide and does something that's no longer required that becomes an issue for sure ... I think it's important for people to have that explained to them when they come here.

The increasingly common practice of employing part-time, casual, and temporary workers from agencies makes it increasingly likely that the staff may not be familiar with the care plan for each resident. A summary sheet for his care plan was tacked up in his room, but he said that staff seldom looked at it. The many part-time and casual workers knew little about him and had no time to check his plan. For a nurse practitioner, having staff ignore the plan was not the major issue. Instead, the problem was the way in which it structured care, took time from it, and limited individual problem solving by staff, who often said that they would like to provide care that responded to individual needs, based on their skills and their knowledge of residents. Asked about what qualities a recreation therapist should possess, a group of family members listed "creative," "intuitive," and "interested in understanding of the elderly and the needs they have." These are all aspects of person-centred care but ones that can be restricted by the emphasis on standardized counting.

This standardization approach has an impact on the entire staff and their relations with residents, which are often rewarding for both. A housekeeper who had previously worked mainly on one floor got to know its residents: "They are so nice, the ones that can still walk around, and they're very friendly. Sometimes

I can be funny with them too [laughs]." But due to the application of efficiency models, she rotated throughout the complex and found it much harder to connect with residents. The fact that her work and the skills involved as well as the social connections she made were largely invisible shored up the notion that she could be moved anywhere.

A nurse also found that the ability to connect, and to know families and residents, worked for everyone involved. She explained, "It's fantastic. You have a chance to build up long-term relationship[s] with them and also with their family. They treat you as family members as well ... Some family members they even tell you what happened in their family, what are their struggles, right?" But standardization, rotating staff, and limited resources make it more difficult to establish the long-term connections that are so central to social care.

In addition, the plans often fail to capture the social aspects that are critical to social care. More than one resident complained about being prevented from staying up at night. A nurse practitioner told us that she had to write a special medical order to allow a woman to watch the ten o'clock news. One woman talked about her mother's concern with her appearance, a non-medical issue too often seen as frivolous. Yet women in particular may be concerned about their clothes, hair, and nails as indicators of dignity.

As one family member explained, inadequate funding formulas based on RAI-MDS meant that staff were pressured to complete their tasks: "They have to rush from one room to another room. They tend to be in a rush and they may not answer the questions that these residents want to ask or need their help sometimes." For another daughter whose father had Alzheimer's, the emphasis on medical care meant, "They're not really doing anything with him to help him with his mind, any of those cognitive games or anything. Basically he's sitting there and he's listening to music I have provided for him but there's no real activities for him that can help him." Asked what was most important about care, a resident responded, "how each resident is an individual ... Everyone has got different ailments and they all tick a different way so you treat them all individually." But the application of the measurement systems does little to promote this individualized care or social care and too often ignores specific needs and patterns related to gender.

What RAI-MDS Means for Workers

Our interviews and observations from a broad cross-section of nursing home staff in various Canadian provinces support contentions by Anna Rahman and Robert Applebaum (2009) and others that RAI-MDS has significantly increased the workload for RNs, licensed practical nurses (LPNs), and HCAs. HCAs note that the demands for additional documentation interfere with providing needed care:

'Too much documentation ... You don't even have time to do certain things but you have to do documentation ... but what are you going to do? You have to do it ... You have to run from binder to binder [to record data]. You have a restraint [to document]. You have what you're taking care of in the morning. You have to do that. You have the snack book. Like we give the dessert out we've got to put that in documentation, you know. It's a lot of writing.

In Ontario, registered practical nurses (known as LPNs elsewhere) most commonly handle coding and entering the information regarding residents' care into the RAI-MDS computer program for each required assessment. They also assist HCAs, who provide most of the direct, daily care, work that becomes more complicated with higher rates of dementia and more complex physical needs among residents (Estabrooks et al. 2015). An LPN shared how stressful it was to fit in the RAI-MDS documenting/coding work:

You've got two or three diabetics that you have to do glucose scan. You have catheter to check. You have dressings, a lot of things, narcotics. The more you have things to do, the more heavy it is, the more demanding it becomes. You have residents that scream all the time. You have residents that fall, residents that's asking to do things, needs to go to the bathroom regularly. So you have all these little things. If you have that going on on the floor plus the MDS it's just so stressful. Very, very stressful.

Documentation stress occurs even at mealtime, with repetitive, undervalued paperwork that diverts attention from care. An HCA stated,

We got the nutritional intake sheets to record that I find ridiculous ... We're all there feeding a patient. To me you report the one who refuse[s] to eat. It's paperwork that's putting us behind because you have to calculate that there ... You still have to record it in your binder so you're doing the same thing times two. Nobody look at it.

And there is no indicator of enjoyment, of chatting, or of satisfaction with the taste of food, to name only a few of the missing measures.

There is a tension between the standardized nature of the RAI-MDS assessment tool and the increasing diversity and complexity of resident needs. On the one hand, recognition is growing that care in this sector must be centred on the individual, with quality of life being the priority. But the one-size-fits-all pressures of standardized assessments can take time away from providing truly resident-centred and/or individualized care (Kontos, Miller, and Mitchell 2010).

Our interviewees pointed out that providing this kind of individualized care is increasingly difficult, given the new assessment demands. The very nature of care work is changing, and crucial aspects of care are not counted in the data. An HCA expressed her frustration in no longer being able to spend time with residents, something that they wanted and were missing: "Before it was more time with the clients. And over the years I realized there's too much paperwork. Too much information to get data, to get some funding for money. We kind of forget the real picture of nursing ... And, you know, patients are human beings. I would not appreciate to be pushed like we push the clients."

HCAs also emphasized the importance of their relationship with residents, stressing that knowing and understanding them, and having the time and support to spend in this way, are critical to providing good care. As one HCA explained, for "many years, they've seen the same resident. They know you. They know you by name. They know everything about you just the same way you know them ... And they put the bell on ... They just want to talk but I can't talk. I can't do that."

Arguing that RAI-MDS has become the only quality measure rather than a quality minimum, Steven A. Levenson (2010, 167) notes that "not everything being measured is meaningful, and only some meaningful things are being measured." Quality of life is idiosyncratic by nature and is intimately linked to residents' histories and backgrounds. Residents identify it as most important to them (Coughlan and Ward 2007). Pushed to concentrate on predetermined tasks rather than responding to the individual needs of residents, staff feel distanced from them, which can discourage them from making judgments based on the most current clinical or personal situations (Colón-Emeric et al. 2010). An HCA from British Columbia outlined the implications of having too little time to spend with residents as people, rather than as individuals who needed their food measured or bed changed:

> I guess I was talking about, um, how residents in residential care as I have experienced it, um, are an underserved population. We do our best but there's always a lot of room for improvement. [*Sighs.*] If I were able to sit and hold the lady's hand, um, to calm her down, um, that was a helpful thing for her in this moment but because of the constraints, the limitations, the time factor and the workload, um, that's just one tiny example of [it]. I guess I was trying to make the point that, um, in residential care we cannot necessarily meet every need. There are unmet needs and I guess I'm talking about not just physical needs. I'm talking about the whole person, the mental, emotional, you know, the three plagues of the elderly, loneliness, boredom, powerlessness.

For a BC nurse practitioner, the assessment tool dominated the nurse's own expertise:

It's weird. It almost is robotic mechanical. Yeah, that's really how I want to describe it. It's robotic mechanical nursing care. If this happens then you do this. If this happens then you do this. The computer is thinking for you and the humanity is lost in it. The thing is people are feeling incapacitated to make their own clinical judgments without having the "I don't know everything about it but the indicator came up." You shouldn't need to have the computer tell you what the problems are with your person. It just seems ridiculous to me because you're the one telling the computer so then the computer can then tell you.

Referring to nurses' use of electronic health records, Olga Petrovskaya, Marjorie McIntyre, and Carol McDonald (2009) argue that when pressured to focus primarily on very specific clinical indicators, they can be discouraged from considering the implications of broader intersections of gender, race, and class. Ultimately, the relations between staff and residents, important to both resident quality of life and staff quality of work, can be undermined when resident-staff engagement becomes primarily about a specific care task or problem. Thus, staff members are responsibilized – in the sense of being held individually responsible – as standardized processes "mediate the relationship between accountable service providers and the individuals whom they seek to help" (Woolford and Curran 2011, 595). Quality becomes a technical and administrative activity, separated or divorced from broader ethical or public accountability underpinnings, as well as from the women who do most of the work.

A BC clinical nurse leader referred to other tensions in the use of standardized assessment tools like RAI-MDS. Although standard terminology and automatic triggering of care plans for specific conditions may be useful prompts for care providers, there can be negative results when the technology supersedes the expertise of the provider:

The care plans can be quite cumbersome to complete on the computer. You know, back in the day when you could sit down and just write it by hand it was a lot faster but then you were having to draw from your own brain which was a good thing. But these days we seem to want to tell them [the care staff] what all the best practices should look like and so we want to give them a pick list of what should be included on the care plan. So there's good and bad to that. You know, are we taking away their ability to think for themselves and requiring them to have that knowledge base and just spoon feeding them with the pick list?

RAI-MDS has increased the discord and tension between and among the members of health care teams. Problems arise when HCAs are not fully involved in the resident assessment tool, and care providers question the ability of the tool to fully capture resident needs.

With increased RAI-MDS coding responsibilities, LPNs are less involved in direct care and must now rely for coding on the reports of HCAs. As a result, the workload for HCAs has increased, and they see LPNs as shirking their responsibilities in hands-on care. One HCA stated,

> It's so funny because they don't know what to put in the computer because they don't know the client anymore so they have to come and ask us. So they're taking our time on top of it to answer their stuff so they look good ... Now the thing I say why should I work like this every day, every day that I have to get up to come here and some they get away with everything like this.

The LPNs also reported experiencing tensions about the time taken away from resident care, the stress of the additional coding work, and the recognition that HCAs resented the change in work responsibilities: "Because they [the LPNs] take a lot of ... time from the residents to come on the computer ... but I don't think they [HCAs] realize the amount of time it takes ... Sometimes it's very stressful because there's so many MDS to do and just like wow!"

Our research also encountered various ways that surveillance has intensified as one response to increased gaming that results from the effort to increase resources (Braithwaite, Makkai, and Braithwaite 2007). Several facilities have adopted computerized daily care recording processes for HCAs. Some supply computer tablets, requiring HCAs simply to click on the appropriate reporting category for each resident once a care task is completed. Often, these systems prevent HCAs from viewing the resident's care history. The justification told to us is that looking at previous charts can bias how HCAs record the present needs of residents. As one administrator explained, "Computerized documentation ... has been so nice because they [HCAs] cannot see what happened the day before. They can't even see what happened the shift before so they're coding for their own observations of that resident on that shift only. And accuracy has improved."

She did not define what she meant by accuracy, and in many instances being able to discover what has happened on previous shifts and days can be crucially important. A clinical nurse specialist in British Columbia suggested why context is important: "I'm used to having a chart and having everything in the chart and progress notes ... Everybody is charting in progress notes. You really have a good running history of what this resident has been presenting like. You know, you can flip back to physicians' orders and you see something in the progress notes and compare. Everything is there."

The new system also allows administration to establish time limits for the reporting and recording of care. It indicates when specific treatments or care assistance should be provided, as well as when they are actually done. Thus, HCAs and others can be monitored, and those who have not charted within the appropriate time can be identified, even when managers are working from home. As one MDS coordinator explained,

> I can audit. I'm auditing ... all the time ... I was auditing her coding last night from home ... So the cut off time for the dinner is 6 p.m. I can see if they've coded it at 10:00 or at 6:01 ... They're supposed to be bringing the tablet into the dining room with them so it may not be every person done at 6:00 ... It just turns pink [to indicate on the coordinator's screen] that "It's [to be done at] this time."

There is no place to document what else was happening on the unit, whether staff members are new to the floor and needing to take time to get to know the resident. In other words, important context is absent from this standardized process.

There are indications that standardized reporting and recording also enables governments to more easily manipulate funding levels. An Ontario MDS co-ordinator shared that the Ministry of Health and Long-Term Care recently reduced the level of funding for residents who were coded in a category requiring extensive care. Acknowledging that "there's always gaming," she suggested that "a lot of homes are probably making it so that their residents fall into that category ... by coding differently."

At every stage from the bedside to the provincial ministry, RAI-MDS supports an efficiency focus through documentation that is monitored and audited. Quality has become a technical, administrative activity, with the emphasis on documentation rather than on care itself. Overall, more responsibility is down-loaded to those who have very little influence over resource decisions.

Conclusion

As a proprietary system reflecting both neo-liberal notions of accountability and the need for more surveillance, RAI-MDS offers a way of exposing the gendered nature and impact of measurement. It is increasingly found in LTRC, a site where the overwhelming majority of workers and residents are women. Yet it rarely takes account of the knowledge and experience of those who do traditional women's work. It does provide some useful data on countable, medical factors. At the same time, it fails to capture and value social care, takes time away from care, emphasizes hierarchy, and stresses standardization that limits options for both residents and care providers. In spite of these tensions, the use of RAI-MDS as an accountability tool for LTRC is expanding rapidly to other jurisdictions.

Acknowledgments

This research was supported by the Social Sciences and Humanities Research Council of Canada as part of its Major Collaborative Research Initiative (file 412-2010-1004). Pat Armstrong of York University was the principal investigator.

Notes

1 Statement made at the Canadian interRAI Conference, Winnipeg, October 6–9, 2014.
2 In 2007, the Performance Improvement and Compliance Branch of the Ministry of Health and Long-Term Care sent all Ontario nursing homes a detailed document entitled "RAI-MDS 2.0 LTC Homes – Practice Requirements," outlining its expectations and practice requirements.

Works Cited

Anttonen, Anneli, and Gabrielle Meagher. 2013. "Mapping Marketisation: Concepts and Goals." In *Marketisation in Nordic Eldercare,* ed. Gabrielle Meagher and Marta Szebehely, 13–22. Stockholm: Stockholm University.
Armstrong, Hugh. 2013. "Neoliberalism and Official Health Statistics: Towards a Research Agenda." In *Troubling Care: Critical Perspectives on Research and Practices,* ed. Pat Armstrong and Susan Braedley, 187–99. Toronto: Canadian Scholars' Press.
Armstrong, Pat, Hugh Armstrong, and Karen Messing. 2009. "Gendering Work? Women and Technologies in Health Care." In *Gender, Health and Technology in Context,* ed. Ellen Balka, Eileen Green, and Flis Henwood, 122–37. Basingstoke, UK: Palgrave.
Armstrong, Pat, Hugh Armstrong, and Krista Scott-Dixon. 2008. *Critical to Care: The Invisible Women in Health Services.* Toronto: University of Toronto Press.
Armstrong, Pat, and Suzanne Day. 2017. *Wash, Wear, and Care: Clothing and Laundry in Long-Term Residential Care.* Montreal and Kingston: McGill-Queen's University Press.
Armstrong, Pat, and Ruth Lowndes. 2018. *Creative Teamwork: Developing Rapid Site-Switching Ethnography.* New York: Oxford University Press.
Braithwaite, John, Toni Makkai, and Valerie Braithwaite. 2007. *Regulating Aged Care: Ritualism and the New Pyramid.* Northampton, MA: Edward Elgar.
CIHI (Canadian Institute for Health Information). 2010. "Depression among Seniors in Residential Care." https://secure.cihi.ca/free_products/ccrs_depression_among_seniors _e.pdf.
–. 2020a. "Canada's Health Care Providers, 2015 to 2019 – Data Tables." December 3. https://www.cihi.ca/en/search?query=Canada%27s+Health+Care+providers.
–. 2020b. "Pandemic Experience in the Long-Term Care Sector: How Does Canada Compare with Other Countries?" June 25. https://www.cihi.ca/en/search?query=Pandemic +Experience+in+the+Long-Term+Care+Sector.
Colón-Emeric, Cathleen S., Donde Plowman, Donald Bailey, Kirsten Corazzini, Queen Utley-Smith, Natalie Ammarell, Mark Toles, and Ruth Anderson. 2010. "Regulation and Mindful Resident Care in Nursing Homes." *Qualitative Health Research* 20, 9: 1283–94.

Coughlan, Rory, and Linda Ward. 2007. "Experiences of Recently Relocated Residents of a Long-Term Care Facility in Ontario: Assessing Quality Qualitatively." *International Journal of Nursing Studies* 44, 1: 47–57. https://doi.org/10.1016/j.ijnurstu.2005.11.022.

Erlandsson, Sara, Palle Storm, Anneli Stranz, Marta Szebehely, and Gun-Britt Trydegård. 2013. "Marketising Trends in Swedish Eldercare: Competition, Choice and Calls for Stricter Regulation." In *Marketisation in Nordic Eldercare*, ed. Gabrielle Meagher and Marta Szebehely, 23–83. Stockholm: Stockholm University.

Estabrooks, Carole A., Janet E. Squires, Heather L. Carleton, Greta G. Cummings, and Peter G. Norton. 2015. "Who Is Looking after Mom and Dad? Unregulated Workers in Canadian Long-Term Care Homes." *Canadian Journal on Aging* 34, 1: 47–59. https://doi.org/10.1017/S0714980814000506.

Fries, Brant E., and Charles J. Fahey. 2003. "Introduction." In *Implementing the Resident Assessment Instrument: Case Studies of Policymaking for Long-Term Care in Eight Countries*, ed. Brant E. Fries and Charles J. Fahey, 1–5. New York: Milbank Memorial Fund.

Gerritsen, Debby L., Nardi Steverink, Dinnus H.M. Frijters, John P. Hirdes, Marcel E. Ooms, and Miel W. Ribbe. 2008. "A Revised Index for Social Engagement for Long-Term Care." *Journal of Gerontological Nursing* 34, 4: 40–48. https://doi.org/10.3928/00989134-20080401-04.

Glenn, Evelyn Nakano. 2010. *Forced to Care: Coercion and Caregiving in America.* Cambridge, MA: Harvard University Press.

Hancock, Trevor, Ron Labonte, and Rick Edwards. 1999. "Indicators That Count! Measuring Population Health at the Community Level." *Canadian Journal of Public Health* 90, suppl 1: S22–26. https://pubmed.ncbi.nlm.nih.gov/10686755/.

Hawes, Catherine, John N. Morris, Charles D. Phillips, Brant E. Fries, Katherine Murphy, and Vincent Mor. 1997. "Development of the Nursing Home Resident Assessment Instrument in the USA." *Age and Ageing* 26, suppl. 2: 19–25.

Health Council of Canada. 2012. *Measuring and Reporting on Health System Performance in Canada: Opportunities for Improvement.* Ottawa: Health Council of Canada.

Kontos, Pia C., Karen-Lee Miller, and Gail J. Mitchell. 2010. "Neglecting the Importance of the Decision Making and Care Regimes of Personal Support Workers: A Critique of Standardization of Care Planning through the RAI/MDS." *Gerontologist* 50, 3: 352–62. https://doi.org/10.1093/geront/gnp165.

Levenson, Steven A. 2010. "The Basis for Improving and Reforming Long-Term Care. Part 4: Identifying Meaningful Improvement Approaches (Segment 2)." *JAMDA* 11, 3: 161–70. https://doi.org/10.1016/j.jamda.2009.12.082.

McMullen, Linda M., and Janet M. Stoppard. 2006. "Women and Depression: A Case Study of the Influence of Feminism in Canadian Psychology." *Feminism and Psychology* 16, 3: 273–88.

Ministry of Health and Long-Term Care. 2022. "Long-Term Care Homes Level-of-Care Per Diem, Occupancy and Acuity-Adjustment Funding Policy." August. https://www.ontario.ca/page/long-term-care-homes-level-care-diem-occupancy-and-acuity-adjustment-funding-policy/.

Mol, Annemarie. 2008. *The Logic of Care: Health and the Problem of Patient Choice.* London: Routledge.

Nitti, Victor W. 2001. "The Prevalence of Urinary Incontinence." *Review of Urology* 3, suppl. 1: S2–S6.

Petrovskaya, Olga, Marjorie McIntyre, and Carol McDonald. 2009. "Dilemmas, Tetra-lemmas, Reimagining the Electronic Health Record." *Advances in Nursing Science* 32, 3: 241–51. https://doi.org/10.1097/ANS.0b013e3181b1056e.

Phillips, Charles D., John N. Morris, Catherine Hawes, Brant E. Fries, Vincent Mor, Marianne Nennstiel, and Vincent Iannacchione. 1997. "Association of the Resident Assessment Instrument (RAI) with Changes in Function, Cognition, and Psychosocial Status." *American Geriatric Society* 45, 8: 986–93.

Rahman, Anna N., and Robert A. Applebaum. 2009. "The Nursing Home Minimum Data Set Assessment Instrument: Manifest Functions and Unintended Consequences – Past, Present, and Future." *Gerontologist* 49, 6: 727–35. https://doi.org/10.1093/geront/gnp066.

Rochon Ford, Anne, and Diane Saibil, eds. 2010. *The Push to Prescribe: Women and Canadian Drug Policy.* Toronto: Women's Press.

Statistics Canada. 2021. "A Profile of Nursing and Residential Care Facilities, 2019." https://www150.statcan.gc.ca/n1/daily-quotidien/210916/dq210916c-eng.htm.

Stosz, Laura, and Iain Carpenter. 2009. "The Use of an Assessment Tool in Care Homes." *Nursing Older People* 21, 1: 24–25. https://doi.org/10.7748/nop.21.1.24.s29.

Sutherland, Jason M., Nadya Repin, and R. Trafford Crump. 2013. *The Alberta Health Services Patient/Care–Based Funding Model for Long Term Care.* Vancouver: UBC Centre for Health Services and Policy Research.

Turcotte, Martin, and Katherine Savage. 2020. "The Contribution of Immigrants and Population Groups Designated as Visible Minorities to Nurse Aide, Orderly and Patient Service Associate Occupations." Statistics Canada. https://www150.statcan.gc.ca/n1/pub/45-28-0001/2020001/article/00036-eng.pdf.

Woolford, Andrew, and Amelia Curran. 2011. "Neoliberal Restructuring, Limited Autonomy, and Relational Distance in Manitoba's Nonprofit Field." *Critical Social Policy* 31, 4: 583–606.

6

Sex, Gender, and Systematic Reviews in Health: Building Critical Engagement

Sari Tudiver, Madeline Boscoe, Vivien Runnels, Lorri Puil, Janet Jull, Stephanie E. Coen, Marion Doull, Vivian Welch, Jennifer Petkovic, Ann Pederson, and Beverley J. Shea

THIS CHAPTER DESCRIBES an initiative to integrate sex- and gender-sensitive methods and measurements into the development, synthesis, and reporting of health evidence. We challenge producers and users of health evidence, including ourselves, to ask how dynamics of sex and gender may be implicated in particular areas of health and illness. Our purpose is to encourage dialogue, reporting, and research to strengthen the quality of evidence used in clinical decisions and in the development of policies and programs. Our primary goal is to improve health outcomes and reduce health inequities, which Margaret Whitehead (1992, 430) defines as "differences in health which are not only unnecessary and avoidable but, in addition, are considered unfair and unjust." In hopes of forging pathways to gender equality, we focus particularly, but not exclusively, on inequities in health that are related to sex and gender.[1] Drawing from the Canadian Institutes of Health Research (CIHR) Institute of Gender and Health, we define *sex* as a construct through which to consider biological attributes and processes, associated with genetic, physical, and physiological features, including differential gene expression, hormonal function, and reproductive sexual anatomy. This definition recognizes variation beyond binary categorizations of male or female. In alignment with CIHR, we use *gender* to refer to socio-culturally constructed roles, behaviours, expressions, and identities of women, girls, men, boys, and gender diverse people. How individuals and groups "understand, experience and express gender" varies widely, and gender identities can be fluid over time. In all societies, gender is associated with the distribution of power and resources, and is institutionalized in complex ways (Canadian Institutes of Health Research 2019). As binary assumptions of these constructs are increasingly challenged, new conceptual approaches, research methods, and measurements are being developed that offer deeper understandings about sex, gender, and the ways in which they are intertwined.

A substantial body of research demonstrates that sex and gender can influence processes related to health: gene expression and cell regulation, drug metabolism, susceptibilities and resilience to particular conditions or illnesses, how disease manifests and is experienced, and access to and use of health care services (Galea et al. 2020; Hreiche, Morissette, and Turgeon 2008; Institute of Medicine 2001; Regitz-Zagrosek and Gebhard 2023; Schiebinger et al. 2011–21; Tannenbaum, Greaves, and Graham 2016). Failure to consider sex and gender in research, technology assessments, clinical decision making, and design and implementation of policies and programs, including those related to workplace health and safety, can waste resources and have detrimental effects on individual and population health. For example, differences in the risk factors and progression of illnesses, such as cardiovascular diseases, some cancers including melanomas, type 2 diabetes, autoimmune disorders, and pain, in particular subpopulations may not be identified and may result in inappropriate management (Coen and Banister 2012; Kautzky-Willer, Harreiter, and Pacini 2016; Messing 2014; Özdemir et al. 2022). Infectious disease outbreaks also reveal sex and gender differences, largely unaddressed in past public health efforts. Having learned from the spread and control of the Human Immunodeficiency Virus (HIV) and the Ebola and Zika viruses, many researchers, front-line workers, and funders called for sex and gender analysis to be an essential part of disease outbreak preparedness and response to the COVID-19 pandemic (Davies and Bennett 2016; Gebhard et al. 2020; Ryan and El Ayadi 2020; Tadiri et al. 2020).

Operationalizing the constructs of sex and gender through robust conceptual approaches, methods, and measurements is integral to the conduct of sound science (Connell 2012; Jahn et al. 2017; Phillips 2008; Rich-Edwards et al. 2018; Tannenbaum et al. 2019; Yakerson 2019). Measurements in health research can estimate a range of relative or absolute risk to indicate how susceptible an individual or population may be to a particular disease or condition and can highlight potential harms in relation to benefits associated with health interventions. Measurements can also indicate clinically relevant differences between and within subpopulations and can provide data about safety, effectiveness, and quality of health care service delivery. However, decisions about *what* to measure, the choice of *which* measurement tools and methods to use, and *how* to present the results are rarely straightforward or transparent, because they incorporate researchers' own disciplinary assumptions and value judgments, and are affected by a range of influences and interests, including research funding (Greenland 2012; Harper et al. 2010). Furthermore, certain issues, such as assessing cultural safety and the appropriateness of health care services for particular populations, cannot be readily quantified but are best understood through the use of qualitative or mixed methods (Drawson, Toombs, and Mushquash 2017; Greenhalgh 2013;

Noyes et al. 2022; Oakley 2000). Below, we describe some of the thinking and practical strategies of the Sex/Gender Methods Group (SGMG),[2] a collaboration to which we belong. It fosters consideration of sex and gender in the planning, conduct, and reporting of research. For nearly two decades, we have worked to bridge the framework and methods of sex- and gender-based analysis (SGBA), rooted in critical social science and feminist theory, with systematic reviews and syntheses of research grounded in a positivist, interpretive paradigm (Denzin and Lincoln 2012; Veenstra 1999).

Building Bridges

When applied to health, SGBA can be used by researchers, health practitioners, and policy-makers to consider fundamental questions about how and why differing subpopulations (e.g., of diverse genders, ages, racialized identities, and other intersecting social locations) experience health conditions and interventions in different or similar ways. SGBA offers a framework and methods to explore the potential relevance of sex and gender to the problem being investigated and gives priority to identifying and addressing long-standing sex- and gender-related inequities in health (Clow et al. 2009; Health Canada 2022; Les Femmes Michif Otipemisiwak 2019; Native Women's Association of Canada 2007, 2020; Treasury Board of Canada Secretariat 2019; Women and Gender Equality Canada 2022).

Systematic reviews critically analyze, combine, and summarize the best available evidence from primary research studies that are relevant to a particular research question. Systematic reviews of research about health interventions are used in developing clinical guidelines for health practitioners, in clinical education, and as a resource for consumers to make informed decisions about their health care. They are also used in formulating social, economic, and health policies that affect individuals and populations and in developing research programs to address identified gaps in knowledge (Graham 2012; Grant and Booth 2009; National Institutes of Health, and National Heart, Lung and Blood Institute 2020; Waters 2009; White and Waddington 2012).

Systematic reviews are widely applied in evidence-based medicine and, more broadly, in evidence-based health care. As characterized by David Sackett et al. (1996, 71), "The practice of evidence-based medicine means integrating individual clinical expertise with the best available external clinical evidence from systematic research." The authors' foundational work emphasizes that clinical expertise "is reflected in many ways, but especially in more effective and efficient diagnosis and in the more thoughtful identification and compassionate use of individual patients' predicaments, rights, and preferences in making clinical decisions about their care" (71). They caution that "without clinical expertise, practice risks becoming tyrannized by evidence, for even excellent external evidence may be inapplicable to or inappropriate for an individual patient" (72). Although the authors stress the value of systematic reviews as a gold standard "for judging whether a treatment does more good than harm" (72), they emphasize that methods must be appropriate to the questions asked and that randomized trials are not always available or appropriate. While Sackett and colleagues did not address sex and gender in their discussion, we suggest that integrating such considerations into evidence-based approaches to health care contributes to more appropriate patient-centred interventions.

Beginnings

The SGMG was formed in 2005 to promote the use of sex- and gender-based analysis in systematic reviews of health interventions (Tudiver et al. 2012). It was a response to two parallel trends in research and policy. First, since the 1990s, many governments, research organizations, and scientific journals in Canada and internationally have instituted policies mandating or recommending that SGBA be considered in the design and reporting of clinical trials, health policies, and programs (European Association of Science Editors 2013; Health Canada 2000, 2013; Heidari et al. 2011; Johnson and Beaudet 2012; National Institutes of Health 2001). Policies promoting SGBA emerged as women's health activists advocated for such changes, and research demonstrating the many ways that sex and gender influence the health and well-being of populations was more widely published (Greaves 2015; Hankivsky, Springer, and Hunting 2018; Morrow, Hankivsky and Varcoe 2008). Second, many governments and research organizations relied on systematic reviews in developing health policies, clinical guidelines, health technology assessments, and research proposals. Our group anticipated a growing body of research addressing sex and gender, as well as increased demand from systematic reviewers, other researchers, and policy-makers for guidance, methods, and tools to conduct rigorous and reliable sex- and gender-based analyses.

To gauge the need for SGBA in systematic reviews, we conducted a preliminary scan of several dozen systematic reviews on a range of health issues. They rarely disaggregated data by sex, commonly referred to the generic "patient" or "person," and failed to consider documented sex and gender differences in the incidence, risk factors, progression, and outcomes of conditions such as cardiovascular and autoimmune diseases, osteoporosis, and HIV/AIDS. No review substantively addressed whether there might be differing treatment or policy implications for women and men, boys and girls. We presented these results at a meeting of systematic reviewers who were affiliated with the Cochrane Collaboration and received encouragement to pursue an education, research, and advocacy initiative that would help systematic reviewers carry out SGBA (Boscoe and Tudiver 2005).

Although we recognized that data pertaining to age, ethnicity, socio-economic status, and other forms of social location were also missing from the reviews we examined, we prioritized working toward gender equity in health. Building upon Hannah Papanek's (1985) insightful metaphor, we conceptualized sex/gender as a "fault line" that cross-cuts other social locations.[3] SGBA provided a framework, methodology, and tools that could, *at a minimum,* encourage systematic reviewers to disaggregate and analyze data by sex,[4] and discuss to whom the evidence did and did not apply. This focus drew on the SGBA expertise in our founding group and a desire to build relationships through mutual learning and to advance achievable change. By addressing gaps pertaining to sex and gender in systematic reviews, we sought to enhance the consideration of sex, gender, and other social locations in future reviews and, eventually, to influence the primary studies on which reviews are based. Somewhat naively, we anticipated that our project would last two or three years.

Systematic Reviews and the Construction of Knowledge

The majority of systematic reviews in health are focused on interventions; others assess prognostic factors, accuracy of diagnostic methods, and epidemiologic associations (Moher et al. 2007; Tricco, Tetzlaff, and Moher 2011). Systematic reviews are often conducted by multidisciplinary research team members who have both topic-specific and methodological expertise, and may include policymakers, consumers, patients, or other interested parties (Concannon et al. 2012; Pollock et al. 2018). Those who conduct systematic reviews identify a question, such as whether the effectiveness or benefits of a treatment or intervention outweigh its potential harms. Next, they determine which types of evidence or study research designs are relevant to the question and choose the appropriate way(s) to identify and then gather the evidence. They appraise the quality of individual studies by taking various forms of bias and other limitations into account, combine and analyze the evidence through a variety of statistical and other methods, and interpret the final results to reach conclusions (Aromataris and Munn 2020; Higgins et al. 2022; Institute of Medicine 2011). The use of a pre-specified protocol, and explicit and transparent methods, help minimize bias during the review process. Meta-analysis – statistical methods to combine and summarize results from different studies – may be conducted when there are adequate data from the primary studies to provide more precise estimates of the effects of an intervention than in single studies. Systematic reviews also determine the consistency of evidence across studies and explore the reasons for heterogeneity in results. By grading the quality or certainty of the totality of evidence and providing a measure of the degree of confidence in the research findings, systematic reviewers can help other researchers, clinicians, and consumers identify what is *not* known about a health intervention and can generate new hypotheses (Guyatt et al. 2008; Guyatt et al. 2013).

Detailed guidance for developing protocols and conducting and reporting systematic reviews is regularly updated and refined. However, critical work in the field of research synthesis points to ways that confidence in systematic reviews and meta-analyses of data can be undermined (Ioannidis 2010, 2016). These critiques call attention to poorly designed or implemented protocols that fail to pre-specify subgroup analyses and to reviews that do not include sufficient information about participants. Systematic reviews *on the same topic* can vary in results and conclusions due to differences in how research questions were framed, search strategies used, eligibility criteria set for study designs and for populations, choice of models of statistical analysis, definitions or end points of study outcomes, and interpretation of results. As well, reviews may be affected by reporting biases in primary research studies such as publication bias (the tendency to publish studies with positive or favourable results but not those with negative or null results), selective outcome reporting (the suppression of information on outcomes such as adverse events), and/or difficulties in accessing grey literature and unpublished data (Dickersin and Chalmers 2011; Every-Palmer and Howick 2014; Institute of Medicine 2011; Kirkham et al. 2018; Mahood, Van Eerd, and Irvin 2014; Wieseler, McGauran, and Kaiser 2010).[5]

Similar criticisms contend that the original goals and premises of evidence-based medicine have been distorted and weakened. Critics cite a "managerial" overemphasis on rules about how evidence should be applied, a corresponding de-emphasis of clinical judgment and compassionate care, corporate influence on the conduct and reporting of research, and waste of resources (Greenhalgh, Howick, and Maskrey 2014; Horton 2015; Ioannidis 2016). Many critics are reaffirming the original principles and practices of evidence-based medicine within a broader framework of "evidence-based health care." Their goals include making research more relevant and responsive to public needs by expanding collaboration among patients, researchers, health professionals, and policy-makers; eradicating publication and other reporting biases, and reducing conflict of interest to ensure that accurate, impartial evidence is accessible for informed decision making; and producing clinical guidelines that are more reliable, relevant, and accessible to end users (Heneghan et al. 2017; Ioannidis et al. 2014).[6] Implementing these goals requires long-term commitment on the part of organizations and their leadership to transform organizational culture through critical reflection, education and training, and sustained political will on the part of regulatory agencies and bodies responsible for safety, quality assessments, professional ethics, transparency, and other standards.

Clinical judgment can be deepened and quality of evidence can be enhanced in evidence-based health care by incorporating more about the context of a particular problem, hypothesis, or question into the research design, analysis, and reporting of primary studies and systematic reviews. Context should include dynamic, intersectional approaches to determine the relevance and/or extent of differences in people's lived experiences over the life course – as sex/gendered beings of various ages, socio-economic status, ethnicities, racialized identities, geographic, and other forms of physical/social location that affect health outcomes and health equity. The type of health infrastructure and resources available to patients or subjects of research is an important determinant of health and should also be described (Edwards and Di Ruggiero 2011). Contextual information is increasingly included in primary studies and systematic reviews that focus on health equity (Bambra et al. 2010; Morton et al. 2016) but is commonly lacking in randomized controlled trials that enroll select participants and in the systematic reviews and meta-analyses based on such trials. To further explore the relevance of context to research and to evidence-based health care, we now interrogate our basic constructs of sex and gender.

Sex, Gender, and the Construction of Knowledge

Distinguishing sex from gender has a relatively recent intellectual history. In the 1960s, a range of scholarly works began to challenge assumptions in the practice of medicine and in biomedical research that viewed biological differences between men and women, and particularly women's reproductive biology, as the primary determinant of their social roles, behaviours, and "destiny" (Bleier 1984; Oakley 2000). Differentiating gender (social roles) from sex (biology) became part of an analytic approach and methodology through which to examine the history of patriarchy, institutional and other power relations, and socio-cultural dimensions of women's lives, including changing gender roles, as distinct from biological and specifically reproductive processes (Connell 2012; Krieger 2003).

Definitions of "sex" and "gender" have become more dynamic and attentive to diversity beyond the binaries of female/male, women/men, and girls/boys, particularly in discourse about gender identity, gender expression, sexual orientation, and self-representations (Keener 2015; Westbrook and Saperstein 2015). As a result, more inclusive and fluid definitions of sex and gender are being used by many scholars, governments, UN agencies, international development and other civil society organizations, and persons working on initiatives promoting human rights and equity, gender equality, and gender mainstreaming.[7]

Although distinguishing sex from gender has proved important to analytic methods and theoretical understandings, these constructs highlight processes that are embodied and intertwined. As Beth Jackson, Ann Pederson, and Madeline Boscoe (2009, 37) express this relationship, "Biological matter (i.e., chromosomes, cells, bodies) do not exist outside of social structures and cultures, and gender relations occur in the physical world. So, we cannot simply extract sex from its social meaning and context, nor can we understand gender apart from its relation to physical bodies." For example, survivors of childhood abuse, including sexual abuse, often experience emotional and physiological sequelae, such as pelvic or neuropathic pain, autoimmune diseases, migraines, and type 2 diabetes (American College of Obstetricians and Gynecologists 2011; Dube et al. 2009; Wilson 2010). Being sensitive to how processes associated with sex and gender are embodied and expressed in physiological and psychosocial conditions can help health care providers and survivors better understand the root causes of these conditions and can contribute to healing.

Our group chose to use the convention sex/gender to emphasize the inter-related processes and structures of these constructs (Tudiver et al. 2012). Other scholars are developing frameworks that accommodate the interrelationships of sex and gender in health research. Anne Hammarström and colleagues (2014, 185) reviewed six theoretical concepts (sex, gender, intersectionality, embodiment, gender equity, and gender equality) that they saw as "central and inter-linked – but problematic and ambiguous in health science." They drew from the work of social epidemiologist Nancy Krieger (2003, 653), who deconstructed some of the ways in which "gender relations influence expression – and inter-pretation – of biological traits" and how "sex-linked biological characteristics can, in some cases contribute to or amplify gender differentials in health." For Krieger (2005, 5), "embodiment" means "how we literally embody, that is, biologically incorporate our lived experience, thereby creating population patterns of health and disease." Her work explores ways to measure the "cumulative interplay" of exposures to experiences such as poverty and discrimination, as well as susceptibilities and resilience over the life course. In doing so, Krieger demonstrates that disease patterns must be understood in the context of differences and similarities among diverse groups, taking into account diversities of sex/gender, social class, race/ethnicity, and geographic and other social locations.

Citing research from social neuroendocrinology, as well as the work of Krieger and others, Kristen Springer, Jeanne Mager Stellman, and Rebecca Jordan-Young (2012) point to the "entanglement" of sex and gender and note that gendered life experiences such as stressors of family obligations, harassment, and poverty have material effects on the body's hormonal and endocrine processes. The authors suggest that sex differences are frequently *assumed* and that "sex" is used as a proxy for mechanisms or processes that should be specified and measured directly. They propose that the entanglement of sex/gender "should be theorized, modeled and assumed until proven otherwise," and they put forward a number of good practice guidelines for examining human health differences (1818). Neuroscientists, social neuroendocrinologists, and other researchers are also grappling with ways to conceptualize, observe, and measure mechanisms and pathways associated with sex hormones to elucidate the complexities of sex differences, sex interactions, hard-wiring, plasticity, malleability, and biopsychosocial stress (Fine et al. 2013; Jordan-Young and Rumiati 2012; Juster 2019; Ritz et al. 2014; van Anders 2015). Building on the work of Sari van Anders, Anne Fausto-Sterling (2019, 532) explores gender/sex, sexual orientation, and identity. She articulates "the idea of gender/sex as a softly assembled dynamic system that comes into being starting in infancy and is maintained through one-on-one interactions with other individuals and via cultural enforcement of gender/sex." Many of these researchers engage creatively with metaphor to explore the multi-dimensionality of sex/gender or gender/sex. Their work resonates with that of cytogeneticist and Nobel laureate Barbara McClintock, who emphasized the critical importance of scientific methods and inquiry of deep immersion in one's subject to cultivate "a feeling for the organism" (Fox Keller 1983, 198), and with pioneering feminist philosophers of science who revealed the ways that social and cultural assumptions about sex and gender influenced which research questions were asked and pursued, and which remained dormant (Fox Keller 1996; Harding 1986; Oakley 2000).

By applying a critical lens of SGBA to assumptions, clinical practices, and how evidence is constructed, researchers can address the implications and limits of measurements. For example, a study of wait times for arthroplasty (surgical replacement of joints, such as knees or hips) found that though women had higher rates of osteoarthritis than men, they were generally less likely to be referred to an orthopedic surgeon, or they were referred after a longer interval. Jackson, Pederson, and Boscoe (2009, 47) ask the research question, "Are interpretations of symptoms and measurements of urgency equitable and valid for women and men across race, ethnicity, class and other important social locations?" They suggest that women may tolerate pain and other symptoms to avoid surgery, thus enabling them to maintain family and other responsibilities. The authors conclude that the presentation of symptoms by patients did differ according to sex and gender and also in the interpretation and diagnoses of these symptoms by practitioners: "The measurement of wait times ('when the clock starts and stops') must take into account women's and men's different journeys through the health care system ... Gender-based analysis may also lead to the identification of more appropriate indicators for wait times, health and health care outcomes" (47–48). A subsequent scoping review of the research on wait times found that limited attention had been paid to issues of sex and gender and called for contextual research on patient trajectories of care for osteoarthritis and related health interventions (Pederson and Armstrong 2015). These research syntheses point to an urgent need to apply sex- and gender-sensitive methods and indicators to address systemic barriers and other obstacles that limit access to quality health services for specific populations.

Engaging with Cochrane

Our group has engaged with Cochrane (previously the Cochrane Collaboration), an independent global network of researchers, practitioners, and consumers in 190 countries, including Canada, who conduct systematic reviews of health interventions.[8] We chose to do so for several reasons. Cochrane founders had demonstrated a strong interest in improving women's health in their first systematic review by synthesizing results of controlled trials of care during and after pregnancy and childbirth (Chalmers, Enkin, and Keirse 1989). As women's health activists, we were familiar with this innovative work. Since its establishment in 1993, Cochrane has earned recognition for detailed guidance in conducting systematic reviews; training and innovation in review methods; regularly updating reviews to ensure currency; and generating tools that assess study quality, grade the strength of findings across studies, and provide an evidence base for knowledge about health interventions and other health care issues (Cassels 2015; Straus et al. 2016). Cochrane's methods also incorporate a focus on applicability of evidence and health equity. The Campbell and Cochrane Equity Methods Group promotes the analysis of equity in systematic reviews to help determine how interventions affect underserved or disadvantaged populations in order to reduce social inequalities in health.[9] Adopting the acronym PROGRESS-Plus for its approach,[10] the Equity Methods Group identifies gender/sex and sexual orientation among the categories of social differentiation across which disadvantage can be measured (Campbell and Cochrane Equity Methods Group n.d.; O'Neill et al. 2014; Tugwell et al. 2010). The founding members of our group had expertise in working on sex/gender issues in community and clinical settings, university research, government, and regulatory environments. Although we routinely produced and used various forms of health evidence, our experience conducting systematic reviews was limited. We saw potential for collaboration with the Equity Methods Group, given our complementary goals and skills (Tudiver et al. 2012).

From the start, we provided working definitions of "sex" and "gender" to promote consistent use of terminology in systematic reviews. To make the case for including sex and gender considerations in health evidence, we regularly updated our files on sex, gender, and health in areas such as cardiovascular and autoimmune diseases and pain. To emphasize the legitimacy of the issues, we cited mandates and policies from Canadian and international governments and research bodies that recognized that past exclusions of women from clinical trials and the failures to address sex and gender differences and similarities in health research could compromise the quality of health evidence used in clinical practice, development of policies and regulations, and future research. Next, we undertook a pilot research study to determine whether and to what degree sex and/or gender were addressed or omitted in Cochrane reviews. When a search of English-language resources revealed no appropriate appraisal tools, we designed one specifically for systematic reviewers who might not be familiar with SGBA. It included thirty-five questions to appraise whether each section of a typical Cochrane review considered sex and/or gender. It used straightforward vocabulary and encouraged comments.

Our pilot study drew a random sample of thirty-eight systematic reviews conducted by the Cochrane Heart, Hypertension and Peripheral Vascular Review Groups and published between 2001 and 2007. The reviews were based on 668 clinical trials, with a total of 473,666 participants. We chose to focus on cardiovascular interventions because of well-documented research pertaining to differences between men and women in age of disease onset, risk factors, symptoms, and in the efficacy and harms of certain drugs and other cardiac treatments. We posited that if cardiovascular reviews revealed little consideration of sex and gender differences, it was likely that Cochrane reviews on other topic areas with less research on sex and gender would display similar omissions (Doull et al. 2010).

The majority of the clinical trials included male and female participants, but this sample of systematic reviews had very low reporting about sex and gender. For example, approximately 70 percent of the reviews provided data about adverse events, but none disaggregated these data by sex or indicated whether this information was available. Only two reviews mentioned gaps in research pertaining to sex or gender, and only one noted possible implications of sex or gender differences for clinical practice. When the words "sex" and "gender" were mentioned (in 13 percent of the reviews), they were used interchangeably and were never defined. Nor was any literature cited to indicate how the concepts might be distinguished. No review referred to participants beyond binary categories of male/female or men/women. We also analyzed a sample of the primary studies included in the reviews to determine whether they considered sex and/or gender: we found the systematic reviews replicated omissions of the primary studies and that reviewers had not identified these omissions (Doull 2009). The strength of these results supported our case for integrating SGBA in systematic review methods. We published our findings (Doull et al. 2010) and reported on the pilot study at seminars and conferences to health researchers, systematic reviewers, and health policy-makers.[11] We sought and received valuable feedback on the appraisal tool from others conducting or using systematic reviews, and we revised it for use as a planning tool in developing systematic review protocols (Doull et al. 2011).

A planning grant from the CIHR provided resources for us to organize a workshop titled "Combining Forces to Improve Systematic Reviews: Gender, Equity and Bias" in the spring of 2011. This invitational workshop brought together individuals with expertise in conducting systematic reviews and those with expertise in SGBA to discuss ways to bridge these approaches and methods. The thirty-four participants included systematic review authors, review group editors and methodologists, biomedical and social science researchers, health practitioners, policy-makers, consumers, and health research funders. They agreed on the need to clarify the concepts of sex, gender, equity, bias, and heterogeneity, which those from differing disciplinary backgrounds interpreted and used in various ways; to explain assumptions underlying certain statistical methods, including when and how to conduct robust subgroup analyses; and to determine whether and how current tools developed and used by Cochrane reviewers for evaluating quality of evidence – such as risk of bias – and health equity could accommodate considerations of sex/gender. In an effort to bridge differing approaches to bias, participants discussed how the omission of evidence pertaining to sex and gender could affect the quality of health evidence and might be a form of methods bias.[12] Consolidating interest in sex/gender and equity, Combining Forces began a dialogue about the challenges of including SGBA in systematic reviews (Runnels et al. 2014).

The workshop marked a critical stage in our group's evolution and engagement with Cochrane. Following the workshop, five of its participants, four of whom were affiliated with Cochrane and had significant experience in conducting systematic reviews, joined the SGMG. These new members added expertise in clinical medicine and pharmacology, and biomedical and social science research, including health geography and knowledge translation. They offered knowledge about Cochrane and suggestions about how best to leverage our work.

Participants at the Combining Forces workshop generated an agenda for future projects. Those working in government policy spheres suggested the format of briefing notes, a communication tool to synthesize information on a subject for non-experts, using language that was clear and action-focused. Our first collaboration involved the development of briefing notes to provide guidance on integrating SGBA into systematic review methods. We focused on three health issues – HIV/AIDS, high blood pressure (hypertension), and musculoskeletal conditions – each of which highlighted different aspects of sex and gender that affect health. HIV causes an infection that can progress to AIDS, with multiple complications and outcomes. Vulnerability to infection, complications or progression, and the ability to access health care vary among groups, including gender diverse subgroups; dynamics of power and coercion can affect transmission of the virus. Hypertension is a common, potentially modifiable cardiovascular risk factor. In addition to gender differences in access to care, men and women under the age of sixty have different baseline risks for primary hypertension, which can be reflected in different rates of cardiovascular complications. Some potential complications (for example, heart attacks) may manifest different symptoms for men and women. Musculoskeletal conditions are multiple and diverse (e.g., lupus, arthritis, osteoarthritis, fibromyalgia) and can be acute or chronic, with demonstrated sex and gender differences in prevalence, immune system response, and the delivery of health care services for the same condition. The editors of the HIV/AIDS, Hypertension, and Musculoskeletal Cochrane Review Groups agreed to collaborate with us in developing the briefing note that was pertinent to their focus (Doull et al. 2014).[13]

The design of briefing notes was based on the premise that users would be sophisticated in research synthesis methods and measurements but would have limited or no familiarity with how sex and gender were conceptualized and operationalized in SGBA. Each briefing note provides key definitions and a rationale for why sex and gender are relevant to the particular topic area. A table on methods and guidance summarizes specific ways that sex and gender could be considered throughout the process of conducting a Cochrane systematic review, from formulating the research question, collecting and analyzing data, presenting results and a summary of findings to interpreting the implications of results. The briefing notes are intended to be as precise as possible to help systematic reviewers operationalize definitions *and* sufficiently nuanced to suggest the complex interrelationships of sex/gender reflected in the rapidly evolving research literature. We balanced concerns that too much information and theory could introduce confusion in how to proceed and result in limited uptake, whereas too little might reinforce the common view of sex and gender solely as variables to be controlled for in multivariate data analysis rather than dynamic processes to be explored and contextualized. Feedback from Cochrane symposia participants and review group members helped refine messages to emphasize the interrelationships of sex/gender and to be more inclusive of gender diverse identities.

The three-page briefing notes tread lightly in tone. They include basic pointers, such as "the terms 'sex' and 'gender' are not interchangeable, but rather, the pathways between these processes should be explored and documented," as well as options for how sex/gender analysis might be applied.[14] They also prompt systematic reviewers to identify and report any unanswered questions or preplanned analyses that could not be conducted because data about sex and gender were not available. Once completed, the notes were distributed to their appropriate review groups and posted on our webpage.

The group then secured funding for a project to assess the extent and nature of reporting about sex and/or gender, including whether SGBA was carried out, in a sample of one hundred Canadian randomized controlled trials, sampled from January 2013 to July 2014. The results of the project, which was designed to assess the primary sources of evidence for systematic reviews, demonstrated poor uptake of sex and gender considerations: 98 percent of studies described the demographic composition of participants by sex, only 6 percent conducted subgroup analysis by sex, and 4 percent reported sex-disaggregated data. No research article defined "sex" or "gender," and none addressed any implications of sex/gender differences or similarities beyond this very basic reporting of data. No studies reported on the inclusion of gender and sexual minorities, including gender non-binary and transgender participants (Welch, Doull, et al. 2017). These findings were consistent with research conducted by a member of our group and her colleague, who found that sex/gender was poorly addressed in the design, analysis, and interpretation of a random sample of randomized controlled trials published in high-impact journals (Phillips and Hamberg 2016). The findings were disheartening, but we recognized the need to build on our previous qualitative work concerning the obstacles that confront researchers and limit the uptake of SGBA (Runnels et al. 2014). We decided to further explore the nature of these stumbling blocks, particularly for scientists who work in the area of cardiovascular diseases. Funded by a CIHR planning grant, we carried out interviews with nineteen federally funded principal investigators of cardiovascular-related diseases to explore barriers and facilitators faced by leaders in the field to integrate considerations of sex/gender into their research. Our qualitative findings will help shed light on processes that may impede the routine consideration of sex/gender, including mechanistic barriers that limit access to sex-based data, funding limits to securing adequate sample sizes for analysis, and the sexist assumptions of socio-cultural structures that shape research questions.[15]

Terms of Engagement

In any context, mainstreaming sex and gender analysis in approach, methodology, and organizational culture presents challenges and productive tensions (Moser and Moser 2005; Sweetman 2012; Walby 2005). Given Cochrane's primary focus on methods and measurements, and the structures of multiple membership groups across continents, incorporating a new approach or method into wider use can be a lengthy and careful process, over many years. There are also disciplinary differences among Cochrane members and variations in receptivity to considering sex, gender, and equity in systematic reviews.

To encourage systematic reviewers to consider new and nuanced questions, concepts, and practices about sex and gender, the SGMG engaged in spaces that are relevant to reviewers and framed its tools and resources to be compatible with the structure and discourse of Cochrane systematic reviews. To our knowledge, we were the first to initiate a dialogue about the added value of SGBA in Cochrane reviews and, through our Combining Forces workshop, to build an agenda for moving forward on these issues. Members of Cochrane review groups and multidisciplinary teams have joined in this dialogue at workshops, on panels at regional and international meetings, and in the development, adaptation, and assessment of sex- and gender-sensitive planning and appraisal tools in research and other projects. The Campbell and Cochrane Equity Methods Group hosts our webpage. Some SGMG members hold leadership positions in Cochrane review and methods groups and in the Campbell Collaboration. Group members have integrated reference to sex/gender into initiatives to add equity considerations to reporting guidelines for randomized controlled trials (CONSORT-Equity) and systematic reviews (PRISMA-Equity), and to methodology used to develop and evaluate clinical, public health, and health system guidelines (Welch et al. 2015; Welch, Akl, et al. 2017; Welch, Norheim, et al. 2017). Since 2019, the chapter on equity in editions of the Cochrane Handbook includes the importance of sex and gender in formulating the question, methods, and design of a Cochrane review, and cites the work of our group (Welch et al. 2022). In 2018, Jennifer Petkovic et al. surveyed 133 Campbell and 555 Cochrane systematic reviews published between August 1, 2016, and July 31, 2017, and identified persistent gaps pertaining to sex and gender, particularly in the reporting of results (Petkovic et al. 2018). This absence of data has important implications for policies and programs based on systematic review evidence. The results of this study may serve as a baseline measure from which improvements in reporting of sex/gender considerations in systematic reviews and trials may be assessed in the future.

In pursuing an incremental, integrative approach, we regularly assess what messages about SGBA could best engage new audiences while encouraging critical inquiry. Without sustained, critical discussion, tools and checklists can be applied superficially and may constrict, rather than stimulate, a dynamic understanding of sex/gender. We recognize the importance of addressing issues such as credibility of subgroup analyses and clinical meaningfulness of differences within and between subpopulations (Wallach et al. 2016). At the same time, we encourage researchers to go beyond analysis of variables to question how current evidence and clinical practice guidelines do or do not address dynamic biological and social processes associated with sex/gender. Further, as discourses and understanding evolve about diverse gender identities, sexual orientations, and self-representations, and their intersection with other determinants of health, we challenge ourselves to note the absence of such information in research, to consider its impacts on the quality of health care services provided to individuals and communities, and to determine what steps we can take to support greater inclusion.[16]

Our efforts to integrate SGBA in the conduct of systematic reviews complement a variety of initiatives in Cochrane. For some time now, teams conducting systematic reviews have broadened their potential sources of evidence beyond randomized controlled trials to encompass syntheses of non-randomized studies and qualitative evidence including realist reviews (Kastner et al. 2016; Noyes et al. 2022; Pawson et al. 2005; Petticrew et al. 2013; Reeves et al. 2013). Acknowledging that consumer perspectives offer important insights about context and experiences of health and illness, Cochrane attempts to involve patients and carers in the review process[17] and accessible, plain-language summaries of systematic reviews are available in multiple languages. As part of a broader movement about data transparency and mitigation of bias, Cochrane has joined with other organizations to support Alltrials[18] in its call for all past and present clinical trials to be registered and their full methods and summary results reported. Cochrane and others also support initiatives to register prospectively all systematic reviews. To mitigate the effects of industry sponsorship on reliability and validity of systematic review evidence, Cochrane has adopted a policy that mandates disclosures of financial and non-financial conflicts of interest. Among the many mandated restrictions, authors working for a related industry cannot serve as a lead author of a review, nor can a review be sponsored by a related industry.[19] As a global organization, Cochrane has acknowledged a need to address systemic barriers to equity, diversity, and inclusion at all levels of the organization and to include and retain people from diverse geographic locations, genders, languages, cultural backgrounds, and perspectives.[20]

Our work also benefits from engagement with researchers in Canada and internationally. For example, our appraisal and planning tools, briefing notes, published work, and written feedback were used by Canadian researchers in a review process to develop metrics for assessing the integration of sex and gender in health research proposals (Day et al. 2017). Members of our group have collaborated with researchers in Germany, seeking guidance in developing a sex and gender checklist and methodology for a systematic review assessing gender-sensitive interventions to promote physical activity and reduce sedentary behaviour in children (Demetriou et al. 2019; Schlund et al. 2021). Cochrane Madrid researchers used a version of our sex and gender appraisal tool for systematic reviews to assess the limited consideration of sex and gender in 113 Cochrane reviews of interventions to prevent health care–associated infections and have sought our input to help refine the tool for future applications (Antequera et al. 2022; López-Alcalde et al. 2019). Researchers in Auckland, New Zealand, drew on the appraisal tool and briefing notes to develop their feminist quality appraisal tool for systematic reviews (Morgan, Williams, and Gott 2017). We regularly contribute methods expertise in assessing research proposals for systematic reviews and help mentor researchers who are unfamiliar with SGBA. Webpage metrics and citations of our publications suggest uptake in Canada and beyond, in areas such as orthopaedic science (Ladd 2016), although it is difficult to assess the nature and depth of impact solely from such data.

Moving Forward

Most members of our group worked on the projects described in this chapter "off the sides of our desks." Drawn by commitment to goals of health equity and social justice, we have sustained the SGMG for close to twenty years. We find satisfaction in collaboration, mutual learning, and supportive relationships. Our members are almost entirely based in Canada, diverse in age, career paths, and interests. The group provides a space within which to raise questions, discuss and explore the complexities of the scientific, historical, political, and sociocultural contexts of sex/gender and related social determinants of health, including the intricate sex/gender pathways and processes of embodiment. We recognize the need to continuously refine, re-examine, and re-contextualize what we discover when evidence comes to light, including evidence of the lived experiences of those whose voices were previously silenced or ignored. We strive to engage in ongoing critique and deeper awareness of the limits of our own perspectives and social locations and to seek out voices beyond our zones of comfort.

In addition to our focus on systematic reviews, members of our group seek to apply what we have learned to other arenas of real-world praxis. This includes integrating sex/gender and intersectional analyses in university-based health research and teaching, including in medical school curricula; in federal government environmental assessments; in working to provide safe affordable housing for people living with psychiatric disabilities; and applying a sex- and gender-based analytic lens to workplace mental health, among many other examples. We also recognize the reductive limitations of measurements, tools, and indicators that through formalized language and structured forms of presentation have the potential to obscure, rather than reveal, the contexts and deeper roots of inequities, including racism, misogyny, and other institutionalized oppressive practices. Indicators and measurements can aid in evaluating which policies and practices are appropriate and culturally safe or inappropriate and harmful to individuals and groups in particular contexts, and can be used to monitor the pace of change toward goals of equity, equality, and standards of quality care. However, such indicators and measurement tools *must* be generated by/with those who have lived experience of oppression and trauma. Incorporating an understanding of these embodied experiences can help to reveal the deeper strata of inequities often embedded and unacknowledged in how a question or problem is framed and in the methods and measurements used to gather, analyze, and interpret evidence.

The documentation of brutality and racism in health care against Indigenous, racialized, and gender-diverse peoples in Canada has become more explicit in public discourse, the subject of features and editorials in medical journals, the wider press, and public inquiries (Evans et al. 2020; Kamel 2021). Such institutionalized violence has always been visible to those who have been its targets and to many others who were penalized for trying to invoke change. Models of health service delivery in community and institutional settings that are sex- and gender-sensitive, culturally safe, and appropriate to those whom they serve have been researched and designed by those with lived experience of institutionalized racism, misogyny, and other forms of oppression (Commission of the National Inquiry into Missing and Murdered Indigenous Women and Girls 2019; Viens 2019). Implementing more just models of care requires strong advocacy to effect political will and resist pushback from interests vested in maintaining the status quo. The future we try to envision is never clear, nor are the goals of health equity assured. Whether within Cochrane or other arenas, we strive to be allies in progressive, collaborative initiatives, contributing sex/gender-sensitive, contextualized evidence about optimal practices in health care, alongside our passion for and commitment to health equity, gender equality, and social justice for all.

Acknowledgments

We thank SGMG members Susan Phillips and Zack Marshall for valuable contributions to revisions for this chapter and Manosila Yoganathan for her input on an earlier draft.

Notes

1   Gender equity is the process of being fair to women, men, girls, boys, and gender-diverse persons. To ensure fairness, measures must often address structural and systemic discrimination that perpetuates stereotypes, unequal treatment, and disparate access to opportunities based on sex/gender. The goal of gender equity is gender equality – to create equal outcomes for all to realize their full human rights and potential, and to benefit

equally, regardless of sex/gender and other social locations. An intersectional analysis can expose the multiple ways that disadvantage, discrimination, and oppression are embodied and expressed in people's lives. Developing gender equality policies with an intersectional approach focuses on the diverse situations and needs of marginalized disadvantaged groups and can lead to more effective strategies for systemic transformation (European Commission, Advisory Committee on Equal Opportunities for Women and Men 2020; Health Canada 2022; Levac et al. 2018).

2 We chose "sex/gender" to emphasize the interrelationship of these concepts. In this chapter, we refer to ourselves as the SGMG or the "group."

3 According to Papanek (1985, 317), "Gender differences are one of the great 'fault lines' of societies – the categories according to which resources are distributed and power allocated within a particular social order. Like geological fault lines, principles of allocations based on gender differences may shift and deepen over time."

4 In this context, disaggregating data by sex referred to binary categories of male and female. Informed by collective work in women's health, we first focused on the lack of reporting about differences or similarities between male and female research subjects and challenged the assumption that evidence from a normative male applied to all. Consideration of diversities beyond the binary emerged later in our work.

5 Including unpublished data can change research outcomes and have implications for clinical practice. For example, a 2014 Cochrane systematic review that included unpublished data reversed findings of benefit for the anti-influenza drug oseltamivir (Tamiflu) (Doshi, Jones, and Jefferson 2012; Jefferson et al. 2014).

6 See the EBM Manifesto at EBMLive, "Better Evidence for Better Healthcare," https://ebmlive.org/manifesto/.

7 See, for example, United Nations Human Rights Office, Free and Equal, "Definitions," https://www.unfe.org/definitions/. We might also ask whether and how concepts that are similar to "sex" and "gender" are understood and expressed in languages other than English and in different cultural paradigms.

8 Global in structure, Cochrane is registered as a not-for-profit organization in the UK. For more on Cochrane, see its website at http://www.cochrane.org.

9 The Equity Methods Group is a joint endeavour between Cochrane and the Campbell Collaboration, which conducts systematic reviews of social welfare, justice, and educational interventions.

10 PROGRESS refers to place of residence, race/ethnicity/culture/language, occupation, gender/sex, religion, education, socio-economic status, and social capital. The "plus" refers to additional personal characteristics, including age and sexual orientation, as well as other domains, such as those that are time-dependent or condition-dependent and may influence opportunities for health. For more information, see Cochrane, "PROGRESS-Plus," https://methods.cochrane.org/equity/projects/evidence-equity/progress-plus.

11 For a listing of our work, see Cochrane, "Sex and Gender Analysis – Publications," http://methods.cochrane.org/equity/sex-and-gender-analysis-publications.

12 We refer here to a broad definition of bias, which may include, for example, research agendas that exclude a segment of the population for which an intervention is intended or that report on a generic "patient" while omitting details about to whom the evidence applies (Pannucci and Wilkins 2010). In connection with systematic reviews, "bias" most commonly refers to methodological issues related to the internal validity of individual studies. Additional forms of meta-bias occur at the level of the systematic review or in sets of studies (Goodman and Dickersin 2011).

13 Briefing notes can be accessed at Cochrane, "Sex and Gender Analysis – Publications," http://methods.cochrane.org/equity/sex-and-gender-analysis-publications.

14   We refer to "sex/gender analysis" rather than "sex- and gender-based analysis" to be consistent with our use of "sex/gender." The terms are basically equivalent.
15   Final reporting on this project is expected in 2023–24.
16   Initiated by SGMG member Dr. Zack Marshall, the Campbell Coordinating Group in Sexual Orientation and Gender Identity is a comprehensive online portal for LGBTQ2SI+ -focused systematic reviews, scoping studies, and evidence maps (LGBTQ2SI+ stands for lesbian, gay, bisexual, trans, queer, two-spirit, intersex, and other diverse sexual orientations and gender identities). See the Knowsy website at https://www.knowsy.ca/.
17   https://cccrg.cochrane.org.
18   Alltrials is an international initiative. For background and membership see http://www.alltrials.net.
19   See https://training.cochrane.org/online-learning/coi-policy/coi-policy-cochrane-library. Whether this initiative is sufficient to promote transparent and full disclosure of all conflicts of interest (financial or other vested interests) so that readers are, at a minimum, aware of potential conflict of interest (COI) and whether it can mitigate the impacts of COI on research results remains to be determined. See Lundh et al. 2017.
20   For further elaboration, see the critical analysis of global health and call to action for addressing health inequities issued by Dr. James (Jimmy) Volmink, founding director of Cochrane South Africa, delivered in the Cochrane Lecture 2022: "Cochrane 2.0: Closing the Health Equity Gap," https://www.cochrane.org/news/recording-2022-cochrane-lecture -jimmy-volmink.

Works Cited

American College of Obstetricians and Gynecologists. Committee on Health Care for Underserved Women. 2011. "Committee Opinion No. 498: Adult Manifestations of Childhood Sexual Abuse." *Obstetrics and Gynecology* 118, 2 pt. 1: 392–95. https://doi.org/10.1097/AOG.0b013e31822c994d.

Antequera, Alba, E. Stallings, R.S. Henry, Jesús López-Alcalde, Vivien Runnels, Sari Tudiver, Peter Tugwell, and Vivian Welch. 2022. "Sex and Gender Appraisal Tool-Systematic Reviews-2 and Participation-to-Prevalence Ratio Assessed to Whom the Evidence Applies in Sepsis Reviews." *Journal of Clinical Epidemiology* 142: 119–32. https://www.jclinepi.com/article/S0895-4356(21)00358-9/fulltext.

Aromataris, Edoardo, and Zachary Munn, eds. 2020. *JBI Manual for Evidence Synthesis.* JBI (Joanna Briggs Institute). https://doi.org/10.46658/JBIMES-20-01.

Bambra, Clare, Marcia Gibson, Amanda Sowden, Kath Wright, Margaret Whitehead, and Mark Petticrew. 2010. "Tackling the Wider Social Determinants of Health and Health Inequalities: Evidence from Systematic Reviews." *Journal of Epidemiology and Community Health* 64, 4: 284–91. https://doi.org/10.1136/jech.2008.082743.

Bleier, Ruth. 1984. *Science and Gender: A Critique of Biology and Its Theories on Women.* Athene Series. Oxford: Pergamon Press.

Boscoe, Madeline, and Sari Tudiver. 2005. "Applying Gender-Based Analysis to Evidence and Policy." Paper presented at the 4th Canadian Cochrane Symposium, Montreal, Quebec, December 2.

Campbell and Cochrane Equity Methods Group. n.d. "About Us – Cochrane Methods Equity." Cochrane. https://methods.cochrane.org/equity/about-us.

Canadian Institutes of Health Research. 2019. "How to Integrate Sex and Gender into Research – CIHR." August 1. https://cihr-irsc.gc.ca/e/50836.html.

Cassels, Alan. 2015. *The Cochrane Collaboration: Medicine's Best-Kept Secret.* Victoria, BC: Agio.

Chalmers, Iain, Murray Enkin, and Marc J.N.C. Keirse, eds. 1989. *Effective Care in Pregnancy and Childbirth.* Vol. 1. *Pregnancy, Parts I–V.* Oxford: Oxford University Press.

Clow, Barbara, Ann Pederson, Margaret Haworth-Brockman, and Jennifer Bernier, eds. 2009. *Rising to the Challenge: Sex- and Gender-Based Analysis for Health Planning, Policy and Research in Canada.* Halifax, NS: Atlantic Centre of Excellence for Women's Health. http://www.nccdh.ca/resources/entry/rising-to-the-challenge.

Coen, Stephanie, and Elizabeth Banister. 2012. *What a Difference Sex and Gender Make: A Gender, Sex and Health Research Casebook.* Ottawa: Institute of Gender and Health of the Canadian Institutes of Health Research. https://dx.doi.org/10.14288/1.0132684.

Commission of the National Inquiry into Missing and Murdered Indigenous Women and Girls. 2019. *Reclaiming Power and Place: The Final Report of the National Inquiry into Missing and Murdered Indigenous Women and Girls.* https://www.mmiwg-ffada.ca/final-report/.

Concannon, Thomas W., Paul Meissner, Jo Anne Grunbaum, Newell McElwee, Jeanne-Marie Guise, John Santa, Patrick H. Conway, Denise Daudelin, Elaine H. Morrato, and Laurel K. Leslie. 2012. "A New Taxonomy for Stakeholder Engagement in Patient-Centered Outcomes Research." *Journal of General Internal Medicine* 27, 8: 985–91. https://doi.org/10.1007/s11606-012-2037-1.

Connell, Raewyn. 2012. "Gender, Health and Theory: Conceptualizing the Issue, in Local and World Perspective." *Social Science and Medicine* 74, 11: 1675–83. https://doi.org/10.1016/j.socscimed.2011.06.006.

Davies, Sara E., and Belinda Bennett. 2016. "A Gendered Human Rights Analysis of Ebola and Zika: Locating Gender in Global Health Emergencies." *International Affairs* 92, 5: 1041–60. https://doi.org/10.1111/1468-2346.12704.

Day, Suzanne, Robin Mason, Cara Tannenbaum, and Paula A. Rochon. 2017. "Essential Metrics for Assessing Sex and Gender Integration in Health Research Proposals Involving Human Participants." *PLoS ONE* 12, 8: e0182812. https://doi.org/10.1371/journal.pone.0182812.

Demetriou, Yolanda, Catherina Vondung, Jens Bucksch, Annegret Schlund, Carolin Schulze, Guido Knapp, Stephanie E. Coen, Lorri Puil, Susan P. Phillips, and Anne K. Reimers. 2019. "Interventions on Children's and Adolescents' Physical Activity and Sedentary Behaviour: Protocol for a Systematic Review from a Sex/Gender Perspective." *Systematic Reviews* 8, 65. https://doi.org/10.1186/s13643-019-0963-2.

Denzin, Norman K., and Yvonna S. Lincoln, eds. 2012. *The Landscape of Qualitative Research.* 4th ed. Thousand Oaks, CA: Sage.

Dickersin, Kay, and Iain Chalmers. 2011. "Recognizing, Investigating and Dealing with Incomplete and Biased Reporting of Clinical Research: From Francis Bacon to the WHO." *Journal of the Royal Society of Medicine* 104, 12. https://doi.org/10.1258/jrsm.2011.11k042.

Doshi, Peter, Mark Jones, and Tom Jefferson. 2012. "Rethinking Credible Evidence Synthesis." *BMJ* 344 (January). https://doi.org/10.1136/bmj.d7898.

Doull, Marion. 2009. "Gender and Systematic Reviews: Phase Two. Primary Study Analysis." Unpublished paper. Ottawa: Canadian Women's Health Network, Working Group on Sex and Gender in Systematic Reviews in Health.

Doull, Marion, Vivien E. Runnels, Sari Tudiver, and Madeline Boscoe. 2010. "Appraising the Evidence: Applying Sex- and Gender-Based Analysis (SGBA) to Cochrane Systematic Reviews on Cardiovascular Diseases." *Journal of Women's Health* 19, 5: 997–1003. https://doi.org/10.1089/jwh.2009.1626.

–. 2011. "Sex and Gender in Systematic Reviews: Planning Tool." Cochrane Methods Equity. http://methods.cochrane.org/sites/methods.cochrane.org.equity/files/public/uploads/SRTool_PlanningVersionSHORTFINAL.pdf.

Doull, Marion, Vivian Welch, Lorri Puil, Vivien Runnels, Stephanie E. Coen, Beverley Shea, Jennifer O'Neill, Cornelia Borkhoff, Sari Tudiver, and Madeline Boscoe. 2014. "Development and Evaluation of 'Briefing Notes' as a Novel Knowledge Translation Tool to Aid the Implementation of Sex/Gender Analysis in Systematic Reviews: A Pilot Study." *PLoS ONE* 9, 11. https://doi.org/10.1371/journal.pone.0110786.

Drawson, Alexandra, Elaine Toombs, and Christopher Mushquash. 2017. "Indigenous Research Methods: A Systematic Review." *International Indigenous Policy Journal* 8, 2. https://doi.org/10.18584/iipj.2017.8.2.5.

Dube, Shanta R., DeLisa Fairweather, William S. Pearson, Vincent J. Felitti, Robert F. Anda, and Janet B. Croft. 2009. "Cumulative Childhood Stress and Autoimmune Diseases in Adults." *Psychosomatic Medicine* 71, 2: 243–50. https://doi.org/10.1097/PSY.0b013e3181907888.

Edwards, Nancy, and Erica Di Ruggiero. 2011. "Exploring Which Context Matters in the Study of Health Inequities and Their Mitigation." *Scandinavian Journal of Public Health* 39, 6: 43–49. https://doi.org/10.1177/1403494810393558.

European Association of Science Editors. 2013. "Gender Policy Committee." http://www.ease.org.uk/about-us/organisation-and-administration/gender-policy-committee.

European Commission, Advisory Committee on Equal Opportunities for Women and Men. 2020. *Opinion on Intersectionality in Gender Equality Laws, Policies and Practices.* Brussels: European Commission. https://commission.europa.eu/system/files/2020-01/opinion_intersectionality_2020_en_0.pdf.

Evans, Michele K., Lisa Rosenbaum, Debra Malina, Stephen Morrissey, and Eric J. Rubin. 2020. "Diagnosing and Treating Systemic Racism." *New England Journal of Medicine* 383, 3: 274–76. https://doi.org/10.1056/NEJMe2021693.

Every-Palmer, Susanna, and Jeremy Howick. 2014. "How Evidence-Based Medicine Is Failing Due to Biased Trials and Selective Publication." *Journal of Evaluation in Clinical Practice* 20, 6: 908–14. https://doi.org/10.1111/jep.12147.

Fausto-Sterling, Anne. 2019. "Gender/Sex, Sexual Orientation, and Identity Are in the Body: How Did They Get There?" *Journal of Sex Research* 56, 4–5: 529–55. https://doi.org/10.1080/00224499.2019.1581883.

Fine, Cordelia, Rebecca Jordan-Young, Anelis Kaiser, and Gina Rippon. 2013. "Plasticity, Plasticity, Plasticity ... and the Rigid Problem of Sex." *Trends in Cognitive Sciences* 17, 11: 550–51. https://doi.org/10.1016/j.tics.2013.08.010.

Fox Keller, Evelyn. 1983. *A Feeling for the Organism: The Life and Work of Barbara McClintock.* New York: W.H. Freeman.

–. 1996. *Reflections on Gender and Science.* New Haven, CT: Yale University Press.

Galea, Liisa A.M., Elena Choleris, Arianne Y.K. Albert, Margaret M. McCarthy, and Farida Sohrabji. 2020. "The Promises and Pitfalls of Sex Difference Research." *Frontiers in Neuroendocrinology* 56: 100817. https://doi.org/10.1016/j.yfrne.2019.100817.

Gebhard, Catherine, Vera Regitz-Zagrosek, Hannelore K. Neuhauser, Rosemary Morgan, and Sabra L. Klein. 2020. "Impact of Sex and Gender on COVID-19 Outcomes in Europe." *Biology of Sex Differences* 11, 1: 29. https://doi.org/10.1186/s13293-020-00304-9.

Goodman, Steven, and Kay Dickersin. 2011. "Metabias: A Challenge for Comparative Effectiveness Research." *Annals of Internal Medicine* 155, 1: 61–62. https://doi.org/10.7326/0003-4819-155-1-201107050-00010.

Graham, Ian D. 2012. "Knowledge Synthesis and the Canadian Institutes of Health Research." *Systematic Reviews* 1, 1: 6. https://doi.org/10.1186/2046-4053-1-6.

Grant, Maria J., and Andrew Booth. 2009. "A Typology of Reviews: An Analysis of 14 Review Types and Associated Methodologies." *Health Information and Libraries Journal* 26, 2: 91–108. https://doi.org/10.1111/j.1471-1842.2009.00848.x.

Greaves, Lorraine. 2015. "Women, Gender, and Health Research." In *Women's Health: Intersections of Policy, Research, and Practice*, 2nd ed., ed. Pat Armstrong and Ann Pederson, 9–30. Toronto: Women's Press.

Greenhalgh, Trisha. 2013. "Why Do We Always End Up Here? Evidence-Based Medicine's Conceptual Cul-de-Sacs and Some Off-Road Alternative Routes." *International Journal of Prosthodontics* 26, 1: 11–15.

Greenhalgh, Trisha, Jeremy Howick, and Neal Maskrey. 2014. "Evidence Based Medicine: A Movement in Crisis?" *BMJ* 348 (June). https://doi.org/10.1136/bmj.g3725.

Greenland, Sander. 2012. "Transparency and Disclosure, Neutrality and Balance: Shared Values or Just Shared Words?" *Journal of Epidemiology and Community Health* 66, 11: 967–70. https://doi.org/10.1136/jech-2011-200459.

Guyatt, Gordon H., Andrew D. Oxman, Regina Kunz, Gunn E. Vist, Yngve Falck-Ytter, and Holger J. Schünemann. 2008. "What Is 'Quality of Evidence' and Why Is It Important to Clinicians?" *BMJ* 336, 7651: 995–98. https://doi.org/10.1136/bmj.39490. 551019.BE.

Guyatt, Gordon H., et al. 2013. "GRADE Guidelines: 11. Making an Overall Rating of Confidence in Effect Estimates for a Single Outcome and for All Outcomes." *Journal of Clinical Epidemiology* 66, 2: 151–57. https://doi.org/10.1016/j.jclinepi. 2012.01.006.

Hammarström, Anne, et al. 2014. "Central Gender Theoretical Concepts in Health Research: The State of the Art." *Journal of Epidemiology and Community Health* 68, 2: 185–90. https://doi.org/10.1136/jech-2013-202572.

Hankivsky, Olena, Kristen W. Springer, and Gemma Hunting. 2018. "Beyond Sex and Gender Difference in Funding and Reporting of Health Research." *Research Integrity and Peer Review* 3, 1: 6. https://doi.org/10.1186/s41073-018-0050-6.

Harding, Sandra. 1986. *The Science Question in Feminism*. Ithaca, NY: Cornell University Press.

Harper, Sam, Nicholas B. King, Stephen C. Meersman, Marsha E. Reichman, Nancy Breen, and John Lynch. 2010. "Implicit Value Judgments in the Measurement of Health Inequalities." *Milbank Quarterly* 88, 1: 4–29. https://doi.org/10.1111/j.1468-0009. 2010.00587.x.

Health Canada. 2000. "Health Canada's Gender-Based Analysis Policy." Public Services and Procurement Canada. http://publications.gc.ca/site/eng/93468/publication. html.

–. 2013. "Guidance Document: Considerations for Inclusion of Women in Clinical Trials and Analysis of Sex Differences." Government of Canada. December 4. https://www. canada.ca/en/health-canada/services/drugs-health-products/drug-products/applications -submissions/guidance-documents/clinical-trials/considerations-inclusion-women -clinical-trials-analysis-data-sex-differences.html.

–. 2022. "Health Portfolio Sex- and Gender-Based Analysis Plus Policy: Advancing Equity, Diversity and Inclusion." https://www.canada.ca/en/health-canada/corporate/ transparency/corporate-management-reporting/heath-portfolio-sex-gender-based -analysis-policy.html.

Heidari, Shirin, Mirjam J. Eckert, Susan Kippax, Quarraisha Abdool Karim, Papa Salif Sow, and Mark A. Wainberg. 2011. "Time for Gender Mainstreaming in Editorial Policies." *Journal of the International AIDS Society* 14, 1: 11. https://doi.org/10.1186/ 1758-2652-14-11.

Heneghan, Carl, Kamal R. Mahtani, Ben Goldacre, Fiona Godlee, Helen Macdonald, and Duncan Jarvies. 2017. "Evidence Based Medicine Manifesto for Better Healthcare." *BMJ* 357 (June): j2973. https://doi.org/10.1136/bmj.j2973.

Higgins, Julian P.T., James Thomas, Jacqueline Chandler, Miranda Cumpston, Tianjing Li, Matthew J. Page, and Vivian A. Welch, eds. 2022. *Cochrane Handbook for Systematic Reviews of Interventions.* Version 6.3. Cochrane. http://www.training.cochrane.org/handbook.

Horton, Richard. 2015. "Offline: What Is Medicine's 5 Sigma?" *The Lancet* 385, 9976: 1380. https://doi.org/10.1016/S0140-6736(15)60696-1.

Hreiche, Raymond, Pierre Morissette, and Jacques Turgeon. 2008. "Drug-Induced Long QT Syndrome in Women: Review of Current Evidence and Remaining Gaps." *Gender Medicine* 5, 2: 124–35. https://doi.org/10.1016/j.genm.2008.05.005.

Institute of Medicine. 2011. *Finding What Works in Health Care: Standards for Systematic Reviews.* Consensus Study Report. Washington, DC: National Academies Press.

Institute of Medicine (US), Committee on Understanding the Biology of Sex and Gender Differences. 2001. *Exploring the Biological Contributions to Human Health: Does Sex Matter?* Edited by Theresa M. Wizemann and Mary-Lou Pardue. Washington, DC: National Academies Press (US). http://www.ncbi.nlm.nih.gov/books/NBK222288/.

Ioannidis, John P.A. 2010. "Meta-Research: The Art of Getting It Wrong." *Research Synthesis Methods* 1, 3–4: 169–84. https://doi.org/10.1002/jrsm.19.

–. 2016. "The Mass Production of Redundant, Misleading, and Conflicted Systematic Reviews and Meta-Analyses." *Milbank Quarterly* 94, 3: 485–514. https://doi.org/10.1111/1468-0009.12210.

Ioannidis, John P.A., Sander Greenland, Mark A. Hlatky, Muin J. Khoury, Malcolm R. Macleod, David Moher, Kenneth F. Schulz, and Robert Tibshirani. 2014. "Increasing Value and Reducing Waste in Research Design, Conduct, and Analysis." *The Lancet* 383, 9912: 166–75. https://doi.org/10.1016/S0140-6736(13)62227-8.

Jackson, Beth E., Ann Pederson, and Madeline Boscoe. 2009. "Waiting to Wait: Improving Wait Times Evidence through Gender-Based Analysis." In *Women's Health: Intersections of Policy, Research and Practice,* ed. Pat Armstrong and Jennifer Deadman, 35–52. Toronto: Women's Press.

Jahn, Ingeborg, Claudia Börnhorst, Frauke Günther, and Tilman Brand. 2017. "Examples of Sex/Gender Sensitivity in Epidemiological Research: Results of an Evaluation of Original Articles Published in JECH 2006–2014." *Health Research Policy and Systems* 15, 1: 11. https://doi.org/10.1186/s12961-017-0174-z.

Jefferson, Tom, et al. 2014. "Neuraminidase Inhibitors for Preventing and Treating Influenza in Adults and Children." *Cochrane Database of Systematic Reviews* 4. https://doi.org/10.1002/14651858.CD008965.pub4.

Johnson, Joy L., and Alain Beaudet. 2012. "Sex and Gender Reporting in Health Research: Why Canada Should Be a Leader." *Canadian Journal of Public Health* 104, 1: e80–e81.

Jordan-Young, Rebecca, and Raffaella I. Rumiati. 2012. "Hardwired for Sexism? Approaches to Sex/Gender in Neuroscience." *Neuroethics* 5, 3: 305–15. https://doi.org/10.1007/s12152-011-9134-4.

Juster, Robert-Paul. 2019. "Sex × Gender and Sexual Orientation in Relation to Stress Hormones and Allostatic Load." *Gender and the Genome* 3: 1–17. https://doi.org/10.1177%2F2470289719862555.

Kamel, Géhane. 2021. *Investigation Report: Law on the Investigation of the Causes and Circumstances of Death for the Protection of Human Life – Concerning the Death of*

Joyce Echaquan. 2020-00275. https://www.coroner.gouv.qc.ca/fileadmin/Enquetes_publiques/2020-06375-40_002__1__sans_logo_anglais.pdf.

Kastner, Monika, Jesmin Antony, Charlene Soobiah, Sharon E. Straus, and Andrea C. Tricco. 2016. "Conceptual Recommendations for Selecting the Most Appropriate Knowledge Synthesis Method to Answer Research Questions Related to Complex Evidence." *Journal of Clinical Epidemiology* 73 (May): 43–49. https://doi.org/10.1016/j.jclinepi.2015.11.022.

Kautzky-Willer, Alexandra, Jürgen Harreiter, and Giovanni Pacini. 2016. "Sex and Gender Differences in Risk, Pathophysiology and Complications of Type 2 Diabetes Mellitus." *Endocrine Reviews* 37, 3: 278–316. https://doi.org/10.1210/er.2015-1137.

Keener, Emily. 2015. "The Complexity of Gender: It Is All That and More ... In Sum, It *Is* Complicated." *Sex Roles* 73, 11: 481–89. https://doi.org/10.1007/s11199-015-0542-5.

Kirkham, Jamie J., Douglas G. Altman, An-Wen Chan, Carrol Gamble, Kerry M. Dwan, and Paula R. Williamson. 2018. "Outcome Reporting Bias in Trials: A Methodological Approach for Assessment and Adjustment in Systematic Reviews." *BMJ* 362 (September): k3802. https://doi.org/10.1136/bmj.k3802.

Krieger, Nancy. 2003. "Genders, Sexes, and Health: What Are the Connections – and Why Does It Matter?" *International Journal of Epidemiology* 32, 4: 652–57. https://doi.org/10.1093/ije/dyg156.

–. 2005. *Embodying Inequality: Epidemiologic Perspectives.* New York: Routledge.

Ladd, Amy L. 2016. "Gendered Innovations in Orthopaedic Science: Sex, Lies, and Stereotype: In Praise of the Systematic Review." *Clinical Orthopaedics and Related Research* 474, 1: 27–30. https://doi.org/10.1007/s11999-015-4577-2.

Les Femmes Michif Otipemisiwak (LFMO)/Women of the Métis Nation. 2019. *Métis-Specific Gender Based Analysis Plus (GBA+) Tool.* Ottawa: National Métis Women's Forum. https://metiswomen.org/wp-content/uploads/2021/06/Metis-Specific-GBA-Tool.pdf.

Levac, Leah, Lisa McMurtry, Deborah Stienstra, Gail Baikie, Cindy Hanson, and Devi Mucina. 2018. *Learning across Indigenous and Western Knowledge Systems and Intersectionality: Reconciling Social Science Research Approaches.* Ottawa: Canadian Research Institute for the Advancement of Women. https://www.criaw-icref.ca/en/product/learning-across-indigenous-and-western-knowledge-systems-.

López-Alcalde, Jesús, Elena Stallings, Sheila Cabir Nunes, Abelardo Fernández Chávez, Mathilde Daheron, Xavier Bonfill Cosp, and Javier Zamora. 2019. "Consideration of Sex and Gender in Cochrane Reviews of Interventions for Preventing Healthcare-Associated Infections: A Methodology Study." *BMC Health Services Research* 19, 1: 169. https://doi.org/10.1186/s12913-019-4001-9.

Lundh, Andreas, Joel Lexchin, Barbara Mintzes, Jeppe B. Schroll, and Lisa Bero. 2017. "Industry Sponsorship and Research Outcome." *Cochrane Database of Systematic Reviews* 2. https://doi.org/10.1002/14651858.MR000033.pub3.

Mahood, Quenby, Dwayne Van Eerd, and Emma Irvin. 2014. "Searching for Grey Literature for Systematic Reviews: Challenges and Benefits." *Research Synthesis Methods* 5, 3: 221–34. https://doi.org/10.1002/jrsm.1106.

Messing, Karen. 2014. *Pain and Prejudice: What Science Can Learn about Work from the People Who Do It.* Toronto: Between the Lines.

Moher, David, Jennifer Tetzlaff, Andrea C. Tricco, Margaret Sampson, and Douglas G. Altman. 2007. "Epidemiology and Reporting Characteristics of Systematic Reviews." *PLOS Medicine* 4, 3: e78. https://doi.org/10.1371/journal.pmed.0040078.

Morgan, Tessa, Lisa Ann Williams, and Merryn Gott. 2017. "A Feminist Quality Appraisal Tool: Exposing Gender Bias and Gender Inequities in Health Research." *Critical Public Health* 27, 2: 263–74. https://doi.org/10.1080/09581596.2016.1205182.

Morrow, Marina, Olena Hankivsky, and Colleen Varcoe, eds. 2008. *Women's Health in Canada: Critical Perspectives on Theory and Policy.* Toronto: University of Toronto Press.

Morton, Rachael Lisa, Iryna Schlackow, Borislava Mihaylova, Natalie Dawn Staplin, Alastair Gray, and Alan Cass. 2016. "The Impact of Social Disadvantage in Moderate-to-Severe Chronic Kidney Disease: An Equity-Focused Systematic Review." *Nephrology, Dialysis, Transplantation* 31, 1: 46–56. https://doi.org/10.1093/ndt/gfu394.

Moser, Caroline, and Annalise Moser. 2005. "Gender Mainstreaming since Beijing: A Review of Success and Limitations in International Institutions." *Gender and Development* 13, 2: 11–22. https://doi.org/10.1080/13552070512331332283.

National Institutes of Health. 2001. "NIH Policy and Guidelines on the Inclusion of Women and Minorities as Subjects in Clinical Research (Amended 2001)." US Department of Health and Human Service, October 9. https://grants.nih.gov/policy/inclusion/women-and-minorities/guidelines.htm.

National Institutes of Health, and National Heart, Lung and Blood Institute. 2020. "About Systematic Evidence Reviews and Clinical Practice Guidelines." US Department of Health and Human Services. https://www.nhlbi.nih.gov/node/80397.

Native Women's Association of Canada. 2007. *Culturally Relevant Gender Based Analysis: An Issue Paper Prepared for the National Aboriginal Women's Summit June 20–22, 2007 in Corner Brook, NL.* Ottawa: Native Women's Association of Canada. https://www.nwac.ca/wp-content/uploads/2015/05/2007-NWAC-Culturally-Relevant-Gender-Based-Analysis-An-Issue-Paper.pdf.

–. 2020. "A Culturally Relevant Gender-Based Analysis (CRGBA) Starter Kit." https://www.nwac.ca/assets-knowledge-centre/A-Culturally-Relevant-Gender-Based-Analysis.pdf.

Noyes, Jane, Andrew Booth, Margaret Cargo, Kate Flemming, Angela Harden, Janet Harris, Ruth Garside, Karin Hannes, Tomás Pantoja, and James Thomas. 2022. "Chapter 21: Qualitative Evidence." In *Cochrane Handbook for Systematic Reviews of Interventions,* Version 6.3, ed. Julian P.T. Higgins, James Thomas, Jacqueline Chandler, Miranda Cumpston, Tianjing Li, Matthew J. Page, and Vivian A. Welch. Cochrane. http://www.training.cochrane.org/handbook.

Oakley, Ann. 2000. *Experiments in Knowing: Gender and Method in the Social Sciences.* New York: New Press.

O'Neill, Jennifer, et al. 2014. "Applying an Equity Lens to Interventions: Using PROGRESS Ensures Consideration of Socially Stratifying Factors to Illuminate Inequities in Health." *Journal of Clinical Epidemiology* 67, 1: 56–64. https://doi.org/10.1016/j.jclinepi.2013.08.005.

Özdemir, B.C., S. Oertelt-Prigione, A.A. Adjei, S. Borchmann, J.B. Haanen, A. Letsch, O. Mir, A. Quaas, R.H.A. Verhoeven, and A.D. Wagner. 2022. "Investigation of Sex and Gender Differences in Oncology Gains Momentum: ESMO Announces the Launch of a Gender Medicine Task Force." *Annals of Oncology* 33, 2: 126–28. https://doi.org/10.1016/j.annonc.2021.11.011.

Pannucci, Christopher J., and Edwin G. Wilkins. 2010. "Identifying and Avoiding Bias in Research." *Plastic and Reconstructive Surgery* 126, 2: 619–25. https://doi.org/10.1097/PRS.0b013e3181de24bc.

Papanek, Hannah. 1985. "Class and Gender in Education-Employment Linkages." *Comparative Education Review* 29, 3: 317–46.

Pawson, Ray, Trisha Greenhalgh, Gill Harvey, and Kieran Walshe. 2005. "Realist Review – A New Method of Systematic Review Designed for Complex Policy Interventions." *Journal of Health Services Research and Policy* 10, 1 (July): 21–34. https://doi.org/10.1258/1355819054308530.

Pederson, Ann, and Pat Armstrong. 2015. "Sex, Gender and Systematic Reviews: The Example of Wait Times for Hip and Knee Replacements." In *Women's Health: Intersections of Policy, Research, and Practice,* 2nd ed., ed. Pat Armstrong and Ann Pederson, 56–72. Toronto: Women's Press.

Petkovic, Jennifer, Jessica Trawin, Omar Dewidar, Manosila Yoganathan, Peter Tugwell, and Vivian Welch. 2018. "Sex/Gender Reporting and Analysis in Campbell and Cochrane Systematic Reviews: A Cross-Sectional Methods Study." *Systematic Reviews* 7, 1: 113. https://doi.org/10.1186/s13643-018-0778-6.

Petticrew, Mark, Eva Rehfuess, Jane Noyes, Julian P.T. Higgins, Alain Mayhew, Tomas Pantoja, Ian Shemilt, and Amanda Sowden. 2013. "Synthesizing Evidence on Complex Interventions: How Meta-Analytical, Qualitative, and Mixed-Method Approaches Can Contribute." *Journal of Clinical Epidemiology* 66, 11: 1230–43. https://doi.org/10.1016/j.jclinepi.2013.06.005.

Phillips, Susan P. 2008. "Measuring the Health Effects of Gender." *Journal of Epidemiology and Community Health* 62, 4: 368–71. https://doi.org/10.1136/jech.2007.062158.

Phillips, Susan P., and Katarina Hamberg. 2016. "Doubly Blind: A Systematic Review of Gender in Randomised Controlled Trials." *Global Health Action* 9, 1: 29597. https://doi.org/10.3402/gha.v9.29597.

Pollock, Alex, Pauline Campbell, Caroline Struthers, Anneliese Synnot, Jack Nunn, Sophie Hill, Heather Goodare, Jacqui Morris, Chris Watts, and Richard Morley. 2018. "Stakeholder Involvement in Systematic Reviews: A Scoping Review." *Systematic Reviews* 7, 1: 208. https://doi.org/10.1186/s13643-018-0852-0.

Reeves, Barnaby C., Julian P.T. Higgins, Craig Ramsay, Beverley Shea, Peter Tugwell, and George A. Wells. 2013. "An Introduction to Methodological Issues When Including Non-Randomised Studies in Systematic Reviews on the Effects of Interventions." *Research Synthesis Methods* 4, 1: 1–11. https://doi.org/10.1002/jrsm.1068.

Regitz-Zagrosek, Vera, and Catherine Gebhard. 2023. "Gender Medicine: Effects of Sex and Gender on Cardiovascular Disease Manifestation and Outcomes." *Nature Reviews Cardiology* 20, 4: 236–47. https://doi: 10.1038/s41569-022-00797-4.

Rich-Edwards, Janet W., Ursula B. Kaiser, Grace L. Chen, JoAnn E. Manson, and Jill M. Goldstein. 2018. "Sex and Gender Differences Research Design for Basic, Clinical, and Population Studies: Essentials for Investigators." *Endocrine Reviews* 39, 4: 424–39. https://doi.org/10.1210/er.2017-00246.

Ritz, Stacey A., David M. Antle, Julie Côté, Kathy Deroy, Nya Fraleigh, Karen Messing, Lise Parent, Joey St-Pierre, Cathy Vaillancourt, and Donna Mergler. 2014. "First Steps for Integrating Sex and Gender Considerations into Basic Experimental Biomedical Research." *FASEB Journal* 28, 1: 4–13. https://doi.org/10.1096/fj.13-233395.

Roseman, Michelle, Katherine Milette, Lisa A. Bero, James C. Coyne, Joel Lexchin, Erick H. Turner, and Brett D. Thombs. 2011. "Reporting of Conflicts of Interest in Meta-Analyses of Trials of Pharmacological Treatments." *JAMA* 305, 10: 1008–17. https://doi.org/10.1001/jama.2011.257.

Runnels, Vivien, Sari Tudiver, Marion Doull, and Madeline Boscoe. 2014. "The Challenges of Including Sex/Gender Analysis in Systematic Reviews: A Qualitative Survey." *Systematic Reviews* 3, 1: 33. https://doi.org/10.1186/2046-4053-3-33.

Ryan, Nessa E., and Alison M. El Ayadi. 2020. "A Call for a Gender-Responsive, Intersectional Approach to Address COVID-19." *Global Public Health* 15, 9: 1404–12. https://doi.org/10.1080/17441692.2020.1791214.

Sackett, David L., William M.C. Rosenberg, J.A. Muir Gray, R. Brian Haynes, and W. Scott Richardson. 1996. "Evidence Based Medicine: What It Is and What It Isn't." *BMJ* 312, 7023: 71–72. https://doi.org/10.1136/bmj.312.7023.71.

Schiebinger, Londa, Ineke Klinge, Hai-Young Paik, Ines Sánchez de Madariaga, Martina Schraudner, and Marcia Stefanick, eds. 2011–21. "Gendered Innovations in Science, Health and Medicine, Engineering and Environment." Stanford University. https://genderedinnovations.stanford.edu/.

Schlund, Annegret, Anne K. Reimers, Jens Bucksch, Catherina Brindley, Carolyn Schulze, Lorri Puil, Stephanie E. Coen, Susan P. Phillips, Guido Knapp, and Yolanda Demetriou. 2021. "Do Intervention Studies to Promote Physical Activity and Reduce Sedentary Behavior in Children and Adolescents Take Sex/Gender into Account? A Systematic Review." *Journal of Physical Activity and Health* 18, 4: 461–68. https://doi.org/10.1123/jpah.2020-0666.

Schroll, Jeppe B., and Lisa Bero. 2015. "Regulatory Agencies Hold the Key to Improving Cochrane Reviews of Drugs." *Cochrane Database of Systematic Reviews.* https://doi.org/10.1002/14651858.ED000098.

Springer, Kristen W., Jeanne Mager Stellman, and Rebecca M. Jordan-Young. 2012. "Beyond a Catalogue of Differences: A Theoretical Frame and Good Practice Guidelines for Researching Sex/Gender in Human Health." *Social Science and Medicine* 74, 11: 1817–24. https://doi.org/10.1016/j.socscimed.2011.05.033.

Straus, Sharon E., Monika Kastner, Charlene Soobiah, Jesmin Antony, and Andrea C. Tricco. 2016. "Introduction: Engaging Researchers on Developing, Using, and Improving Knowledge Synthesis Methods: A Series of Articles Describing the Results of a Scoping Review on Emerging Knowledge Synthesis Methods." *Journal of Clinical Epidemiology* 73 (May): 15–18. https://doi.org/10.1016/j.jclinepi.2016.01.031.

Sweetman, Caroline. 2012. "Introduction." *Gender and Development* 20, 3: 389–403. https://doi.org/10.1080/13552074.2012.743266.

Tadiri, Christina P., Teresa Gisinger, Alexandra Kautzky-Willer, Karolina Kublickiene, Maria Trinidad Herrero, Valeria Raparelli, Louise Pilote, and Colleen M. Norris. 2020. "The Influence of Sex and Gender Domains on COVID-19 Cases and Mortality." *CMAJ* 192, 36: E1041–E45. https://doi.org/10.1503/cmaj.200971.

Tannenbaum, Cara, Robert P. Ellis, Friederike Eyssel, James Zou, and Londa Schiebinger. 2019. "Sex and Gender Analysis Improves Science and Engineering." *Nature* 575, 7781: 137–46. https://doi.org/10.1038/s41586-019-1657-6.

Tannenbaum, Cara, Lorraine Greaves, and Ian D. Graham. 2016. "Why Sex and Gender Matter in Implementation Research." *BMC Medical Research Methodology* 16 (October): 145. https://doi.org/10.1186/s12874-016-0247-7.

Treasury Board of Canada Secretariat. 2019. "Integrating Gender-Based Analysis Plus into Evaluation: A Primer (2019)." https://www.canada.ca/en/treasury-board-secretariat/services/audit-evaluation/evaluation-government-canada/gba-primer.html.

Tricco, Andrea C., Jennifer Tetzlaff, and David Moher. 2011. "The Art and Science of Knowledge Synthesis." *Journal of Clinical Epidemiology* 64, 1: 11–20. https://doi.org/10.1016/j.jclinepi.2009.11.007.

Tudiver, Sari, Madeline Boscoe, Vivien E. Runnels, and Marion Doull. 2012. "Challenging 'Dis-Ease': Sex, Gender and Systematic Reviews in Health." In *What a Difference Sex and Gender Make: A Gender, Sex and Health Research Casebook,* ed. Stephanie Coen and Elizabeth Banister, 25–33. Ottawa: Institute of Gender and Health of the Canadian Institutes of Health Research.

Tugwell, Peter, Mark Petticrew, Elizabeth Kristjansson, Vivian Welch, Erin Ueffing, Elizabeth Waters, Josiane Bonnefoy, Antony Morgan, Emma Doohan, and Michael P. Kelly. 2010. "Assessing Equity in Systematic Reviews: Realising the Recommendations of the Commission on Social Determinants of Health." *BMJ* 341 (September): c4739.

van Anders, Sari M. 2015. "Beyond Sexual Orientation: Integrating Gender/Sex and Diverse Sexualities via Sexual Configurations Theory." *Archives of Sexual Behavior* 44, 5: 1177–213. https://doi.org/10.1007/s10508-015-0490-8.

Veenstra, Gerry. 1999. "Different Wor(l)ds: Three Approaches to Health Research." *Canadian Journal of Public Health* 90, suppl. 1: S18–S21.

Viens, Jacques. 2019. "Public Inquiry Commission on Relations between Indigenous Peoples and Certain Public Services in Québec: Listening, Reconciliation and Progress, Final Report." Gouvernement du Québec. https://www.cerp.gouv.qc.ca/index.php?id=2&L=1.

Walby, Sylvia. 2005. "Gender Mainstreaming: Productive Tensions in Theory and Practice." *Social Politics* 12, 3: 321–43. https://doi.org/10.1093/sp/jxi018.

Wallach, Joshua D., Patrick G. Sullivan, John F. Trepanowski, Ewout W. Steyerberg, and John P.A. Ioannidis. 2016. "Sex Based Subgroup Differences in Randomized Controlled Trials: Empirical Evidence from Cochrane Meta-Analyses." *BMJ* 355 (November). https://doi.org/10.1136/bmj.i5826.

Waters, Elizabeth. 2009. "Evidence for Public Health Decision-Making: Towards Reliable Synthesis." *Bulletin of the World Health Organization* 87: 164.

Welch, Vivian A., et al. 2022. "Chapter 16: Equity and Specific Populations." In *Cochrane Handbook for Systematic Reviews of Interventions,* Version 6.3, ed. Julian P.T. Higgins, James Thomas, Jacqueline Chandler, Miranda Crumpston, Tianjing Li, and Vivian A. Welch. Cochrane. http://www.training.cochrane.org/handbook.

Welch, Vivian A., Elie A. Akl, et al. 2017. "GRADE Equity Guidelines 1: Considering Health Equity in GRADE Guideline Development: Introduction and Rationale." *Journal of Clinical Epidemiology* 90 (October): 59–67. https://doi.org/10.1016/j.jclinepi.2017.01.014.

Welch, Vivian, Marion Doull, et al. 2017. "Reporting of Sex and Gender in Randomized Controlled Trials in Canada: A Cross-Sectional Methods Study." *Research Integrity and Peer Review* 2, 1: 15. https://doi.org/10.1186/s41073-017-0039-6.

Welch, Vivian A., Ole F. Norheim, Janet Jull, Richard Cookson, Halvor Sommerfelt, Peter Tugwell, and CONSORT-Equity and Boston Equity Symposium. 2017. "CONSORT-Equity 2017 Extension and Elaboration for Better Reporting of Health Equity in Randomised Trials." *BMJ* 359 (November): j5085. https://doi.org/10.1136/bmj.j5085.

Welch, Vivian, Mark Petticrew, Jennifer Petkovic, David Moher, Elizabeth Waters, Howard White, Peter Tugwell, and the PRISMA-Equity Bellagio Group. 2015. "Extending the PRISMA Statement to Equity-Focused Systematic Reviews (PRISMA-E 2012): Explanation and Elaboration." *International Journal for Equity in Health* 14 (October): 92. https://doi.org/10.1186/s12939-015-0219-2.

Westbrook, Laurel, and Aliya Saperstein. 2015. "New Categories Are Not Enough: Rethinking the Measurement of Sex and Gender in Social Surveys." *Gender and Society* 29, 4: 534–60. https://doi.org/10.1177/0891243215584758.

White, Howard, and Hugh Waddington. 2012. "Why Do We Care about Evidence Synthesis? An Introduction to the Special Issue on Systematic Reviews." *Journal of Development Effectiveness* 4, 3: 351–58. https://doi.org/10.1080/19439342.2012.711343.

Whitehead, Margaret. 1992. "The Concepts and Principles of Equity and Health." *International Journal of Health Services* 22, 3: 429–45. https://doi.org/10.2190/986L-LHQ6 -2VTE-YRRN.

Wieseler, Beate, Natalie McGauran, and Thomas Kaiser. 2010. "Finding Studies on Reboxetine: A Tale of Hide and Seek." *BMJ* 341 (October): c4942. https://doi.org/10. 1136/bmj.c4942.

Wilson, Debra Rose. 2010. "Health Consequences of Childhood Sexual Abuse." *Perspectives in Psychiatric Care* 46, 1: 56–64. https://doi.org/10.1111/j.1744-6163.2009.00238.x.

Women and Gender Equality Canada. 2022. "What Is Gender-Based Analysis Plus?" https://women-gender-equality.canada.ca/.

Yakerson, Alla. 2019. "Women in Clinical Trials: A Review of Policy Development and Health Equity in the Canadian Context." *International Journal for Equity in Health* 18, 1: 56. https://doi.org/10.1186/s12939-019-0954-x.

7

Violence against Women: A Measure of Inequality

Lee Lakeman, Holly Johnson, Diana Majury,
and Manuela Popovici

IN THIS CHAPTER, we four feminists (a front-line worker, a legal scholar, and two social science researchers) examine the data, methods, and analytic tools regarding violence against women (VAW) that we have gleaned from over three decades of work on the subject. Our reflections focus on a half-century of feminist VAW activism in Canada, starting in the 1970s. Although all of us have at least some front-line, some legal, and some research experience, we come from very different backgrounds and work in very different contexts. This combination of feminist perspectives and joint activism has been critical to the successes of the women's movement in Canada and is perhaps uniquely Canadian. We see this chapter as a starting point in our articulation of what we believe, based on experience and research – that VAW is the lynchpin of women's inequality and that gender equality is essential to the eradication of VAW.

The collection of data on incidents of violence against women in Canada has played an important role in enabling feminists to see the bigger picture – the prevalence and devastation of VAW – and to better understand VAW patterns and factors and their interconnection with other forms of women's inequality. Since the 1970s, dramatic statistics have helped feminists persuade others – government, policy-makers, the public – that VAW and its widespread and long-term impacts on women's lives are serious and urgent problems. The data spoke to the number of incidents of VAW; rather than concentrating on prevention, responses focused on services for the victims and punishment for the perpetrators, aligning with neo-liberalism's emphasis on the individual and individual responsibility. In this climate, the stress on data grew to the point that quantitative data came to be treated as ends in themselves, required to retain existing VAW services and to maintain waning attention on the issue. In the current age of measurement, the data have become the story rather than a tool to assist in piecing the story together. Data collection and even minimal data analysis are resource intensive, absorbing much time and energy from feminists, as well as depleting the limited funds available for feminist services and research. These expenditures would be worthwhile if we were growing and learning and making new connections, if we were expanding our knowledge of the causes of VAW and of what can be done to reduce/eliminate it. However, expenditures on data collection may be ineffective, even counter-productive, if we are simply protecting the status quo by confirming what we already know.

Other chapters in this volume outline the limitations, even dangers, of over-reliance on indicators, measurement, and quantitative data with respect to specific instances of women's inequality – the narrowing of focus, the siloing effect, decontextualization, knowledge monopolization, obfuscation, and the hierarchization that measurement facilitates. These critiques, as well as the acknowledged benefits that can be gained from data and measurement, provide the context for this chapter, in which we argue that the time has come for a more holistic, intersectionality-based approach to women's inequality and to the building of women's substantive equality. Such an approach would focus on the interconnections and interdependencies among the component pieces of women's inequality. Measurement and data no doubt have a role to play in articulating and implementing this more complex approach, but the methods and tools will need to be more sophisticated and more sensitive to nuance and complexity. The measurement project needs to shift from documenting inequality to helping in the creation of equality.

From its inception, the Canadian VAW movement asserted that VAW is a cornerstone of women's inequality, that VAW not only springs from women's inequality but holds the rest of women's oppression in place and vice versa. Under that assertion, male violence against women is framed as a gender inequality issue, and gender inequality is understood to be enforced by male violence. Yet policy aimed at reducing violence or providing safety or aid to women rarely tackles the underlying causes of gender inequality. And conversely, policies designed to address other sites of women's inequality (unequal pay, daycare, housing, employment) seldom pay attention to the role of VAW as it relates to those issues. Although policies and services may provide temporary assistance and support to individual women and may hold a small minority of individual men accountable, they have no systemic impact on violence; they do not alter gendered power relations or other social, economic, and legal structures that sustain gender inequality. Far from benignly maintaining the status quo, a good many policies and services actually exacerbate inequalities.

That violence is the lynchpin of women's inequality, and that it functions to maintain the oppression and subordination of women, is clear to those who provide support to, or advocate on behalf of, abused and sexually assaulted women. This is evident in the lived experiences of these women and their interactions with male partners, police, courts, social welfare, housing and immigration policies, and society at large. But these connections have been documented only sporadically by feminist services and researchers and not at all by others. And this documentation is made more difficult in the current neo-liberal political context in which equality claims based on systemic disadvantage have been delegitimized, the self-sufficient citizen/consumer is exalted, and the notion that violence is a product of anything other than individual action or misadventure is easily dismissed (Brodie 2008; Morrow, Hankivsky, and Varcoe 2004). For feminists, the numbers bespeak a deeply rooted systemic issue, whereas neo-liberal policy-makers see them as individual aberrations to be routed case by case. Knowing how to gather and utilize evidence to demonstrate the structural underpinnings and interconnections with male violence against women, and to sustain those connections, is critical for fundamental and lasting change for women, and more challenging than one might think.

In an analysis of seventy countries, Mala Htun and S. Laurel Weldon (2012) find that autonomous women's movements and the institutionalization of feminist ideals are critical for developing policies that address issues of significance to women's lives. Indeed, they are more essential than left-of-centre governments, women in government, or macro-level economic factors. This emphasizes the importance of recognizing feminism as comprised of "epistemic communities" with expertise and policy-relevant knowledge (otherwise known as "practice-based evidence") that has been accumulated over decades of supporting sexually assaulted and abused women (Coy, Kelly, and Dustin 2015; Walby 2011), and engaging that expertise to effect change. Searching for and incorporating this expertise are essential if decision-makers and holders of institutional power are to enact policies that are helpful and not harmful to women and that aim at structural, not just individual, change.

Over the course of the last thirty-odd years, the epistemic community of feminist anti-VAW advocates has presented its arguments in a variety of fora, linking VAW to other forms of women's oppression. However, as the women's movement, we have not substantiated a full and ongoing analysis of that interrelationship. In responding to demands from funders and to VAW naysayers, our efforts have been limited largely to gathering statistics that define and measure the prevalence of VAW. Although this remains an ongoing task of some significance, the narrow focus on counting individual incidents fails to capture the full impact of VAW on every aspect of each and every woman's life and in some ways may make that impact less visible. We need to turn our attention to developing a fulsome equality analysis of VAW that demonstrates how it functions to enforce women's inequality. Measurement will be part of this analysis, but measurement of VAW is complex and political, and it insidiously shapes social reality (Kimmel 2002; Merry and Coutin 2014). We need to be clear about the role we see for measurement and to develop a methodology that is up to the difficult task.

We start the chapter at the root of feminist method – with the front line, with our history of receiving, intervening in, and recording women's experiences and women's stories. The front line is the bedrock of our epistemic community and the place where our understanding of and theorizing about violence and VAW have been shaped. Social science research on VAW improved dramatically when it was grounded in the front lines and in women's stories and when the researchers did not shy away from the political implications of their findings. Feminist legal advocacy improved significantly when it was no longer done in isolation but in coalition, informed by data, experiences, and theory from the front lines, and when the advocates did not shy away from the political implications of their arguments. Feminist front-line support and advocacy bring the power, integrity, and promise of the women's movement to each woman's fight when they engage both law and social science research on her behalf and when front-line workers connect her struggle for liberty to that of other women.

Starting at the Front Line

Until the 1970s, VAW hid in plain sight. Even the women's movement had little data or understanding beyond the pain of each woman who experienced rape, wife assault, incest, and/or prostitution. Neither Simone de Beauvoir's 1949 *The Second Sex* (1989) nor Kate Millett's *Sexual Politics* (1968) included VAW in their early articulations of patriarchy. They did not yet know its frequency or function.

The Royal Commission on the Status of Women travelled throughout Canada in the late 1960s, inviting women to express what was holding them back from "equality." Although many women presented personal testimony about sexist violence, not one of the commission's resolutions mentioned VAW (Royal Commission on the Status of Women 1970). The commission did not understand its significance in women's oppression or its connection with their inequality.

But feminists came to know, to understand, to see the significance. In Canada, the second wave of the women's movement sprang from the cracks between histories of a welfare state, the peace activism of anti-nuclear feminists of an earlier generation, and liberal political traditions in Canadian politics. The post-war economic boom meant that money was available for state-funded social development, and the global revolts of baby boomers coming of age compelled the Canadian government to concede some reforms even as the swing to the right was gathering power.

Almost instantaneously in the context of modern feminist gatherings and uprising, North American comprehension of sexist violence broke through the patriarchal obfuscation: consciousness-raising groups in the late 1960s, rape speak-outs in the 1970s, second-wave feminist publications throughout the 1970s, and most importantly, the first North American women's centres, rape crisis centres (Toronto Rape Crisis Centre and Vancouver Rape Relief in 1973), and women's shelters (in Toronto, Woodstock, Vancouver, and Winnipeg in 1974) emerged. By 1976, Diana Russell's organizing of the Vienna International Tribunal of Crimes against Women had added an international perspective and raised the questions within the frame of women's human rights (Russell and Van de Ven 1976). Feminist front-line workers and feminist researchers collected and analyzed data on the rates of VAW and the forms it took. Those data provided the evidence that supported women's claims and their demands for funding and for change.

Theory about violence, borrowed from the New Left and from the American Black civil rights struggles, was reformulated and employed to address the questions: How often does VAW happen? What are the dynamic human relations between men and women? What results in VAW? What is needed to end the violence and to change the relations? But perhaps we might have asked more clearly, What is the force created by the individual acts of male violence? What function does it play? What is the interaction between VAW and the oppression of women as a group? What is the relation between violence against one woman and the subjugation of all women? What is the relationship between VAW and other forces of women's oppression, such as economic forces or social cultural forces? Does sexist violence hold those gendered relations in place? How can we measure? What should we measure? These are all questions about the relationship between VAW and women's inequality and about how we might demonstrate that relationship. Equality is central to this analysis, but as we came to learn, equality is not a simple or straightforward concept.

Substantive Equality

Historically, equality has been equated with sameness, a belief that is still commonly held. Nicholas Mark Smith (2011) argues that when we say that we are all equal, we are asserting a basic level of sameness that all humans share, which requires that everyone be treated with concern and respect. On one level, this is a concrete assertion, but it provides little direction as to what equality actually means or looks like in practice. Smith (2011, 2) posits that there is "an abstract notion of equality, a belief in the equal worth of human beings, about which there is widespread (although sometimes implicit rather than explicit) agreement, and a large range of specific equalities about which there is much disagreement." Thus, as a starting point, we have general agreement on a basic and abstract, but not meaningless, value/principle. Beyond that, we have huge debates over virtually everything to do with equality. Equality is the justification – it provides the terms of the debate or the bottom line, but it does not tell us what to do. We cannot simply assert equality and think we have won the argument – the argument, with respect to a specific inequality, requires "sophisticated moral analysis" (Smith 2011, 10).

Equality advocates have rejected sameness both as a simple answer to the meaning of equality and as an analytic tool. In their view, the sameness that underlies the equality principle, providing the rationale for mutual respect and concern, does not dictate what respect looks like in practice. This treat-people-who-are-the-same-the-same model – now referred to as formal equality – remains the dominant understanding of equality among the general public. However, for those who are committed to an equality that means respect and concern for all, the formal equality model is woefully inadequate.

In trying to escape the limitations of formal equality, feminists were drawn to the idea of equity, as a concept related to equality but not tied into the restricting sameness that haunts it. Equity is a derivative from the word "equality" (a translation of the French word *equité* from a Latin root meaning "even, just, and equal"), and its current definition aligns with fairness and impartiality rather than equality: "the quality of being fair or impartial; fairness; impartiality."[1] Its synonyms include disinterest, equitableness, fair-mindedness, justness, even-handedness, objectivity, justice, and probity. If we adopted equity rather than equality as our basic value, the notions of impartiality, fairness, and particularly objectivity would give rise to new and somewhat different, but no less troublesome, problems of interpretation and application from those attached to the sameness in equality.

"Equity" was brought into common usage as a substitute for "equality" by Justice Rosalie Abella (1984) through her report on employment equity. She introduced the term "employment equity" as a more expansive and flexible, as well as a more palatable, substitute for the much maligned, much misunderstood American term "affirmative action." The hope for equity in this context was to go beyond the limitations of formal equality and to address the underlying systemic inequalities in the employment context (Sheppard 2010). Although we cannot be sure that the shift in terminology reduced resistance to the more concrete and proactive forms of employment equity, the language of employment equity did open up dialogue and legislative possibilities (at least in the short term) that might otherwise have been rejected under blanket resistance to the perceived evil of affirmative action.

Whatever the benefits of invoking equity in the context of employment/ affirmative action, developments in the language of equality have overtaken the need for a full-scale substitution. The Abella Report was released in 1984, two years after equality had been enshrined as a Canadian constitutional value in section 15 of the Charter of Rights and Freedoms but five years before the first Supreme Court of Canada decision on section 15 did for equality what Abella probably could not have done through the medium of a government report.[2] The court interpreted Canada's constitutional equality guarantee as a guarantee of substantive equality, as this approach to equality has since come to be known. Substantive equality starts with the recognition of inequality and its historical context and focuses on implications and result, not treatment. It is a systemic approach to equality. This was a hugely positive and significant step forward in terms of equality rights for marginalized and oppressed peoples in Canada. On the basis of much deep thinking, consultation, analysis, and advocacy, equality advocates argued before the court for a meaning of equality that would be more flexible, contextual, and proactive than the long-standing formal approach defined in terms of likes being treated alike. The court was able to see that employing the dominant group as the standard of measurement and assessing who was close enough to that standard to warrant being treated the same (formal equality) was an approach that would, in many situations, entrench existing inequalities and would further marginalize those who were most different from the dominant group. It was this formal approach to equality that Abella avoided through the adoption of equity and that the Supreme Court explicitly rejected in favour of substantive equality. We no longer need equity as a substitute; we no longer need a substitute; substantive equality provides a solid base.

The movement away from formal equality has taken us into uncertainty and seriously complicated the expectation of being able to recognize and know equality easily. Substantive equality rejects the positivist approach of counting and measuring the similarities that constitute equality as sameness. We are now faced with a much more complex undertaking. The uncertainty now attached to equality has given rise to the perceived need to provide some indication of the meaning of equality in the name itself. In proposing alternatives, such as basic equality, inclusive equality, complex equality, and real equality, authors are responding to the uncertainty that continues to inhere in equality even with the adjective "substantive."[3] Although uncertainty does mean lack of predictability and possible confusion, it is the uncertainty of equality that demands that its proponents engage in sophisticated moral analysis. And sophisticated moral analysis seems like a good thing to demand of ourselves. At the very least, it is not clear that the search for a different/better adjective moves us forward in terms of clarity. Perhaps the goal should be to (re)claim equality simpliciter –

equality alone in all of its complexity and uncertainty – and to engage in the public education project of disaggregating equality and sameness so that equality can stand alone unmodified and unencumbered by sameness. In the interim, we are content to work with "substantive equality," the language endorsed by the Supreme Court of Canada.

The challenge then becomes – or rather remains – how to move this theorizing in the language of substantive equality into public consciousness and how to document the interconnections that the theory requires. A critical mass of feminist lawyers collaborated with front-line women's organizations to intervene in cases to press the courts to use the Charter of Rights and Freedoms to address VAW (CASAC 2004).[4] The prevalence and impacts of VAW needed to be demonstrated time and again in each of these cases; statistics were critical to laying this foundation. We continued to need quantitative data to ground our equality arguments. However, given the restricted word count and language allowed by a legal factum, only a sliver of space was left for these groups to make the more complex argument that VAW is an equality issue inextricably tied to other issues of women's inequality.[5] These kinds of efforts have been piecemeal and truncated; we have not yet developed a substantive equality framework that addresses the interconnectedness of women's inequalities.

Back to the Front Lines

In Canada, front-line workers do not have the necessary resources to provide full documentation of VAW as an equality issue. Front-line feminists intervene as allies to support each woman who calls an anti-violence centre. They record the stories and see connections between parts of each woman's burden and between the stories women tell. Anti-violence centres count incidents and the numbers of women violated in the context of supporting them. It is critical that they do so because women report to feminist centres tens of times more frequently than they report to legal or medical authorities. Front-line workers, using their ground-breaking standpoint, speculated that half of heterosexually partnered women had suffered a blow from a husband or male common-law partner, that upward of one-quarter of girls had endured sexual assaults before adulthood – much of it incest by their fathers – that VAW was so common as to be a normal experience of women, and that to fear attack was to be mindful. The amount of violence staggered those who looked. And it still does. As renowned feminist Beatrix Campbell (2014, 84) states, "Confronting intimate atrocities is treacherous politics; it has to withstand the perpetrators' power, the listeners' flood of fear, awe and disgust. It has to overcome shame, strategic silence and retraction. The effort of telling and listening must be reciprocal;

only if society's secrets become public knowledge can society know itself and change itself."

Activists listen not just to numbers but to stories told of yesterday and of forty years before, stories of women's courage and insight, wisdom and vigour, endurance and resistance. Women in support groups debate the impacts of the institutions of the family, compulsory heterosexuality, religion, and education; whether women's economic insecurity makes them more susceptible to violence; how violence impoverishes women and compounds race and class oppression; whether men are brutal and aggressive by nature; and whether the social creation of masculinity is at all changeable. Survivor stories illustrate the functions of violence. Whereas it was, and is, crucial to start with the stories, the numbers became vitally important – for our understanding, for public education, for policy, and for funding.

One challenge of the 1970s was how to fund the new feminist centres while simultaneously protecting their independent capacity to collect, count, and analyze the information and to organize women to act and advocate. Government and the professions wanted the raw numbers and the referrals, but they were less interested in the stories that generated social and political upheaval. Accusations of bias and threats to funding grew as feminists exposed the normalcy of sexist violence, its strategic significance, and the social and legal impunity with which men committed VAW (DuBois 2012; Johnson 2012).

Divisions widened between political activists and professionals regarding how to think about VAW. Gillian Walker (1990, 31) describes an early Vancouver conflict, a clear example of the divide between activists and professionals that has continued to worsen since Walker wrote about it:

> On the one side, the grounding assumptions named men as doing the beating, questioning the basis of women's oppression in the family and the part played by social institutions in maintaining that oppression. On the other, those who could not accept this analysis wanted to read wife-battering as an indictment of outdated sex roles, traditional attitudes, and inadequate institutional procedures, to be remedied by professional interventions at appropriate levels.

Feminist front-line praxis wove together groupings of victims, women's activism, and VAW organizations. As Norma Jean Profitt (2000) documents, women's self-organized activism was healing. For feminists, liberatory actions and mutual education were elements in revealing sexist violence and diminishing its impact. The interrelationship of sex and gender with other sites of women's oppression – race, class, disability, and sexuality – was woven into feminist analysis and practice. But this intersectional approach made the data collection much more complicated. The complications of feminist analysis were resisted by those whose response to the staggering VAW numbers was simply to "fix" the victims and punish the perpetrators. The medical and legal professions in Canada blunted the transformative possibilities by absorbing women's demands into the status quo, framing them solely as justifications for victim services controlled by the regimes of health care (mostly mental health) and crime control (mostly law and order and piecemeal law reform). A decade of fierce struggle followed over the public naming, understanding, authorizing, categorizing, and consequent responses to VAW (Walker 1990).

In 1989, Marc Lépine killed fourteen women engineering students and an employee at l'École Polytechnique in Montreal, enraged that feminists had interfered with his masculine entitlement. Women took to the streets in every Canadian city to mourn and protest both his acts of VAW and the official response to them. So adamant and numerous were those public incidents of feminism that an all-party subcommittee of parliamentarians called hearings into the "War on Women" (House of Commons Sub-Committee on the Status of Women 1991). Each of the national women's equality advocacy groups that had been granted federal funding during the previous decade presented to the subcommittee the results of its own praxis and theorizing on VAW that led to the recognition that sexist violence was a controlling factor in women's social standing as a group.

Under the same pressure from women in the street, the federal government established the Canadian Panel on Violence against Women, appointing individuals with experience in women's service delivery as its members. Their mandate, budget, and composition – well short of those of a royal commission – limited the possibility of a full and proper inquiry and forestalled the potential for social transformation. In the endless cycle of having to (re)prove the problem, the panel spent much of its report documenting the prevalence of VAW in Canada. Although it failed to contend with the power structures of sex, race, and class in which that violence was lodged, the report did not contradict the assertion of the movement that sexist violence held women down. VAW as the grounding of women's inequality was implicit in the report but was not the analytic frame.

At the annual National Action Committee (NAC) on the Status of Women convention in 1993, the women's movement critiqued the panel for its failures and united behind the anti-violence wing in adopting "99 Federal Steps toward an End to Violence against Women" (Lakeman 1992). Parliament declared December 6 a National Day of Remembrance on Violence against Women but ignored even the least contentious of the recommendations of both the panel and the movement's proposed ninety-nine steps. Canadian governments at all levels degendered and professionalized responses to VAW, under the guise of "mainstreaming" (CASAC 2004). The federal government directed funds to gathering VAW data, with a focus on ascertaining occurrence numbers. In a sense, this one-time infusion of funding into data collection produced critical evidence of the everyday violence that women endure, but media and government interpretations quickly degenerated to counting individual incidents of spousal violence or sexual assault, unencumbered by social context.

In 1991, in the name of a fair trial for the (male) accused, the Supreme Court of Canada struck down the rape shield laws that protected complainants in a sexual assault trial from being cross-examined on their past sexual history.[6] This was the first in a series of sexual assault cases in which feminists battled against liberal notions of formal equality, over the value of the Charter to women (given that it had been invoked against women in these cases), and over how courts judge women who complain of sexual violence (Boyle et al. 2000; CASAC 2004). In the 1994 *O'Connor* case, the Supreme Court held that any records (school, therapy, rape crisis centre) of the complainant in a sexual assault trial could be subpoenaed.[7] In response, rape crisis workers defied the government, the courts, and the defence bar by shredding their files when threatened that the files would be used in court to discredit the women who contacted them (Gotell 2008; Lakeman 2005). At stake was the political relationship between front-line workers and violated women. One consequence of that protracted struggle is that fewer independent centres keep records for fear of having them subpoenaed and misused by the courts. Many stories have been lost, important stories that provide the context for the numbers as well as the connections needed to develop and sustain a substantive equality analysis. Quantitative data continued to be collected but without the detailed information that revealed individual instances of violence and cruelty as examples of the larger problem of systemic inequality.

During the mid-1990s, economic and political changes restructured Canada. The federal government downloaded most of the responsibility for social programs to the provinces, without the parallel downloading of funds to support existing or new social welfare programs and without adopting national protections against growing inequality. This restructuring included the end of the policy of national consultations with civil society as a normal practice, the release of the provinces from their obligations to uphold national standards, and the termination of the Canada Assistance Plan funding. The loss of this funding resulted in cuts to welfare provisions such as transition houses, as well as cuts to welfare rates to individuals and to individual entitlements. Cuts also ended the full funding of Status of Women Canada (SWC). The trickle down from this resulted in cuts to every provincial Status of Women department, which in turn led to cuts to all women's centres across the country (initially federally funded as equality initiatives) and to all national and regional women's groups.

The restructuring of Canada by conservatives to please global market forces trumped our local achievements and equality claims as female citizens. State funding structures disaggregated and discredited feminist front-line knowledge by wrenching "service" to violence victims away from women's aspirations to freedom from sexist violence. Service was the exclusive focus; advocacy was prohibited. Funding streams separated the forms of VAW so as to align with categories and approaches that the professions understood. Medicine continued to pathologize both women victims and violent men. Law continued to dismiss or traumatize women complainants and to provide most men with impunity. Both continued to isolate and individualize the few incidents of violence that they accepted as such, naming each as a distinct crime and a distinct wound but ignoring the context and plague of it. Statistics had helped to expose the issue of VAW, but they had also facilitated its absorption into mainstream services and structures. The VAW numbers were the problem to be addressed – not the culture of inequality that produced and perpetuated them. Caught up in the ongoing process of supplying data to justify their continued existence, service providers became inured to the travesty of having endlessly to prove and reprove the ubiquity of VAW. The legacy of this period of fragmentation and decontextualization remains with us to this day, making attempts to demonstrate the systemic link between violence and inequality that much harder.

The work done before the 1990s was key to how the movement conceived of violence. The 1990s were knife-edge years in which the pan-Canadian women's movement, like its sisters abroad, forced VAW onto the public agenda, but these were also the years in which the movement to establish women's equality and to end VAW was imperilled. Although the approach of the Canadian women's movement to reform initiatives became more sophisticated – it selected those initiatives that were consistent with transformation – the movement's democratic influence on government was all but eliminated (Brodie 2008; Lakeman 2005). Canada cut the remaining vestiges of domestic mechanisms for monitoring and/or promoting women's "equal" citizenship. Ministries charged with improving the status of women at the national and provincial levels collapsed, as did their budgets and programs. The federal government downloaded responsibility for services to the provinces and territories (and sometimes municipalities), abandoning its equality obligations. Funding withdrawals and refusals to consult punished women's groups for their protests and made pan-Canadian organizing largely impossible. Within a few years, the infrastructure of national women's groups was diminished or gone.

Evidence from the Social Sciences

Meanwhile, feminist social scientists worked parallel to, and in partnership with, grassroots women's organizations to document women's lived experiences in ways that researchers hoped would speak truth to decision-makers in a language they would understand and act upon. By bringing a feminist-inspired orientation to the tools of traditional social science research, researchers have been able to incorporate feminist goals into research processes and to transform research tools. They developed new methodologies that were grounded in women's realities, with the result that questions were better worded to describe women's experiences, and protocols prioritized women's safety and reduced and responded to the emotional impacts of telling their stories of violence. These research tools helped challenge not only status quo patriarchal discourse and policy making, but also androcentric research methods and the unexamined assumptions and biases behind them. Feminist social scientists recruited sexually assaulted and abused women and their advocates in the production of knowledge claims; in doing so, they exposed the dominant power structures behind mainstream research tools (Randall and Haskell 1995; Russell 1982). They helped to make visible social and political inequalities in both methods and truth claims about women's lives, in the realms of labour and income, unpaid work and family, poverty, health, and male violence (Harnois 2013).

Naming male VAW, making women's experiences visible and making them count, has been a central and ongoing struggle for feminist researchers (Kelly and Radford 1996). After a rather promising start, these attempts met with fierce resistance. The more challenging task of making visible the function that male violence holds in women's lives and the interconnections to gender inequality has never really had traction.

Following the Montreal massacre, when the federal government focused on the need to know more about male VAW, feminist advocates were invited as an epistemic community to have direct input into the questions, wording, and methodology of the first-ever national survey on violence against women, conducted by Statistics Canada in 1993 (Johnson 1996). Abused and sexually assaulted women were recognized as experts on their own lived realities and as the best possible source of advice on how, in the context of a telephone survey, women could be engaged to talk about these deeply personal violations in ways that would guarantee results that accurately reflected the prevalence, contexts, impacts, outcomes, and decisions they made to resist violence, all the while respecting their right to safety and minimizing the possibility of triggering emotional or other harms.

This survey and its results were a significant step forward in contextualizing VAW as a systemic problem, with roots in broader patriarchal power structures.

It was the first, and one of the very few surveys, to situate women's experiences of sexual and physical assaults within a context of sexual harassment and controlling and emotionally abusive behaviours.[8] This approach was grounded in Liz Kelly's (1988) early work, which theorized a continuum of violence that put social science language around how everyday sexual harassment functions as a reminder to women of their subordinate status – a form of social control that refuses to be named. Men have long used violence as a tool to silence and demean women who dare to transgress boundaries around male privilege. Harassment that limits women's freedom in the public sphere has inevitably found fertile new ground in the online world in the form of vicious verbal attacks and threats and routine misogyny, all in an effort to stifle women's voices and their right to participate in public and political spaces (Filipovic 2007). This hate speech is used to keep patriarchal power structures in place. Even though we can see this social control in operation, it is difficult to document. We do not have sufficiently comprehensive models to enable us to explore how violence upholds women's oppression and inequality or to measure those interconnections. The promising work on developing methods that would capture the interconnections of gendered inequalities was undermined and discredited as the radical implications of the analysis began to emerge. The issue was not about a few, or even a lot of, aberrant men; this was about fundamental social change.

The Statistics Canada VAW survey was the first of its kind to situate male partner violence within a context of coercive control. But this too has largely been lost, as intimate partner violence has been degendered and individualized in the name of "objectivity." Evan Stark (2007) describes coercive control as a form of entrapment in which men are able to draw on societal-level gender inequality to enforce the obedience of female partners in all aspects of their lives – economic, social, freedom of movement, and sexual – thus constraining women's lives without ever having to resort to blows, although the occasional punch entrenches male authority and ensures compliance. Excusing and denying the context for male violence – the male subjugation of women – keeps the focus firmly on individual men as aberrations rather than as enforcers of social and political structures.

Very briefly and sporadically, some individuals in positions of state power saw grassroots feminists as a legitimate epistemic community, with recognized expertise and policy-relevant knowledge, even if not political influence (Brodie 2008). But soon the ground defining legitimacy shifted and it now includes self-identified anti-feminists, such as men's and fathers' rights groups, as well as mainstream professionals who speak from a degendered and individualized framework that is divorced from structural inequalities (Walby 2011). In a reassertion of patriarchal power, groups whose explicit goal is to roll back gender equality gains and who deny that patriarchal power structures have anything to do with violence have gained the ear of governments while grassroots feminists, with their direct experience working alongside abused and sexually assaulted women, are painted as marginal and extreme (Dragiewicz 2008). Before long, the innovative methodology and the shockingly high prevalence rates produced by the 1993 survey that had been proclaimed as ground breaking and essential for policy and political action were derided as irredeemably flawed and dismissed as a threat to the social order (Johnson 2015). Even though this survey provided the impetus for similar work in many countries individually, and collectively through international comparative projects, it has not been repeated in Canada. The focus on women's equality was lost when Canada reverted to a gender-neutral approach. In a recent initiative to measure "gender-based" violence broadly (Cotter and Savage 2019), Statistics Canada invited feminist academic researchers to redesign questions related to intimate partner violence that should prevent the ease with which sexual and physical violence can be disentangled from coercive control (Ford-Gilboe et al. 2016). Acts of male violence that threaten women daily, including sexual harassment, stalking, and misogynistic attacks, have been reinstated in the redesign. Whereas this return to a more comprehensive understanding of intimate partner violence is in line with feminist analysis, it will be undermined by the gender-neutral approach with which it is to be applied. Measurement models that would permit us to link VAW to other sites of women's oppression in a comprehensive way have yet to be developed and tested.

Substantive equality requires a structural, intersectional approach in order to capture and contend with the complex realities of women's experiences. Although all women are possible targets of male violence, some are disproportionately so due to a combination of interrelated disadvantage, exclusion, and multiple devalued social identities based on poverty, race, ethnicity, immigration status, colonization, sexual orientation, and disability (CRIAW 2013; Horvath and Kelly 2007). Relatedly, social science research has shown that policies around child welfare, family law, housing, criminalization of women, employment equity, and social assistance exacerbate women's vulnerability to and the impacts of male violence.

Take social assistance as an example: In Ontario, cuts to social spending resulted in welfare benefits that amounted to roughly one-third of Statistics Canada's low-income cut-off, a conservative poverty measure (Mosher and Evans 2006). Research with sixty-four abused women who had experience with social assistance in Ontario concluded that access to adequate financial resources that is dependent neither on the batterer's co-operation nor labour market participation is critical to the safety of women abused in their intimate relationships. Without such access many abused women and their children remain locked in abusive relationships with no hope of escape, or are forced to trade subjugation to abuse for abject poverty, homelessness, and profound social exclusion. (Mosher and Evans 2006, 162)

And, we would add that adequate financial resources are critical for all women, to avoid being targeted for violence in the first place.

The link between welfare and violence extends to access to housing and to child custody and circles back to violence. Due to shifts in social welfare policy in Alberta, four thousand women were turned away from shelters during an eighteen-month period, more severely injured women showed up at shelters, and women had to relinquish their children to violent partners because the latter could support the children and the women could not (Morrow, Hankivsky, and Varcoe 2004). The maximum government-funded stay in most shelters for abused women is three or four weeks, and across Canada, a lack of safe and affordable housing and second-stage housing for women who are leaving emergency shelters renders them vulnerable to losing children to child protection authorities or to violent partners (Tutty et al. 2009). Violence therefore increases vulnerability to homelessness, and homelessness increases the risk of staying with or returning to a violent partner (Novac 2006). Policies that prioritize abused women for social housing can backfire: in most instances, they must apply for housing within three months of leaving an abusing partner, which penalizes those who flee to friends or relatives, moving among short-term stays (Novac 2006).

Child protection services have the authority to apprehend children from women who do not have adequate housing, thereby punishing them for their poverty. Furthermore, child protection policies increase risk and danger to women and children when they hold women accountable for failing to protect children from witnessing their father's violence (Strega and Janzen 2013). Legislation is gender-neutral (citing the responsibilities of "parents"), but the implementation of the law is biased against women. Holding the "non-offending" parent responsible for protecting children assumes that women have easy access to resources and that these resources will stop the violence (Strega and Janzen 2013). The power and control of abusive men are extended to the state when women are unable to live independently and care for and maintain custody of their children. The state essentially violates its own zero-tolerance policy on domestic violence when abused women are penalized by welfare policies that restrict their choices (Mosher et al. 2004). Lack of freedom for women is held in place by male violence and by social policies that continue in a circular dance, each reinforcing the other. Women who are further marginalized by race, ethnicity, class, and/or sexuality continue to be additionally constrained and restrained by this policy/violence dance that in effect increases their marginalization and their vulnerability to male violence.

Conclusion

In the 1960s, a new "wave" of women came forward to give and to receive help in dealing with men who battered and raped girls and women. By the 1970s, violated women were coming forward in hundreds, then thousands. The women's movement in Canada responded by inventing anti-rape centres and transition houses, by incorporating demands for social, political, and economic interventions in feminist national lobbying plans, and by theorizing about the nature of VAW, oppression, and patriarchy. Each of these actions influenced the others. The direct actions of housing and assisting abused individual women provided new information for lobbying strategies and for theory. Feminist theory also shaped the standards of services, insisting that even the best feminist services are only a part of the necessary attack on patriarchy. We are now in need of new global theory, new global strategies, and renewed Canadian anti-violence institutions guided by an equality analysis and an autonomous movement. We are in need of a comprehensive substantive equality analysis of inequality.

Equality advocates clearly understand VAW as an issue that is rooted in inequality. At the basic level, the argument is simple and clear: women are disproportionately the victims of domestic violence and sexual assaults, and men are disproportionately the perpetrators.[9] Measurement and statistics have supported this claim since 1993. But a substantive equality analysis requires more. It requires us to look at the issue systemically, contextually, and intersectionally; to make connections with other aspects of women's inequality; to look cross-culturally and cross-nationally. It requires us to take into account that unequal employment and pay, unequal housing, unequal parenting, and unequal access to the rule of law endanger women and advantage men. It also requires us to look at how the lack of a job or income or adequate housing leaves women with no choice but to live with a dangerous man, and how women's positions in race, class, and gender hierarchies leave them open to discrimination and unable to call on the rule of law.

We need data to help us see and understand connections, but the data we need are not necessarily the same as those required by funders or kept by other sources. Authorities record interpersonal crimes and injuries and document professional responses. But those data are individualized and degendered. Even the data collected by feminist researchers are susceptible to what anthropologists

Sally Engle Merry and Susan Bibler Coutin (2014, 8) call "the paradox of quantification." As they explain,

> focusing on a specific and ranked set of acts makes measurement easier and comparison more possible. It usefully reveals the extent of violent acts. However, by relying on the list of acts, the objective comparison loses critical information on the experience and perspective of the person herself. It is a proxy for the experience of violence. It effaces the very phenomenon these measures seek to expose: the extent to which women's everyday lives and experiences are affected by the possibility and practice of violence. This is the paradox of quantification.

We in Canada are caught in this paradox. The constraints imposed by limited government funding and by the government and institutional focus on counting the numbers of specific acts of VAW have rendered invisible the quotidian and systemic nature of the violence and its role in inducing and supporting other forms of women's inequality. We have copious data that document the extent of violent acts against women. But, despite their appalling size, these numbers depict only an individualized and partial picture of VAW. This "proxy for the experience of violence" has led to individualized and partial responses. The numbers cannot stand alone; they need to be embedded in their social and political context. Front-line VAW workers possess the missing critical information, plus the knowledge and expertise to provide the full picture. Researchers need to develop methods that will better capture that information, that will capture the full experience of the violence and its impacts on women's lives and women's (in)equality. In the absence of this information, we are incapable of developing meaningful or effective anti-VAW policy.

No professional or intellectual discipline other than feminism retains a commitment to ending VAW or to establishing women's equality as integral to its definition as a discipline. There is no category and no combination of categories in any discipline that aggregates these incidents of violence as the force we call violence against women. Front-line activists have documented those incidents and their contexts in story form; social science research has measured and analyzed amounts of violence and moments of inequality; feminist legal scholars and lawyers have used those data to develop equality-based arguments and have advocated for women's freedom from violence using an equality analysis. However, at present no method allows us to link incidents of VAW (rape, incest, wife battering, sexual harassment, and the violence of prostitution) to the overall repression of women's lives.

This chapter emanates from our desire to bring this interconnectivity to the forefront and to at least begin the conversation about how we can demonstrate the interconnections of women's wide-ranging inequalities and the central role of VAW in creating and maintaining these inequalities. VAW is more than the number of incidents, more than the statistics, horrifying as they may be. What we have learned is that VAW is a dynamic and pervasive social force that affects the lives of all women. The challenge for us as feminist anti-VAW activists and researchers is how to use the data, both current and future, to demonstrate the function of VAW, not only as a force whose power derives from women's oppression, but also as a force that holds women's oppression in place.

Acknowledgments

We thank Liz McIntyre and Sarmatha Sathianathan for their contributions in preparing this chapter. This research was supported by the Social Sciences and Humanities Research Council of Canada through the Community First: Impacts of Community Engagement Project.

Notes

1 https://www.dictionary.com/browse/equity.
2 *Andrews v Law Society of British Columbia*, [1989] 1 SCR 143.
3 The term "basic equality," adopted by Smith, was taken from Jeremy Waldron "to refer to the abstract belief in human worth" (Smith 2011, 2). Colleen Sheppard (2010) coined the term "inclusive equality" to include a substantive, procedural, and relational approach to the inequalities we experience. Karin Van Merle (2008, 141) explores Henk Botha's notion of "complex equality" that takes account of the interrelatedness between equality and many other values – for example, democracy and social justice – in order to reach a better understanding of the "moral, political and material dimensions of equality."
4 The lawyers were active in the Women's Legal Education and Action Fund (LEAF) and in the National Association of Women and the Law. The women's organizations included the Canadian Association of Sexual Assault Centres, Disabled Women's Network (DAWN/RAFH), and the Native Women's Association of Canada.
5 LEAF's website (https://www.leaf.ca/) provides case summaries and facta for the cases in which it has intervened.
6 *R v Seaboyer; R v Gayme*, [1991] 2 SCR 577.
7 *R v O'Connor*, [1995] 4 SCR 411.
8 The recent European Union twenty-eight-country survey is an exception, as it is the first survey since 1993 to include sexual harassment (FRA 2014).
9 There are exceptions: some women are perpetrators of intimate and sexual violence and some men are victims. However, this fact does not negate the gendered nature of intimate and sexual violence or mean that it is not an equality issue. See *Janzen v Platy Enterprises*, [1989] 1 SCR 1252.

Works Cited

Abella, Rosalie Silberman. 1984. *Report of the Commission on Equality in Employment*. Ottawa: Government of Canada.
Beauvoir, Simone de. 1989. *The Second Sex*. New York: Vintage Books.
Boyle, Christine, Lee Lakeman, Sheila McIntyre, and Elizabeth Sheehy. 2000. "Tracking and Resisting Backlash against Equality Gains in Sexual Offence Law." *Canadian Woman Studies* 20: 72–83.

Brodie, Janine. 2008. "We Are All Equal Now: Contemporary Gender Politics in Canada." *Feminist Theory* 9, 2: 145–64. https://doi.org/10.1177/1464700108090408.

Campbell, Beatrix. 2014. *End of Equality.* London: Seagull Books.

CASAC (Canadian Association of Sexual Assault Centres). 2004. *Canada's Promises to Keep: The Charter and Violence against Women.* Vancouver: CASAC.

Cotter, Adam, and Laura Savage. 2019. "Gender-Based Violence and Unwanted Sexual Behaviour in Canada, 2018: Initial Findings from the Survey of Safety in Public and Private Spaces." Juristat, December 5. https://www150.statcan.gc.ca/n1/en/pub/85-002-x/2019001/article/00017-eng.pdf?st=Ik54uj6z.

Coy, Maddy, Liz Kelly, and Holly Dustin. 2015. "A Feminist 'Epistemic Community' Re-shaping Public Policy: A Case Study of the End Violence against Women Coalition." In *Critical Issues on Violence against Women: International Perspectives and Promising Strategies,* ed. Holly Johnson, Bonnie S. Fisher, and Véronique Jaquier, 244–55. Oxford: Routledge.

CRIAW (Canadian Research Institute for the Advancement of Women). 2013. "Factsheet: Violence against Women in Canada." Accessed April 9, 2014. http://criawicref.ca/sites/criaw/files/VAW_ENG_long_final_0.pdf.

Dragiewicz, Molly. 2008. "Patriarchy Reasserted: Fathers' Rights and Anti-VAWA Activism." *Feminist Criminology* 3, 2: 121–44. https://doi.org/10.1177/1557085108316731.

DuBois, Teresa. 2012. "Complaints of Police Investigation of Sexual Assault: How Far Have We Come since Jane Doe?" In *Sexual Assault in Canada: Law, Legal Practice, and Women's Activism,* ed. Elizabeth Sheehy, 195–214. Ottawa: University of Ottawa Press.

Filipovic, Jill. 2007. "Blogging While Female: How Internet Misogyny Parallels 'Real-World' Harassment." *Yale Journal of Law and Feminism* 19: 295–303.

Ford-Gilboe, Marilyn, C. Nadine Wathen, Colleen Varcoe, Harriet L. MacMillan, Kelly Scott-Storey, Tara Mantler, Kelsey Hegarty, and Nancy Perrin. 2016. "Development of a Brief Measure of Intimate Partner Violence Experiences: The Composite Abuse Scale (Revised) – Short Form (CASR-SF)." *BMJ Open* 6, 12. https://bmjopen.bmj.com/content/6/12/e012824.

FRA (European Union Agency for Fundamental Rights). 2014. *Violence against Women: An EU-Wide Survey.* Luxembourg: Publications Office of the European Union.

Gotell, Lise. 2008. "Tracking Decisions on Access to Sexual Assault Complainants' Confidential Records: The Continued Permeability of Subsections 278.1–278.9 of the *Criminal Code*." *Canadian Journal of Women and the Law* 20, 1: 111–54.

Harnois, Catherine E. 2013. *Feminist Measures in Survey Research.* Los Angeles: Sage.

Horvath, Miranda, and Liz Kelly. 2007. *From the Outset: Why Violence Should Be a Priority for the Commission for Equality and Human Rights.* London: End Violence against Women.

House of Commons Sub-Committee on the Status of Women. 1991. *The War against Women.* Ottawa: Government of Canada.

Htun, Mala, and S. Laurel Weldon. 2012. "The Civic Origins of Progressive Policy Change: Combating Violence against Women in Global Perspective, 1975–2005." *American Political Science Review* 106, 3: 548–69. https://doi.org/10.1017/S0003055412000226.

Johnson, Holly. 1996. *Dangerous Domains: Violence against Women in Canada.* Toronto: Nelson Canada.

–. 2012. "Limits of a Criminal Justice Response: Trends in Police and Court Processing of Sexual Assault." In *Sexual Assault in Canada: Law, Legal Practice and Women's Activism,* ed. Elizabeth Sheehy, 613–34. Ottawa: University of Ottawa Press.

–. 2015. "Degendering Violence." *Social Politics* 22, 3: 390–410. https://academic.oup.com/sp/article-abstract/22/3/390/1623093.

Kelly, Liz. 1988. *Surviving Sexual Violence.* Cambridge: Polity Press.

Kelly, Liz, and Jill Radford. 1996. "Nothing Really Happened: The Invalidation of Women's Experiences of Sexual Violence." In *Women, Violence and Male Power: Feminist Activism, Research and Practice,* ed. Marianne Hester, Liz Kelly, and Jill Radford, 19–33. Buckingham: Open University Press.

Kimmel, Michael S. 2002. "'Gender Symmetry' in Domestic Violence: A Substantive and Methodological Research Review." *Violence against Women* 8, 11: 1332–63. https://doi.org/10.1177/107780102237407.

Lakeman, Lee. 1992. "Women, Violence and the *Montréal Massacre.*" In *Twist and Shout: A Decade of Feminist Writing in This Magazine,* ed. Susan Crean, 92–101. Toronto: Second Story.

–. 2005. *Obsession, with Intent: Violence against Women.* Montreal: Black Rose Books.

Merry, Sally Engle, and Susan Bibler Coutin. 2014. "Technologies of Truth in the Anthropology of Conflict." *American Ethnologist* 41, 1: 1–16. https://doi.org/10.1111/amet.12055.

Millett, Kate. 1968. *Sexual Politics.* Boston: New England Free Press.

Morrow, Marina, Olena Hankivsky, and Colleen Varcoe. 2004. "Women and Violence: The Effects of Dismantling the Welfare State." *Critical Social Policy* 24, 3: 358–84. https://doi.org/10.1177/0261018304044364.

Mosher, Janet, and Pat Evans. 2006. "Welfare Policy: A Critical Site of Struggle for Women's Safety." *Canadian Woman Studies* 25, 1–2: 162–66.

Mosher, Janet, Pat Evans, Margaret Little, Eileen Morrow, Jo-Anne Boulding, and Nancy VanderPlaats. 2004. *Walking on Eggshells: Abused Women's Experiences of Ontario's Welfare System.* Toronto: Woman and Abuse Welfare Research Project.

Novac, Sylvia. 2006. *Family Violence and Homelessness: A Review of the Literature.* Ottawa: National Clearinghouse on Family Violence, Public Health Agency of Canada.

Profitt, Norma Jean. 2000. "Survivors of Woman Abuse: Compassionate Fires Inspire Collective Action for Social Change." *Journal of Progressive Human Services* 11, 2: 77–102. https://doi.org/10.1300/J059v11n02_05.

Randall, Melanie, and Lori Haskell. 1995. "Sexual Violence in Women's Lives: Findings from the Women's Safety Project, a Community-Based Survey." *Violence against Women* 1, 1: 6–31. https://doi.org/10.1177/1077801295001001002.

Royal Commission on the Status of Women. 1970. *Report of the Royal Commission on the Status of Women in Canada.* Ottawa: Government of Canada.

Russell, Diana E. 1982. "The Prevalence and Incidence of Forcible Rape and Attempted Rape of Females." *Victimology: An International Journal* 7, 1–4: 81–93.

Russell, Diana E., and Nicole Van de Ven. 1976. *Crimes against Women: Proceedings of the International Tribunal.* Berkeley: Russell.

Sheppard, Colleen. 2010. *Inclusive Equality: The Relational Dimensions of Systemic Discrimination in Canada.* Montreal and Kingston: McGill-Queen's University Press.

Smith, Nicholas Mark. 2011. *Basic Equality and Discrimination: Reconciling Theory and Law.* Farnham: Ashgate.

Stark, Evan. 2007. *Coercive Control: The Entrapment of Women in Personal Life.* New York: Oxford University Press.

Strega, Susan, and Caitlin Janzen. 2013. "Asking the Impossible of Mothers: Child Protection Systems and Intimate Partner Violence." In *Failure to Protect: Moving beyond Gendered Responses,* ed. Susan Strega, Julia Krane, Simon Lapierre, Cathy Richardson, and Rosemary Carlton, 49–76. Winnipeg: Fernwood.

Tutty, Leslie M., et al. 2009. *"I Built My House of Hope": Best Practices to Safely House Abused and Homeless Women*. Calgary: Resolve Alberta.

Van Merle, Karin. 2008. "Haunting (In)Equalities." In *Rethinking Equality Projects in Law: Feminist Challenges*, ed. Rosemary Hunter, 125–46. Oxford: Hart.

Walby, Sylvia. 2011. *The Future of Feminism*. Cambridge: Polity Press.

Walker, Gillian. 1990. *Family Violence and the Women's Movement: The Conceptual Politics of Struggle*. Toronto: University of Toronto Press.

8

Measuring Violence against Women: A Multi-Scalar Portrait of Recent Developments, Practices, and Issues

Maggie FitzGerald

INDICATORS ARE "STATISTICAL measures that are used to consolidate complex data into a simple number or rank that is meaningful to policy makers and the public" (Merry 2011, S86). Although they provide a simplified measure to grapple with complex data, the processes of creating and implementing indicators are riddled with challenges, particularly when it comes to social phenomena. This chapter aims to analyze some of these challenges through a case study of the ways in which violence against women (VAW) is quantified and measured at various scales. How do differing approaches to measuring VAW come to define and constitute what is understood as VAW? Who is involved in the development of these surveys, indicators, and measurements? Which organizations use these measurements? At what scale does the indicator operate? And what are the limitations of these measurements?

Measurement and the Challenge of Vernacularization

A few definitional points are merited here. Whereas measurement can be an important tool that can shape political agendas and draw attention to a variety of gender equality issues (Walby 2005), as the chapters in this volume reveal (see in particular Chapters 1, 3, 4, and 9), "measurement is never an innocent act" (Buss 2015, 381; see also Mohr and Ghaziani 2014, 237). Measurement, instead, is complicated by the fact that it is both technical and political, as Linda Briskin points out in Chapter 9 of this volume. The technical aspects of measurement – for example, the mechanisms through which data are collected and made available, and the logistics of attempting to organize disparate data from different contexts in a way that renders them comparable – are rarely straightforward. They involve complex social processes through which determinations are made about what counts and what does not. These determinations, of course, are political, as are their outcomes. In the pursuit of measurement, "categories of people and behaviour are created to enable counting, comparison, and ranking to take place, affecting how problems are defined and emerge as worthy of attention" (Buss 2015, 381). As will become evident below, the political nature of measurement can give rise to numerous specific issues, including generative governance effects, such as when indicators change the behaviours they are meant to measure (Espeland and Sauder 2012, 86; see also Introduction to this volume). A failure to capture intersectional experiences can also occur, as decisions are made to render data commensurable.

Of vital importance for what follows is the challenge of vernacularization. To make data comparable across contexts, measurement devices like indicators must be able to travel across geographies and move across scales. However, as Peggy Levitt and colleagues (2013) point out, this travelling is rarely straight-forward; instead, it involves complicated processes of translation through which meaning is created by connecting global ideas to the local (see also Zwingel 2013, 115). Specifically, Levitt et al. (2013) call this process "vernacularization." In reviewing the differing ways that VAW is measured internationally, region-ally, and supranationally, as well as at various scales in the Canadian context, this chapter, first and foremost, highlights the problem of vernacularization. As global ideas enter into differing locales and operate in and across different scales, they are refashioned; "there is a mismatch between the way [VAW] is understood in the vernacular and the kinds of measurements that take place at [a variety of] levels" (Merry 2016, 110–11; see also Merry and Coutin 2014). Yet, when indicators are presented abstracted from context, these "mismatches" across scales are obfuscated. This multi-scalar portrait of VAW indicators thus seeks to foreground the consequences of vernacularization and to illustrate how the process of indicator translation can lead to additional measurement issues related to commensurability and decontextualization, which ultimately impede the capture of VAW in all its myriad forms.

Measuring VAW Internationally

At the international level, the measurement of VAW is most visible in the variety of indicators developed by the United Nations (UN). A relatively recent phe-nomenon, the push to develop indicators related to VAW was a response to national and transnational feminist activism in the 1980s and 1990s that defined VAW as a human rights violation (Merry 2016, 46) and that understood it as perhaps the most prevalent and tolerated form of gender inequality (Shaw 2006). More precisely, this activism led to the gradual recognition of VAW as a human rights issue by various branches of the UN system, particularly by the Committee on the Elimination of Discrimination against Women. The committee monitors progress for women in the countries that are parties to the 1979 Convention on the Elimination of Discrimination against Women (Committee on the

Elimination of Discrimination against Women 2009). The central means of monitoring this progress is through national reports submitted by the parties within one year of ratifying or acceding to the convention and every four years thereafter. The committee is also a key player in identifying any issues affecting women, notably through its general recommendations.

In 1989, the committee identified VAW as an important issue (general recommendation 12), and in 1992, it adopted general recommendation 19, which, among other things, "requires national reports to the Committee to include statistical data on the incidence of VAW" (Committee on the Elimination of Discrimination against Women 2009).[1] This call to enhance the collection of quantitative data on VAW has since been echoed by the UN General Assembly on several occasions, and it has led to other questions: What is the best way to collect these data? What should be measured? What methodologies should be employed? How can we ensure that the results are comparable across contexts and time? With the exception of the "WHO Multi-Country Study on Women's Health and Domestic Violence against Women" (Garcia-Moreno et al. 2005), few studies used "standardized methodologies in a diverse set of countries in order to arrive at comparable statistics" (UN Statistics Division 2014, 3). In 2006, the UN secretary-general's study on all forms of VAW (UN 2006) noted these concerns and recommended that the UN "undertake to support the development of unified methods and standards for data collection, provide technical support to countries and build capacity of national statistical offices, and promote existing methods and good practices to ensure that the principles of sound data collection are met" (UN Statistics Division 2014, 3).

UN Guidelines for Producing Statistics on VAW

In 2014, to address this task of developing unified methods and standards for data collection on VAW, the UN Statistics Division released a report titled "Guidelines for Producing Statistics on Violence against Women" (henceforth called "Guidelines"). It was a detailed methodological guide "to assist countries in assessing the scope, prevalence and incidence of violence against women" (UN Statistics Division 2014, iii). The Friends of the Chair of the Statistical Commission on indicators on VAW had been established in the previous year to assist with the development of the report; this group produced a list of core indicators for which data should be collected and presented it in a report (UN 2010).

The definition of VAW used in "Guidelines" and the indicators proposed by the Friends of the Chair rely on the language used in the UN Declaration on the Elimination of Violence against Women, which describes VAW as "any act of gender-based violence that results in, or is likely to result in, physical, sexual or psychological harm or suffering to women, including threats of such acts, coercion or arbitrary deprivation of liberty, whether occurring in public or in private life" (UN 1993, art. 1). "Guidelines" supplements this definition with the one employed by the Beijing Platform for Action (UN 1996, 44, paras. 113–15), specifying that

> acts of violence against women include violation of the human rights of women in situations of armed conflict, such as systematic rape, sexual slavery and forced pregnancy, as well as forced sterilization, coercive/forced use of contraceptives, female infanticide and prenatal sex selection. The definition also encompasses acts of violence unique to specific contexts, such as dowry-related violence and female genital mutilation. (UN Statistics Division 2014, 11)

The core indicators used in "Guidelines" (UN Statistics Division 2014, 15) are as follows:

i   Total and age specific rate of women subjected to physical violence in the last 12 months by severity of violence, relationship to the perpetrator and frequency

ii   Total and age specific rate of women subjected to physical violence during lifetime by severity of violence, relationship to the perpetrator and frequency

iii   Total and age specific rate of women subjected to sexual violence in the last 12 months by severity of violence, relationship to the perpetrator and frequency

iv   Total and age specific rate of women subjected to sexual violence during lifetime by severity of violence, relationship to the perpetrator and frequency

v   Total and age specific rate of ever-partnered women subjected to sexual and/ or physical violence by current or former intimate partner in the last 12 months by frequency

vi   Total and age specific rate of ever-partnered women subjected to sexual and/ or physical violence by current or former intimate partner during lifetime by frequency

vii   Total and age specific rate of women subjected to psychological violence in the past 12 months by the intimate partner

viii   Total and age specific rate of women subjected to economic violence in the past 12 months by the intimate partner

ix   Total and age specific rate of women subjected to female genital mutilation.

Both the definition of VAW and the core indicators employed in "Guidelines" raise concerns. First, though the definition is quite broad, it is poorly translated to the indicators. For instance, the focus of these indicators is on interpersonal

VAW, which means that broader systemic forms of VAW, such as state violence by the military and police, are not captured (Merry 2016, 62). The indicators also erase the contextual specificity of interpersonal VAW, such as the interplay of love and fear (Merry 2016, 62). As a result, the list of indicators, in practice, defines VAW "much more narrowly than the global women's movement does" (Merry 2016, 62).

This narrowing of what counts as VAW is a direct consequence of commensuration. Wendy Espeland and Michael Sauder (2012, 91) explain that "commensuration is a process fundamental to measurement that entails turning qualities into quantities that share the same metric." This process can be difficult; for example, even if it were possible to count the incidences of female genital mutilation (extremely unlikely, given the underground nature of the practice), translating the fears and psychological damages that accompany it into quantities would be far more complicated. As a result, aspects and qualities of VAW are reduced or erased through commensuration processes.

Commensuration also poses a distinct challenge, given that indicators – most notably at the international scale – are meant to provide a means to compare phenomena across contexts. On the one hand, indicators (and the data behind them) must be collected and constructed in such a way that they can travel across contexts to allow for comparison. At the same time, as noted above, indicators must be able to translate to different locales in order to travel across contexts, which involves complex processes of vernacularization. For example, when the Bangladesh Bureau of Statistics (2013) conducted a survey on VAW, it used the UN Statistics Division standard questionnaire so that the results could be compared internationally. However, using the questionnaire posed a major challenge, as researchers needed to customize and translate it to fit the socio-economic and cultural contexts of Bangladesh; words such as "dowry," "rape," and "violence" were avoided (Hossen 2014, 8) because they were sensitive in the Bangladeshi context.

A second drawback of the "Guidelines" definition of VAW is that it does not discuss the axes of difference that shape women's lives – and their experiences of violence. Race, sexuality, disability, class, and gender identity are not analyzed explicitly, yet they are known to influence and indeed constitute experiences – including experiences of violence – in unique and varying ways (Lépinard 2014; McCall 2005). In other words, the indicators do not use an intersectional lens to assess the rates of VAW; except for providing measurements according to age groupings, they do not assess VAW in relation to other identity markers such as race, sexuality, ethnicity, disability, and class. This omission erases significant aspects of VAW, including the fact that differing axes of power are co-constitutive of VAW and thus cannot be separated out from these experiences.

Such erasures point to a broader concern: when it is too hard to categorize and measure a phenomenon (or simply when phenomena are not measured due to political processes that deem them unworthy of measurement), certain problems are rendered invisible. As Sally Merry and Susan Coutin (2014, 12) write, "Experiences that cannot be made commensurable or that cannot be documented cannot be measured. In effect, such experiences are disappeared from the analysis." This disappearing is not without consequence. Most obviously, an accurate picture of VAW is not captured, given that certain experiences are rendered invisible. Equally significant, however, are the ways in which these omissions may operate through the generative effects of indicators and measurement, whereby measurement devices come to frame and mobilize particular understandings of the phenomena being measured. In this case, the definitions of VAW and the related core indicators employed by "Guidelines" act as important framing devices (van Eerdewijk and Roggeband 2014, 59) that shape understandings of and discussions around VAW more generally (especially for countries that are obliged to report on VAW).

The UN Secretary-General's Database

In 2006, the UN General Assembly adopted resolution 61/143, calling upon the UN system and member states to intensify efforts to eliminate VAW. Paragraph 19 of this resolution requested that the UN secretary-general establish a database that included data from the member states on all forms of VAW; this call was echoed in subsequent resolutions, and countries were also urged to supply the data required for this database. In February 2008, the secretary-general launched his campaign to end VAW, which was to continue until 2015 to coincide with the target deadline for the millennium development goals (UN Women 2012).[2] As a part of this campaign, the UN secretary-general's database was developed and launched in 2009 (UN Women 2016b). A press release for the launch explained that a central benefit of the database was to "encourage exchange on initiatives and ideas, and the transfer of promising practices" related to eliminating VAW (UN 2009).

In 2016, in accordance with the adoption of the 2030 Agenda for Sustainable Development, the database was updated, redesigned, and relaunched as the Global Database on Violence against Women (UN Women 2016b). One of the UN's sustainable development goals (SDGs) is to "achieve gender equality and empower all women and girls." A sub-goal of this is to "eliminate all forms of violence against all women and girls in the public and private spheres, including trafficking and sexual and other types of exploitation" (UN General Assembly 2015, 18). Two indicators will be used in relation to this sub-goal:

a Proportion of ever-partnered women and girls aged 15 years and older subjected to physical, sexual or psychological violence by a current or former intimate partner, in the last 12 months, by form of violence and by age group and;

b Proportion of women and girls aged 15 years and older subjected to sexual
violence by persons other than an intimate partner, in the last 12 months, by
age group and place of occurrence. (UN Statistical Commission 2016, 21)

These two indicators are similar to the three main indicators included in the
secretary-general's database, which are discussed below.

The main source of data for this database consisted of responses by countries
to a questionnaire on VAW issued by the UN in 2012 (UN Women 2012).
Employing the UN definition of VAW, the questionnaire asked member states
to identify and describe (in a hundred words or less) institutional, legal, legislative frameworks and other mechanisms that had been implemented to address
VAW (UN Women 2012). States were strongly encouraged to provide this information, but the database does not monitor the effectiveness of these infrastructures. The questionnaire and the database are managed by the Ending VAW
section of UN Women (UN Women 2012).

The database is supplemented by data on the prevalence of VAW from reports
by various UN human rights bodies (UN Women 2016a). Based on these data
sets, three indicators were provided for each country: physical and/or sexual
violence from an intimate partner during the last twelve months; lifetime
physical and/or sexual violence from an intimate partner; and lifetime sexual
violence from a non-partner (UN Women 2016a). Significantly, however, these
indicators are not necessarily equivalent across countries. For example, in
Armenia the second indicator is the proportion of ever-partnered women aged
fifteen to fifty-nine who have experienced intimate partner physical and/or
sexual violence at least once in their lives. For Australia, the same indicator is
the proportion of women aged over eighteen who have experienced intimate
partner physical and/or sexual violence at least once in their lifetime (UN
Women 2016b). These two indicators thus measure different things; nonetheless, they are called by the same name and are rendered comparable by the
database.

The database illustrates another dimension of indicators: "the governing effects of measurement regimes" (Buss 2015, 382). Judith Kelley and Beth
Simmons (2015, 57) explain the concept of reactivity as "the tendency for people
to change their behaviour in response to being evaluated." On a larger scale,
reactivity can be used to effect discipline by defining "what is appropriate,
normal, and to what we should aspire" (Espeland and Stevens 2008, 414). By

distilling VAW into three main indicators and providing an easy means to compare countries, this database serves as a disciplining tool. Countries are easily comparable and can be ranked according to whether they are complying with the UN SDGs. It is also interesting to note that one does not even need to look at the actual values of the indicators to draw comparisons across countries. An interactive map on the home page reports how many indicators are available for each country (many countries report more than the three indicators above). In a world where indicators are highly valued, this creates the appearance that countries with more available data are doing more to address VAW than those with less data.

By prioritizing rankings, this database and its indicators serve as a way to govern the behaviour of countries. To improve their rankings, governments may adapt their policies and behaviours to comply with the UN SDGs, adjust their reporting practices, or both. Although this can effect real changes that reduce the prevalence of VAW, it may also simply produce better numbers without dealing with the substantive issue. For instance, collecting more data, though valuable in some sense, does not necessarily correspond to any improvement in terms of addressing VAW. Furthermore, the governing function of indicators is important to keep in mind so as to foreground the reality that they are not, and cannot be, objective measurement tools. Rather, the governance effect of measurement (Merry 2011, S84) – demonstrated by databases like this – emphasizes how certain successful indicators become influential, change the very behaviours they purport to measure (Espeland and Sauder 2012, 86), and are therefore a power-laden tool, as opposed to a neutral, objective, and apolitical measurement device.[3]

Supranational and Regional Measurement of VAW

The measurement of VAW at the supranational level is best exemplified through a variety of measurement initiatives in Europe. In 2011, the Convention on Preventing and Combating Violence against Women and Domestic Violence was adopted in Istanbul by the Council of Europe Committee of Ministers (Bonewit 2016). Known as the Istanbul Convention, it defines and criminalizes both VAW and domestic violence and calls for all member states to collect disaggregated statistical data at regular intervals on all forms of VAW (Council of Europe 2011, 10, art. 11).

The Istanbul Convention is legally binding and has been ratified by twenty-two member states of the Council of Europe (Council of Europe 2016a). To demonstrate their progress, member states must submit reports to the council. These reports are based on an open-ended questionnaire sent to the parties to the convention;[4] the first completed report, covering the years 2014–15, was released in September 2016 (Council of Europe 2016b). It requires parties to provide quantitative and qualitative data on a variety of issues related to VAW, with a special focus on measures taken to combat it. As outlined in the questionnaire, VAW includes psychological violence, stalking, physical and sexual violence, rape, forced marriage, female genital mutilation, forced abortion, forced sterilization, sexual harassment, and domestic VAW, which is defined as physical, sexual, psychological, or economic violence that occurs in a domestic unit, regardless of whether the perpetrator lives with the victim (Council of Europe 2016c).

These reporting requirements will probably change the landscape of measuring VAW. Not only are countries legally required to strengthen their capacity to collect data for reporting, but the ways in which they collect, quantify, organize, and present data will become an important site for monitoring their progress in meeting their treaty obligations. An early response prior to the Istanbul Convention was a European Union survey, which was conducted in 2008, six years before the convention came into force. It responded to a call for data on VAW made by an ad-hoc committee to the convention.

Violence against Women: A European Union Survey

In 2008, the Council of Europe released the "Final Activity Report" of the Task Force to Combat Violence against Women, Including Domestic Violence.[5] The report noted the absence of comprehensive data on VAW and called for all member states "to systematically collect and analyse all types of data on violence against women, producing indicators that can support decision-making and intervention and monitor and evaluate the implementation of policies and measures" (Council of Europe 2008, 84, recommendation 5.3.5.). In response to this call, the European Union Agency for Fundamental Rights undertook a European Union (EU)–wide survey on VAW and released the results in a 2014 report titled "Violence against Women: An EU-Wide Survey" (FRA 2014).[6] The report was based on interviews with forty-two thousand women across the twenty-eight EU member states (FRA 2014, 3). They provided both quantitative and qualitative data on the prevalence and consequences of physical and sexual violence, psychological partner violence, stalking, sexual harassment, violence in childhood, fear of victimization, and attitudes and awareness of VAW (FRA 2014, 5–6). The survey was developed with the help of experts from a variety of bodies, including the World Health Organization, the European Institute for Crime Prevention and Control, Eurostat, European Institute for Gender Equality, and the UN Office for Drugs and Crime.

It included common indicators, such as prevalence rates of various types of physical and sexual violence, as well as some less common indicators. For instance, it gave statistics related to the emotional impacts of VAW, including the percentage of women who had worried about possible assault by strangers or partners during the last year and the percentage of women who had avoided certain situations and places (such as being alone with a colleague, leaving the house, or going home) for fear of physical or sexual assault (FRA 2014, 139, 144). These indicators are valuable in that they allowed women to judge and express the severity of their experiences of VAW. Instead of statisticians determining, for instance, that the number of physical abuses reflected the severity of VAW, women who had experienced violence could articulate how it had affected their lives. Of course, percentages alone cannot fully reflect such impacts, and emotional effects are not easily translated into quantities; in fact, attempts to quantify emotions may only serve to trivialize and diminish the complexities of experiences of violence. By including these aspects of VAW in the report, however, the survey furnished a more robust picture of the multi-faceted ways that VAW manifests and influences the lives of women.

It also provided indicators related to specific groups of women, based on sexual orientation, disability, health, and migrant backgrounds. For example, the indicators dealt with the prevalence of various forms of violence according to women's self-declared sexual orientation (heterosexual/straight, lesbian, bisexual, or other), their assessment of their disability and health (no disability or health concerns versus some disability or health concerns), and their assessment of their migrant background (citizen or non-citizen and length of time in the country of residence) (FRA 2014, 184–90). Although the indicators still isolated each variable (for instance, they did not calculate the prevalence of VAW for women who identified as bisexual and migrant), they moved toward better capturing the complexities of VAW and its intersections with axes of difference, as opposed to measuring VAW for women as a homogenized group.

The European Union Agency for Fundamental Rights intends to make the data sets from this survey available for public use via the internet. The aim is "to provide policy makers with the robust and comparable data they need to shape informed, targeted policies" to combat VAW (FRA 2016). The survey is unique in attempting to capture the prevalence of VAW in a harmonized and comparable way across all EU member states (European Institute for Gender Equality 2015, 119), and the European Institute for Gender Equality has used data from the report to calculate a sub-domain of its Gender Equality Index. The European Parliament also cited the data in its recent report on VAW (Bonewit 2016). The ways in which these data have been used by third parties demonstrate how measurements and indicators can travel, circulating, framing, and (re)producing knowledge in a variety of spaces and contexts.

Global and Regional Estimates of Violence against Women

A final example of an initiative to measure VAW at a regional level is the report "Global and Regional Estimates of Violence against Women" (Garcia-Moreno et al. 2013), developed by the World Health Organization, the London School of Hygiene and Tropical Medicine, and the South African Medical Research Council. The report focuses exclusively on measuring interpersonal VAW, understood as physical and/or sexual intimate partner violence and non-partner sexual violence, as well as the health effects of such violence. The authors write that

> physical violence is defined as: being slapped or having something thrown at you that could hurt you, being pushed or shoved, being hit with a fist or something else that could hurt, being kicked, dragged or beaten up, being choked or burnt on purpose, and/or being threatened with, or actually, having a gun, knife or other weapon used on you. Sexual violence is defined as: being physically forced to have sexual intercourse when you did not want to, having sexual intercourse because you were afraid of what your partner might do, and/or being forced to do something sexual that you found humiliating or degrading. (Garcia-Moreno et al. 2013, 4–5)

On the basis of this focus, the report produces three main indicators: global and regional prevalence estimates of intimate partner violence; global and regional prevalence of non-partner sexual violence; and combined estimates of the prevalence of intimate partner violence and non-partner violence (Garcia-Moreno et al. 2013, 16–20). In comparison to the EU-wide survey, which includes emotional violence, this report generally focuses on physical manifestations of violence (although its definition of sexual violence does include feelings of fear and humiliation).

A point of interest regarding this study is that it did not collect primary data. Rather, it compiled its data from previous studies published between 1998 and 2010, as well as from data sets (Garcia-Moreno et al. 2013, 11). One potential issue with this approach is that the studies may have used different methodologies and definitions of VAW to gather their data. For instance, the report notes that "estimates based on *any author's definition* of sexual violence were included" (Garcia-Moreno et al. 2013, 12, emphasis added). The problem here is that vernacular definitions of sexual violence may produce disparate responses. As a result, data from different surveys may not be completely reconcilable, and attempting to do so may result in distortions of the data. Perhaps more importantly, this methodology of creating indicators based on existing data exemplifies what Merry (2016, 7) calls "data inertia." This occurs when existing data determine what an indicator can measure; "the way categories are created and measured often depends on what data are available" (Merry 2016, 7). By relying on already existing data, Garcia-Moreno et al. (2013) reproduce – and, as noted above, may even distort – the categories, measurements, and findings put forth by pre-existing studies on VAW.

Measuring VAW Nationally: The Canadian Case

In the early 1990s, Statistics Canada developed and implemented the first large-scale national survey of intimate partner VAW (Johnson 2015, 395). Since then, Statistics Canada has remained a leader in measuring VAW. Its most recent report, "Measuring Violence against Women" (Sinha 2013),[7] is the third contribution of the Federal-Provincial-Territorial Status of Women Forum and Statistics Canada toward measuring VAW. The first two were "Assessing Violence against Women" (Statistics Canada 2002) and "Measuring Violence against Women" (Statistics Canada 2006).

Although the 2013 report followed the broad definition of VAW provided by the UN (1993), the types of violence that it examined "are largely limited to those acts that reach the criminal threshold" (Sinha 2013, 4). This is mainly because it relied heavily on police-reported surveys, which use Criminal Code definitions of VAW, for its data. This again illustrates that though measurement processes and techniques can and do travel across scales, they often cannot be directly transposed onto a given context, either due to data availability, culturally specific meanings, or other contextual factors.

A well-known drawback of depending on police-reported surveys is that certain crimes, such as sexual assaults, commonly do not come to the attention of police (Sinha 2013, 12). As a result, the 2013 report used self-reported data from the General Social Survey on victimization as its second source of data. This source complemented the police-reported survey data, as self-reporting often includes incidents of victimization that are unreported and under-reported to the police, as well as information about other types of abuse (such as financial or emotional), the consequences of VAW, and the use of social services (Sinha 2013, 5).

The indicators produced by the report mainly measured the prevalence and severity of VAW, although descriptive analysis of risk factors associated with VAW, statistics related to its impact, and responses to it were discussed. The report demonstrated that quantitative and qualitative data could be used together to provide a robust picture of VAW. For instance, it noted that for every 100,000 women, 1,207 had been subjected to violence, only slightly higher than the rate for men (1,151 victims per 100,000 men). However, it supplemented this statistic with information about the types of violence that women were more likely than men to experience, such as sexual assault, stalking, and criminal harassment (Sinha 2013, 11).

The report also provided a (partially) intersectional analysis of VAW. For instance, it noted that "where possible, data are disaggregated by geographic and population groupings to provide a sense of the diversity of women's experiences of victimization. These can include variations by region, age, Aboriginal identity, and sexual orientation" (Sinha 2013, 6).

Measuring VAW for Specific Groups and Local Contexts

Smaller, more localized studies of VAW are difficult to find, particularly when it comes to studies that develop indicators. This is due to a couple of factors. For one, conducting data collection and surveys is expensive and time consuming – small organizations and research projects are often unable to gather the data necessary to produce indicators. Second, new indicators are continually being generated, creating a competitive ecology in which certain indicators become successful, widely accepted, and used, "while the vast majority of indicators search in vain for global interest and influence" (Merry 2016, 16). Even when alternative indicators exist, they are often difficult to disseminate widely. Finally, indicators that are "consistent with dominant understandings" (Johnson 2015, 393) of the phenomena being measured, or that create rankings that "conform to widely accepted views of good and bad performance among countries" (Merry 2016, 17), often have the greatest credibility. In consequence, indicators that challenge dominant understandings are often less likely to gain currency and to circulate.

For example, Douglas Brownridge conducted a study, published in the academic journal *Violence against Women* in 2006, that reported some indicators related to the prevalence of violence against women with disabilities in Canada. Brownridge (2006, 817) found that during the five years preceding the data collection, women with disabilities reported 1.4 times the rate of violence than women without disabilities. In addition, they were especially vulnerable to severe acts of violence by their partners. Brownridge noted that "male partners of women with disabilities were about 2.5 times more likely to behave in a patriarchal dominating manner and about 1.5 times more likely to engage in sexually proprietary behaviours than were male partners of women without disabilities" (818). However, this situation often goes undetected by investigators, as the prevailing assumption is that women with disabilities are celibate and thus cannot experience violence from an intimate partner (817). In other words, dominant misconceptions limit what is studied and measured.

Missing and Murdered Indigenous Women: A National Overview

One study that has gained much attention in Canada and that focuses on a particular group of women is the Royal Canadian Mounted Police report "Missing and Murdered Aboriginal Women: A National Operational Overview" (RCMP 2014), which was followed up by "Missing and Murdered Aboriginal Women: 2015 Update to the National Operational Overview" (RCMP 2015).[8] Notably this report, and related investigations on the crisis of missing and murdered Indigenous women in Canada, is the result of much political lobbying and activism by Indigenous women and their allies (Native Women's Association of Canada 2010).

The 2014 RCMP report compiled data from "law enforcement holdings from across all police jurisdictions in Canada" (RCMP 2014, 6) to develop rates that measured both murdered and missing women. It found that, from 2001 to 2014, the average homicide rate for Aboriginal women was six times higher than for female homicide victims who were not Aboriginal (Miladinovic and Mulligan 2015). Furthermore, Aboriginal females made up about 11.3 percent of missing females in Canada and represented roughly 16.0 percent of all female homicide victims; this is far greater than their representation in Canada's female population (RCMP 2014, 8–9).[9] The report provided measures of the types of violence to which Indigenous women were subjected. For example, 32 percent of female Aboriginal homicide victims died as a result of a beating, a cause of death reported almost twice as often for them as for their non-Aboriginal counterparts (RCMP 2014, 10). The data were also broken down into geographic categories, indicating that Aboriginal female victims were overrepresented in the Prairie provinces and the territories (Miladinovic and Mulligan 2015).

The report noted that collecting information about origin and identity, and thus determining whether a person was Indigenous, posed a significant challenge to measuring the violence. Policies aimed at protecting the privacy of victims had resulted in under-reporting of Aboriginal identity (Miladinovic and Mulligan 2015). Further, asking police to make judgments about ethnicity and identity is problematic, and can lead to situations whereby people are assigned an identity that they themselves do not claim (RCMP 2014, 21). Lastly, the report noted that "differences in police practice between agencies make it hard to create a data set that is comparable across jurisdictions" (RCMP 2014, 21). Thus, though "the policing community has amended their policies which prevented the reporting of Aboriginal identity of victims and person[s] accused" (Miladinovic and Mulligan 2015), significant problems remain in categorizing people based on identity. If a person is unable or unwilling to identify as Indigenous, the determination of this identity is left to the judgment of police.

This may skew subsequent measurements based on identity, especially given the ways in which racism shapes perceptions of Indigeneity and the fact that systemic racism exists in Canadian police forces (McNeilly 2018). The 2015 update to the report, for instance, noted that "eight cases [of missing Indigenous women] were captured in the updated data set as a result of file reviews of these historical cases. The reasons for the lack of inclusion in the 2014 Overview are attributable to *Aboriginal origin not originally captured,* files not previously reported or files not current on [the Canadian Police Information Centre]" (RCMP 2015, 12, emphasis added).

West Coast Legal Education and Action Fund Gender Equality Report Card

As a final example of measuring VAW in a localized context, the West Coast chapter of the Women's Legal Education and Action Fund (LEAF) produced the "BC Gender Equality Report Card" (2020), which assessed the British Columbia government's progress in six issue areas affecting the rights of women and people who face gender discrimination. One issue area was "freedom from gender based violence." In its report for 2019–20, the chapter awarded the government a D+ grade for its performance in addressing gender-based violence (in its grading scale, A+ was the highest score and F was a fail). Its assessment explicitly highlighted the government's failure to fund services for survivors of violence, to budget dedicated funds for acting on the Calls for Justice of the National Inquiry into Missing and Murdered Indigenous Women and Girls, and to adopt the rights-based framework for responding to sexual assault that community groups have been calling for (LEAF, West Coast chapter, 2020, 6).

This type of measurement is clearly distinct from the indicators reviewed above. It did not seek to capture the prevalence of VAW in an indicator that could be used for comparative purposes (and notably, it used a broader understanding of gender-based violence, as opposed to VAW). Instead, the report card employed an indicator (in the form of a letter grade) to assess the government's response to gender-based violence. In so doing, it offered, I suggest, an alternative way to mobilize measurement toward gender equality ends. Though measurement will (perhaps unavoidably) involve issues of commensurability, decontextualization, and vernacularization, it may be worth considering how developing more tools to assess and measure responses to VAW/gender-based violence – in contrast to incidences and prevalence of VAW – could prove fruitful for holding those in power accountable as we work toward gender equality. As the authors of Chapter 7 in this volume argue, there is potential for data and measurement to tell a larger story about VAW.

Conclusion

Measuring VAW is an important task; it helps make aspects of VAW visible and provides a means to compare, contrast, and discuss the extent of this phenomenon around the world. In so doing, indicators and other measurement devices can have positive impacts, as they raise awareness about the extent of the issue and can be used to help inform policies directed at preventing and addressing VAW in a variety of contexts. However, as this overview demonstrates, processes of vernacularization often result in a plethora of ways to approach the measurement of VAW and the subsequent development of indicators, especially across various scales. Each of these methodologies has varying strengths and weaknesses, and involves different issues and challenges, including problems related to commensurability, decontextualization, and governance effects. Given these concerns, it is imperative that we strive continually "to understand the strengths and the limitations of quantitative knowledge and to compare and assess different indicators" (Merry 2016, 26). Commitment to this type of ongoing critical reflection on quantitative knowledge will create space both to improve our measuring techniques and to illuminate what is missing and obscured when we rely solely on indicators as a means to understand and address important social issues such as VAW. In other words, we must foreground the techniques and processes involved in acts of counting and calculation, and the ways in which they operate at different scales, so that we can analyze and begin to understand more fully the consequences of measurement (Merry and Coutin 2014).

Acknowledgments

I wish to thank the Social Sciences and Humanities Research Council for funding that facilitated this research and Rob Currie-Wood and Diana Majury for helpful comments on an earlier version of the chapter.

Notes

1 Although limitations of space preclude a full discussion of the topic, it is again important to highlight that the inclusion of VAW on the UN agenda was largely the result of transnational feminist activism (Merry 2016; Moghadam 2015).
2 The campaign to end VAW appears to be linked to the development goals, but none of them are actually related to VAW. Goal 3 is to "promote gender equality and empower women," but the specific target is to eliminate gender disparity in primary and secondary education, and the indicators used to measure progress related to this target are the ratio of girls to boys in all levels of education; ratio of literate women to literate men; share of women in wage employment in the non-agricultural sector; and proportion of seats held by women in national parliaments (Millennium Project 2006).
3 In addition to the UN's various efforts to develop VAW indicators, numerous gender inequality indices also circulate at the international level, including the UN's Gender Inequality Index (GII), the Organisation for Economic Co-operation and Development's Social Institutions and Gender Index (SIGI), the World Economic Forum's Global Gender

Gap Index (GGI), and Social Watch's Gender Equity Index (GEI). Some, such as the SIGI, include measurements of VAW; others do not (the GII, GGI, and the GEI). Although a strong argument can be made that the inclusion of various measurements of VAW is important when attempting to capture a portrait of gender inequality more generally, gender inequality indices that do measure VAW combine these measurements with other sub-indices to create a single all-encompassing indicator representing gender inequality more broadly. As a result, I do not discuss them in detail here; instead, I focus specifically on indicators, surveys, and reports that are solely dedicated to the measurement of VAW at various scales.

4 The Council of Europe refers to this as a questionnaire, but it is more akin to a guideline, as it simply lists the various topics on which countries should report.

5 The task force was established as a part of the Istanbul Convention.

6 To my knowledge, as of December 2022 this was the most recent European Union survey of VAW.

7 To my knowledge, as of December 2022 this was the most recent Statistics Canada report measuring VAW.

8 The political movement to address the epidemic of missing and murdered Indigenous women in Canada originally referred to missing and murdered Aboriginal women. I follow suit in most of this discussion to reflect the wording in the two RCMP reports analyzed here, though I sometimes use "Indigenous" in accordance with current norms.

9 For instance, Aboriginal females made up only 4.3 percent of the Canadian population in 2011 (RCMP 2014, 7).

Works Cited

Bangladesh Bureau of Statistics. 2013. "Report on Violence against Women (VAW) Survey 2011." Accessed July 30, 2016. http://203.112.218.66/WebTestApplication/userfiles/Image/Latest%20Statistics%20Release/VAW_Survey_2011.pdf.

Bonewit, Anne. 2016. *The Issue of Violence against Women in the European Union.* Brussels: European Parliament. http://www.europarl.europa.eu/RegData/etudes/STUD/2016/556931/IPOL_STU(2016)556931_EN.pdf.

Brownridge, Douglas A. 2006. "Partner Violence against Women with Disabilities: Prevalence, Risk, and Explanations." *Violence against Women* 12, 9: 805–22. https://doi.org/10.1177/1077801206292681.

Buss, Doris. 2015. "Measurement Imperatives and Gender Politics: An Introduction." *Social Politics* 22, 3: 381–89. https://doi.org/10.1093/sp/jxv030.

Committee on the Elimination of Discrimination against Women. 2009. "Committee on the Elimination of Discrimination against Women." UN Women. Accessed August 19, 2016. http://www.un.org/womenw/atch/daw/cedaw/committee.htm.

Council of Europe. 2008. *Final Activity Report: Task Force to Combat Violence against Women, Including Domestic Violence.* Strasbourg: Council of Europe. https://www.coe.int/t/dg2/equality/domesticviolencecampaign/Source/Final_Activity_Report.pdf.

–. 2011. *Council of Europe Convention on Preventing and Combating Violence against Women and Domestic Violence.* Strasbourg: Council of Europe. https://rm.coe.int/CoERMPublicCommonSearchServices/DisplayDCTMContent?documentId=090000168046031c.

–. 2016a. "Chart of Signatures and Ratifications of Treaty 210." Accessed August 23, 2016. http://www.coe.int/en/web/conventions/full-list/-/conventions/treaty/210/signatures.

–. 2016b. "Evaluations." http://www.coe.int/en/web/istanbul-convention/evaluation.

–. 2016c. "Questionnaire on Legislative and Other Measures Giving Effect to the Provisions of the Council of Europe Convention on Preventing and Combating Violence against Women and Domestic Violence." Strasbourg: Group of Experts on Action against Violence against Women and Domestic Violence. https://rm.coe.int/CoERMPublicCommon SearchServices/DisplayDCTMContent?documentId=09000016805c95b0.

Espeland, Wendy Nelson, and Michael Sauder. 2012. "The Dynamism of Indicators." In *Governance by Indicators: Global Power through Quantification and Rankings,* ed. Kevin E. Davis, Angelina Fisher, Benedict Kingsbury, and Sally Engle Merry, 86–109. Oxford: Oxford University Press.

Espeland, Wendy Nelson, and Mitchell L. Stevens. 2008. "A Sociology of Quantification." *European Journal of Sociology* 49, 3: 401–36. https://doi.org/10.1017/S0003975609000150.

European Institute for Gender Equality. 2015. *Gender Equality Index 2015.* Vilnius, Lithuania: European Institute for Gender Equality. http://eige.europa.eu/sites/default/files/documents/mh0215616enn.pdf.

FRA (European Union Agency for Fundamental Rights). 2014. "Violence against Women: An EU-Wide Survey." Accessed August 3, 2016. http://fra.europa.eu/sites/default/files/fra-2014-vaw-survey-main-results-apr14_en.pdf.

–. 2016. "Equality and Non-discrimination." http://fra.europa.eu/en/theme/gender.

Garcia-Moreno, Claudia, Henrica A.F.M. Jansen, Charlotte Watts, Mary Ellsberg, and Lori Heise. 2005. *WHO Multi-Country Study on Women's Health and Domestic Violence against Women.* Geneva: WHO. https://apps.who.int/iris/handle/10665/43309.

Garcia-Moreno, Claudia, Christina Pallitto, Karen Devries, Heidi Stöckl, Charlotte Watts, and Naeemah Abrahams. 2013. *Global and Regional Estimates of Violence against Women: Prevalence and Health Effects of Intimate Partner Violence and Non-Partner Sexual Violence.* Geneva: WHO. http://apps.who.int/iris/bitstream/10665/85239/1/9789241564625_eng.pdf.

Hossen, Alamgir. 2014. *Measuring Gender-Based Violence: Results of the Violence against Women (VAW) Survey in Bangladesh.* Dhaka: Bangladesh Bureau of Statistics. http://unstats.un.org/unsd/gender/Mexico_Nov2014/Session%203%20Bangladesh%20paper.pdf.

Johnson, Holly. 2015. "Degendering Violence." *Social Politics* 22, 3: 390–410. https://doi.org/10.1093/sp/jxv021.

Kelley, Judith G., and Beth A. Simmons. 2015. "Politics by Number: Indicators as Social Pressure in International Relations." *American Journal of Political Science* 59, 1: 55–70. https://doi.org/10.1111/ajps.12119.

LEAF, West Coast chapter. 2020. *BC Gender Equality Report Card 2019/2020.* Vancouver: West Coast LEAF. http://www.westcoastleaf.org/work/bc-gender-equality-report-card-2019-2020/.

Lépinard, Éléonore. 2014. "Doing Intersectionality: Repertoires of Feminist Practices in France and Canada." *Gender and Society* 28, 6: 877–903. https://doi.org/10.1177/0891243214542430.

Levitt, Peggy, Sally Engle Merry, Rosa Alayza, and Mercedes Crisostomo Meza. 2013. "Doing Vernacularization: The Encounter between Global and Local Ideas of Women's Rights in Peru." In *Feminist Strategies in International Governance,* ed. Gulay Caglar, Elisabeth Prugl, and Susanne Zwingel, 127–43. New York: Routledge.

McCall, Leslie. 2005. "The Complexity of Intersectionality." *Signs* 30, 3: 1771–800. https://doi.org/10.1086/426800.

McNeilly, Gerry. 2018. *Broken Trust: Indigenous People and the Thunder Bay Police Service.* Toronto: Office of the Independent Police Review Director. http://oiprd.on.ca/wp-content/uploads/OIPRD-BrokenTrust-Final-Accessible-E.pdf.

Merry, Sally Engle. 2011. "Measuring the World: Indicators, Human Rights, and Global Governance." *Current Anthropology* 52, suppl. 3: S83–S95.

–. 2016. *The Seductions of Quantification: Measuring Human Rights, Gender Violence, and Sex Trafficking.* Chicago: University of Chicago Press.

Merry, Sally Engle, and Susan Bibler Coutin. 2014. "Technologies of Truth in the Anthropology of Conflict." *American Ethnologist* 41, 1: 1–16. https://doi.org/10.1111/amet.12055.

Miladinovic, Zoran, and Leah Mulligan. 2015. "Homicide in Canada, 2014." Statistics Canada. Accessed August 2, 2016. http://www.statcan.gc.ca/pub/85-002-x/2015001/article/14244-eng.htm#a13.

Millennium Project. 2006. "Goals, Targets and Indicators." UN Secretary-General and UN Development Group. Accessed August 21, 2016. http://www.unmillenniumproject.org/goals/gti.htm#goal1.

Moghadam, Valentine M. 2015. "Transnational Feminist Activism and Movement Building." In *The Oxford Handbook of Transnational Feminist Movements,* ed. Rawwida Baksh and Wendy Harcourt, 53–81. Oxford: Oxford University Press.

Mohr, John, and Amin Ghaziani. 2014. "Problems and Prospects of Measurement in the Study of Culture." *Theoretical Sociology* 43: 225–46.

Native Women's Association of Canada (NWAC). 2010. *What Their Stories Tell Us: Research Findings from the Sisters in Spirit Initiative.* Ottawa: NWAC. https://nwac.ca/wp-content/uploads/2015/07/2010-What-Their-Stories-Tell-Us-Research-Findings-SIS-Initiative.pdf.

RCMP (Royal Canadian Mounted Police). 2014. *Missing and Murdered Aboriginal Women: A National Operational Overview.* Ottawa: Government of Canada. https://www.rcmp-grc.gc.ca/en/missing-and-murdered-aboriginal-women-national-operational-overview.

–. 2015. *Missing and Murdered Aboriginal Women: 2015 Update to the National Operational Overview.* Ottawa: Government of Canada. https://www.rcmp-grc.gc.ca/en/missing-and-murdered-aboriginal-women-2015-update-national-operational-overview.

Shaw, D. 2006. "Women's Right to Health and the Millennium Development Goals: Promoting Partnerships to Improve Access." *International Journal of Gynecology and Obstetrics* 94, 3: 207–15. https://doi.org/10.1016/j.ijgo.2006.04.029.

Sinha, Maire, ed. 2013. *Measuring Violence against Women: Statistical Trends.* Ottawa: Canadian Centre for Justice Statistics, Statistics Canada. http://www.statcan.gc.ca/pub/85-002-x/2013001/article/11766-eng.pdf.

Statistics Canada. 2002. *Assessing Violence against Women: A Statistical Profile.* Ottawa: Statistics Canada. https://www2.gnb.ca/content/dam/gnb/Departments/eco-bce/WEB-EDF/Violence/PDF/en/Statusofwomen.pdf.

–. 2006. *Measuring Violence against Women: Statistical Trends 2006.* Ottawa: Statistics Canada. http://www.statcan.gc.ca/pub/85-570-x/85-570-x2006001-eng.pdf.

UN (United Nations). 1993. "Declaration on the Elimination of Violence against Women." United Nations General Assembly. https://www.ohchr.org/en/instruments-mechanisms/instruments/declaration-elimination-violence-against-women.

–. 1996. *Report of the Fourth World Conference on Women: Beijing, September 4–15, 1995.* New York: United Nations. http://www.un.org/womenwatch/daw/beijing/pdf/Beijing%20full%20report%20E.pdf.

–. 2006. *Ending Violence against Women: From Words to Action.* New York: Study of the Secretary-General, UN. http://www.un.org/womenwatch/daw/public/VAW_Study/VAWstudyE.pdf.

–. 2009. "Deputy Secretary-General Launches Database on Violence against Women, Hailing It as First Global 'One-Stop Shop' for Information on Measures by Member States."

Press release, March 5. Accessed August 22, 2016. http://www.un.org/press/en/2009/dsgsm446.doc.htm.

–. 2010. *Report on the Meeting of the Friends of the Chair of the United Nations Statistical Commission on Statistical Indicators on Violence against Women.* New York: United Nations Statistics Division. http://www.un.org/womenwatch/daw/vaw/IssuesFocus/Report-of-the-Meeting-of-the-Friends-of-the-Chair-February-2010.pdf?Open&DS =E/CN.3/2009/13&Lang=E.

UN General Assembly. 2015. Resolution adopted by the General Assembly on 25 September 2015 Resolution 70/1. Accessed August 22, 2016. http://www.un.org/ga/search/view_doc.asp?symbol=A/RES/70/1&Lang=E.

UN Statistical Commission. 2016. *Report of the Inter-Agency and Expert Group on Sustainable Development Goal Indicators.* New York: UN Economic and Social Council. https://digitallibrary.un.org/record/821651?ln=en#record-files-collapse-header.

UN Statistics Division. 2014. *Guidelines for Producing Statistics on Violence against Women.* New York: United Nations Economic and Social Affairs. http://unstats.un.org/unsd/gender/docs/Guidelines_Statistics_VAW.pdf.

UN Women. 2012. "United Nations Secretary-General's Coordinated Database on Violence against Women: Questionnaire to Member States." https://www.un.org/womenwatch/daw/vaw/v-q-member.htm#quest.

–. 2016a. "About." Accessed August 14, 2016. http://evaw-global-database.unwomen.org/en/about.

–. 2016b. "Global Database on Violence against Women." http://www.evaw-global-database.unwomen.org/en.

van Eerdewijk, Anouka, and Conny Roggeband. 2014. "Gender Equality Norm Diffusion and Actor Constellations: A First Exploration." In *Gender Equality Norms in Regional Governance: Transnational Dynamics in Europe, South America and Southern Africa,* ed. Anna van der Vleuten, Anouka van Eerdewijk, and Conny Roggeband, 42–65. New York: Palgrave Macmillan.

Walby, Sylvia. 2005. "Measuring Women's Equality in a Global Era." *International Journal of Social Science* 57, 184: 371–87.

Zwingel, Susanne. 2013. "Translating International Women's Rights Norms: CEDAW in Context." In *Feminist Strategies in International Governance,* ed. Gulay Caglar, Elisabeth Prugl, and Susanne Zwingel, 111–26. New York: Routledge.

9

Gender Equality Measurement, Collective Agency, and Trade Unions: A Way Forward

Linda Briskin

MEASURING AND MONITORING gender and women's equality through a variety of quantitative indices are seen by Plantenga and Remery to "promote equal opportunities, increase gender awareness and induce countries to take specific actions" (2013, 50). In recent years, recognition of the importance of gender data has increased. At the launch of the UN Women Count Data Hub in 2019, Anita Bhatia said, "In the drive to get better gender equality outcomes, and to really push for women's empowerment, we need gender data."[1]

This chapter provides an extensive but not exhaustive overview of gender equality indices. Two key concerns emerge: first, the conflation of measures of gender equality and assessments of women's rights and status; and second, the focus on *individual* empowerment used in almost all international indices, the indicator for which is frequently political representation. The chapter proposes an alternative frame of *collective agency* as a measurable dimension that shifts attention from those institutions that reproduce gender inequality to those that promote gender equality.

The second part of this chapter argues that trade unions are a key institutional vehicle for women's collective agency and voice. Union membership increases women's income and reduces the gender pay gap, a central dimension in all gender equality indices. It also improves the quality and conditions of working life. Union membership, then, helps progress women's status, supports gender equality, and offers a valuable measure of women's collective agency.

Gender Equality Indices

Three essential questions provide reference points for an overview of the indices that measure women's equality: How is gender equality understood? What dimensions are seen as relevant? And what indicators operationalize or measure them? Appendix 9.1 charts the indices and highlights historical shifts regarding which dimensions are considered relevant. It includes the Gender Inequality

Index (GII) and others from the United Nations Development Programme (UNDP), the Gender Equity Index (GEI) from Social Watch, the Global Gender Gap Index (GGI) from the World Economic Forum (WEF), the Gender Status Index (GSI) from the Economic Commission for Africa, the European Gender Equality Index from the European Institute for Gender Equality, the Social Institutions and Gender Index (SIGI) from the Organisation for Economic Co-operation and Development (OECD), the Cingranelli-Richards Human Rights Dataset (CIRI), the Environment and Gender Index from the International Union for the Conservation of Nature, the Gender Results Framework (GRF) from Canada, and the Sustainable Development Goals Index from Equal Measures 2030.

Gender equality is typically understood in terms of outcomes, with reference to "levels of achievement between women and men on a given gender indicator" (EIGE 2013, 13). The most common way of measuring it is via gender gaps. For example, the World Economic Forum (WEF 2020, 45) explains that its Global Gender Gap Index,

> is designed to measure gender-based gaps in access to resources and opportunities in countries, rather than the actual levels of the available resources and opportunities in those countries. We do this to disassociate the Global Gender Gap Index from countries' levels of development. In other words, the index is constructed to rank countries on their gender gaps not on their development level.

The measurement of gender equality independent of levels of development is common to many such indices. Also common is that "no distinction is made as to the direction of this gap ... The target is the equality point ... whether a gap is to the advantage of women or men" (EIGE 2013, 13). So, for example, a situation in which men outperform women will be rated in the same way as one in which women outperform men. As a result, the frame of gender gaps is often agnostic on what constitutes well-being. Social Watch (2012b), which prepares the Gender Equity Index, comments:

> Social Watch measures the gap between women and men, not their well-being. Thus, a country in which young men and women have equal access to the university receives a value of 100 on this particular indicator ... A country in which boys and girls are equally barred from completing primary education would also be awarded a value of 100. This does not mean that the quality of education in both cases is the same. It just establishes that, in both cases girls are not less educated than boys.

Social Watch (2012b) rightly points out that, with such an approach, "the lack of equity cannot be justified by a lack of resources ... Regardless of income levels, each country can reduce gender disparity through adequate policies ... Equality in the structure of opportunities in a society is a goal that must and can be pursued regardless of economic power."

UN: Gender-Sensitive Measures of Well-Being and Human Development

Several indices from the United Nations Development Programme do attempt to assess well-being and human capabilities. For example, the Human Development Index (HDI), introduced in 1990, measured whether people lead a long and healthy life (longevity), are educated and knowledgeable, and enjoy a decent standard of living. The HDI did not originally address gender differences. However, in 1995, the UNDP's Gender-Related Development Index was added and considered the same dimensions adjusted for gender inequalities. It tracked "overall human development and included a penalty for gender gaps in human development – that is, a gender-sensitive measure of human development" (Klasen and Schüler 2011, 3). Given the dimensions used in the Human Development Index, the GDI was not a direct measure of gender inequality.

UN: Measures of Gender Inequality

Also in 1995, the UN introduced the Gender Empowerment Measure (GEM). Unlike the GDI, which measured gender-related human development, GEM measured women's relative empowerment. Although it also adopted the penalty approach, the GEM highlighted dimensions significant for women's equality: political participation and decision-making power, economic participation and decision-making power, and power over economic resources.

In 2010, the UNDP replaced the GEM with the Gender Inequality Index. Unlike the GEM, which was available for only 75 countries, it covers 137 countries. It also uses somewhat different dimensions: reproductive health, empowerment, and labour market participation. As with the GDI and the GEM, the GII captures the loss of achievement in key dimensions due to gender inequality. In 2021, the UNDP reported that the world average score on the GII was almost 47 percent, reflecting a percentage loss in achievement across the three dimensions due to gender inequality.[2]

Canada: Measures of Gender Equality

Introduced in 2018 by the Canadian government, the Gender Results Framework highlights six key areas where change is required to advance gender equality: education and skills development; economic participation and prosperity;

leadership and democratic participation; gender-based violence and access to justice; poverty reduction, health, and well-being; and gender equality around the world.[3] Each measure includes objectives, indicators, and available data, and government initiatives to address the issue. The Leadership and Democratic Participation section of the GRF offers data on women in senior management, women entrepreneurs, women holding seats on company boards, women in elected office and ministerial positions, women in the justice system as law enforcement, security, and intelligence officers, and judges.[4]

Statistics Canada also launched a statistics hub on gender, diversity, and inclusion, which tracks, in part, Canada's progress on the GRF indicators.[5] The government claims that whenever possible, and in time, the indicators will include intersecting identity factors such as disability, gender identity, sexual orientation, Indigenous identity, immigrant status, and visible minority status.[6] Statistics Canada periodically publishes "Women in Canada: A Gender-Based Statistical Report," with the latest version appearing in 2018.[7] The report employs gender gap methodology, although some intersectional data on First Nations, Inuit, and Métis women, immigrant women, and visible minority women are included.

Canada is represented in the international indices described above. For example, the GEI of Social Watch computes a value for the gender gap in each of the three areas (education, economic activity, and empowerment) using a scale from 0 (when, for example, no women are educated and all men are) to 100 (perfect equality). In 2012, Canada had an overall rating of 0.80, with 1 for education, 0.83 for economic activity, and 0.57 for empowerment (Social Watch 2012a). Canada's GII ranking dropped from thirteenth in 2020 to fifteenth in 2021, with a score of .069.[8] On the Global Gender Gap Index 2023 from the World Economic Forum, Canada ranked thirtieth, with a score of .770. This involved a rank change of –5.[9]

Limits of Gender Gap Measures

Gender gap measurement has obvious value. However, it is not unproblematic for assessing and exploring women's equality and empowerment. First, although both common sense and previous research point to a closing of gender gaps, evidence suggests that using a comparison of women and men as a measure of equality is increasingly questionable. Gaps may be closing, with no concomitant increase in well-being. As a European Commission report (Bettio et al. 2012, 11–12) stated, "the levelling down of gender gaps in employment, unemployment, wages and poverty ... does not reflect progress in gender equality as it is based on lower rates of employment, higher rates of unemployment and reduced earnings for both men and women." The report's conclusion questioned "whether 'gender gaps' adequately capture trends in gender equality in recessionary times" (206).

Second, the implicit assumption of gender gap approaches is that the conditions of men are the standard against which women's status should be measured (EIGE 2013, 7). Third, the range of women-specific issues, which are not distributional in nature, is not captured by gender gap measurement. For example, "the GEM is not concerned with issues related to the body and sexuality, nor to religious, cultural or legal issues. Left out are issues of ethics, women's rights and care ... The GEM is not concerned with the violation of women's rights and does not measure, for instance, whether the United Nations CEDAW is ratified or adhered to" (Charmes and Wieringa 2003, 432). Finally, gender gaps do not capture the differences among women based on class, racialization, citizenship, and ability. Approaches grounded in gender equality measured by gender gaps in achievement may be inherently flawed and may not offer an adequate reference point for exploring women's status.

Alternative Measures of Gender Inequality

A number of relatively new indices examine data on women's equality in more nuanced ways than gender gap methodology. The Georgetown Institute's Women, Peace and Security Index (WPSI) (first published in 2017 and updated in 2019 and 2021) offers a global ranking of 167 countries. Canada placed twelfth among the twelve best-performing countries.[10] The index incorporates three basic dimensions of women's well-being – inclusion (economic, social, political); justice (formal laws and informal discrimination); and security (at the family, community, and societal levels). Unlike gender gap methodologies, it measures women's well-being captured through eleven indicators, some of which are

---

In the justice dimension of the Georgetown index, legal discrimination is measured by the aggregate score for laws and regulations that limit women's ability to participate in society or the economy or that differentiate between men and women.

Also in the justice dimension, discriminatory norms are measured by the percentage of men who disagreed with the proposition "It is perfectly acceptable for any woman in your family to have a paid job outside the home if she wants one."

In the security dimension, community safety is measured by the percentage of women who report that they "feel safe walking alone at night in the city or area where you live" (Georgetown Institute for Women, Peace and Security 2019, 12).

---

unique and unusual. The box above shows how the WPSI measures legal dis-crimination, discriminatory norms, and community safety.

The European Gender Equality Index focuses on dimensions of work, money, knowledge, time, health, and power (EIGE 2019),[11] with satellite indices on violence against women and intersecting inequalities differentiated from the main index "because [they do] not measure gaps between women and men" (EIGE 2017, 23).

For the years 1981–2014, the Cingranelli-Richards Human Rights Dataset contains standards-based quantitative information on the respect displayed by governments for fifteen internationally recognized human rights in 202 countries (CIRI Human Rights Data Project 2014).[12] The CIRI can be sorted by various indices, such as women's economic rights, political rights, and social rights (see Appendix 9.1).

The 2013 Environment and Gender Index (EGI) is a project of the Global Gender Office of the International Union for Conservation of Nature (IUCN). The index measures country performance at the intersection of gender, environ-ment, and sustainable development, using the following dimensions: livelihood, ecosystem, gender-based rights and participation, governance, gender-based education and assets, and country-reported activities in regards to the Con-vention on the Elimination of All Forms of Discrimination against Women (CEDAW). The introduction points out that "environmental programs and policies often include gender in a token manner or as an afterthought, limited to reporting on women's participation, listing them as beneficiaries, or focusing on women as victims" (IUCN 2013, 12).

Equal Measures 2030 brings together data to highlight a gendered perspective on the sustainable development goals (SDGs) of the UN (poverty, hunger, health, education, gender equality, water and sanitation, energy, work and economic growth, industry, infrastructure and innovation, inequality, cities and commun-ities, climate, peace and institutions, and partnerships).[13] The SDGs were adopted by all UN member states in 2015, and a fifteen-year plan to achieve them was established.[14] The SDG Gender Index from Equal Measures 2030 includes fifty-one indicators to assess the SDGs of the UN and covers 129 countries.[15] Some indicators are gender-specific, whereas others are not, but all have a dispropor-tionate effect on girls and women. On the 2019 Equal Measures scale, Canada ranked eighth, with a total score of 85.8 (see Appendix 9.1). The 2023 Equal Measures report concluded: "The world won't reach gender equality until at least 2108 – nearly a century later than we'd hoped" (Equal Measures 2030 2023, 3).

Of the indices considered, four refer to violence against women (VAW), which suggests a growing recognition that gender gaps are insufficient to reveal the complexity of women's experiences and status. Despite the inclusion of VAW, these indices point to the paucity or lack of data. Since 2009, the Social Institutions and Gender Index from the Organisation for Economic Cooperation and Development has included physical integrity as a dimension (measured by violence against women, female genital mutilation, and reproductive integrity). Since 2017, the Women, Peace and Security Index has included intimate partner violence, community safety, and organized violence in its security measure. Since 2018, the Canadian Gender Results Framework has included gender-based violence, using indicators of harassment-free workplaces, numbers of women victims of intimate partner violence and sexual assault, victims of childhood maltreatment, femicide by an intimate partner, police reporting of violent crimes, numbers of Indigenous women and girls who are victims of violence, and increased accountability and responsiveness of the Canadian criminal justice system.[16] A 2020 report from Equal Measure 2030 presents data on women's perceptions of safety at night. The European Gender Equality Index has a satellite index on VAW, although it is not yet fully populated with data.[17]

Women's Power, Equality, and Empowerment

The indicators used to measure many of the gender equality dimensions, particularly income and labour force participation, have been subject to extensive analyses and criticisms (see, for example, Beneria and Permanyer 2010; Charmes and Wieringa 2003; Klasen and Schüler 2011). However, the discourses of power and empowerment embedded in many of these indices have not been explored, nor have the political and economic indicators used to operationalize and measure them. Further, the distinctions between gender equality, women's status, and women's empowerment have not been examined. In connection with the GEM, Jacques Charmes and Saskia Wieringa (2003, 433) comment, "The major problem of the GEM lies in its validity as a measure of empowerment. The crucial question is on what understanding of power is the GEM built? How is empowerment conceptualised?"[18]

The shift from the language of "power" to "empowerment" occurred with the Gender Inequality Index in 2010, after which the World Economic Forum and Social Watch followed suit. However, empowerment is not defined at a conceptual level in these indices. Yet, assumptions are implicit about what conditions support women's empowerment (for example, education, representation, and/ or labour force participation) and what indicators measure it (share of women in parliamentary seats, on boards, in technical positions). For example, the fifth UN sustainable development goal, on gender equality development, includes women's representation in national parliaments and in managerial positions.[19]

The GII includes an empowerment dimension, which is measured by higher education attainment levels and shares of parliamentary seats held by each sex.[20]

Linking these indicators to empowerment, often based on common sense and taken-for-granted thinking, is rarely interrogated. In this regard, the WEF draws a disturbing distinction between gender equality and women's empowerment: the first is measured by the gap between women and men in the chosen indicators, and the second is measured by whether "women are 'winning' the 'battle of the sexes' ... and outperforming men in particular indicators" (Hausmann et al. 2013, 4). This statement highlights the confusion over the meanings of women's empowerment.

What Representations Matter

What is evident from Appendix 9.1 is that the most significant dimension of "empowerment" is demographic or descriptive representation.[21] The most common indicators are shares of parliamentary seats and positions as senior officials and managers. Indices that differentiate political and economic power often measure economic power by the gender gap in members of boards and members of the Central Bank (see, for example, the European Gender Equality Index). Hanny Cueva Beteta (2006, 222) points out the class bias:

> The GEM uses female presence on national parliaments, institutions that normally concentrate national elites with access to education, as well as political and economic networks. This is also the case for the female share of economic decision-making positions ... As a result, the existence of gender inequality among the less economically advantaged population – which is usually greater – is simply not accounted for.

Perhaps the most complex and sensitive set of representation measures is in the Gender Status Index from the Economic Commission for Africa (ECA 2011). It divides political power into two domains – the public sector and civil society – and its forms of representation for the public sector are extensive (see Appendix 9.1). Furthermore, the index recognizes that "public power has to come to terms with new forms of power residing in the civil society" (ECA 2011, 25), and it includes demographic representation in civil society, as measured by the number of women who are traditional rulers or who hold senior positions in political parties, trade unions, employers' associations, and non-governmental organizations.

Although the indicators used to measure women's empowerment have a narrow focus, the findings are unequivocal. For all indices, the greatest gender gap occurs on the political empowerment dimension. The 2012 GEI computed a world value for education of seventy-one (or "low"), for economic participation forty-two ("very low"), and for political empowerment a mere seventeen ("critical") (Social Watch 2012b). The 2023 Global Gender Gap Index from the World Economic Forum found that the 146 countries it covered had closed 96 percent of the gender gap in health outcomes and 95.2 percent of the gap in educational attainment. However, on economic participation and political empowerment, the gap remained wide: only 60.1 percent of the economic outcomes gap and only 22.1 percent of the political outcomes gap had been closed.[22] On the indicator of the proportion of women who held ministerial or cabinet-level senior government roles, the 2020 report from Equal Measures 2030 (2020, 15) found that forty countries had "slid backwards since 2001." The dismal outcomes on women's representation highlight the continuing importance of these measures.

Women's Collective Agency

Undoubtedly, descriptive representation remains an end in itself, an important mechanism for voice, and a means to increase democracy. Beteta (2006, 224) comments, "Increasing gender equality in political representation (including national parliaments) is a matter of justice ... It contributes to the legitimacy of political regimes and provides role-models for girls and women, changing attitudes, opinions and behaviour of women and men in the process." However, as demonstrated by an extensive literature, demographic representation is not a particularly effective instrument for increasing or measuring women's equality (see, for example, Briskin 2014).[23]

Electoral strategies and demographic profiles offer only narrow mechanisms for social, political, and organizational change; they overestimate the impact of individual women in political parties, boardrooms, and unions. They also convey a limited view of what constitutes agency and political empowerment. Further, as gender demographics improve, they can be used to suggest, mistakenly, that great strides toward equality have been made. In fact, maintaining a narrow focus on representation may limit the capacity to envision mechanisms that more effectively support an equality and rights agenda.

Empowerment measures need to consider not only achievements of women as individuals, that is, individual agency, but also vehicles for collective agency. Naila Kabeer (1999, 13) concludes that "most of the measures of empowerment found in the literature ... are defined at the level of the individual." She asks, "How do changes in ... women's representation in parliament, for instance, translate into the greater political agency of women?" (10). Sakiko Fukuda-Parr

(2003, 309, 314) also points to the importance of moving beyond a focus on individual action and toward collective action, which, "especially in the form of social movements, has been the essential motor behind progress in achieving major policy shifts necessary for human development, such as the recognition of gender equality, the need to protect the environment, or the promotion and protection of a comprehensive set of human rights." A growing body of research, both qualitative and quantitative, supports this view. One excellent example is a thirty-year study that tracked public policies on VAW in seventy countries from 1975 to 2005; unusually, it employed quantitative measures (Htun and Weldon 2012). It asked, "Why do some governments have more comprehensive policy regimes than others?" (548). Its results were unequivocal: "Autonomous mobilization of feminists in domestic and transnational contexts – not leftist parties, women in government, or national wealth – is the critical factor accounting for policy change (548) ... These effects of autonomous organizing are more important ... than women's descriptive representation inside the legislature or the impact of political parties" (563–64). This suggestive research shifts attention from individual achievements and the gender gap to collective agency. A policy recommendation in the Equal Measures 2023 report supports this approach: "Invest in, create space for, and listen to feminist organizations and movements." It concludes: "Little progress on women's rights would have been made without pressure and advocacy from these organizations and movements."[24] The foundational assumption is that the more societies support women's collective agency, the greater the likelihood of reducing the gender gap and advancing their rights.

Thus, the concept of *collective agency* offers an alternative to the language of empowerment and the indicator of political representation that is used in almost all the international indices. As M. Hewson (2010, 13) explains, agency "refers to the experience of acting, doing things, making things happen, exerting power, being a subject of events, or controlling things." Hewson differentiates between individual agency (individuals acting) and collective agency: "When individuals collaborate they create collective entities; insofar as such entities engage in effectual activity, they become collective agencies" (13). This chapter, then, distinguishes between the individual empowerment dimension, which improves women's situation in only a marginal way, and collective agency, which enhances their status, rights, and voice, and helps to progress their equality. The paradigm of collective agency requires a shift from outcomes to means.

From Outcomes to Means

The World Economic Forum distinguishes between outcomes and means, or inputs. Its Global Gender Gap Index evaluates countries based on outcomes rather than inputs or means. Our aim is to provide a snapshot of where men and women stand with regard to some fundamental outcome indicators related to basic rights such as health, education, economic participation and political empowerment. Indicators related to country-specific policies, rights, culture or customs – factors that we consider "input" or "means" indicators – are not included in the index. (WEF 2020, 5)

Most indices focus on outputs. However, SIGI, introduced in 2009 by the OECD (n.d.),[25] does not take up outcomes, well-being, or levels of achievement, because it argues that doing so "neglects the question of the origins of these inequalities." Rather, it highlights the institutional basis of gender inequality to show "how social institutions affect gender inequality; thus, it focuses not on gendered outcomes, but on institutions that affect such outcomes" (Klasen and Schüler 2011, 8). For SIGI, the key measures are discriminatory family code, restricted physical integrity, son bias, restricted resources and entitlements, and restricted civil liberties (see Appendix 9.1). The SIGI website suggests that "by capturing discriminatory social institutions, policy-makers can understand and identify the often invisible areas where resources and interventions should be targeted to promote gender equality, poverty reduction and development" (OECD 2018).

Like SIGI, this chapter argues for a focus on means rather than outcomes, and also on institutions that affect outcomes, rather than on individual achievements. However, unlike SIGI, it explores institutions that promote gender equality rather than reproduce inequality. The rest of the chapter focuses on one such institution: trade unions.

Trade Unions Improve Women's Status

The 2005 United Nations report "Gender Equality: Striving for Justice in an Unequal World" (UNRISD 2005, 167) confirms the significance of social movements and civil society institutions for advancing women's equality: "Women's activism in civil society is the main force behind women-friendly legislative change, and underpins the efforts of feminists in public office." However, unlike a focus solely on autonomous women's movements adopted by Htun and Weldon (2012), the UN report points out that "a significant amount of female mobilization and solidarity occurs outside women-dominated organizations. Trade unions, political parties, state-sponsored mass organizations, and civil-society groups with other agendas may advocate on behalf of their women members" (UNRISD 2005, 168). Trade unions are a key labour market institution. They have an impact on households and workplaces, and they influence education, health, and public policy. Operating at multiple levels and geographies, they undertake collective bargaining and external campaigns to transform the conditions of work and workplaces, and to promote social justice more broadly. Simultaneously, they engage in institutional transformations to reshape their own policies, practices, and culture.

The International Labour Organization (ILO) (2009, 161) points out that in civil society, "It is through participation that women and men can achieve decent and productive work in conditions of freedom, equity, security and human dignity." Trade unions are a key arena for such participation. Patrick Flavin, Alexander Pacek, and Benjamin Radcliff (2010) examined fourteen industrial democracies to test the proposition that unions improve the quality of life for citizens. Their conclusions were unequivocal: "Organized labor makes a positive contribution to the quality of life of citizens in industrial democracies." The authors note that "levels of life satisfaction vary directly with union density and union membership, even when salient economic conditions and other important national level characteristics are controlled for ... It is the most vulnerable members of society who are most positively affected by membership in and the influence of organized labor in the industrial world" (446–47).

Guy Mundlak and Hila Shamir (2014) confirmed the importance of trade unions for vulnerable workers. Discussing migrant care workers, the authors found that unions played an important role in establishing industrial citizenship and enhancing political agency, despite the intimate nature of their work, its gendered character, and the vulnerabilities that stemmed from their migration status. Research, then, supports the view that not only does collective bargaining improve the wages and working conditions of union members, but union membership also increases life satisfaction.[26] By extension, union membership contributes to human development and agency, and offers a *measure* of well-being. On these grounds alone, union membership should be a significant dimension for measuring gender equality, particularly in the United Nations Development indices based on Amartya Sen's capability approach, which argues that people "must be empowered to have a voice in the major decisions that shape their lives" (Charmes and Wieringa 2003, 427).

Unions are uniquely situated to promote both social transformation and the institutional mainstreaming of equality. Despite their commitments to equality policies and practices, and their multi-levelled structural and institutional resources, they are under-theorized and often underrated as instruments of equality and agency. In discussions of measuring gender equality, their potential merits little or no attention (Briskin 2011). Evidence suggests, however, that they are a key institution for enhancing women's collective agency, voice, empowerment, and equality.[27]

Collective Bargaining

Union women's organizing has expanded union issues beyond the economic, made visible the permeable boundaries between the public and private, and set new and often successful bargaining agendas that attempt to gender all collective bargaining demands. Such organizing has challenged the generic worker and increasingly insisted not only on a recognition of the significance of gender, but also of other marginalized identities.

Innovative initiatives on violence against women demonstrate the success of such organizing and the flexibility and potential of collective bargaining as an equity tool. They also underscore that unions are not narrowly focused on economic issues (Briskin 2006). Unifor, Canada's largest private sector union, with more than 315,000 members, has developed exemplary programs. Its Women's Advocate program deals with women's concerns around violence, harassment, or any other form of discrimination. It was first negotiated in 1993 at Ford, Chrysler, and General Motors,[28] and is part of a Domestic Violence at Work Policy and Program. Unifor currently has over 350 women's advocates in collective agreements in school boards, airlines, manufacturing, paper mills, shipyards, hospitals, nursing homes, long-term care homes, casinos, and rail facilities in both female- and male-dominated workplaces (Unifor n.d., 2, 4). Unifor has also developed language for and won protection against disciplinary procedures for women who lose time at work due to abusive family situations. Unifor has produced an extensive pamphlet on the program and a report titled "Bargaining a Domestic Violence Policy and Program."[29]

Such initiatives are happening in many countries. A 2017 report on eleven countries by the European Trade Union Confederation (ETUC) found eighty collective agreements and workplace policies that addressed violence and harassment at work, with a particular focus on sexual harassment (Pillinger 2017, 25).

Union Advantage

Union membership increases women's income and reduces the gender pay gap, a central dimension in all gender equality indices. Although many factors determine wages and job quality (such as education, workplace size, industry, and so forth), union coverage is a key element in improving wage levels and economic equality. In Canada, women union members earned $6.88 per hour more than women without unions. What is known as the "union advantage" translates into $552.5 million more paid to women each week.[30] Union membership also has monetary advantages for racialized women. In 2007, unionized African Canadian women earned $186 per week and Indigenous women $179 per week more than their non-unionized peers.[31] Economist Andrew Jackson (2005, 9) notes,

> Unionization is associated with formalized and equitable pay and promotion structures as well as layoff rules which tend to minimize some of the most overt forms of discrimination on the basis of gender and race, and many unions have consciously tried to promote pay and employment equality for their lower paid and women members through bargaining ... Unionized workers are also most likely to benefit from legislated pay and employment equality laws than are non union workers because unions have the resources to make these laws effective.

Unionized women have better working conditions and more control over their work, safer workplaces, predictable hours, access to health and pension benefits, opportunities for training and education, and some degree of job security through their collective agreements.[32] The social benefits and entitlements beyond earnings that affect employees' standard of living are often referred to as the social wage.[33]

Union advantage data unequivocally highlight benefits and protections for unionized workers and point to numerous positive outcomes of unionization. I argue, then, that union membership is a significant proxy indicator of women's equality.

Trade Unions Support Women's Collective Agency

In addition to changing workplace relations and conditions through collective bargaining, the four themes explored below highlight union support for women's collective agency and voice.[34]

Commitment to Equality in Union Policy and Constitutions/Rule Books

Unions express their commitments to equality in their policies and constitutions/rule books. In 2007, the ETUC, which represents eighty-two union organizations in thirty-six European countries, plus twelve industry-based federations, adopted a Charter on Gender Mainstreaming in Trade Unions. It states:

> Gender equality is an essential element of democracy in the workplace and in society. The ETUC and its affiliates confirm their commitment to pursue gender equality as part of their broader agenda for social justice, social progress and sustainability in Europe, and therefore adopt a gender mainstreaming approach as an indispensable and integral element of all their actions and activities. (ETUC 2007)

Over the last forty years, the Canadian union movement has produced extensive materials on equality-related issues. The last decade has witnessed a remarkable increase in union policy on racism, homophobia, sexism, and more recently on transphobia and ableism (Hunt and Rayside 2007).

Union Practice as Democratic Institutions

Trade union women have fought for the democratization of unions through leadership and representational strategies. Not only do unions support women's collective agency, but union women's collective leadership has enhanced the equality potential of unions. As a result of resolute organizing by women, unions have undertaken democratizing initiatives to transform their culture and organizational practices to ensure fairness and representation for equality-seeking members.

A dual strategy for democratization has emerged: first, the election of more women and members of other equality-seeking groups to union leadership positions through affirmative action, positive action, and proportionality initiatives; and second, constituency organizing (sometimes called separate or self-organizing) to represent the interests of and mobilize women and other equality-seeking groups. This dual strategy highlights the distinction between individual empowerment (via leadership) and collective agency (via constituency organizing) (Briskin 2014).

Women's committees are widely institutionalized in trade unions, at many levels and in most countries. In fact, over the past forty years, constituency organizing inside unions has brought together members of equality-seeking groups – women, people of colour, Indigenous people, people with disabilities, and lesbian, gay, bisexual, and transgendered people – to increase their skills, self-confidence, and political power. An extensive literature documents and explores the contributions of this organizing. In Canada, through constituency organizing, women have promoted women's leadership, challenged traditional leaderships to be more accountable, encouraged unions to be more democratic and participatory, forced them to take up women's concerns as union members and as workers – through policy initiatives and at the negotiating table – and helped to transform union relationships with social movements (Briskin 1999, 2002; Hunt and Rayside 2007; Kainer 2009).[35] Constituency organizing enhances women's *collective* agency.

Unions as Equality Resources

Unions operate as equality resources at numerous levels and geographies – at local, regional, national, transnational, and global levels. At the transnational level, eleven global union federations organized by sector and industry represent millions of workers in almost every country in the world, and each has an active women's committee (Global Unions n.d.). In addition, the International Trade Union Confederation, the umbrella organization to which the global unions belong, represents 200 million workers in 163 countries and territories; it too has an active equality program. Each level offers explicit and often constitutionalized commitments to democratic practice and equality. These multi-layered and resourced structures support women's collective agency and enhance union capacity as equality vehicles.

Unions as Social Movements

Htun and Weldon (2012, 549, 552, 555) emphasize the importance of autonomous feminist movements in shaping policy on VAW. They suggest that such movements "develop oppositional consciousness, imagine new forms of social organization, and mobilize broad societal action to generate understanding and support." Although trade union women's organizing operates in an institutionalized rather than an autonomous context, the parallels are striking. The degree of institutionalization of unions suggests that unions are not themselves social movements. However, constituency organizing inside unions (such as women's committees) mirrors social movement practice in many ways: around participatory democracy and consensus decision making, the sharing of skills and knowledge, active leadership development, and broad visions for social change. It is also the case that beginning in the 1970s, around issues such as pay equality, affirmative action, sexual harassment and VAW, childcare, and reproductive rights, Canadian union women formed alliances and coalitions across unions and with social movements, contesting the isolationist tendencies in the union movement and legitimizing coalition building with groups outside it.

The fact that unions operate at multiple levels offers great potential for transnational advocacy. Ground-breaking transnational initiatives, such as the Pay Equity Now! Campaign launched in 2000 by the Public Service International, highlight cross-union, cross-border, and union-community coalition work in Europe, Africa, Asia, and Latin America. Jane Pillinger (2005, 592) writes that the campaign

> culminated in national and global actions and campaigns which have had various impacts, including agenda setting for unions, employers and governments, raised public awareness through lobbying, and information campaigns about gender inequalities. *Pay Equity Now!* has also focused on how issues such as living minimum wages, poverty alleviation and the valuing of women's work through practical gender pay equity initiatives can be used as a tool for organizing and recruiting women.

The pay equity campaign is instructive on a number of levels. It demonstrates the importance of unions as equality resources at numerous levels and geographies, their policy and research concerns, the potential of collective bargaining to address low-paid work, and union commitments to leadership training, constituency organizing, and coalition work.

The Patriarchal Character of Unions

Common sense views often erroneously assume that unions are patriarchal institutions run by men who ignore the concerns of women and other marginalized workers. In fact, in many countries including Canada, women now make up the majority of union membership. In 2019 in Canada, 53 percent of union members were women.[36] Further, "trade unions are the largest collective organization of women across the world" (Pillinger and Wintour 2019, 2).

Although women's organizing has undeniably transformed unions, this is not to suggest that the struggle over patriarchal, homophobic, and racist cultures, policies, and practices has been resolved (see Briskin et al. 2014). Like the fight against racism, challenging patriarchal practices is an ongoing battle in every social, political, and economic institution. Karl Gardner (2022, 4) points out that "despite being organizations founded on principles of justice and solidarity, unions are not immune from the structural forces of capitalism, settler colonialism, heteropatriarchy, and white supremacy that continue to influence Canadian society."

However, deeply embedded democratic mechanisms in unions and the mobilization of union women and Black, Indigenous, and racialized workers help make visible misogynist and racist transgressions of some union leadership, as well as racist and sexist practices and policies. Gardner (2022, 4) concludes that unions "are gradually becoming committed advocates for anti-racism and equity in the workplace." Regardless, even "patriarchal" unions offer women significant advantages in relation to improving wages, working conditions, pensions, and sick leave. They also enhance women's collective agency and voice.

To dismiss unions erases the agency of women unionists who have achieved considerable success in both challenging and transforming them. In fact, extensive research demonstrates the often dramatic impact of union women and other equality-seeking groups on the practices, policies, and discourse of unions in many Western countries.

Data to Measure Women's Collective Agency via Trade Unions

Macro Indicators

Many scholars who explore and agencies that manage gender equality indices lament the lack of appropriate data. They call for accessible data sources that monitor progress over time and support inter-country comparisons (for example, Plantenga and Remery 2013). Boris Branisa and colleagues (2013, 32) point specifically to the lack of gender-disaggregated statistics and the fact that "data may be unavailable, unreliable, or noncomparable."

However, data on unionization by gender are readily available. The ILO database of labour statistics provides many data sets for 230 countries, areas, and territories on more than a hundred indicators, including trade union density rate by sex (as a percent of employees).[37] Statistics Canada puts out periodic information on unionization, which includes a variety of measures disaggregated by sex (Galarneau and Sohn 2013).[38] Data on unionization by gender can certainly be used as a measure of, or proxy for, collective agency.

Significant to this collective agency paradigm, especially in the current context in which unions around the world are under considerable attack, are data that indicate access to unionization, the right to collective representation, and the right to bargain collectively as part of freedom of association. The Worker's Rights Dataset of the CIRI contains such data. The CIRI Human Rights Data Project (2014) states that "workers should have freedom of association at their workplaces and the right to bargain collectively with their employers ... A score of 0 indicates that workers' rights were severely restricted; a score of 1 indicates that workers' rights were somewhat restricted; and a score of 2 indicates that workers' rights were fully protected during the year in question." In 2011, on the CIRI measure, Canada received a score of 1. In fact, it has a dismal record, despite ratifying the 1948 ILO Freedom of Association and Protection of the Right to Organise Convention.[39] Restrictive labour laws have also been expanding in recent years, which certainly limit women's collective agency.[40] On existing world indices, Canada scores quite high. If an index were to include the right to union representation and its attendant protections, Canada's score would drop considerably – a stark reminder that what is measured influences the profile that emerges. Lack of widespread access to collective agency limits improvements in the status of women in Canada.

On a positive note, the 2019 Sustainable Development Goals Gender Index developed by Equal Measures 2030 includes "extent of freedom of association and collective bargaining rights in law" as an indicator to measure women's progress on work and economic growth (SDG 8). This is the first index to link collective bargaining rights directly to women's advancement. As Equal Measures 2030 (2019, 30) notes, "women constitute the largest number of workers in precarious employment in both the developed and developing world, and collective bargaining, though relatively under-researched, can be critical to non-discrimination in the workplace, equal pay for work of equal value, and parental leave rights. Many top scoring countries overall on the 2019 SDG Gender Index have strong collective bargaining rights."

Institutional Indicators

Also significant are institutional indices that assess unions in terms of their degree of support for women's rights and collective agency. Such data should include:

- equality demographics of membership, local and central leadership, union staff and committee membership, and in confederation and transnational union structures
- programs to ensure equality representation such as affirmative action, designated seats, and proportionality measures; structures of representation such as women's committees and other constituency structures
- constitutionalization of equality (equality and mainstreaming clauses in union constitutions, rule books, and charters)
- equality audits of collective agreements, including documenting collective bargaining gains in specified areas for women and monitoring mechanisms for the implementation of equality provisions; and
- finally, measures to ensure equality bargaining practices including desegregation of the collective bargaining committees to include women and members of other equality-seeking groups, and constitutionalized links between women's committees and collective bargaining committees. (Briskin 2014)

Some national unions and union confederations have done excellent work in documenting some of these measures. Data collection initiatives by the Trades Union Congress (TUC) in the United Kingdom provide a national model. In 2001, TUC passed a historic motion to change its constitution to include a commitment to equality as a condition of affiliation with it. At the same time, it established a comprehensive biannual equality auditing process. The 2016 equality audit examined union progress in bargaining for equality around equal pay, flexible work, pensions, and bullying and harassment (Trades Union Congress 2016). The TUC Equality Audit in 2022 highlighted the promotion of equality in union membership, structures and processes to ensure they reflect the diversity of the membership (Trades Union Congress 2022).

The 2007 Gender Mainstreaming Charter adopted by the ETUC commits to an annual survey to highlight the need for gender mainstreaming in trade unions and to assess progress in reducing the gender "representation gap" in union organizations. These annual surveys are probably the most comprehensive done by any union in the world (ETUC 1999, 2003, 2019; see also Sechi 2007). These reports document leadership demographics and mechanisms of mainstream-ing, including implementation and dissemination measures, and the existence and powers of women's committees.

In Canada, data on such measures are very scarce. Since the government abandoned the Corporations and Labour Unions Act report in 1995, there are no reliable figures on women's participation in trade union leadership. Only limited data are forthcoming from Canadian unions on many of the institutional indicators. The last collection of cross-union data, *Advancing Equity by the Numbers and Reporting on Past Promises* (Canadian Labour Congress 2011), was a survey of affiliates of the Canadian Labour Congress, modelled on the TUC audits.

As part of the project to highlight the role of unions in advancing women's equality and empowerment, I propose a *Women's Equality and Trade Unions Index* sponsored by the ILO to bring together gendered union density data with institutional indicators of gender equality in unions in the 230 countries in-cluded in the ILO database of labour statistics.[41]

Conclusion

Traditional gender measurement indices focus on the gender gap, and/or on those institutions that reproduce gender inequality and heighten women's victimization. This chapter promotes a collective agency paradigm which high-lights institutions that support women's equality, in particular, trade unions. Unionization is a valuable measure of women's collective agency, and also a vehicle for progressing women's status and increasing gender equality.

This approach shifts the discourse from individual to collective agency, problematizes the commonsense strategic emphasis on increasing numbers of women in politics and corporate leadership, and promotes a wider recogni-tion of both the potential and the contribution of unions to women's empower-ment and equality. The focus on unions and collective agency directs attention away from political representation as a measure of empowerment to economic representation as empowerment, and offers a more fully realized understanding of agency itself.

Practices of measurement are both technical and political. Invariably, the choice of dimensions and indicators affects the vision of gender equality and the policy initiatives that it produces. Currently, conservative governments around the world are dramatically reducing not only what data are collected but also access to data. Robert Brym and Howard Ramos (2013) suggest that, in Canada, "increasingly, facts are ignored, suppressed, or distorted to suit government ideol-ogy." In such a context, and as part of the project of enhancing women's status and rights, it is imperative to call for and support new initiatives to measure, understand, and support women's equality.

What data are collected, and how, both reveal and conceal. Certainly, John Kenneth Galbraith was correct when he remarked that "if it is not counted, it tends not to be noticed."[42] Not only are documentation and measurement important parts of developing, defending, and monitoring equality initiatives, but they are also organizing and educational tools, and they provide a reference point for transnational comparisons and campaigns. A final comment: In the context of the COVID-19 pandemic and the ongoing climate crisis, moving beyond the individual is critical to understanding and addressing systemic inequalities that are engendered by racialization, marginalization, vulnerability, homophobia, and class. The project of revisioning social and political relations and mobilizing communities of resistance depends upon embracing and reinvigorating all forms of collective agency.[43]

Appendix 9.1

Indices on gender equality

Source	Index	Dimensions	Indicators
United Nations Development Programme (UNDP)	Gender-Related Development Index (GDI), introduced in 1995	*Long and healthy life	Measured by life expectancy at birth
		*Knowledge	Measured by adult literacy rates and the combined secondary and tertiary gross enrolment ratios
		*Decent standard of living	Measured by estimated earned income in purchasing power parity US$
United Nations Development Programme (UNDP)	Gender Empowerment Measure (GEM), introduced in 1995	*Political participation and decision-making power	Measured by women's and men's percentage shares of parliamentary seats
		Economic participation and decision-making power	**Measured by women's and men's percentage shares of positions as legislators, senior officials, and managers, and by women's and men's percentage shares of professional and technical positions**
		*Power over economic resources	Measured by women's and men's estimated earned income
United Nations Development Programme (UNDP)	Gender Inequality Index (GII), introduced in 2010 to replace GEM and GDI	*Reproductive health	Measured by the maternal mortality ratio and the adolescent fertility rate
		Empowerment	**Measured by the share of parliamentary seats held by each sex and by secondary and higher education attainment levels**
		*Labour market	Measured by the labour market participation rate
World Economic Forum	Global Gender Gap Index (GGI), introduced in 2005	*Economic participation and opportunity	
		Sub-domain: Participation gap	Measured by labour force participation rates
		Sub-domain: Remuneration gap	Measured by ratio of estimated female-to-male earned income (and a qualitative variable calculated through the World Economic Forum's Executive Opinion Survey [wage equality for similar work])

Organisation	Index	Sub-domain	
		Advancement gap	**Measured by the ratio of women to men among legislators, senior officials, and managers, and the ratio of women to men among technical and professional workers**
		*Political empowerment	**Measured by the ratio of women to men in minister-level positions and the ratio of women to men in parliamentary positions. Also ratio of women to men in terms of years in executive office (prime minister or president) for the last fifty years**
		*Educational attainment	Measured by female literacy rate, the female net primary-level enrolment, the female net secondary-level enrolment, and the female gross tertiary-level enrolment, all taken in ratio to the corresponding male value
		*Health and survival	Measured by sex ratio at birth and ratio of female healthy life expectancy over the male value
Social Watch	Gender Equity Index (GEI), introduced in 2007	*Education	Measured by literacy rate, enrolment rate in primary education, enrolment rate in secondary education, and enrolment rate in tertiary education
		*Economic activity	Measured by rate of economic activity and estimated perceived income
		*Empowerment	**Measured by share of women in technical positions, in management and government positions, in parliament, and in ministerial-level positions**
Organisation for Economic Co-operation and Development (OECD)	Social Institutions and Gender Index (SIGI) (excludes OECD countries), introduced in 2009	*Family code	Measured by legal age of marriage, early marriage, parental authority, inheritance
		*Civil liberties	Measured by access to public space, political voice
		*Physical integrity	Measured by violence against women, female genital mutilation, reproductive integrity
		*Son bias	Measured by missing women, fertility preference

Source	Index	Dimensions	Indicators
Cingranelli-Richards Human Rights Dataset (CIRI)	Cingranelli-Richards Human Rights Dataset (CIRI), from 1981 to 2011	*Resources and entitlements	Measured by access to land, to bank loans and credit, and to property other than land
		Women's political rights	The right to vote The right to run for political office The right to hold elected and appointed government positions The right to join political parties The right to petition government officials
		Women's economic rights	Equal pay for equal work Free choice of profession or employment without the need to obtain a husband or male relative's consent The right to gainful employment without the need to obtain a husband or male relative's consent Equality in hiring and promotion practices Job security (maternity leave, unemployment benefits, no arbitrary firing or layoffs) Non-discrimination by employers The right to be free from sexual harassment in the workplace The right to work at night The right to work in occupations classified as dangerous The right to work in the military and the police force
		Women's social rights	The right to equal inheritance The right to enter into marriage on the basis of equality with men The right to travel abroad The right to obtain a passport The right to confer citizenship to children or a husband The right to initiate a divorce

European Institute for Gender Equality	European Gender Equality Index, introduced in 2013		The right to own, acquire, manage, and retain property brought into marriage The right to participate in social, cultural, and community activities The right to an education The freedom to choose a residence/domicile Freedom from female genital mutilation of children and adults without consent Freedom from forced sterilization
		*Work	
		Sub-domain: Participation	Measured by full-time equivalent employment rate and duration of working life (years)
		Sub-domain: Segregation	Measured by sectoral segregation
		Sub-domain: Quality of work	Measured by flexibility of working time, health and safety, and training at work
		*Power	
		Sub-domain: Political power	**Measured by gender gap in parliamentary representation; regional assemblies/ministerial representation**
		Sub-domain: Economic power	**Measured by gender gap in members of boards and members of the Central Bank**
		Sub-domain: Social power	
		*Money *Knowledge *Time	
Canada	Gender Results Framework (GRF) (2018)	*Education and skills development	Measured by more diversified educational paths and career choices Reduced gender gaps in reading and numeracy skills among youth, including Indigenous youth Equal lifelong learning opportunities and outcomes for adults

Source	Index	Dimensions	Indicators
		*Economic participation and prosperity	Measured by increased labour market opportunities for women, especially in underrepresented groups Reduced gender wage gap Increased full-time employment of women Equal sharing of parenting roles and family responsibilities Better gender balance across occupations More women in higher-quality jobs, such as permanent and well-paid jobs
		***Leadership and democratic participation**	**Measured by women in senior management, as entrepreneurs, holding seats on company boards, in elected office and ministerial positions, in the justice system as law enforcement, security, and intelligence officers, and judges**
		*Gender-based violence and access to justice	Measured by harassment-free workplaces Fewer women are victims of intimate partner violence and sexual assault Fewer victims of childhood maltreatment Fewer women killed by an intimate partner Increased police reporting of violent crimes Fewer Indigenous women and girls are victims of violence Increased accountability and responsiveness of the Canadian criminal justice system
		*Poverty reduction, health, and well-being	Fewer vulnerable individuals living in poverty Fewer women and children living in food-insecure households Fewer vulnerable individuals lacking stable, safe, and permanent housing Child and spousal support orders enforced More years in good health Improved mental health

Equal Measures 2030	Sustainable Development Goals Gender Index (2019)	*Gender equality (SDG 5)	Measured by child, early, and forced marriage Perceptions of partner violence Legal grounds for abortion **Women in parliament** **Women in ministerial roles**
		*Work and economic growth (SDG 8)	Measured by wage equality Women in vulnerable work Collective bargaining rights in law Laws on women's workplace equality Women's ownership of bank accounts
		*Health (SDG 3)	Measured by maternal mortality Adolescent birth rate Access to family planning Improved access to contraception for young people and reduced adolescent birth rate
		*Education (SDG 4)	Measured by girls' primary school progression Girls' secondary education completion Young women not in education, employment, or training Women's literacy
		*Poverty *Hunger *Water and sanitation *Energy *Industry, infrastructure, and innovation inequality *Cities and communities *Climate *Peace and institutions *Partnerships	

Note: The bolded sections highlight areas related to empowerment and representation.

Notes

1 UN Women, "UN Women Launches Women Count Data Hub," September 24, 2019, https://data.unwomen.org/news/un-women-launches-women-count-data-hub. See UN Women, "Making Every Woman and Girl Count: 2019 Annual Report," July 23, 2020, https://data.unwomen.org/publications/women-count-annual-report-2019.

2 United Nations Development Programme, "Gender Inequality Index (GII)," https://hdr.undp.org/data-center/thematic-composite-indices/gender-inequality-index#/indicies/GII.

3 Government of Canada, "Gender Results Framework," https://cfc-swc.gc.ca/grf-crrg/index-en.html.

4 "Leadership and Democratic Participation," https://women-gender-equality.canada.ca/en/gender-results-framework/leadership-democratic-participation.html.

5 Statistics Canada, Gender, Diversity and Inclusion Statistics (GDIS) Hub, https://www.statcan.gc.ca/eng/topics-start/gender_diversity_and_inclusion.

6 Statistics Canada, Gender, Diversity and Inclusion Statistics (GDIS) Hub, https://www.statcan.gc.ca/eng/topics-start/gender_diversity_and_inclusion.

7 Statistics Canada, "Women in Canada: A Gender-Based Statistical Report," https://www150.statcan.gc.ca/n1/pub/89-503-x/89-503-x2015001-eng.htm.

8 United Nations Development Programme, "Gender Inequality Index (GII)," https://hdr.undp.org/data-center/thematic-composite-indices/gender-inequality-index#/indicies/GII.

9 World Economic Forum, *Global Gender Gap Report 2023,* https://www.weforum.org/reports/global-gender-gap-report-2023/, 11.

10 For more information on Canada's rankings, see https://giwps.georgetown.edu/country/canada/.

11 European Institute for Gender Equality, "Gender Statistics Database," https://eige.europa.eu/gender-statistics/dgs/browse/index.

12 http://www.humanrightsdata.com/.

13 Equal Measures 2030, "Our Impact Report," January 2023, https://www.equalmeasures2030.org/.

14 https://www.un.org/sustainabledevelopment/development-agenda/.

15 Equal Measures 2030, "Our Impact Report," January 2023, https://www.equalmeasures2030.org/.

16 https://women-gender-equality.canada.ca/en/gender-results-framework/gender-based-violence-access-justice.html.

17 European Institute for Gender Equality, "Gender-Based Violence," https://eige.europa.eu/gender-based-violence. Mala Htun and Laurel Weldon (2012) present a global comparative and quantitative analysis of policies on VAW over four decades.

18 Empowerment in the GEM has been variously understood as a measure of women's opportunities (Plantenga and Remery 2013), their role as agents (GEI), their political, economic, and social participation (Charmes and Wieringa 2003), and their access to levers of power (Beneria and Permanyer 2010), among others.

19 United Nations, "5 Gender Equality: Achieve Gender Equality and Empower All Women and Girls," https://unstats.un.org/sdgs/report/2020/goal-05/.

20 United Nations Development Programme, "Gender Inequality Index (GII)."

21 This chapter examines only how the indicators of empowerment and representation are operationalized in these indices. There is an extensive literature on women's representation. See, for example, Briskin (2014), which differentiates between what I call representational democracy and representational justice.

22 https://www.weforum.org/reports/global-gender-gap-report-2023/, 5.

23 The scholarship on women and politics distinguishes between women's descriptive and substantive representation, the former "counting and accounting for the numbers of women in political institutions" and the latter "exploring whether, and under what conditions, representatives 'act for' women" (Childs, Webb, and Marthaler 2010, 201). Since there is no guarantee that acting for women will result in successful policy outcomes, substantive representation is also disaggregated into process and outcome – that is, a distinction between "the process of acting for women and the fact of changing policy outcomes" (Franceschet and Piscopo 2008, 394–95).

24 "SDG Index Mini Report," https://www.equalmeasures2030.org/.

25 The SIGI is drawn from the OECD Gender, Institutions and Development Database, a tool to determine and analyze obstacles to women's economic development. It covers a total of 160 countries and comprises an array of sixty indicators on gender discrimination. The OECD (n.d.) points out that "the database's true innovation is the inclusion of institutional variables that range from intrahousehold behaviour to social norms. Information on cultural and traditional practices that impact on women's economic development is coded so as to measure the level of discrimination."

26 Examining the relationship between union decline and the growth of inequality in the United States, Bruce Western and Jake Rosenfeld (2011, 513) conclude that "the decline of organized labor explains a fifth to a third of the growth in inequality."

27 For further discussion on unions and collective agency, see Linda Briskin (2023).

28 https://www.unifor.org/unifors-ground-breaking-womens-advocate-program.

29 https://www.unifor.org/resources/our-resources/unifor-womens-advocate-program -booklet and https://www.unifor.org/unifors-ground-breaking-womens-advocate-program.

30 Canadian Labour Congress, "Build Worker Power," https://canadianlabour.ca/what-unions -do/build-worker-power/.

31 Ontario Federation of Labour, "Women and Unions: The Benefits," 2008.

32 CUPE, "Top Ten Union Advantages," https://cupe.ca/top-10-union-advantages.

33 The Unions Module of the Gender and Work Database includes an excellent statistical primer and demonstration on Canadian union advantage data. See Gender and Work Database, "Conceptual Guide to the Unions Module," http://www.genderwork.ca/gwd/ modules/unions/.

34 For a detailed examination of these themes, see Linda Briskin (2011).

35 For the United Kingdom, see, for example, Geraldine Healy and Gill Kirton (2000); Jill C. Humphrey (2000); and Jane Parker (2006).

36 Statistics Canada, "Union Coverage by Industry, Annual (x1,000)," Table 14-10-0070-01, https://www150.statcan.gc.ca/t1/tbl1/en/tv.action?pid=1410007001.

37 The trade union density rate conveys the number of union members as a percentage of the total number of persons in paid employment. https://ilostat.ilo.org/topics/union -membership/.

38 Statistics Canada, "Union Coverage by Industry," Table 14-10-0132-01, https://www150. statcan.gc.ca/t1/tbl1/en/tv.action?pid=1410013201.

39 International Labour Organization, "Co87 – Freedom of Association and Protection of the Right to Organise Convention, 1948 (No. 87)," https://www.ilo.org/dyn/normlex/en/f? p=NORMLEXPUB:12100:0::NO::P12100_ILO_CODE:C087. For countries that have ratified this convention, see International Labour Organization, "Ratifications of Co87 – Freedom of Association and Protection of the Right to Organise Convention, 1948 (No. 87)," http://www.ilo.org/dyn/normlex/en/f?p=1000:11300:0::NO:11300:P11300_ INSTRUMENT_ID:312232. The absence of the United States is noteworthy.

40   For more on Canada's dismal record with the ILO convention, see Canadian Foundation for Labour Rights, "Canada's Record at the ILO," http://www.labourrights.ca/issues/fact3 -canadas-record-ilo. On restrictive labour law in Canada, see http://www.labourrights. ca/issues/restrictive-labour-laws-canada.

41   Data on women's movements (for example, on the numbers of non-governmental and community-based women's organizations, as well as on their funding) would complement unionization as measures of women's collective agency (see, for example, Htun and Weldon 2012).

42   Quoted at https://www.ohchr.org/Documents/Issues/HRIndicators/AGuideMeasurement ImplementationIntroduction_en.pdf.

43   Recent research suggests that the best strategy to close the racial health gap, especially in relation to COVID, is to unionize workers. Jennifer Interlandi, "The Coronavirus Race Gap, Explained," *New York Times,* October 4, 2020.

Works Cited

Beneria, Lourdes, and Iñaki Permanyer. 2010. "The Measurement of Socio-Economic Gender Inequality Revisited." *Development and Change* 41, 3: 375–99. https://doi.org/10. 1111/j.1467-7660.2010.01648.x.

Beteta, Hanny Cueva. 2006. "What Is Missing in Measures of Women's Empowerment?" *Journal of Human Development* 7, 2: 221–41. https://doi.org/10.1080/14649880600768553.

Bettio, Francesca, Marcella Corsi, Carlo D'Ippoliti, Antigone Lyberaki, Manuela Samek Lodovici, and Alina Verashchagina. 2012. *The Impact of the Economic Crisis on the Situation of Women and Men and on Gender Equality Policies.* Brussels: European Commission. https://op.europa.eu/en/publication-detail/-/publication/4a10e8f6-d6d6 -417e-aef5-4b873d1a4d66/language-en.

Branisa, Boris, Stephan Klasen, Maria Ziegler, Denis Drechsler, and Johannes Jütting. 2013. "The Institutional Basis of Gender Inequality: The Social Institutions and Gender Index (SIGI)." *Feminist Economics* 20, 2: 29–64. https://doi.org/10.1080/13545701.2013.850523.

Briskin, Linda. 1999. "Autonomy, Diversity, and Integration: Union Women's Separate Organizing in North America and Western Europe in the Context of Restructuring and Globalization." *Women's Studies International Forum* 22, 5: 543–54. https://doi.org/10. 1016/S0277-5395(99)00053-9.

–. 2002. "The Equity Project in Canadian Unions: Confronting the Challenge of Restructuring and Globalization." In *Gender, Diversity and Trade Unions: International Perspectives,* ed. Fiona Colgan and Sue Ledwith, 28–47. London: Routledge.

–. 2006. *Equity Bargaining/Bargaining Equity.* Toronto: Centre for Research on Work and Society, York University. http://www.yorku.ca/lbriskin/pdf/bargainingpaperFINAL 3secure.pdf.

–. 2011. "Trade Unions, Collective Agency and the Struggle for Women's Equality: Expanding the Political Empowerment Measure." In *Making Globalization Work for Women: Women Workers' Social Rights and Trade Union Leadership,* ed. Valentine M. Moghadam, Suzanne Franzway, and Mary Margaret Fonow, 214–43. New York: State University of New York Press.

–. 2014. "Strategies to Support Equality Bargaining *inside* Unions: Representational Democracy and Representational Justice." *Journal of Industrial Relations* 56, 2: 208–27. https://doi.org/10.1177/0022185613517472.

–. 2023. "The Royal Commission and Unions: Leadership, Equality, Women's Organizing and Collective Agency." In *Feminism's Fight: Challenging Politics and Policies in Canada since 1970,* ed. Barbara Cameron and Meg Luxton, 279–303. Vancouver: UBC Press.

Briskin, Linda, Sue Genge, Margaret McPhail, and Marion Pollack. 2014. "Austerity, Gender Equality and Canadian Unions." In *Orchestrating Austerity: Impacts and Resistance*, ed. Donna Baines and Stephen McBride, 66–78. Winnipeg: Fernwood.

Brym, Robert, and Howard Ramos. 2013. "Actually, Now's the Perfect Time to 'Commit Sociology.'" iPolitics. https://www.ipolitics.ca/news/actually-nows-the-perfect-time -to-commit-sociology.

Canadian Labour Congress. 2011. *Advancing Equity by the Numbers and Reporting on Past Promises*. Ottawa.

Charmes, Jacques, and Saskia Wieringa. 2003. "Measuring Women's Empowerment: An Assessment of the Gender-Related Development Index and the Gender Empowerment Measure." *Journal of Human Development* 4, 3: 419–35. https://doi.org/10.1080/14649 88032000125773.

Childs, Sarah, Paul Webb, and Sally Marthaler. 2010. "Constituting and Substantively Representing Women: Applying New Approaches to a UK Case Study." *Politics and Gender* 6, 2: 199–223. https://doi.org/10.1017/S1743923X10000048.

CIRI Human Rights Data Project. 2014. "CIRI Human Rights Data Project." http://www. humanrightsdata.com.

ECA (Economic Commission for Africa). 2011. *The African Gender and Development Index: Promoting Gender Equality in Africa*. Addis Ababa: ECA.

EIGE (European Institute for Gender Equality). 2013. *Gender Equality Index*. Vilnius, Lithuania: EIGE. http://eige.europa.eu/sites/default/files/Gender-Equality-Index -Report.pdf.

–. 2017. *Gender Equality Index 2017: Methodological Report*. Luxembourg: Publications Office of the European Union.

–. 2019. "Gender Equality Index." Accessed October 19, 2020. https://eige.europa.eu/gender -equality-index/2019.

Equal Measures 2030. 2019. *Harnessing the Power of Data for Gender Equality: Introducing the 2019 SDG Gender Index*. Surrey, UK: Equal Measures 2030. Accessed October 19, 2020. https://www.equalmeasures2030.org/2019-sdg-gender-index-report/.

–. 2020. *Bending the Curve towards Gender Equality by 2030*. Surrey, UK: Equal Measures 2030. https://www.equalmeasures2030.org/2020-bending-the-curve-report/.

–. 2023. "Our Impact Report." https://www.equalmeasures2030.org/.

ETUC (European Trade Union Confederation). 1999. *The 'Second Sex' of European Trade Unionism*. Brussels: ETUC.

–. 2003. *Women in Trade Unions: Making the Difference*. Brussels: ETUC. https://www.etuc. org/en/study-women-trade-unions-making-difference.

–. 2007. *ETUC Charter on Gender Mainstreaming in Trade Unions*. Brussels: ETUC. https:// www.etuc.org/en/etuc-charter-gender-mainstreaming-trade-unions.

–. 2019. "ETUC Annual Gender Equality Survey 2019." March 21. https://www.etuc.org/ en/circular/etuc-annual-gender-equality-survey-2019.

Flavin, Patrick, Alexander C. Pacek, and Benjamin Radcliff. 2010. "Labor Unions and Life Satisfaction: Evidence from New Data." *Social Indicators Research* 98, 3: 435–49. https:// doi.org/10.1007/s11205-009-9549-z.

Franceschet, Susan, and Jennifer M. Piscopo. 2008. "Gender Quotas and Women's Substantive Representation: Lessons from Argentina." *Politics and Gender* 4, 3: 393–425. https://doi.org/10.1017/S1743923X08000342.

Fukuda-Parr, Sakiko. 2003. "The Human Development Paradigm: Operationalizing Sen's Ideas on Capabilities." *Feminist Economics* 9, 2–3: 301–17. https://doi.org/10.108 0/1354570022000077980.

Galarneau, Diane, and Thao Sohn. 2013. "Long Term Trends in Unionization." Statistics Canada. Accessed October 19, 2020. http://www.statcan.gc.ca/pub/75-006-x/2013001/article/11878-eng.htm.

Gardner, Karl. 2022. *Advancing Equity and Racial Justice in Canadian Workplaces and Labour Unions.* Toronto: York University. https://www.yorku.ca/research/glrc/wp-content/uploads/sites/425/2022/11/Final-Report-Advancing-Equity-and-Racial-Justice-in-Canadian-Workplaces-and-Labour-Unions.pdf.

Georgetown Institute for Women, Peace and Security. 2019. "Women, Peace and Security Index (2019–20)." Accessed October 19, 2020. https://giwps.georgetown.edu/the-index/.

Global Unions. n.d. "Global Unions." Accessed October 19, 2020. http://www.global-unions.org/?lang=en.

Hausmann, Ricardo, Laura D. Tyson, Yasmina Bekhouche, and Saadia Zahidi. 2013. *The Global Gender Gap Report.* Cologne, Switzerland: World Economic Forum. http://www3.weforum.org/docs/WEF_GenderGap_Report_2013.pdf.

Healy, Geraldine, and Gill Kirton. 2000. "Women, Power and Trade Union Government in the UK." *British Journal of Industrial Relations* 38, 3: 343–60. https://doi.org/10.1111/1467-8543.00168.

Hewson, M. 2010. "Agency." In *Encyclopedia of Case Study Research,* ed. Albert J. Mills, Gabrielle Durepos, and Elden Wiebe, 13–17. Thousand Oaks, CA: Sage.

Htun, Mala, and S. Laurel Weldon. 2012. "The Civic Origins of Progressive Policy Change: Combating Violence against Women in Global Perspective, 1975–2005." *American Political Science Review* 106, 3: 548–69. https://doi.org/10.1017/S0003055412000226.

Humphrey, Jill C. 2000. "Self-Organization and Trade Union Democracy." *Sociological Review* 48, 2: 262–82. https://doi.org/10.1111/1467-954X.00215.

Hunt, Gerald, and David Rayside, eds. 2007. *Equity, Diversity and Canadian Labour.* Toronto: University of Toronto Press.

International Labour Organization (ILO). 2009. *Gender Equality at the Heart of Decent Work.* International Labour Conference, 98th Session. Geneva: ILO. http://www.ilo.org/wcmsp5/groups/public/---ed_norm/---relconf/documents/meetingdocument/wcms_105119.pdf.

IUCN (International Union for the Conservation of Nature). 2013. *The Environment and Gender Index Report.* Gland, Switzerland: IUCN. https://portals.iucn.org/library/node/45092.

Jackson, Andrew. 2005. *Work and Labour in Canada: Critical Issues.* Toronto: Canadian Scholar's Press.

Kabeer, Naila. 1999. *The Conditions and Consequences of Choice: Reflections on the Measurement of Women's Empowerment.* Paper 108. Geneva: United Nations Research Institute for Social Development. http://www.unrisd.org/80256B3C005BCCF9/(httpAuxPages)/31EEF181BEC398A380256B67005B720A/$file/dp108.pdf.

Kainer, Jan. 2009. "Gendering Union Renewal: Women's Contributions to Labour Movement Revitalization." In *Unions, Equity, and the Path to Renewal,* ed. Janice R. Foley and Patricia L. Baker, 15–38. Vancouver: UBC Press.

Klasen, Stephan, and Dana Schüler. 2011. "Reforming the Gender-Related Development Index and the Gender Empowerment Measure: Implementing Some Specific Proposals." *Feminist Economics* 17, 1: 1–30. https://doi.org/10.1080/13545701.2010.541860.

Mundlak, Guy, and Hila Shamir. 2014. "Organizing Migrant Care Workers in Israel: Industrial Citizenship and the Trade Union Option." *International Labour Review* 153, 1: 93–116. https://doi.org/10.1111/j.1564-913X.2014.00198.x.

OECD (Organisation for Economic Co-operation and Development). 2018. "What Is SIGI?" https://www.genderindex.org.

–. n.d. "Gender, Institutions and Development Database (GID-DB) 2019." https://stats. oecd.org/Index.aspx?DataSetCode=GIDDB2019.

Parker, Jane. 2006. "Towards Equality and Renewal: Women's Groups, Diversity and Democracy in British Unions." *Economic and Industrial Democracy* 27, 3: 425–62. https://doi.org/10.1177/0143831X06065963.

Pillinger, Jane. 2005. "Pay Equity Now! Gender Mainstreaming and Gender Pay Equity in the Public Services." *International Feminist Journal of Politics* 7, 4: 591–99. https:// doi.org/10.1080/14616740500284599.

–. 2017. *Safe at Home Safe at Work: Trade Union Strategies to Prevent, Manage and Eliminate Work-Place Harassment and Violence against Women.* Brussels: European Trade Union Confederation. https://www.etuc.org/en/document/safe-home-safe-work-final-report -national-country-studies.

Pillinger, Jane, and Nora Wintour. 2019. *Collective Bargaining and Gender Equality.* Newcastle upon Tyne, UK: Agenda.

Plantenga, Janneke, and Chantal Remery. 2013. "Measuring Gender Equality within the European Union." In *Gender and the European Labour Market,* ed. Francesca Bettio, Janneke Plantenga, and Mark Smith, 36–50. London: Routledge.

Sechi, Cinzia. 2007. *Women in Trade Unions in Europe: Bridging the Gaps.* Brussels: European Trade Union Confederation. https://www.etuc.org/sites/default/files/English _complet_1.pdf.

Social Watch. 2012a. "GEI and Per Capita Income." http://www.socialwatch.org/node/ 14371.

–. 2012b. "Measuring Inequity: The 2012 Gender Equity Index." http://www.socialwatch. org/node/14366.

Status of Women Canada. 2018. *Women in Canada: A Gender-Based Statistical Report.* 7th ed. Ottawa: Government of Canada. https://www150.statcan.gc.ca/n1/pub/89 -503-x/89-503-x2015001-eng.htm.

Trades Union Congress (TUC). 2016. *TUC Equality Audit 2016 Report.* London: TUC. https://www.tuc.org.uk/research-analysis/reports/tuc-equality-audit-2016-report.

–. 2018. *TUC Equality Audit 2018.* London: TUC. https://www.tuc.org.uk/research -analysis/reports/tuc-equality-audit-2018.

–. 2022. *TUC Equality Audit 2022.* https://www.tuc.org.uk/research-analysis/equality/ tuc-equality-audit/EqualityAudit2022.

Unifor. n.d. *Bargaining a Domestic Violence Policy and Program.* Toronto: Unifor.

UNRISD (United Nations Research Institute for Social Development). 2005. *Gender Equality: Striving for Justice in an Unequal World. Policy Report on Gender and Development: 10 Years after Beijing.* Geneva: United Nations. https://digitallibrary.un.org/ record/542951?ln=en.

WEF (World Economic Forum). 2020. *The Global Gender Gap Report 2020.* Geneva: WEF. https://reports.weforum.org/global-gender-gap-report-2020/.

Western, Bruce, and Jake Rosenfeld. 2011. "Unions, Norms, and the Rise in U.S. Wage Inequality." *American Sociological Review* 76, 4: 513–37. https://doi.org/10.1177/ 0003122411414817.

10

Trade Policy and Gender Equality Measurement: The Canadian Government's Inclusive Trade Strategy

Laura Macdonald and Nadia Ibrahim

FREE TRADE AGREEMENTS (FTAs) have typically been approached as gender-blind instruments that, according to their advocates, raise living standards around the globe for both men and women. FTAs have been promoted as part of a broader package of neo-liberal pro-market economic reforms, involving privatization, deregulation, advancement of financial flows, cutbacks in the provision of public services, and the reduction of the role of the state in the economy. Trade policies adopted as part of this neo-liberal agenda include not just tariff reduction, but also provisions that encourage the liberalization of trade in services, and the inclusion of intellectual property rights, investor-state dispute settlement mechanisms that amplify the power of firms vis-à-vis states, and other measures to increase trade and investment flows in bilateral, regional, and global trade agreements.

As part of the response to the faltering legitimacy of these neo-liberal policies, however, actors around the globe have turned their attention to their gender-specific impacts and have proposed measures to ensure that women receive more of the benefits of liberalized trade. For example, the European Union (EU) for several years has attempted to adopt a more "gender responsive" form of trade policy by integrating provisions and objectives related to gender into several FTAs and has also included gender-related language in FTA preambles. In March 2018, the vast majority of EU members approved a motion in the EU Parliament called "Gender in EU Trade Agreements." It stated that future trade agreements would feature a gender equality chapter, include women's rights, and support the economic independence of women (Larouche-Maltais and MacLaren 2019, 3–4). In addition, in December 2017, at the eleventh World Trade Organization (WTO) ministerial conference, 118 WTO members and observers agreed to support the Buenos Aires Declaration on Trade and Women's Economic Empowerment. The declaration acknowledged "the importance of incorporating a gender perspective into the promotion of inclusive economic growth, and the key role that gender-responsive policies can play in achieving sustainable socioeconomic development." It added "that inclusive trade policies can contribute to advancing gender equality and women's economic empowerment, which has a positive impact on economic growth and helps to reduce poverty" (WTO 2017). It also called for improved methods for evaluating the gender impact of trade measures and proposals.

Efforts to promote a gender-based analysis of trade agreements are a relatively recent phenomenon compared to other types of public policy discussed in this collection.[1] Resistance to integrating gender concerns into trade policy has been quite strong, given the highly technocratic and neo-liberal character of the policy area (see Hannah, Roberts, and Trommer 2022). Given this, consideration of how to measure the gender impact of trade policies is still in its early stages. The dominance of quantitative tools such as computable general equilibrium (CGE) modelling to measure the likely impact of trade policies poses particular challenges for integrating a gender perspective, especially as these methods are extremely difficult for the average citizen to understand or respond to. The Canadian government, in fact, has been a world leader in pioneering new methods for evaluating the gender impact of trade and for mainstreaming gender considerations into trade policy. As we discuss in this chapter, it is important to carefully assess the government's methods to measure and evaluate the actual or potential impact of trade policies on gender disparities. A narrow approach to measuring this impact not only risks obscuring the whole picture (i.e., the broader gendered effects of trade), but it also limits the potential for meaningfully advancing gender equality. Indeed, it may serve to reinforce existing inequities and the dominant neo-liberal trade paradigm.

In this chapter, we examine efforts to mainstream gender and gender-sensitive evaluation tools in Canadian trade policy. Our research is based on government statements, documents, and interviews with six representatives of Canadian women's, development, labour, and research organizations. We selected organizations with active research or advocacy programs on international trade and approached staff who were responsible for their organization's trade file. Our semi-structured interviews provided insights into questions surrounding the gendered impacts of trade policy, the nature and effectiveness of Canada's approach to mainstreaming gender in trade policy, and suggestions for advancing gender equality in (and accompanying) trade policy. Perspectives from civil society provide an indication of how to develop more holistic approaches to gender mainstreaming and measurement of gender impacts of trade. Inclusion of civil society voices is important to recognize alternative forms of knowledge and expertise in what is still a highly elitist and technocratic field. These groups have also been pushing governments away from a tendency to focus on the needs of women entrepreneurs and toward a consideration of the gendered impacts of trade agreements and policy on a broader range of actors, including workers in both the formal and informal sectors, caregivers, and public service providers. Additionally, we were participant observers in a consultation on gender and trade policies at Global Affairs Canada, organized by Oxfam Canada, and one of the authors has been invited to participate in a new Global Affairs Canada consultative mechanism, the Gender and Trade Advisory Group, which was launched in the fall of 2020.

Feminist Analysis of International Trade

Mainstream economic analysis and trade policy making implicitly assume that trade is gender-neutral and that policies to explicitly address gender discrimination are not required in trade policy. On the rare occasions when they do consider gender, neoclassical economic studies imply that trade liberalization in developing countries should be particularly beneficial to women. According to this approach, trade liberalization will place pressures on industries and firms that discriminate against women workers, since this restriction on the potential labour supply keeps their costs artificially high. Liberalization will thus increase international competition and result in greater incorporation of women into the labour force (see Elson, Grown, and Çagatay 2007, 35–38).

Substantial evidence from feminist and heterodox economists challenges this mainstream assumption.[2] For example, numerous studies in semi-industrialized countries show the persistence of gender gaps in manufacturing sector wages that have increasingly been integrated into world markets (Osterreich 2007; Seguino 2000). The United Nations Conference on Trade and Development (UNCTAD 2017, xi) notes that amplifying the labour force participation of women without enacting demand-side policies and structures to absorb them "worsens gender segregation in labour markets and encourages the crowding of women into low-value-added, informal service sector activities." For instance, Lilia Domínguez-Villalobos and Flor Brown-Grossman (2010, 55) argue that in the case of Mexico, increased trade after the implementation of the North American Free Trade Agreement (NAFTA) did not translate into improved gender equality, despite the rapid expansion of women's entry into paid employment.

Numerous studies have demonstrated the negative impacts of trade liberalization on women, employing quantitative analysis of its effects on various economic sectors (see, for example, Aguayo-Tellez 2011; Fontana 2007; Korinek 2005; United Nations WomenWatch 2011). Based on gender-disaggregated data, these studies show that women and other marginalized groups are particularly hard hit by the negative dimensions of these liberalization policies. Trade policy–induced changes to employment, taxation, public services, and consumption have marked effects on women, who already face substantial barriers. They may affect the gender-based distribution of paid and unpaid work in households. Although to some extent, neo-liberal policies have contributed to the increase of women's participation in paid employment, they have also led to the prevalence of low-wage and precarious jobs, the internationalization of reproductive and care work, the intensification of women's workloads (the double shift), and the feminization of poverty. Cuts to public services such as education, health care, and childcare have a disproportionate impact on women, who tend to be most dependent on public services.

The rollback of public services also adds to the workload for many women, who are traditionally responsible for much of this service provision (Spieldoch 2007). It is important to note that these policies have a more pronounced impact on the most vulnerable women – women of colour, Indigenous women, (im)migrant women, trans women, and women with disabilities. The adoption of intersectional approaches to evaluating the impact of trade liberalization and the development of alternative strategies are therefore essential. Trade liberalization may disrupt sectors and markets where women are active, thus jeopardizing their employment and pushing them into unregulated and poorly compensated jobs in the informal sector (González 2017; United Nations WomenWatch 2011). Furthermore, the rise in women's labour force participation, which is often associated with increased trade, may reduce their time spent on domestic/care work or leisure and damage their health (Fontana 2007). Increased global competition as a result of trade liberalization may put pressure on women employees and women-run enterprises to make upgrades despite their difficulties in accessing credit, technical knowledge, and marketing networks (United Nations WomenWatch 2011).

Considerable progress has been made, as this discussion reveals, in analyzing the ways in which new trade policies may affect men and women differently. To achieve more transformational policies, however, it is necessary to develop an analysis of the indicators and tools that have been used to measure and evaluate trade policies and their gendered assumptions. As Erin Hannah, Adrienne Roberts, and Silke Trommer (2022, 1371) argue, existing approaches to trade policy tend to reinforce neo-liberal orthodoxy partly because the policies are embedded in a technocratic episteme, in which a relatively closed group of experts "cement and reproduce the norms, consensual scientific knowledge and ideological beliefs that constitute the orthodoxy." Understanding methods of measurement can provide a valuable tool to challenge the myth that trade is gender-neutral and help reveal inequities that were invisible in the trade regime because there was no effort to measure them. Measurement can help us to illustrate the disproportionate impacts and experiences of trade on diverse groups of Canadian women (for example, policies to increase women-owned export businesses' access to credit).

Problematizing Measurement in International Trade Policy

The so-called technical turn to measurement in policies and practices that promote gender equality, discussed in the Introduction to this volume, conforms in some ways with the dominant logic that has prevailed in trade policy and macro-economic policy more broadly for decades. With this lens, we see that trade agreements and policies themselves have been used as a form of measurement – to quantify trading relationships and the flow of goods and services, and to establish tariffs, quotas, and penalties. By problematizing these tools and the dominant paradigm, we can see that these rules/measures are not objective or neutral but rather are informed by neo-liberal assumptions. They also impose a particular set of (neo-liberal) rules (such as deregulation and privatization), which we know have unequal impacts (e.g., on the global South), including along gender differences.

The most prevalent approach to evaluation of new trade policies for many years has been the use of CGE models (which are also employed to assess the possible impact of other policy measures, such as environmental policies). These models use computer-based simulations to calculate the future state of the global economy (or of any country or region analyzed), to forecast computationally the impact of policies such as trade liberalization on key economic variables, including income and expenditure flows. Lars Nilsson (2018, 158), the European Commission's deputy head of the Chief Economist and Trade Analysis Unit, maintains that "CGE models have been the workhorse for assessing the economy-wide impact of trade liberalization for more than three decades." The advantage of these models, he argues, is that they provide a method of looking at the linkages between the international and domestic production of goods and services, taking into account the consumption and investment decisions of firms, consumers, and governments across sectors, as well as the fact that different sectors compete for capital, land, and labour (158). As their name applies, these techniques must be "computable." In other words, they require the use of "numerical" data and results (De Ville and Siles-Brügge 2015, 657).

CGE models have been criticized for decades, even in mainstream economics, partly because some see them as having been employed to exaggerate the gains from trade liberalization (see discussion in Nilsson 2018, 160–62). Heterodox economists have levelled strong critiques of the theoretical assumptions underlying the models. For example, Canadian political economist Jim Stanford (2010, 22) argues that a CGE model is not an empirical investigation at all: it is an elaborate simulation model, whose results are fully dependent on the *a priori* theoretical specifications and quantitative parameters built into the model by its designers. Numbers can be attached to any such set of theoretical specifications, but the mere act of attaching numbers to arbitrarily specified theoretical relationships in no way makes it grounded or reliable as a quantitative depiction of the real world economy.

Stanford (2010, 23–24) lists some of the "dubious assumptions" that are built into such models – that they fully employ all factors, including labour; that factor pricing is uniform; that demand and macro-economic policies do not matter; that "society can be described by a single 'representative' household with comparable tastes, purchasing habits, and factor supply decisions"; that there is no capital mobility between countries; that trade is balanced; and that products are differentiated by place of origin. The findings of models based on such highly idealized assumptions cannot be accepted, argues Stanford, because the assumptions are unrealistic.

Another way of understanding the role of modelling techniques comes from a constructivist international political economy approach. In their analysis of the use of CGE modelling in the discursive framing of the proposed Transatlantic Trade and Investment Partnership between the EU and the United States, Ferdi De Ville and Gabriel Siles-Brügge (2015) draw upon the "ideational turn" in the study of political economy. As they suggest, claims that the agreement will yield substantial economic gains for both parties, based on CGE modelling techniques, have been repeatedly used to justify FTAs in the face of civil society concerns. Referring to the work of economic sociologist Jens Beckert, they contend that these models "represent an important exercise in the 'management of fictional expectations.'" This phrase conveys the idea that even though the social world is fundamentally uncertain, economic actors use such models to promote their own objectives (De Ville and Siles-Brügge 2015, 656–57). The inherent complexity of the models hides the high level of uncertainty on which they are based and also makes them extremely impervious to examination or criticism by non-economists. The "black box" character of economic modelling may thus smuggle in many assumptions based on neo-liberal ideology and the interests of firms or other actors in a way that is largely sheltered from criticism based on broader social objectives.

Critiques of CGE techniques from heterodox and constructivist political economists have overlooked, however, the gendered nature of many of the assumptions and data on which these models (and the consequent strategies of measurement that are employed to produce them) are based. Overlooking these biases may lead to the problematic assumption that better models can be produced if only better numbers are included. Indeed, this approach has been adopted in recent attempts by the Canadian government to incorporate gender-based analysis plus (GBA+) into new trade policies, as we discuss below. The current approach to gender and trade adopts a narrow understanding of both the gendered impacts of trade and the tools for advancing gender equality (for example, by focusing almost exclusively on the impact of liberalization on women entrepreneurs and business owners in Canada). Although paying attention to these aspects is important, it is not sufficient to advance broad-based gender equality, as it ignores other impacts including that on women workers in the developing world.

Some serious attempts have been made to adapt CGE approaches to integrate feminist concerns (see Hannah, Roberts, and Trommer 2018). Marzia Fontana (2007), for example, applies a CGE model that distinguishes female from male labour based on gender-disaggregated data and includes household work and leisure as sectors, to simulate the effects of an elimination of tariffs in Zambia and Bangladesh. More recently, UNCTAD (2017) developed a Trade and Gender Toolbox to provide a systematic framework for carrying out an *ex ante* analysis of how a given trade policy would affect women. The toolbox includes a CGE model but expands its traditional use by incorporating such indicators as gender equality in employment, education, and social protection. Data are taken from sources such as censuses and education, labour market, health, and political participation statistics.

UNCTAD (2019) discusses the methodology adopted in the toolbox, recognizing some of the many limitations on the available data. For example, it points out that though "labour market characteristics are collected at the individual level, economic outcomes such as consumption, income, welfare spending receipt, tax payment, living conditions, etc. are often collected at the household level without considering their incidence at the individual level, which would allow for a gender analysis" (14). Indicating the need for much more extensive surveys of firms and households, and for greater study of gender dynamics in the informal sector, it recognizes that few surveys focus on "non-material aspects of well-being such as agency, cultural norms, social relations, [and] household decision-making power" (14). Moreover, the study notes the difficulty of incorporating the impact of non-tariff measures into CGE analysis. Given that such an approach has a "high likelihood of obtaining spurious results," it analyzes only the impact of the removal of tariffs, rather than examining the wide range of other measures involved in contemporary trade agreements (11). The UNCTAD toolbox currently supplies the most advanced method for evaluating the gender impact of trade policies. Even so, UNCTAD itself recognizes the real limitations of the availability of adequate gender-disaggregated data that accurately reflect women's position in the economy and the limits of a CGE approach for studying real-world trade politics. Nonetheless, as discussed below, although the Canadian government has attempted to employ a gender-sensitive approach to evaluating trade policy, it still relies heavily on the CGE methodology.

Canadian Trade Policy, "Inclusive Trade," and Gender Equality Measurement

Winning the federal election of 2015, the Liberal Party under Justin Trudeau formed a majority government and was re-elected with a minority government in 2019 and 2021. The government adopted a feminist perspective, appointed a gender-balanced cabinet, and has promoted gender mainstreaming across its departments using a GBA+ approach to integrate intersectional perspectives. After an extensive process of consultation, Global Affairs Canada (2017) announced that Canada had adopted a Feminist International Assistance Policy. The government also initially espoused what it termed a "Progressive Trade Agenda," claiming that it entailed "an open and transparent process, and maintaining an ongoing dialogue with a broad range of civil society and other stakeholders, including small and medium-sized businesses, women-owned enterprises, non-governmental organizations, and Indigenous peoples and northern communities" (Government of Canada 2017, 4). Subsequently, Ottawa backed away from the word "progressive," referring instead to its "inclusive" approach to trade policy, with similar content:

> Canada is advancing an inclusive approach to trade that seeks to ensure that the benefits and opportunities that flow from trade are more widely shared, including with under-represented groups such as women, SMEs [small- and medium-sized enterprises] and Indigenous peoples.[3] By providing more opportunities for more hard-working Canadians to succeed, Canada is creating wealth and jobs for the middle class. (Government of Canada 2019b)

The Liberal government's commitment to an inclusive approach to trade, as well as its broader feminist foreign policy, serves several political objectives: it rebrands Canadian policy and distances it from both the Harper government's record and that of the Trump administration in the United States; it reaffirms the rhetorical presentation of Canada as a "good state"; and it appeals to women voters (see Parisi 2020).

The government's support for mainstreaming gender in trade policy is not entirely new. In fact, Canada played a leading role in pushing for incorporation of gender-based analysis into global trade policies in the 1990s. These efforts sprang not solely from state initiatives, but also from pressure from a highly active and critical Canadian women's movement. During the debates on the Canada-US FTA (which entered into force in 1989) and the subsequent NAFTA, the National Action Committee on the Status of Women (NAC), a national feminist organization, demanded that the agreement be rejected, in part because of its harmful effects on women. Both FTAs passed, but the efforts of women's groups did introduce gender concerns into public debates on trade policy early on, and after the Beijing Conference of 1995, the Liberal government of Jean Chrétien committed to gender mainstreaming. Due to all these developments, Canada played an active role in other multilateral organizations in calling for gender mainstreaming in trade policy. For example, in 1997, when Canada chaired the Asia-Pacific Economic Cooperation (APEC), that organization committed to gender mainstreaming.[4] The Canadian International Development Agency (CIDA) successfully lobbied for the establishment of a Women Leaders' Network in APEC, making APEC the only multilateral economic body of the time to incorporate gender mainstreaming (Gabriel and Macdonald 2005, 82; Leblond and Fabian 2017).

Nevertheless, the implementation of gender mainstreaming occurred even as the Chrétien government moved to cut its funding for women's organizations as part of its neo-liberal reforms. In the mid-2000s, Canadian feminists argued that this change had increasingly sidelined women's movements from the policy process (Gabriel and Macdonald 2005; Rankin and Wilcox 2004). Efforts (however limited) to mainstream gender concerns into Canadian trade policy came to a halt under the Conservative government of Stephen Harper (2006–15). In the fall of 2006, Ottawa cut $15 million from Status of Women Canada's (SWC) budget and altered its funding guidelines so that organizations engaged in advocacy, lobbying, or research work became ineligible for support. At the same time, its policy guidelines required that applicants for SWC funding must demonstrate that they contributed to the economic well-being of women (Mann 2016). These dramatic cutbacks and the political exclusion of feminist voices from policy making undermined the capacity of the Canadian women's movement in general and meant that few feminist advocacy groups survived to address trade issues.

The push for a gendered approach to trade policy has been revived and expanded under the Trudeau government, as a signature element of its inclusive trade agenda. It employed the language of "smart economics" to justify the policy, underlying the broader benefits to society of gender equality (Chant and Sweetman 2012). A Global Affairs Canada (2018) document, "Highlighting Gender in Trade," thus states,

Research shows that gender equality can create large economic benefits, as increased female labour force participation and increased female education leads to a more productive workforce and increased investment. Experience has also shown that trade agreements, and the cooperation that they have facilitated to reduce barriers to trade, have created positive economic outcomes for their signatories. However, significant gender-related barriers, which limit or distort trade, still exist. These barriers represent missed trade-related opportunities for economic growth in national and international economies. By working to remove them, women's economic empowerment and gender equality stand to benefit.

Moreover, these benefits are measured and portrayed in quantitative terms, based, for example, on growth rates, export numbers from women-owned businesses, and increased women's labour force participation. Elements that might require a different form of measurement and evaluation (such as women's empowerment) are ignored.

Another signature aspect of the Liberal government's approach was the gender chapter in the Canada-Chile Free Trade Agreement of 2017, which was based largely on the 2016 Chile-Uruguay agreement. The Canada-Chile gender chapter recognizes that "improving women's access to opportunities and removing barriers in their countries enhances their participation in national and international economies." It establishes an agenda of shared learning and cooperation, as well as a joint committee to oversee progress. In line with the idea of gender mainstreaming as smart economics, the chapter includes commitments to cooperate in such areas as "encouraging capacity-building and skills enhancement of women at work, in business, and at senior levels in all sectors of society (including on corporate boards)"; "improving women's access to, and participation and leadership in, science, technology and innovation, including education in science, technology, engineering, mathematics and business"; "promoting financial inclusion and education as well as promoting access to financing and financial assistance"; "advancing women's leadership and developing women's networks"; and "promoting female entrepreneurship" (Government of Canada 2019a).

To be fair, further down the list are such measures as "advancing care policies and programs with a gender and shared social responsibility perspective," "conducting gender-based analysis," and "sharing methods and procedures for the collection of sex-disaggregated data, the use of indicators, and the analysis of gender-focused statistics related to trade" (Government of Canada 2019a). However, the chapter includes no mechanisms for enforcement of any of these commitments and makes no attempt to develop shared standards.

The Trudeau government's "inclusive" approach to trade policy was severely tested by the 2016 election of President Donald Trump and his threat to rip up

NAFTA. The Trump administration eventually settled on renegotiating the agreement, after push-back from labour, big business, and both Canada and Mexico. Despite then–trade minister Chrystia Freeland's promise to pursue a gender chapter in the renegotiated NAFTA, the Canadian negotiators rapidly dropped this demand once the talks were seriously under way, probably responding to strong opposition from the US Trade Representative's office. Instead, the Canada–United States–Mexico Agreement (CUSMA) (Government of Canada 2019c) makes occasional references to the topic, as in its chapter on small- and medium-sized enterprises (Chapter 25), in which the parties agree to collaborate on promoting small businesses owned by underrepresented groups, including women, Indigenous people, and youth. The only chapter that addresses the links between gender and trade in any substantive fashion is the one that deals with labour (Chapter 23). The inclusion of this chapter in the main text of the agreement, rather than as a side-accord, does represent an improvement over NAFTA because its contents can be enforced through state-to-state dispute settlement.

Importantly, the chapter recognizes the three governments' commitment to the International Labour Organization's fundamental labour rights, including "the elimination of discrimination in respect of employment and occupation." It also encompasses the goals of eliminating discrimination in employment and occupation and promoting women's equality in the workplace. The labour chapter features other progressive objectives such as cooperating to address "gender-related issues in the field of labour and employment," including eliminating discrimination in employment and wages and promoting equal pay for equal work; consideration of gender issues related to occupational safety and health, including childcare and nursing mothers; and preventing gender-based workplace violence and harassment (Government of Canada 2019c, art. 23.12:5(j)). As Linda Briskin notes in Chapter 9 of this volume, trade unions are an often-overlooked tool for advancing women's equality. The inclusion of stronger mechanisms for promoting labour rights in the CUSMA (compared to NAFTA, where labour rights were included only in an unenforceable side-accord) as well as the gender equity provisions in the Mexican labour reform of 2019 thus represent important steps forward in promoting gender and working-class equity in North America.

Unfortunately, an attempt to have the CUSMA encompass protection of workers against employment discrimination on the basis of sexual orientation provoked an angry reaction from some Republicans, who threatened to block the deal if the provision were included (Dobush 2018). As a result, the three countries were asked to implement the policies that each "considers appropriate to protect workers," effectively gutting the article by making it voluntary.

Global Affairs Canada (GAC) developed new, more sophisticated approaches to CGE modelling of trade agreements to take gender into account using gender-disaggregated data, as displayed in its 2019 evaluation of the likely implications of a potential trade agreement with the Mercado Común del Sur (Mercosur), also known as the Southern Common Market, an economic bloc consisting of Argentina, Brazil, Paraguay, and Uruguay (Government of Canada 2019d).[5] Its efforts still shared some of the problems associated with these modelling techniques, as discussed above, and were less holistic than the UNCTAD toolbox in the type of data considered. The Office of the Chief Economist of GAC carried out a quantitative analysis of the likely impact of a Canada-Mercosur agreement on women and "other sub-groups in the population." The data were drawn from the Statistics Canada census, its Labour Force Survey and other surveys, and also included input from stakeholder consultations. The evaluation considered the impact on Canadian women only, not South American women, and determined that the net impact would be positive for them, since "the sectors projected to add the most jobs – services, including retail/wholesale trade – would generate disproportionately larger demands for female workers than male workers (3,810 jobs created for women compared to 1,896 jobs created for men)." The economic impact evaluation concluded by touting the benefits of the agreement in glowing terms, even though the model had projected a quite limited impact: "The expansion of trade with Mercosur countries would drive economic gains, generate jobs, promote gender balance in the economy, encourage youth employment and increase the number of SMEs in Canada. All these effects would support a broader sharing of the benefits of the agreement, including among traditionally under-represented groups in the economy and trade" (Government of Canada 2019d).

This approach represents an improvement on the gender-blind evaluation of trade policy and was supplemented with a qualitative analysis of the entire agreement, which identified chapters in which gender concerns could be addressed, if the Mercosur bloc agreed (Government of Canada 2019d). The government also launched an online consultation on the nexus between gender and trade (in which only twenty people participated) and held a roundtable in Toronto on the topic, with eight "leading experts of various backgrounds." These processes may have raised some important concerns, but they do not represent a robust consultation process.[6]

In a webinar with Canadian and Chilean officials, held as one of the cooperation activities mandated by the trade and gender chapter of the Canada-Chile FTA, an economist from the Office of the Chief Economist of GAC highlighted the benefits of collecting gender-disaggregated data from the outset and of developing a plan to measure socio-economic effects of the potential

FTA. He stated that "it was a best practice in order to show citizens how trade as [sic] the potential to benefit everyone" (Global Affairs Canada 2020). This is an example of the phenomenon discussed by Hannah, Roberts, and Trommer (2022, 1377), who argue that impact assessment exercises are often used to "legitimate, rather than interrogate, trade-policy choices in the public debate." These efforts do not seriously address the anticipated or demonstrated disproportionate negative impacts of trade policy choices on women or other disadvantaged groups raised by feminist activists and scholars. Whereas the Trudeau government's feminist approach has thus resulted in some innovative policies, it ignores the limitations to CGE models and fails to consider possible negative impacts of liberalized trade agreements.

Alternative Approaches to Evaluating the Gender Impacts of International Trade

As an alternative to Liberal government policies, civil society organizations advocate for a more transformational approach to gender mainstreaming, including a more comprehensive and holistic approach to measurement and evaluation of trade policies. Our interviews with representatives from women's, labour, and other non-governmental groups provided insights into questions around the gendered impacts of trade policy broadly, the nature and effectiveness of Canada's "inclusive approach to trade," and recommendations for improvement. The interviews took place in Ottawa in 2018 (see list of interviews on page 241). We have decided to anonymize the interview subjects to protect their identities.

Most of the civil society representatives we spoke with viewed stand-alone gender chapters in trade agreements as a positive step, at least in theory. They are a symbolic recognition of (or commitment to) gender equity. However, because they are purely symbolic, they have a limited capacity to improve the lives of the women whom trade agreements affect. Citing the example of the Canada-Chile gender chapter, interviewees suggested that the language of such chapters was weak and purely aspirational, as the largely voluntary provisions lacked effective enforcement mechanisms – the "teeth" required to realize the stated goals (Interviewees 2, 4, and 5). The Canada-Chile chapter restates the parties' commitment to existing international agreements, but rather than establishing a corresponding enforcement mechanism, it merely expresses the parties' "intent to implement" the commitment. According to Interviewee 1, a trade union representative, this is an example of "traditional weaselly words and phrases that give the illusion that social provisions of trade are taken seriously or given the same weight as other rights in the trade framework." Furthermore, gender chapters can create the "nuts and bolts" or lines of authority (such as gender committees) for programs or policies to promote gender rights, but funding and processes must be in place for the initiatives to take effect in a timely fashion (Interviewee 3).

As well, our interviewees believed that the gender chapters were congruent with neo-liberalism in targeting a small group of women (entrepreneurs or business owners) who would access or benefit from trade opportunities. This may be important, but it does not respond to the needs of the majority of women. Nor does it benefit them. In fact, most vulnerable workers – those performing unpaid or low-wage care, informal, and/or precarious work – are women. Gender chapters also fail to address (or ameliorate) the negative impacts of trade (Interviewees 2, 4, and 5). According to Intervieweee 4, another trade union representative, the government's approach to trade policy is "a really great exercise in public relations, but there seems to be nothing of substance behind it ... The gender chapter especially aligns with the general positioning of the Trudeau government. They want to be seen as the first feminist government [in Canada] ... On trade, but also on many issues, their rhetoric is much stronger than the follow-through."

The interviewees suggested that gender chapters should include effective enforcement mechanisms and appropriate resources to realize the stated goals. Regarding the aspirational nature of many gender and other social provisions, Interviewee 1 stated, "it's fine to be aspirational and speak to important issues, but I think there's a conversation now about the role of enforceable standards and actually using trade or trade agreements as a lever to put teeth into [other] international agreements [that lack] enforcement mechanisms."

Like many observers, our interviewees noted the problems with top-down approaches to policy making and the inadequacy of consultation processes. The Trudeau government claims to be more transparent than its predecessor(s) and to engage in more public consultation. Although there has been a marked improvement, including stakeholder consultation groups, interviewees identified some significant limitations. For example, Interviewee 4 noted that though the government established a labour consultation group during the NAFTA renegotiation, there was no equivalent for gender rights (such a group was finally created in the fall of 2020). Interviewee 5, a representative of a development organization, described the situation to that date as displaying a lack of "meaningful consultation" with civil society. This contrasted with other negotiations, such as those involving climate change, in which civil society groups were actively engaged, could read draft text, and could present alternatives.

The lack of adequate consultation mechanisms may also reflect the demobilization and/or underfunding of feminist organizations. As discussed above, women's movements' focus on trade issues has diminished since their high level of involvement during the initial Canada-US FTA and NAFTA negotiations in the late 1980s and early 1990s. According to two interview participants, this probably occurred because the resources and capacity of many groups became so limited, with the result that few people were working on trade and gender research (Interviewees 2 and 5). It can also be difficult to mobilize members, supporters, or the broader public around trade issues due to their complex and seemingly abstract nature. As Interviewee 4 remarked, trade issues had an "amorphousness" that made mobilization very difficult.

Interviewees did see some elements of the government's attempt to mainstream gender as positive, but felt that there was much room for improvement to advance gender equity through trade policy, as well as through complementary laws and policies. They suggested various ways in which trade policy could be bettered to advance gender equity, including both liberal elements and more transformative elements.

Union interviewees underscored the importance of enforceable labour chapters that considered gender dimensions to protect workers' rights, including for migrant workers. This may include negotiating provisions to enforce (or preserve policy space for) pay equity, parental leave, and more (Interviewee 1). Interviewee 4 suggested that "a strong gender chapter depends on a strong labour chapter." These interview participants also emphasized the necessity of protecting public services (Interviewees 2 and 4). However, it is important to note that they still expressed some doubt about whether adding gender chapters (or other social chapters) to trade agreements would sufficiently address both the gendered effects of trade liberalization and the broader critiques of free trade.

For example, a key consideration for furthering gender equality (and other progressive goals) is the preservation of future policy space, which may be endangered by such elements as investor state dispute settlement mechanisms that may prevent or discourage governments from creating new laws in the public interest. In debates surrounding investment protection and regulatory cooperation provisions, this concern is often referred to as the "chilling effect" that the provisions have on public interest regulations, particularly those related to environmental protection, public health, consumer protection, and food safety. To combat this trend, participants argued, Canada must negotiate to preserve future policy space, a step that is particularly imperative for future policies, such as a universal childcare program or pharmacare (Interviewee 2). Quantitative approaches such as CGE modelling techniques are incapable, however, of evaluating the possible impact of regulatory chill, and so far GAC has not considered such concerns in its GBA+ approach to inclusive trade.

In relation to such concerns, interview subjects also mentioned the importance of alternative approaches to measurement and evaluation of trade policies.

Nearly all of them agreed with the government's adoption of gender mainstreaming but argued that GBA+ should be integrated into an entire agreement or trade policy agenda, as well as across government departments. An essential element of advancing gender equality was applying gender-based analysis of trade deals before and after agreements were finalized, as well as ongoing analysis and evaluation. Interviewee 2, a labour representative, pointed to the lack of gender-based analysis or gender impact assessment of trade agreements to date. As noted above, the government has been working toward developing GBA+ for prospective new trade agreements, such as the one with Mercosur and the renegotiated NAFTA. A more thorough approach, however, would require analysts to question some of the underlying assumptions of a CGE modelling exercise to include a more expansive and multi-faceted approach to evaluation.

In this line, some interviews led to a broader discussion of the need for a transformational overhaul of (or alternative to) the current model for international trade and cooperation. Interviewee 1 called for "a fundamental rethinking or reforming of the global trading system. It's not about fixing one [chapter] or the other, but rethinking the ideology that underpins it all." Similarly, Interviewee 5, a development organization representative, posited that "a truly progressive trade agenda would require a rethinking of the fundamental objectives of a trading relationship ... [that] would involve placing human rights, etc. at the foundation." Merely "adding women and stirring" to quantitative approaches to measuring the impact of trade agreements cannot consider such deeper implications of the contemporary global trade regime.

Conclusion

As this chapter shows, the use of statistical techniques and quantitative methodologies in the "technical turn to measurement" is nothing new, since for years governments have depended on CGE modelling to evaluate and justify trade agreements. This approach relies upon the mobilization of a vast range of data to project how a given change in trade policy (normally the removal of tariffs) will affect public well-being (measured in terms of such indicators as employment levels and wages). Efforts to deploy such techniques to measure gendered outcomes are in their infancy. Ottawa is at the forefront of global attempts to develop both gender-sensitive approaches to modelling trade policy outcomes and new policies such as gender chapters and mainstreaming of gender initiatives throughout trade agreements. These important initiatives begin seriously to address the inequitable implications of new trading relationships and the problems of measurement and evaluation based on gender-blind data.

Perhaps the most sophisticated approach to this issue is that of the UNCTAD toolbox. Ottawa's economic analysis thus far is based on analyzing a more limited range of impacts, primarily those that affect employment and wages, as well as the proportion of women-owned export businesses. Nevertheless, even the UNCTAD approach fails to entirely address the weaknesses identified by critics of CGE modelling techniques, who point to their unrealistic assumptions. It may be the case that the more easily measurable impacts (for example, the number of women-owned export businesses) shape how we understand the gendered aspects of trade, whereas the harder-to-measure social phenomena (such as the effect of deregulation and austerity on women's work, including care work, and the chilling effect of investor state dispute settlement and regulatory cooperation) remain invisible. A more satisfactory approach from a feminist perspective should move beyond the use of statistical evidence to incorporate a range of qualitative and sectoral studies to gain a richer understanding of how change in the global economy affects the lives of women and other marginalized groups. They should also address the gender impacts of trade agreements on women in all of the signatory states, and not just those in the country doing the analysis – in this case, Canada. As our interviewees insisted, it is also important to develop new models of consultation that bring in alternative perspectives on the benefits of trade measures and the need for measures that mitigate negative impacts.

Acknowledgments

The authors thank the Social Sciences and Humanities Research Council of Canada for its financial support through the Partnership Development Grant, "Alternatives to Austerity." We also thank Scott Sinclair for his support and contributions to earlier versions of this chapter, Jim Stanford, Adrienne Roberts, and Christina Gabriel for their comments on an earlier draft, and Stephen McBride and other members of the "Alternatives to Austerity" research group.

Notes

1 However, the Canadian government did attempt to address gender disparities in trade during the early 2000s (Gabriel and Macdonald 2005; Leblond and Fabian 2017). See also Irene van Staveren (2007) for an early attempt to develop a systematic approach to measuring the impact of changes in trade relations on gender disparities.
2 "Heterodox" refers to various theoretical approaches to the study of economics that differ from or critique the assumptions of the neoclassical school, which has been dominant in most university economics departments for several decades.
3 For a discussion of efforts to incorporate Indigenous concerns in trade agreements, see Patricia Goff (2017) and Leah Sarson (2019).
4 See Jacqui True (2008) for a discussion of gender mainstreaming in APEC.
5 Venezuela was previously a full member of Mercosur but was suspended in 2016.

6 Note that Global Affairs Canada has gone some way toward addressing some of the concerns expressed by interviewees since the time when the interviews took place, for example with the creation of the Gender and Trade Advisory Group in 2020.

List of Interviews

Interviewee 1. Labour union representative. Ottawa, March 27, 2018.
Interviewee 2. Labour union representative. Ottawa, February 22, 2018.
Interviewee 3. Think tank representative. Ottawa, March 7, 2018.
Interviewee 4. Labour union representative. Ottawa, March 14, 2018.
Interviewee 5. Development NGO representative. Ottawa, February 21, 2018.

Works Cited

Aguayo-Tellez, Ernesto. 2011. "The Impact of Trade Liberalization Policies and FDI on Gender Inequalities: A Literature Review." World Bank Open Knowledge Repository. http://hdl.handle.net/10986/9220.

Chant, Sylvia, and Caroline Sweetman. 2012. "Fixing Women or Fixing the World? 'Smart Economics,' Efficiency Approaches, and Gender Equality in Development." *Gender and Development* 20, 3: 517–29.

De Ville, Ferdi, and Gabriel Siles-Brügge. 2015. "The Transatlantic Trade and Investment Partnership and the Role of Computable General Equilibrium Modelling: An Exercise in 'Managing Fictional Expectations.'" *New Political Economy* 20, 5: 653–78.

Dobush, Grace. 2018. "'New NAFTA' Was Supposed to Include Robust LGBTQ Protections. But the U.S. Has All but Nullified Them in a Footnote." Yahoo! Finance, December 4. https://finance.yahoo.com/news/apos-nafta-apos-supposed-robust-110329102. html.

Domínguez-Villalobos, Lilia, and Flor Brown-Grossman. 2010. "Trade Liberalization and Gender Wage Inequality in Mexico." *Feminist Economics* 16, 4: 53–79.

Elson, Diane, Caren Grown, and Nilüfer Çagatay. 2007. "Mainstream, Heterodox, and Feminist Trade Theory." In *The Feminist Economics of Trade*, ed. Irene van Staveren, Diane Elson, Caren Grown, and Nilüfer Çagatay, 33–52. London: Routledge.

Fontana, Marzia. 2007. "Modeling the Effects of Trade on Women, at Work and at Home: Comparative Perspectives." In *The Feminist Economics of Trade*, ed. Irene van Staveren, Diane Elson, Caren Grown, and Nilüfer Çagatay, 117–39. London: Routledge.

Gabriel, Christina, and Laura Macdonald. 2005. "Managing Trade Engagements? Mapping the Contours of State Feminism and Women's Political Activism." *Canadian Foreign Policy Journal* 12, 1: 71–88.

Global Affairs Canada. 2017. "Canada's Feminist International Assistance Policy." https://www.international.gc.ca/world-monde/assets/pdfs/iap2-eng.pdf?_ga=2.181571879. 1613153013.1614105895-2052678147.1614105895.

–. 2018. "Highlighting Gender in Trade." https://www.international.gc.ca/gac-amc/publications/blueprint_2020-objectif_2020/highlighting_gender_trade-mettre_accent_sur_genre_commerce.aspx?lang=eng.

–. 2020. "Activity Report: Gender Based Analysis Plus (GBA+): Canada-Mercosur FTA Negotiations.'" https://www.international.gc.ca/trade-commerce/gender_equality -egalite_genres/gba-canada-mercosur-acs.aspx?lang=eng.

Goff, Patricia M. 2017. *Bringing Indigenous Goals and Concerns into the Progressive Trade Agenda.* Knowledge Synthesis Grant 2017 Report. https://www.wlu.ca/academics/faculties/faculty-of-arts/faculty-profiles/patricia-goff/ksg-report.pdf.

González, Arancha. 2017. "How Gender Affects SMEs' Participation in International Trade." In *Redesigning Canadian Trade Policies for New Global Realities,* Vol. 6, ed. Stephen Tapp, Ari Van Assche, and Robert Wolfe, 583–92. Montreal: Institute for Research on Public Policy.

Government of Canada. 2017. "Government Response to the Sixth Report of the Standing Committee on International Trade: The Trans-Pacific Partnership Agreement: Benefits." July 19. https://www.ourcommons.ca/content/Committee/421/CIIT/GovResponse/ RP9072707/421_CIIT_Rpt06_GR/421_CIIT_Rpt06_GR-e.pdf.

–. 2019a. "Appendix II: Chapter N *bis:* Trade and Gender." https://international.gc.ca/ trade-commerce/trade-agreements-accords-commerciaux/agr-acc/chile-chili/fta -ale/2017_Amend_Modif-App2-Chap-N.aspx?lang=eng.

–. 2019b. "Canada's Inclusive Approach to Trade." https://www.international.gc.ca/gac -amc/campaign-campagne/inclusive_trade/index.aspx?lang=eng.

–. 2019c. "Canada–United States–Mexico Agreement." https://www.international.gc.ca/ trade-commerce/trade-agreements-accords-commerciaux/agr-acc/cusma-aceum/ text-texte/toc-tdm.aspx?lang=eng.

–. 2019d. "Summary of Initial GBA+ for Canada-Mercosur FTA Negotiations." https:// www.international.gc.ca/trade-commerce/gender_equality-egalite_genres/gba_plus _summary-acs_plus_resume.aspx?lang=eng.

Hannah, Erin, Adrienne Roberts, and Silke Trommer. 2018. *Gendering Global Trade Governance through Canada-UK Trade Relations.* Knowledge Synthesis Grant: Final Report. https://www.academia.edu/43617551/Knowledge_Synthesis_Grant_Final_ Report_Gendering_Global_Trade_Governance_through_Canada_UK_Trade_ Relations.

–. 2022. "Gender in Global Trade: Transforming or Reproducing Global Trade Ortho- doxy?" *Review of International Political Economy* 29, 4: 1368–93.

Korinek, Jane. 2005. "Trade and Gender: Issues and Interactions." OECD Trade Policy Papers, No. 24. Paris: OECD Publishing. https://doi.org/10.1787/826133710302.

Larouche-Maltais, Alexandre, and Barbara MacLaren. 2019. *Making Gender-Responsive Free Trade Agreements.* Ottawa: Conference Board of Canada.

Leblond, Patrick, and Judit Fabian. 2017. *Modernizing NAFTA: A New Deal for the North American Economy in the Twenty-First Century.* CIGI Papers 123. Waterloo, ON: Centre for International Governance Innovation. https://www.cigionline.org/sites/default/files/ documents/Paper%20no.123web.pdf.

Mann, Ruth M. 2016. "The Harper Government's New Right Neoliberal Agenda and the Dismantling of Status of Women Canada and the Family Violence Initiative." *Inter- national Journal for Crime, Justice and Social Democracy* 5, 2: 50–64.

Nilsson, Lars. 2018. "Reflections on the Economic Modelling of Free Trade Agreements." *Journal of Global Economic Analysis* 3, 1: 156–86.

Osterreich, Shaianne. 2007. "Gender, Trade and Development: Labor Market Dis- crimination and North-South Terms of Trade." In *The Feminist Economics of Trade,* ed. Irene van Staveren, Diane Elson, Caren Grown, and Nilüfer Çagatay, 55–78. London: Routledge.

Parisi, Laura. 2020. "Canada's New Feminist International Assistance Policy: Business as Usual?" *Foreign Policy Analysis* 16, 2: 163–80.

Rankin, L. Pauline, and Krista D. Wilcox. 2004. "De-gendering Engagement? Gender Mainstreaming, Women's Movements and the Canadian Federal State." *Atlantis* 29, 1: 52–58.

Sarson, Leah. 2019. "'You Cannot Trade What Is Not Yours': Indigenous Governance and the NAFTA Negotiations." *American Review of Canadian Studies* 49, 2: 332–47.

Seguino, Stephanie. 2000. "Gender Inequality and Economic Growth: A Cross-Country Analysis." *World Development* 28, 7: 1211–30.

Spieldoch, Alexandra. 2007. *A Row to Hoe: The Gender Impact of Trade Liberalization on Our Food System, Agricultural Markets and Women's Human Rights.* Geneva: Friedrich-Ebert-Stiftung. https://www.files.ethz.ch/isn/47736/2007-01-01_Row ToHoe_EN.pdf.

Stanford, Jim. 2010. *Out of Equilibrium: The Impact of EU-Canada Free Trade on the Real Economy.* Ottawa: Canadian Centre for Policy Alternatives. https://www.policy alternatives.ca/publications/reports/out-equilibrium.

True, Jacqui. 2008. "Gender Mainstreaming and Regional Trade Governance in Asia-Pacific Economic Cooperation (APEC)." In *Global Governance: Feminist Perspectives,* ed. Shirin M. Rai and Georgina Waylen, 129–59. London: Palgrave Macmillan.

UNCTAD (United Nations Conference on Trade and Development). 2017. *Trade and Development Report 2017. Beyond Austerity: Towards a Global New Deal.* New York: UNCTAD. https://unctad.org/en/pages/PublicationWebflyer.aspx?publicationid=1852.

–. 2019. *Making Trade Policies Gender-Responsive: Data Requirements, Methodological Requirements and Challenges.* New York: UNCTAD. https://unctad.org/system/files/official-document/ditc2019d1_en.pdf.

United Nations WomenWatch. 2011. "Gender Equality and Trade Policy." Accessed November 20, 2017. http://www.un.org/womenwatch/feature/trade/index.html.

van Staveren, Irene. 2007. "Gender Indicators for Monitoring Trade Agreements." In *The Feminist Economics of Trade,* ed. Irene van Staveren, Diane Elson, Caren Grown, and Nilüfer Cağatay, 257–76. London: Routledge.

WTO (World Trade Organization). 2017. "Joint Declaration on Trade and Women's Economic Empowerment on the Occasion of the WTO Ministerial Conference in Buenos Aires in December 2017." https://www.wto.org/english/tratop_e/womenandtrade_e/buenos_aires_declaration_e.htm#:~:text=The%20proponents%20of%20the%20Buenos,encouraging%20women's%20participation%20in%20trade.

11

Advancing Intersectional Considerations in Measuring Gender Equality: A Community Vitality Index in Labrador

Leah Levac, Deborah Stienstra, Petrina Beals, and Jessica McCuaig

IN 2012, WOMEN IN Happy Valley–Goose Bay, Labrador, which lies at the head of Lake Melville on the traditional lands of the Innu and Inuit, were facing the imminent construction of an 824 megawatt hydroelectric dam on the Lower Churchill River. This prompted substantial concerns about the well-being of women in the community, given the consequences of past waves of so-called development (Stienstra 2015), and motivated a participatory research collaboration between these women and researchers from the University of Guelph, who set out to track well-being from the perspective of women. The team, including the authors of this chapter, built on the research and relationships developed through FemNorthNet to produce and implement a feminist intersectional participatory research process to generate a well-being framework and index called a community vitality index (CVI).[1] Described in more detail below, feminist intersectional participatory research is both a theoretical and a methodological orientation to research. It respects principles of feminist intersectionality (drawn from Dhamoon 2011; Hankivsky 2012; and others), community-based participatory research (Israel et al. 2005), and feminist participatory action research (Reid and Frisby 2008). We also used relational leadership theory (Fairhurst and Uhl-Bien 2012; Uhl-Bien 2006) to consider the project's potential for facilitating leadership practices and capacities that are important to social change work (Ospina and Foldy 2010). In response to women's historical exclusion from economic agenda setting and local decision making, we aimed to embed the voices and preferences of diverse women in the decision-making processes that affect their lives.

This case study presents the process of developing the CVI. In keeping with the focus of this book, we highlight the challenges of, and potential for new approaches to, technocratic measurement in gender equality. Ultimately, we suggest that localized well-being frameworks and indices such as the CVI, produced through participatory processes that make a point of including diverse women and that push against some of the risks of the technocratic turn in gender equality measurement (see, for example, Republic of Vanuatu 2010), are a promising way to advance women's well-being and thus gender equality in Canada. However, in keeping with the ground laid in the Introduction, we also recognize that the neo-liberal logics underpinning indicator culture pose a threat to how women's well-being is understood in policy discussions. For instance, a technocratic approach to understanding well-being – privileging experiences that can be quantified – can "[drive] society in certain directions and even [determine] the policy agendas of governments" (Republic of Vanuatu 2010, 2). Further, as the authors of the Introduction to this volume note, "indicator culture involves the abstraction of information from context and the mobilization of this information in a way that has generative effects in terms of behaviours and knowledge production" (page 5). Still, though inappropriate measures can drive society away from advances in gender equality, measures that accurately reflect women's experiences may have the opposite effect. Relatedly, we see two key reasons for employing a technocratic measurement approach. First, by grounding technocratic measurement tools in discourses that accurately reflect how women want their lives to be portrayed and discussed, we advance more equitable discourses about them. This helps to address persistent Western cultural norms that degrade their equality. Second, by framing women's well-being experiences through indicators, we can generate a privileged form of data, thus allowing us to engage in policy debates and decisions with increasing impact. As Ann Janette Rosga and Margaret Satterthwaite (2009, 258) point out, "some of the core problems [such as drifts toward potentially quantifiable data over more substantive considerations] inherent in the indicators project would still be present even if quantitative indicators were banished."

The Town, the Dam, and the Impacts

Happy Valley–Goose Bay (HV-GB) is in the midst of significant economic restructuring. At the heart of this change is the multi-billion-dollar hydroelectric project that dams the Lower Churchill River, also known as Mista-Shipu in Innu. Although HV-GB has a population of only eight thousand, it is the second-largest town in Labrador, which is part of the province of Newfoundland and Labrador. Labrador covers nearly 300,000 square kilometres but has a population of just over thirty thousand. HV-GB is its government and service hub, and is home to people who identify as Innu of Nitassinan, Nunatsiavut Inuit, NunatuKavut Inuit, new immigrants, and Labradorians, people who settled in Labrador over the years and who think of it as home. The town is experiencing significant population changes shaped by the hydroelectric project. In addition to this rapid economic change, its geography and cultural diversity add to its complexity. The same is true of its political context – consisting of Indigenous, federal, provincial, and municipal governments. Whether the hydroelectric project will be beneficial or harmful is a controversial matter across these governments and among local people. Certainly, there is much hope that it will bring employment opportunities for locals, including women. There is also concern, however, that women will bear disproportionate burdens resulting from the project.

For example, people are concerned about the negative socio-economic impacts, including strain on local infrastructure, increasing incidence of illegal drug use, altered access to traditional food sources, and lack of appropriate housing. These and other issues are well documented in literature examining the gendered and intersectional impacts of resource extraction and development (Manning et al. 2018; Stienstra et al. 2016) and were noted in the final report of the Lower Churchill Joint Environmental Assessment Review Panel (Canadian Environmental Assessment Agency et al. 2011), though never adequately addressed.

Better understanding women's well-being is thus particularly important because, in the absence of a clear articulation of it, women's concerns (including those noted above) are easily dismissed, and efforts to address well-being in the community may fail to take women's experiences into account, especially those who are often rendered invisible, such as Indigenous women and women with disabilities. Community participants' articulation of this problem highlights the importance of understanding women's well-being as part of advancing gender equality. Effectively, women's well-being needs cannot be addressed if we fail to understand them, and gender equality is elusive in environments that disproportionately burden women's well-being.

Tracking Women's Well-Being during Labrador's Economic Restructuring

In 2007, the Government of Newfoundland and Labrador released "The Future of Our Land. A Future for Our Children. A Northern Strategic Plan for Labrador," a document that foreshadowed the development of the Lower Churchill hydroelectric project. Probably because the government had decided to "consider recommendations from Aboriginal Women's conferences" (Government of Newfoundland and Labrador 2007, 10) and to include the Women's Policy Office as part of the plan's advisory committee, the plan acknowledged a persistent lack of appropriate services for women in Labrador (20, 64), as well as their underrepresentation in the labour market (21). It also called for attention to childcare needs and for training on gender-based analysis to facilitate appropriate service provision for women (41). Overall, however, the plan lacked a gendered and intersectional foundation, and it failed to acknowledge women as agents in advancing Labrador. Their primary positioning as victims in need of services was predictable but inadequate.

In 2011, the Joint Environmental Assessment Review Panel released its recommendations for the Lower Churchill hydroelectric project, one of which was "social effects needs assessment and research" (Canadian Environmental Review Agency et al. 2011, 291). In this, it had clearly responded to a presentation made by Petrina Beals, then executive director of the Mokami Status of Women Council (Mokami Status of Women Council 2011) and an ongoing collaborator in this research. The panel report acknowledged that "baseline data regarding the existing levels of alcohol and drug abuse and related sexual assault and family violence [are] not available" (xxviii), and that "women's groups ... [had] already [seen] many unaddressed problems and would expect more if the project proceeded" (xxviii). It concluded that there was "the potential for adverse effects resulting from high wage employment, including increased substance abuse, and sexual assault, family violence and adverse effects on women and children [and that] these effects would be difficult to monitor because of the lack of data and because, by nature, the effects are often hidden" (xxviii). The report suggested that "mitigation must include a research element" (xxviii), and it recommended that the provincial government should "conduct a social effects needs assessment, including an appropriately resourced participatory research component, that would determine the parameters to monitor, collect baseline data, and provide recommendations for social effects mitigation measures and an approach to on-going monitoring" (291). The Government of Newfoundland and Labrador (2012, 24) accepted "the intent of the recommendation" but noted that "aspects of the recommendation [were] beyond the control of the Department, specifically conducting the research."

The panel's insightful – yet unheeded – call opened the door to a role for participatory research in determining what parameters to monitor, collecting baseline data, and providing recommendations for social effects mitigation. In response, and after several months of discussions with women in the community, we set out to develop a locally relevant, feminist intersectionality informed framework to track changes to the well-being of women in HV-GB. We called the framework a "community vitality index" (CVI) to flag the necessity of women's well-being to the life of the community.

Several regional, national, and international tools have been designed to measure well-being. In Newfoundland and Labrador, comprehensive accessible data are publicly available through a website portal called Newfoundland and Labrador Community Accounts.[2] These and other well-being frameworks imply a definition of well-being through the indicators on which they focus.

Community Accounts includes eight domains: health; social relationships; income, consumption, and leisure; employment and working conditions; education, literacy, skills, and training; society, culture, politics, and justice; community safety and social vitality; and demographics (May 2007). The system, which tracks and aggregates data, allows users to manipulate search areas by municipality, economic zone, and region. It is an innovative tool of tremendous value to the social planning efforts of communities. Still, one of its primary limitations is its reliance on available data. For example, it does not include on-reserve members of the Innu Nation in Labrador, and some of the data are not gender disaggregated. In addition, the data are insufficiently sensitive to local considerations, to women's social positions, and to important geographic and cultural realities that permeate the North. Further, the conceptual foundation of Community Accounts is not gendered; it does not use a definition of well-being that reflects women's diverse experiences.

These weaknesses are not unique to Community Accounts. The Canadian Index of Wellbeing (Michalos et al. 2011), the Inuvialuit Health Indicators (Inuvialuit Regional Corporation 2011), and the First Nations Community Wellbeing Index (McHardy and O'Sullivan 2004) all suffer similar shortcomings. Each is useful in some way, but none provide an intersectional, localized picture of well-being that reflects women's understandings of it. Further advances are necessary to encompass the complex realities of the lives of northern women with diverse identities. This approach to identity and its interaction with sociopolitical and economic systems is offered by intersectionality (Dhamoon 2011; Hankivsky 2012; McCall 2005). Liz Eckermann (2000), Pauktuutit Inuit Women of Canada, Derek Rasmussen, and Jessica Guillou (2012), and others suggest that considering identity is important to recognizing the contextual factors that affect women's well-being and therefore to developing intersectional well-being indicators and frameworks.

In addition to definitional limitations, existing well-being indices do not sufficiently recognize the context in which well-being is produced and/or sustained. Of particular relevance for our research, northerners often live in remote and isolated communities, depend heavily on the land for cultural and physical sustenance, and travel significant distances to access supports and services.

Our Theoretical Commitments

Our feminist intersectional participatory research process addresses some limitations of current well-being frameworks while striving to advance the role of women in Labrador's strategic agenda. We understand that women with diverse identities are experts in the complex realities that affect their well-being, and that their experiences are best captured by feminist intersectionality and through community-based approaches to research. Using a feminist intersectional lens allows us to undertake what Rita Kaur Dhamoon (2011, 231) refers to as a "critique of the work and effects of power." It also enables us to satisfy our collective interest in influencing policy decisions that shape the lives of women.

Community-based participatory research (Israel et al. 2005) "demand[s] a research practice within the emancipatory perspective, a practice that fosters the democratic participation of community members" (Wallerstein and Duran 2008, 27). In this paradigm, we use feminist participatory action research, noting that the goals of feminism and participatory research are compatible, especially in terms of developing strategies for change (Frisby, Maguire, and Reid 2009). Finally, our focus on change draws on, and adds to, literature about social change organizations and relational leadership. Sonia Ospina and Erica Foldy (2010, 300) note that "creating inclusive, open and equitable processes and structures to maintain a diversity of voices and the deep participation of ... members is a deliberate leadership practice in most social change organizations." Building on this, Ospina et al. (2012) explain that social change leadership has the explicit goal of developing policies that advance social justice, in part by responding to systemic inequities. They, and others (Fairhurst and Uhl-Bien 2012; Uhl-Bien 2006), subscribe to a relational theory of leadership, which understands leadership as developing mutually in relationships. Leadership, from this perspective, is a process of co-creating leadership practices and practitioners, rather than the established set of practices of an individual.

Our Feminist Intersectional Participatory Research Process

Despite its relatively linear presentation here, the development of the CVI was both iterative and flexible, and it evolved with our understanding of the well-being of women in HV-GB and of the dynamic relationships and networks at play. To implement this research and leadership process, we began by hiring Petrina Beals, one of this chapter's co-authors, as a community-based research assistant. She was instrumental in helping to identify a wide range of potential research collaborators.

Literature Review

While we built our community collaboration, we also undertook a literature review, which focused on several areas, including factors affecting women's well-being, existing indices of well-being and technocratic approaches to measuring it, and women's leadership and advocacy. The breadth of our review helped inform the context of our research, our methods, and our outcomes.

Existing research recognizes that several factors play a role in women's well-being.[3] This literature prompted discussions throughout the development process and informed the final CVI. Our review of literature on women's leadership and advocacy guided our decision to approach this work not only as research, but also as a leadership process. For example, we benefited from the knowledge that women's activism is shaped by place-based factors and identity constructs (Reed 2010; Side 2005), and that women may require new forums for action where diversity is accepted and encouraged (Frisby, Maguire, and Reid 2009), or where they are encouraged to reach out to each other through existing social networks (Tastsoglou and Miedema 2003).

In reviewing well-being indices, we found that they did not fully encompass the definition and experiences of women in Happy Valley–Goose Bay. For instance, the Canadian Index of Wellbeing (n.d.) uses a series of indicators across eight domains (community vitality, democratic engagement, education, environment, healthy populations, leisure and culture, living standards, and time use), which capture – in broad terms – the dimensions of well-being we discussed in our collaboration. However, it does not explicitly define well-being, and some of its indicators, such as for the environment domain, do not take important points into account, such as human-nature relations. In sum, no existing index engaged with all the priorities raised by women during the creation of the CVI.

During our review, we also deepened our understanding of the paradoxes that come with technocratic approaches to measuring women's well-being as a component of gender equality. As noted earlier, we ultimately accept that engaging with technocratic measurement approaches is necessary but recognize that we must push against the risks of technocracy, including the neo-liberal underpinnings of indicator culture. Anthropologist Sally Engle Merry (2011, S85) notes several challenges, including that the use of indicators can "replace judgments on the basis of values or politics with apparently more rational decision making." In other words, evidence produced through indicators may be misleading because it seems value-free, even though it is not. She also writes that indicators "tend to ignore individual specificity and context in favor of superficial but standardized knowledge" (S86). Daniel Kaufmann and Aart Kraay (2007) suggest principles for guiding the development of indicators, including submitting them to rigorous public and academic scrutiny. In response to these and other concerns, we proceeded through the research with great intentionality and suggest that our feminist intersectional participatory process itself helps to counter these and other concerns, pushing against the challenges of technocratic approaches to gender equality measurement.

The Recruitment Process

To avoid essentializing women while also capturing a wide range of their experiences, identities, and positions, we drew on Jan Trost's (1986) description of stratified sampling for qualitative studies, which includes identifying factors that could be important for shaping the experiences of participants (such as age, Indigenous identity, presence of disability, socio-economic status), to guide our recruitment efforts. We also relied on a modified snowball sampling approach, which "uses a small pool of initial informants to nominate other participants who meet the eligibility criteria for a study" (Given 2008). In our case, this included drawing on Petrina's existing networks, along with inviting participants to recommend other participants. Through this process, we invited women to become involved with the community collaborative and/or the front-line research (as workshop participants/collaborators).

The small community collaborative or community advisory group consisted of local women who reviewed the work to ensure its relevance to the community. Although its membership has changed over the years, community advisers continue to offer guidance, contacts, suggestions, and information to ensure that relevant contextual and identity-based factors are not overlooked. For example, they identified an opportunity to collaborate with the local college's community studies program during the early stages of the research. They also proposed data collection approaches and helped to build community connections. More recently, they supported ongoing data analysis.

Initially, twenty-six participants/collaborators were involved in two, two-day workshops that were at the heart of developing the CVI. One workshop was held with ten women who were students at the HV-GB campus of the College of the North Atlantic. The second involved sixteen women from the community, thirteen of whom attended the entire workshop, whereas the remaining three attended parts of it. Participants were between the ages of eighteen and sixty, and they came from diverse socio-economic and cultural backgrounds. They also had diverse family compositions, physical and mental abilities, sexual orientations, and educational backgrounds.

Data Collection

Data used to inform the development of the CVI were collected and progressively analyzed during the two workshops, the Labrador Wellness annual general meeting (AGM), a redrafting of the CVI and the initial drafting of an

Table 11.1

Data collection and analysis overview

Research stage	Data collection method	Date
Workshops	Audio-recordings of group discussions Discussion notes taken by participants Flip chart notes from large group discussions Murals/visual representations of well-being Lead researcher and research assistant field notes Evaluation questionnaires Participants' written definitions of well-being	March 2013
Labrador Wellness AGM	Flip chart notes from large group discussions Participant identity questionnaires (using Turning Point© technology) Rankings of factors affecting well-being	April 2013
CVI redraft and initial survey draft	Literature review of existing survey tools	September 2012–September 2013
Training and CVI piloting	Audio-recordings of group discussions Lead researcher and research assistant field notes Completed surveys Audio-recordings of one-on-one discussions	December 2013 – March 2014

accompanying survey, and workshop participant training and community pilot. Each stage in the research process, including data collection methods used, is outlined in Table 11.1 and described below.

The design of the two workshops drew from a number of resources, including literature that described practices of engaging with diverse stakeholders in community decisions (e.g., Four Worlds Centre for Development Learning 2000; Izurieta et al. 2011). It also highlighted the importance of providing people from historically marginalized groups, including women, with special supports to facilitate their participation (Frusciante and Siberon 2010; Jones and Presler-Marshall 2012). This literature, along with our collective past experiences, allowed us to tailor our process specifically for the participants to provide a safe space to discuss issues, be empowered, challenge gender stereotypes, learn engagement skills, and build relationships/networks (Jones and Presler-Marshall 2012). Additionally, we drew heavily on Petrina's past experiences to inform the logistics of the workshops. The goals were to

- create a definition of well-being that resonated with diverse local women
- gather stories that highlighted women's well-being experiences
- determine categories of well-being that captured women's stories and definitions
- identify individual and contextual factors that affected women's well-being.

We used several inclusion strategies in the design and implementation of the workshops, with the intent of putting intersectionality into practice. For example, workshop locations were easy to access, and all participants received a stipend as a way of compensating them for contributing their knowledge. Meals, transportation, and childcare were also provided. We rented an additional room where women could go to take a break, recharge their energy, or speak with a support person (other participants who received small additional stipends) as needed.

Using the data gathered during the workshops, we conducted a thematic analysis to create an initial draft of the CVI. We looked for repetition, similarities, and differences (Ryan and Bernard 2003). The initial draft and final version of the CVI consisted of five components of well-being – physical, emotional, spiritual, mental/intellectual, and cultural – each of which was accompanied by its own definition (see Table 11.2).

The Labrador Wellness AGM was hosted by the Labrador Wellness Coalition. During a workshop offered at the AGM, we collected suggestions for revisions to the initial draft of the CVI. Participants from health and wellness agencies across the region received information about the project and a copy of the draft CVI. Working with the provincial Office of Public Engagement and using a series of activities, along with Turning Point technology,[4] thirty participants offered their thoughts about the draft CVI by completing an identity survey and considering the draft definitions and components of well-being. They also prioritized several factors identified as being important to well-being using a modified Delphi technique (Linstone and Turoff 2002).[5]

Developing the identity questions for inclusion in the CVI survey was one of the most difficult parts of the data collection process. We feared essentializing respondents but knew that asking about their identities would enable us to consider how characteristics beyond gender informed their definitions of well-being. To address our concerns, we asked them to tell us about how they identified themselves, as opposed to telling us how they might be classified (e.g., "Please

Table 11.2

Key components of the community vitality index

	Description	Associated image/presentation
Core definitions	Women's diversity: "Many Indigenous women, including Innu, Nunatsiavut Inuit, and NunatuKavut Inuit women call HV-GB home. There is also a large population of Labradorians; people who were born and raised in Labrador but who do not identify with one particular culture. Many women moved to Labrador for family and/or work reasons. The military base was one of the primary reasons that women moved to HV-GB. Some women moved to HV-GB from other parts of Canada for jobs ... Recently, there has been an increase in immigrant women, especially from the Philippines, who are working in service industries, and who call Labrador home" (workshop participants, March 17, 2013). Well-being: "depends on having the opportunity to enjoy and develop a healthy and sustainable relationship with the environment. Having the ability to value yourself ... having a sense of safety and security, and having access to appropriate food, housing, resources, finances, and support services. Having a social support network and being free from violent relationships ... having or being able to learn coping mechanisms; being able to make choices about what's best for you and your family; having access to information and resources; and social acceptance of diverse identities are also critically important ... Having a space to meet to share and learn with other women is also important. Overall wellbeing is made up of: (1) physical; (2) emotional; (3) mental/intellectual; (4) spiritual; and (5) cultural wellbeing" (Levac and Members of the CVI Steering Committee 2018, 5).	Inuksuk (ᐃᓄᒃᓱᒃ in Inuktitut): symbol used by Inuit people and other northern Indigenous people; "represents the meaning of our well-being in our culture; that every rock has its own unique shape and connects together like a puzzle, and every piece needs each other to build an Inuksuk. We need all these domains to shape our well-being" (workshop participant, March 11, 2013).
Supplemental definitions	Physical well-being: strength, health, endurance, and feeling well; using our body to get us through life; not about physical beauty or ability; being able to have a healthy lifestyle, including healthy diet and body; having appropriate housing (Levac and Members of the CVI Steering Committee 2018, 5–6).	Snowshoe: makes it possible to travel, hunt, visit, and build strength.

	Emotional well-being: inner strength; includes valuing yourself; being able to have control over your overall well-being, and having a healthy image of yourself; requires access to social support (Levac and Members of the CVI Steering Committee 2018, 6).	Spider's web: strong connections that we build; can be supportive but can turn negative and trap us (e.g., abusive relationships).
	Mental/intellectual well-being: knowledge and wisdom gained through family, education, elders, and life experience; being able to value the thoughts of people we trust and trusting ourselves when we disagree with the people close to us; capable of making life's decisions or having someone we trust and we choose who can help us; how we react to other people and how we accept, and are accepted by, others (Levac and Members of the CVI Steering Committee 2018, 6).	Womb: the first drum that every human hears is the beating of the mother's heart; the first net that protects us all.
	Spiritual well-being: lies within us and comes from our connections to land and people; includes self-acceptance and respect for others, and ability to practise and experience love (having compassion for others), joy (having a song in your heart), long-suffering (being patient and perseverant), kindness (being thoughtful to others without seeking reward), faithfulness (a commitment to being true and loyal), gentleness (consideration for the feelings of others), self-control, and energy (your hand to the world, or your aura) (Levac and Members of the CVI Steering Committee 2018, 7).	Dream catcher: Ojibwa in origin, it lets good dreams pass through while snaring bad ones, which are then erased by the light of day.
	Cultural well-being: freedom to practise your own culture and to belong to a cultural group; identity framing; results from being valued for the differences that define us and our beliefs, our history, and our roots (Levac and Members of the CVI Steering Committee 2018, 7).	Fishing net: Reliance on fish in our traditional diets; important to all cultural groups in Labrador; signifies clean water.
Survey	Sixty-eight questions about respondents' identity, all related to each of the five categories of well-being in the framework; based on participants' definitions and discussions about well-being and drawn from existing well-being surveys.	Presented as an electronic survey tool.
Stories	Specific examples of how well-being is manifested in the lives of Labrador women; stories gathered through discussions at community workshops and through community pilot.	Stories presented as audio or text clips in final CVI.

tell us about your sexual orientation. Do you identify as a lesbian?" versus "I am a lesbian").

We had trouble constructing our question about cultural identities. Three Indigenous Peoples claim or hold land rights in Labrador – Nunatsiavut Inuit, NunatuKavut Inuit, and the Innu of Nitassinan. As well, many non-Indigenous people have long histories in Labrador and identify as "Labradorian," even more so than as Canadian. To address this and other challenges, we rejected the term "cultural background" in favour of simply using "background." We thus avoided a singular construction of culture and encouraged respondents to "choose all that apply," recognizing that people can associate with many backgrounds. We worded the question as follows:

Please tell us about your background. I consider myself (choose all that apply) ...
 a) Nunatsiavut Inuit
 b) NunatuKavut Inuit[6]
 c) Innu
 d) Labradorian
 e) Newfoundlander
 f) Canadian
 g) Recent Immigrant
 h) I don't identify with any of these backgrounds.

In nearly every identity question, respondents could choose "I don't identify with any of these [backgrounds, groups, etc.]" to ensure that no one was forced to select an inappropriate label. We also had a substantive discussion about the term "two-spirited," which does not fit well in Western constructions of gender and sexual orientation, but is commonly used in Western contexts to "refer to [an Indigenous] person who identifies as having both a masculine and a feminine spirit, and is used by some Indigenous people to describe their sexual, gender and/or spiritual identity" (Re:searching for LGBTQ2S+ Health 2023). Ultimately, we decided to include the option of identifying as two-spirited in the questions about gender and about sexual orientation, recognizing this as an imperfect solution.

Using the data gathered to this point, we redrafted the CVI framework. It included a visual representation of well-being (Figure 11.1),[7] descriptions of women's diversity and well-being, and definitions of categories of well-being (Table 11.2). To accompany the framework, we used our collected data to create a survey (an index) to gather information about the community's well-being. We included questions drawn not only from participant contributions, but also from existing well-being surveys, where appropriate.

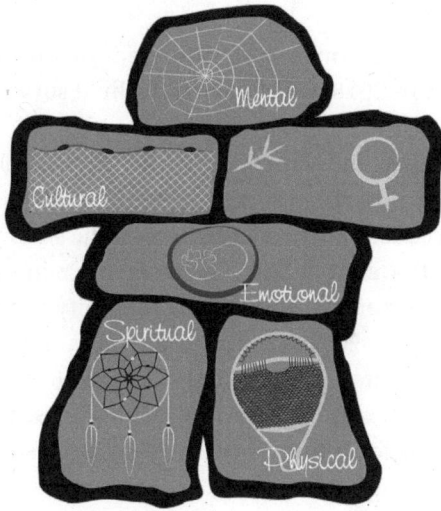

Figure 11.1 The visual representation of the community vitality index

This stage in the process was facilitated by Jessica McCuaig, another research assistant and co-author of this chapter, who meticulously sorted through existing well-being indicators, matched them with concepts highlighted by workshop participants, and used participants' language to touch on identified aspects of well-being. The draft survey posed 8 identity questions and contained 164 questions that corresponded to the CVI framework. It was piloted in the community by workshop participants, who met with approximately fifty women between January and March 2014 to ask them to fill out the questionnaire and provide feedback on it. As we discuss in more detail below, we grappled – and continue to grapple – with the decision to use a survey as a data collection tool, given its limitations with regards to reflecting holistically on women's experiences.

For the community pilot, interested participants from the initial workshops completed a half-day training session on research ethics, data collection, and the contents of the CVI. During the session, they also completed the draft survey themselves to check for clarity and to provide feedback. Next, they took the framework and the survey to other women in HV-GB and asked them to complete the survey, review the framework, and provide feedback. This gave us the opportunity to validate the survey, adding to its internal strength and its external credibility. Workshop participants could reassert their collective ownership over the project and engage in dialogue with other local women, sharing and gathering new knowledge related to their well-being. The ongoing involvement of workshop participants, but especially at this stage, allowed the resulting CVI to "maintain ... the deep participation of ... members [which] is a deliberate leadership practice in most social change organizations" (Ospina and Foldy 2010, 300).

The Final CVI

Feedback gathered through the community pilot informed final revisions to the CVI framework and survey. In 2018, we launched the final survey, which contained eleven identity-related questions (regarding age, gender, background) and sixty-eight questions spread across the five domains of well-being. Community-wide, 127 people who identified as women or two-spirit completed the survey. After undertaking a collaborative data analysis of the survey results (Levac, Pin, and Rochefort 2020), we produced five mini-reports in which we organized the results according to thematic areas that community advisers had identified as important (Buchnea et al. 2022; Kennedy et al. 2022a, 2022b, 2022c, 2022d). We are also considering strategies to make the data publicly available so that female residents of HV-GB can use them to identify both trends in women's well-being and the needs for future research. Ideally, the survey will be repeated in the future so that changes to women's well-being can be identified and monitored. The goal of these efforts is to ensure that the CVI remains relevant and useful to the community (Israel et al. 2005), and available to facilitate social change.

Countering Challenges of Gender Equality Measurement through the Creation of the CVI

At least three elements of the process and resulting CVI contribute to pushing against the challenges of gender equality measurement: conceptual clarity and relevance, maintaining a meaningful and equitable collaboration, and facilitating agency and relational leadership. These elements help to advance more accurate discourses about the well-being experiences and preferences of women in the community. They also provide a foundation for producing data that can help to inform policy decisions.

Conceptual Clarity and Relevance

Reflective of well-being concepts that are important to women with diverse identities, the CVI illustrates how they want to talk about their own experiences while also framing how others talk about the subject. This is a key component of addressing one challenge of the technocratic turn, that "decisions about [how to measure things] depend on who is present to discuss [the issue], who can speak with experience, and what templates and models are available and known to the expert groups who develop them" (Merry n.d., 1).

Participating women's definitions of well-being included several important features (summarized in Table 11.2). For example, they highlighted its dependence on human-land relationships, as opposed to environment-related indicators in other indices that focus on biophysical features and personal behaviours.

Their definitions also drew heavily on ideas related to self-worth and self-esteem (having the ability to value yourself), as well as the notion of choice (being able to choose what is best for you and your family), which do not feature strongly in the indices we reviewed. The definition of mental/intellectual well-being developed through our research emphasizes the paradoxical nature of social networks. Women's definitions were also interconnected. As one woman explained,

> everything really does relate to everything else. There were so many other things that could go under all five of the categories ... I mean if you don't have safe or affordable housing for your children, then how are you going to pass on your cultural knowledge if your kids are sick and you're being abused. In order to have wellbeing, you have to have, you know, you want your kids to be safe and have a good education and to learn their culture and their traditions ... And you know, they're our heart so it adds up emotionally. But if you don't have one, if you don't have all five, you don't have wellbeing. (workshop participant, March 17, 2013)

As noted earlier, women's definitions of well-being directly informed the development of the survey. For example, this appeared in survey items such as "How often are you able to get wild food or country food if you want it?" and "I feel comfortable being open about my beliefs and practicing my spirituality in my community."

The visual representation of the CVI framework (Figure 11.1) highlights women's nuanced and integrated understandings of well-being. For participants, the Inuksuk represents balance (all stones must fit together to form a stable structure), uniqueness, direction (we all benefit from collective guidance), and connection to the earth. Traditionally, Inuksuks are genderless, but the women who developed the CVI suggested that this particular Inuksuk is woman. The images contained in its stones and accompanying the five dimensions of well-being – various types of nets – are symbolic for many reasons. Like a woman's well-being, a net is best when all its connections are strong. A net does not work properly if it has holes in it or if strands are missing. But nets are also paradoxical: they represent safety because they can catch you but also danger, because you can get caught in them. The stone without a net contains a symbol often used to represent "woman," as well as a black spruce twig, which is also depicted on the Labrador flag. The black spruce tree is common across Labrador.

Maintaining a Meaningful and Equitable Collaboration

Throughout the process, we strove to maintain equitable power distribution among members of the team. This was important for addressing the challenges of technocratic gender equality measurement because it allowed us to include local residents' voices in the development of the indicators (Kaufmann and Kraay 2007). To enforce our commitment to meaningful and equitable inclusion, we used mutual assistance pacts instead of participant consent forms. In the pacts, participants could indicate how they wanted their stories and contributions to be acknowledged in the final research. Each pact could be uniquely tailored to preferences that we could accommodate (i.e., being named as a storyteller, being involved in subsequent rounds of data analysis). This approach drew on participatory research practices and on the principles of ownership, control, access, and possession (First Nations Information Governance Centre 2023). Retaining the language of participants throughout the development process is another example of honouring our commitment to equitable collaboration because it allowed them to see the resulting discourse as their own. This also facilitated agency and relational leadership. Finally, discussions about the presentation of survey data in ways that avoided essentializing or generalizing women's experiences figured centrally in the ongoing work of the community collaborative.

Facilitating Agency and Relational Leadership

The women who were involved in developing the CVI participated not only in a collaborative research process, but also in a relational leadership process. Relational leadership challenges hierarchical understandings by rejecting the need for defined positions of authority and recognizing leadership as an evolving and context-specific process, created through relationships. Workshop participants cited their involvement in the process as important to their well-being. They were able to "connect with other women, hear [each other's] stories and gain growth and understanding through the experience" (workshop participant, March 17, 2013).

They also validated the importance of having their voices heard:

> There was something too we were talking about ... the voices. Because I thought that was a very important part because we as women sometimes get shut down or people say ugly things and we just want to leave ... and you believe what they got to say ... So we thought we'd put "voices" in there under mental [well-being] was it, so we put it under mental [well-being] because a lot of women just get shut down and don't get heard. (workshop participants, March 17, 2013)

Challenges in the Process

Certain challenges undermined our efforts to push against the limitations of technocratic approaches to gender equality measurement. For example, developing a technical measure of well-being can sometimes be used simply to shoehorn women's well-being into dominant masculine policy discussions. This evokes a question raised by Michelle Fine and María Elena Torré (2004) – does implementing participatory research from within institutions such as universities inevitably undermine its emancipatory potential? Ultimately, along with Fine and Torré (2004), we find that the risks are outweighed by the possible benefits of reform. We also worried that we would overpromise and underdeliver, a common ethical dilemma of participatory research. Two related challenges presented themselves. The first was managing disparate design priorities; we had to be responsive to community partner needs but also to the requirement for rigour and cost effectiveness (Izurieta et al. 2011). In response, we developed a survey to track changes to women's well-being, but we also aimed to reflect feminist research methodologies and use qualitative methods to capture nuance and complexity. Our respect for the community's perspective is illustrated in the development and final presentation of the framework, which includes images and stories of well-being. The second challenge was that our research is oriented to the future, whereas many of the needs of women in HV-GB are immediate. As one woman pointed out, "I've never seen a housing crisis like I've seen here ... navigating and finding out where services are or if services even exist ... if you're not safe and you don't have a place to sleep" (workshop participant, March 16, 2013). The participants also recognized this tension, but some continued to engage in the process, in the hope that the longer-term work would help to address their needs. Finally, though local women identified creating a survey as a way of generating information that could complement community knowledge – most often available in the form of stories – it nevertheless also introduced challenges such as the risk of reducing their experiences to average well-being scores, an outcome that runs contrary to women's complex understandings of their well-being. To navigate this paradox in our ongoing work, as mentioned above, we continue to have regular discussions about how to avoid essentializing women's experiences while presenting the resulting data. The thematic mini-reports noted above are an example of these efforts.

Conclusion

Our research challenged the risks of the technocratic turn in gender equality measurement. We did not reject the utility that technical measures of abstract social concepts such as well-being can offer to advancing gender equality. Neither were the paradoxes and tensions inherent in this approach invisible to us. The Lower Churchill hydroelectric project is changing the community of HV-GB and is an important reminder of the necessity of engaging with, and trying to change, dominant discourses about women, about community well-being, and about the impacts of economic restructuring. Our CVI is useful not only for community members, but also for community leaders and policy-makers who are interested in addressing the impacts associated with the dam. The feminist intersectional participatory process that guided us challenged the risks of the technocratic turn in gender equality measurement. Specifically, by defining well-being with a diverse group of women in the community, we ensured that historically excluded voices were present to discuss the issue (Merry 2011). By trying to maintain a meaningful and equitable collaboration with community members, we ensured that both residents of HV-GB and academics scrutinized the indicators (Kaufmann and Kraay 2007).

This work also highlights the valuable contributions of northern women with diverse identities when they are positioned as experts in the complex realities that affect their lives. This promotes relational leadership, whereby leadership practices and practitioners are developed through relationships. Ultimately, we were able not only to amplify women's voices, but also to uncover an important connection between participatory research and relational leadership.

Our research illustrates the importance of attending to women's experiences and local context when considering well-being. Indeed, we argue that localized community-developed indices offer a promising alternative way of measuring gender equality. Relatedly, we suggest that adopting nuanced forms of measurement will shift how we discuss and consider what constitutes gender equality. But on their own, these tools cannot correct the dominant discourses that exclude women's well-being or undermine the neo-liberal logics of indicator culture. In fact, at least partially because of the privileging of economic benefits (for a few) over gender equity and equality, some women in HV-GB already face significant threats to their well-being.

Besides our ongoing efforts in HV-GB, work is under way to implement our process elsewhere, with communities that have learned about the development of the CVI and are interested in better understanding their own well-being, using a feminist intersectional perspective. The CVI and its development are part of a broader wave of community-level well-being monitoring that is unfolding across Canada. With its feminist intersectional foundation, our process can make an important contribution to the design of future well-being monitoring projects, which will no doubt develop, given that communities are under growing pressure to produce more data in support of their arguments about their well-being needs. Because technocratic measures shape our ideas about what constitutes well-being and equality, they also influence the possibilities for gendered policy responses. Generic frameworks do not reflect local women's contexts. Using a feminist intersectional participatory approach in the development of technocratic tools is thus a promising way to advance women's well-being and gender equality.

Acknowledgments

We acknowledge that our work spans many territories, including that of the Innu and Inuit in what is now known as Labrador, and the treaty territory of the Mississaugas of the Credit, where the University of Guelph is located. We also acknowledge the tremendous work of the Labrador women who were involved in this research. The CVI is a product of their ideas about, and experiences with, well-being. Without their generous contributions of time and thought, it would never have existed. Thanks also to the helpful comments from the book's editors and two anonymous reviewers, and to the Social Sciences and Humanities Research Council of Canada for funding this research.

Notes

1 See the project homepage at FemNorthNet, https://www.criaw-icref.ca/our-work/research-projects/femnorthnet/.
2 See the portal's homepage at Newfoundland and Labrador Community Accounts, http://nl.communityaccounts.ca/.
3 These include ethno-cultural racial identity: Bombak and Bruce (2012); Hendrickson, Kilbourn, and Ontario Women's Health Network (2011); gender and sexual orientation: Fredriksen-Goldsen, Kim, and Barkan (2012), Hendrickson, Kilbourn, and Ontario Women's Health Network (2011); presence of disability: Fredriksen-Goldsen, Kim, and Barkan (2012); mental health issues and stigmatization: MacMillan et al. (2008), Maiese (2002), Westfall (2011); environmental factors: Sheppard and Hetherington (2012); ability/opportunity to participate in decision making: Kaiser, Kaiser, and Barry (2009); and engagement in cultural activities: Parlee, Berkes, and the Teetl'it Gwich'in Renewable Resources Council (2005), Sheshatshiu Innu First Nation (2011).
4 Turning Point© technology is an electronic voting system that can be used in large groups to record individuals' answers to questions and to present the aggregated results to the group immediately. It is typically used in classrooms to facilitate student participation.
5 The Delphi technique allows a group to collectively prioritize items for inclusion in a survey or a set of indicators using the aggregated results of an individual ranking process.
6 In the original survey, we used the term "Southern Inuit and/or Métis" based on advice from community collaborators. This was more widely used than "NunatuKavut Inuit" at the time.
7 The image was created by Monica Peach, funded by the Government of Nunatsiavut, and conceptualized by women who participated in the development of the CVI. It has been published in Leah Levac and Jacqueline Gillis, "Northern Women's Conceptualizations of Wellbeing: Engaging in the 'Right' Policy Conversations," in *Creating Spaces of Engagement: Policy Justice and the Practical Craft of Deliberative Democracy,* ed. Leah Levac and Sarah Marie Wiebe (Toronto: University of Toronto Press, 2020), 94–116.

Works Cited

Bombak, Andrea E., and Sharon G. Bruce. 2012. "Self-Rated Health and Ethnicity: Focus on Indigenous Populations." *International Journal of Circumpolar Health* 71, 1. http://dx.doi.org/10.3402/ijch.v71i0.18538.

Buchnea, Amanda, Annalise Kennedy, Jacqueline Gillis, and Leah Levac. 2022. *The Wellbeing of Women-Identifying Nunatsiavut Beneficiaries in and around Happy Valley–Goose Bay.* Ottawa: Canadian Research Institute for the Advancement of Women. https://www.criaw-icref.ca/publications/the-wellbeing-of-women-identifying-nunatsiavut-beneficiaries-in-and-around-happy-valley-goose-bay/.

Canadian Environmental Assessment Agency, Lower Churchill Hydroelectric Generation Project Joint Review Panel, Newfoundland and Labrador Department of Environment and Conservation, Government of Newfoundland and Labrador, and Intergovernmental Affairs Secretariat. 2011. *Report of the Joint Review Panel: Lower Churchill Hydroelectric Generation Project, Nalcor Energy, Newfoundland and Labrador.* Ottawa: Canadian Environmental Assessment Agency.

Canadian Index of Wellbeing. n.d. "Domains and Indicators." https://uwaterloo.ca/canadian-index-wellbeing/what-we-do/domains-and-indicators.

Dhamoon, Rita Kaur. 2011. "Considerations on Mainstreaming Intersectionality." *Political Research Quarterly* 64, 1: 230–43. https://doi.org/10.1177/1065912910379227.

Eckermann, Liz. 2000. "Gendering Indicators of Health and Well-Being: Is Quality of Life Gender Neutral?" *Social Indicators Research* 52: 29–54.

Fairhurst, Gail T., and Mary Uhl-Bien. 2012. "Organizational Discourse Analysis (ODA): Examining Leadership as a Relational Process." *Leadership Quarterly* 23, 6: 1043–62. https://doi.org/10.1016/j.leaqua.2012.10.005.

Fine, Michelle, and María Elena Torré. 2004. "Remembering Exclusions: Participatory Action Research in Public Institutions." *Qualitative Research in Psychology* 1, 1: 15–37. https://doi.org/10.1191/1478088704qp003oa.

First Nations Information Governance Centre. 2023. "The First Nations Principles of OCAP®." https://fnigc.ca/ocap-training/.

Four Worlds Centre for Development Learning. 2000. *The Community Story Framework: A Tool for Participatory Community Analysis.* Cochrane, AB: Four Worlds Centre for Development Learning.

Fredriksen-Goldsen, Karen I., Hyun-Jun Kim, and Susan E. Barkan. 2012. "Disability among Lesbian, Gay, and Bisexual Adults: Disparities in Prevalence and Risk." *American Journal of Public Health* 102, 1: e16–e21. https://dx.doi.org/10.2105%2FAJPH.2011.300379.

Frisby, Wendy, Patricia Maguire, and Colleen Reid. 2009. "The 'F' Word Has Everything to Do with It: How Feminist Theories Inform Action Research." *Action Research* 7, 1: 13–29. https://doi.org/10.1177/1476750308099595.

Frusciante, Angela, and Carmen Siberon. 2010. "Constructing Collaborative Success for Network Learning: The Story of the Discovery Community Self-Assessment Tool." *Foundation Review* 2, 1: 53–71. https://doi.org/10.4087/FOUNDATIONREVIEW-D-10-00003.

Given, Lisa M. 2008. "Snowball Sampling." The Sage Encyclopedia of Qualitative Research Methods. https://methods.sagepub.com/reference/sage-encyc-qualitative-research-methods/n425.xml.

Government of Newfoundland and Labrador. 2007. *The Future of Our Land. A Future for Our Children. A Northern Strategic Plan for Labrador.* St. John's: Government of Newfoundland and Labrador. https://caid.ca/NorStrPlaNorLab2007.pdf.

–. 2012. *Government of Newfoundland and Labrador's Response to the Report of the Joint Review Panel for Nalcor Energy's Lower Churchill Hydroelectric Generation Project.* St. John's: Government of Newfoundland and Labrador. https://www.gov.nl.ca/ecc/files/env-assessment-projects-y2010-1305-response-to-panel-report.pdf.

Hankivsky, Olena, ed. 2012. *An Intersectionality-Based Policy Analysis Framework.* Vancouver: Institute for Intersectionality Research and Policy, Simon Fraser University.

Hendrickson, Tekla, Barbara Kilbourn, and Ontario Women's Health Network (OWHN). 2011. *Our Words. Our Health. Health Research Knowledge Translation: Including the Voices of Ontario Women.* Toronto: OWHN.

Inuvialuit Regional Corporation. 2011. "Inuvialuit Research." https://indicators.inuvialuit.com.

Israel, Barbara A., Eugenia Eng, Amy J. Schulz, and Edith A. Parker, eds. 2005. *Methods in Community-Based Participatory Research for Health.* San Francisco: Jossey-Bass.

Izurieta, Arturo, Bevlyne Sithole, Natasha Stacey, Hmalan Hunter-Xenie, Bruce Campbell, Paul Donohoe, Jessie Brown, and Lincoln Wilson. 2011. "Developing Indicators for Monitoring and Evaluating Joint Management Effectiveness in Protected Areas in the Northern Territory, Australia." *Ecology and Society* 16, 3: 9. http://dx.doi.org/10.5751/ES-04274-160309.

Jones, Nicola, and Elizabeth Presler-Marshall. 2012. "Governance and Poverty Eradication: Applying a Gender and Social Institutions Perspective." *Public Administration and Development* 32, 4–5: 371–84. https://doi.org/10.1002/pad.1618.

Kaiser, Margaret M., Katherine Laux Kaiser, and Teresa L. Barry. 2009. "Health Effects of Life Transitions for Women and Children: A Research Model for Public and Community Health Nursing." *Public Health Nursing* 26, 4: 370–79. https://doi.org/10.1111/j.1525-1446.2009.00792.x.

Kaufmann, Daniel, and Aart Kraay. 2007. *Governance Indicators: Where Are We, Where Should We Be Going?* World Bank Policy Research Working Paper 4370. Washington, DC: World Bank. http://papers.ssrn.com/sol3/papers.cfm?abstract_id=1019685.

Kennedy, Annalise, Amanda Buchnea, Leah Levac, and Olivia Flegg. 2022a. *Environment and Women's Wellbeing in HV-GB.* Ottawa: Canadian Research Institute for the Advancement of Women. https://www.criaw-icref.ca/publications/environment-womens-wellbeing-in-hv-gb/.

–. 2022b. *Food, Water and Women's Wellbeing in HV-GB.* Ottawa: Canadian Research Institute for the Advancement of Women. https://www.criaw-icref.ca/publications/food-water-womens-wellbeing-in-hv-gb/.

–. 2022c. *Social Supports and Women's Wellbeing in HV-GB.* Ottawa: Canadian Research Institute for the Advancement of Women. https://www.criaw-icref.ca/publications/social-supports-womens-wellbeing-in-hv-gb/.

–. 2022d. *Spirituality, Culture and Women's Wellbeing in HV-GB.* Ottawa: Canadian Research Institute for the Advancement of Women. https://www.criaw-icref.ca/publications/spirituality-culture-womens-wellbeing-in-hv-gb/.

Levac, Leah, and Members of the CVI Steering Committee. 2018. *Community Vitality Index (CVI): Overview.* Ottawa: Canadian Research Institute for the Advancement of Women. https://www.criaw-icref.ca/wp-content/uploads/2021/05/CVI-Overview.pdf.

Levac, Leah, Laura Pin, and Julie Rochefort. 2020. "Understanding Community Data in Community." Live Work Well Research Centre. Accessed December 12, 2022. https://liveworkwell.ca/news/2020/11/understanding-community-data-community.

Linstone, Harold A., and Murray Turoff, eds. 2002. *The Delphi Method: Techniques and Applications.* http://www.foresight.pl/assets/downloads/publications/Turoff_Linstone.pdf.

MacMillan, Harriet L., Ellen Jamieson, Christine A. Walsh, Maria Wong, Emily J. Faries, Harvey McCue, Angus B. MacMillan, David R. Offord, and the Technical Advisory Committee of the Chiefs of Ontario. 2008. "First Nations Women's Mental Health: Results from an Ontario Survey." *Archives of Women's Mental Health* 11: 109–15. https://doi.org/10.1007/s00737-008-0004-y.

Maiese, Deborah R. 2002. "Healthy People 2010 – Leading Health Indicators for Women." *Jacobs Institute of Women's Health* 12, 4: 155–64. https://doi.org/10.1016/S1049-3867(02)00140-8.

Manning, Susan M., Patricia Nash, Leah Levac, Deborah Stienstra, and Jane Stinson. 2018. *A Literature Synthesis Report on the Impacts of Resource Extraction for Indigenous Women.*

Ottawa: Canadian Research Institute for the Advancement of Women. https://www.criaw-icref.ca/wp-content/uploads/2021/04/Impacts-of-Resource-Extraction-for-Indigenous-Women.pdf.

May, Doug. 2007. *Determinants of Well-Being.* St. John's: Memorial University and Newfoundland and Labrador Statistics Agency. https://nl.communityaccounts.ca/pdf_files/DeterminantsOfWellBeing-06.pdf.

McCall, Leslie. 2005. "The Complexity of Intersectionality." *Signs* 30, 3: 1771–800. https://www.jstor.org/stable/10.1086/426800.

McHardy, Mindy, and Erin O'Sullivan. 2004. *First Nations Community Well-Being in Canada: The Community Well-Being Index (CWB), 2001.* Ottawa: Strategic Research and Analysis Directorate, Indian and Northern Affairs Canada.

Merry, Sally Engle. 2011. "Measuring the World: Indicators, Human Rights, and Global Governance." *Current Anthropology* 52, suppl. 3: S83–S95. https://doi.org/10.1086/657241.

–. n.d. "Chapter 4: Measuring Violence against Women." University of Victoria. http://www.law.uvic.ca/demcon/2012%20readings/violence%20ag%20women.pdf.

Michalos, Alex, et al. 2011. "The Canadian Index of Wellbeing: Technical Paper." University of Waterloo. https://uwaterloo.ca/canadian-index-wellbeing/sites/ca.canadian-index-wellbeing/files/uploads/files/Canadian_Index_of_Wellbeing-TechnicalPaper-FINAL.pdf.

Mokami Status of Women Council. 2011. *Out of the Rhetoric and into the Reality of Local Women's Lives: Submission to the Environmental Assessment Panel on the Lower Churchill Hydro Development.* Ottawa: Canadian Research Institute for the Advancement of Women. https://www.criaw-icref.ca/publications/out-of-the-rhetoric-and-into-the-reality-of-local-womens-lives/.

Ospina, Sonia, and Erica Foldy. 2010. "Building Bridges from the Margins: The Work of Leadership in Social Change Organizations." *Leadership Quarterly* 21, 2: 292–307. https://doi.org/10.1016/j.leaqua.2010.01.008.

Ospina, Sonia, Erica Foldy, Waad El Hadidy, Jennifer Dodge, Amparo Hofmann-Pinilla, and Celina Su. 2012. "Social Change Leadership as Relational Leadership." In *Advancing Relational Leadership Research: A Dialogue among Perspectives,* ed. Mary Uhl-Bien and Sonia M. Ospina, 255–302. Charlotte, NC: Information Age.

Parlee, Brenda, Fikret Berkes, and the Teetl'it Gwich'in Renewable Resources Council. 2005. "Health of the Land, Health of the People: A Case Study on Gwich'in Berry Harvesting in Northern Canada." *EcoHealth* 2: 127–37. https://doi.org/10.1007/s10393-005-3870-z.

Pauktuutit Inuit Women of Canada, Derek Rasmussen, and Jessica Guillou. 2012. "Developing an Inuit-Specific Framework for Culturally Relevant Health Indicators Incorporating Gender-Based Analysis." *Journal of Aboriginal Health* 8, 2: 24–35.

Reed, Maureen G. 2010. "Taking Stands: A Feminist Perspective on 'Other' Women's Activism in Forestry Communities of Northern Vancouver Island." *Gender, Place and Culture* 7, 4: 363–87. http://dx.doi.org/10.1080/713668882.

Reid, Colleen, and Wendy Frisby. 2008. "Continuing the Journey: Articulating Dimensions of Feminist Participatory Research (FPAR)." In *The Sage Handbook of Action Research: Participative Inquiry and Practice,* ed. Peter Reason and Hilary Bradbury, 93–105. Los Angeles: Sage.

Republic of Vanuatu. 2010. "Alternative Indicators of Well-Being for Melanesia: Changing the Way Progress Is Measured in the South Pacific." Pacific Data Hub. https://microdata.pacificdata.org/index.php/catalog/531/related-materials.

Re:searching for LGBTQ2S+ Health. 2023. "Two-Spirit Community." http://lgbtqhealth. ca/community/two-spirit.php.

Rosga, Ann Janette, and Margaret Satterthwaite. 2009. "The Trust in Indicators: Measuring Human Rights." *Berkley Journal of International Law* 27, 2: 253–315. http://dx.doi. org/10.2139/ssrn.1298540.

Ryan, Gery W., and H. Russell Bernard. 2003. "Techniques to Identify Themes." *Field Methods* 15, 1: 85–109. https://doi.org/10.1177/1525822X02239569.

Sheppard, Amanda J., and Ross Hetherington. 2012. "A Decade of Research in Inuit Children, Youth, and Maternal Health in Canada: Areas of Concentrations and Scarcities." *International Journal of Circumpolar Health* 71, 1. http://dx.doi.org/10.3402/ijch. v71i0.18383.

Sheshatshiu Innu First Nation. 2011. *Mmu Uauitetau Tipatshimuna. It Takes a Community to Raise a Child: A Sheshatshiu Innu First Nation Report on a Community Health Needs Assessment.* Sheshatshiu, NL: Sheshatshiu Innu First Nation.

Side, Katherine. 2005. "Snapshot on Identity: Women's Contributions Addressing Community Relations in a Rural Northern Irish District." *Women's Studies International Forum* 28, 4: 315–27. https://doi.org/10.1016/j.wsif.2005.04.016.

Stienstra, Deborah. 2015. "Northern Crises: Women's Relationships and Resistances to Resource Extractions." *International Feminist Journal of Politics* 17, 4: 630–51. https:// doi.org/10.1080/14616742.2015.1060695.

Stienstra, Deborah, Leah Levac, Gail Baikie, Jane Stinson, and Susan M. Manning. 2016. *Gendered and Intersectional Implications of Energy and Resource Extraction in Resource-Based Communities in Canada's North.* Ottawa: Canadian Research Institute for the Advancement of Women. https://www.criaw-icref.ca/wp-content/uploads/2021/04/ Gendered-and-Intersectional-Implications-of-Energy-and-Resource-Extraction-in -Resource-Based-Communities.pdf.

Tastsoglou, Evangelia, and Baukje Miedema. 2003. "Immigrant Women and Community Development in the Canadian Maritimes: Outsiders Within?" *Canadian Journal of Sociology* 28, 2: 203–34. https://doi.org/10.2307/3341459.

Trost, Jan E. 1986. "Statistically Nonrepresentative Stratified Sampling: A Sampling Technique for Qualitative Studies." *Qualitative Sociology* 9, 1: 54–57. https://doi.org/10.1007/ BF00988249.

Uhl-Bien, Mary. 2006. "Relational Leadership Theory: Exploring the Social Processes of Leadership and Organizing." *Leadership Quarterly* 17, 6: 654–76. https://doi.org/10.1016/ j.leaqua.2006.10.007.

Wallerstein, Nina, and Bonnie Duran. 2008. "The Theoretical, Historical, and Practice Roots of CBPR." In *Community-Based Participatory Research for Health: From Process to Outcomes,* 2nd ed., ed. Meredith Minkler and Nina Wallerstein, 25–45. New York: Jossey-Bass.

Westfall, Rachel. 2011. *Dimensions of Social Inclusion and Exclusion in Yukon, 2010.* Whitehorse: Yukon Bureau of Statistics. https://www.yumpu.com/en/document/ view/22339933/dimensions-of-social-inclusion-and-exclusion-in-yukon-2010.

Contributors

Hugh Armstrong is a professor emeritus of social work and political economy at Carleton University. His publications include numerous journal articles and book chapters and, with Pat Armstrong, several books, including *The Double Ghetto: Canadian Women and Their Segregated Work* and their co-edited volume, *The Privatization of Care: The Case of Nursing Homes*. He proudly sits on the board of the Ontario Health Coalition.

Pat Armstrong is a distinguished research professor emeritus at York University. A feminist political economist who studies social policy, women and work, as well as health and social services, she has led multiple research projects conducted in partnership with multiple organizations, especially with unions. Her recent books include *Unpaid Work in Nursing Homes: Flexible Boundaries; Wash, Wear, and Care: Clothing and Laundry in Long-Term Residential Care* (with Suzanne Day); and *The Privatization of Care: The Case of Nursing Homes* (with Hugh Armstrong).

Petrina Beals (she/her) is a proud mother and grandmother. She is the executive director of Violence Prevention Labrador, based in Happy Valley–Goose Bay (HV-GB), Labrador. She is a lifelong feminist advocate, and the past executive director of Mokami Status of Women Council, also in HV-GB. Petrina worked for several years as a research associate on the Community Vitality Index project described in Chapter 11.

Madeline Boscoe, RN, DU, is a founding member of the Cochrane-affiliated Sex and Gender Methods Group. She is a senior leader and advocate, leading and supporting successful regional and national efforts for policy and services that meet women's needs, such as publicly funded midwifery and improved drug and device regulation. She served as the founding executive director of the Canadian Women's Health Network and Winnipeg Women's Health Clinic's Advocacy Program and was the first chair of the CIHR Institute of Gender and Health Knowledge Translation Committee. She is the recipient of an honorary doctorate from the University of Ottawa and the Governor General's Award in Commemoration of the Persons Case in 2011.

Linda Briskin is a professor emeritus at York University. Her research interests include feminist pedagogies; equality bargaining; gendering worker militancies; women's organizing inside trade unions; and leadership and representation. She has been a feminist and union activist for many decades. Her commitment to social justice has framed her scholarship and inspired her teaching. She is also a writer and fine art photographer. Her photographs have been published widely (https://www.lindabriskinphotography.com/). Her fiction and creative non-fiction has appeared in many literary journals.

Jacqueline Choiniere, RN, PhD, is an associate professor in the School of Nursing at York University. Her research explores the influence of political, economic, and social forces on the conditions of care and work. Recent publications include *Health Matters: Evidence, Critical Social Science and Health Care in Canada* (co-edited with Eric Mykhalovskiy, Pat Armstrong, and Hugh Armstrong), and "Accessing Nursing Home Care: Unpaid Work in Ontario and Sweden" (co-authored with Petra Ulmanen and Ruth Lowndes), in *Unpaid Work in Nursing Homes: Flexible Boundaries* (edited by Pat Armstrong).

Stephanie E. Coen, PhD, is an associate professor in the School of Geography at the University of Nottingham, UK. Her interdisciplinary research uses participatory and arts-based methods to investigate gendered inequities in physical activity/sport and socio-environmental influences on young people's health.

Marion Doull, PhD, is a senior policy adviser with the Canadian Federal Public Service. Prior to joining the public service, Marion worked as a post-doctoral researcher at the University of British Columbia where her work focused on gender, sexual health, and health disparities among young people. Marion is a founding member of the Cochrane-affiliated Sex/Gender Methods Group.

Maggie FitzGerald is an assistant professor in the Department of Political Studies at the University of Saskatchewan. Her research focuses on the ethics of care, global ethics and international political theory, decolonial ethics, and feminist political economy. Her work has appeared in journals such as *Ethics* *and Social Welfare; Atlantis: Critical Studies in Gender, Culture, and Social Justice;* and *International Journal of Care and Caring.* She is the author of *Care and the Pluriverse: Rethinking Global Ethics.*

Christina Gabriel is a professor in the Department of Political Science and the Institute of Political Economy at Carleton University. Her research interests include citizenship, migration, gender and politics, and regional integration. She has contributed chapters and articles on issues such as migration, border control, transnational care labour, and North American regional integration. She is the co-author of *Containing Diversity: Canada and the Politics of Immigration in the 21st Century* (with Yasmeen Abu-Laban and Ethel Tungohan).

Joan Grace is a professor of political science at the University of Winnipeg. Her work explores the processes and institutions of government policy development, as well as state-society relationships in the Canadian parliamentary system. She is a co-editor of the *Handbook on Gender and Federalism* and author of scholarly articles published in *Parliamentary Affairs* and *Canadian Public Administration.*

Nadia Ibrahim is a staff representative at a national labour union. She was formerly the coordinator of the Trade Justice Network and worked as a researcher on a variety of topics, including the impacts of trade agreements on gender equality, public services, the environment, and food and agriculture systems. Nadia holds an MA in political economy from Carleton University and a BA in global political economy from the University of Manitoba.

Holly Johnson retired from the Department of Criminology at the University of Ottawa in 2018. Her research examined women's experiences of male violence and criminal justice and social responses to it using a variety of methodologies. She was lead investigator on national and international comparative surveys on violence against women. She also contributed to the UN guidelines for statistical indicators on male violence against women as well as numerous UN advisory groups.

Janet Jull, OT Reg (ON), PhD, is an assistant professor at Queen's University, and an affiliate investigator at the Ottawa Hospital Research Institute. Janet develops and evaluates shared decision-making tools and approaches to support client-centred care, and investigates collaborative research practices.

Lee Lakeman organized against male violence at Vancouver Rape Relief and Women's Shelter from 1978 to 2012. An honorary member of the collective, Lee is completing a history of thirty-five years of the collective's work on topics including the invention of anti-rape centres, consciousness raising, rape law reform, transition house standards, the impact of the Charter, the Justice department consultations in the 1990s, anti-feminist backlash, the Montreal Massacre, prostitution and pornography industries, and the conflict between sex and gender ideologies.

Leah Levac (she/her) is a mother, dog-lover, associate professor in political science at the University of Guelph, and Canada Research Chair (Tier 2) in Critical Community Engagement and Public Policy. Across her research and teaching – with community organizations, northern and Indigenous women, municipal governments, students, and others – she explores how collaborative research responding to community-identified concerns can transform colonial public policy making. She is the co-editor of *Creating Spaces of Engagement: Policy Justice and the Practical Craft of Deliberative Democracy.*

Laura Macdonald is a professor in the Department of Political Science and the Institute of Political Economy at Carleton University. She has published widely on such issues as the role of non-governmental organizations in development, gender and trade, global civil society, social policies and citizenship struggles in Latin America, Canadian development assistance, and Canada–Latin American relations. Her recent work looks at transnational activism in North America around labour rights, migration, and human rights in Mexico.

Diana Majury is a retired professor from Carleton University's Department of Law and Legal Studies. As a feminist, she researched, taught, and was active in the areas of equality law, human rights, and violence against women.

Jessica McCuaig (she/her) currently leads the Disability Navigator pilot program at the University of Michigan, which focuses on improving the accommodations experience and access for faculty and staff with disabilities. Prior to working at U-M on diversity, equity, and inclusion initiatives, Jessica was a consultant and project manager for non-profit organizations focused on access, stakeholder engagement, and policy-related research.

Marika Morris is a research, evaluation, and training consultant and an adjunct research professor in the School of Canadian Studies at Carleton University. She is a former federal public servant and has worked for members of parliament and gender equality organizations. Her clients are mainly Inuit organizations, health organizations, and organizations devoted to preventing gender-based violence. She is a member of Statistics Canada's Advisory Committee on Social Conditions.

Ann Pederson, PhD, is the director of Population and Global Health at BC Women's Hospital and Health Centre in Vancouver. She is an adjunct professor at the School of Population and Public Health, UBC, and at Simon Fraser University's Faculty of Health Sciences. Ann's work focuses on improving the health care response to gender-based violence and parents' and clinicians' experiences related to stillbirth. She has co-edited several books, including *Making It Better: Gender Transformative Health Promotion*.

Jennifer Petkovic, PhD, is the coordinator of the Campbell Equity Methods Group and Cochrane Equity Thematic Group and an affiliate investigator at the Bruyère Research Institute. Her research interests include health equity and stakeholder engagement methods in evidence synthesis and guidelines.

Manuela Popovici is a research assistant with the violence against women hub of the Community First: Impacts of Community Engagement Project. She works in the area of human rights and equity, both domestically and internationally.

Lorri Puil, MD, PhD, is a physician-scientist and an adjunct professor in the School of Population and Public Health in the Faculty of Medicine at the University of British Columbia (UBC). She is a member of the UBC Therapeutics Initiative and an editor of Cochrane Hypertension. She teaches quantitative research synthesis methods and evaluates health care interventions for Canadian and international policy-makers. Her interests include methods for incorporating sex/gender and equity considerations into the synthesis of health research to inform decision making.

L. Pauline Rankin is a professor in the School of Canadian Studies and Provost and Vice-President (Academic) at Carleton University. Her research spans various aspects of gender and politics, with specific interest in domestic and global applications of gender mainstreaming, gender activism, and gender equality measurement. She is a co-editor of *We Still Demand! Redefining Resistance in Sex and Gender Struggles* (with Patrizia Gentile and Gary Kinsman).

Stephanie Redden held the 2019–20 Human Trafficking and Modern Day Slavery Postdoctoral Fellowship at Yale University's Gilder Lehrman Center for the Study of Slavery, Resistance, and Abolition. In 2021, she was a visiting scholar with the Institute of Political Economy at Carleton University. Her work has been published in a number of edited books, as well as in the *International Feminist Journal of Politics* and *Globalizations*.

Vivien Runnels, PhD, has been a senior researcher for several years at the Faculties of Social Sciences and Medicine, University of Ottawa, and, more recently, a senior research adviser at Saint Paul University. She was a founding member of the Cochrane-affiliated Sex/Gender Methods Group. As author and editor, Vivien has made a number of contributions on issues that primarily concern social justice and health equity.

Beverley Shea, PhD, is a clinical investigator at the Ottawa Health Research Institute and an adjunct professor at the Department of Epidemiology and Public Health at the University of Ottawa. She is an editor for the Cochrane Musculoskeletal Review Group and co-convenor for the Cochrane non-randomized methods working group. Beverley is also a clinical scientist at the Bruyère Research Institute and led the development of AMSTAR, an instrument for assessing the quality of systematic reviews.

Deborah Stienstra holds the Jarislowsky Chair in Families and Work at the University of Guelph, where she is the director of the Live Work Well Research Centre and a professor of political science. She is the author of *About Canada: Disability Rights*. Her research and publications explore the intersections of disabilities, gender, childhood, and Indigenousness, identifying barriers to, as well as possibilities for, engagement and transformative change.

Liam Swiss is a professor of sociology at Acadia University. His research examines foreign aid, global development, Canadian development policy, and gender equality. His research has appeared in journals such as the *American Sociological Review, Social Forces, Social Science Research*, and *World Development*. He is the author of *The Globalization of Foreign Aid: Developing Consensus*.

Rebecca Tiessen is a professor in the School of International Development and Global Studies at the University of Ottawa. She has also been a faculty member at Dalhousie University and Canada Research Chair at the Royal Military College of Canada. Her publications focus on gender and development, feminist foreign policy, and youth as agents of change. One of her scholarly collections includes a special issue (free, open access) titled *Innovations in Gender Equality and Women's Empowerment: Understanding the Role of International Development Volunteers* *as Transnational Actors* (https://www.nomos-elibrary.de/10.5771/978374 8924951/innovations-in-gender-equality-and-women-s-empowerment).

Sari Tudiver, PhD, is an Ottawa-based researcher, writer, and women's health advocate. Fascinated by the challenges of generating and sharing knowledge across discourses and sectors, she has worked in academic and community health settings, with international development civil society organizations, and for the Canadian federal government in health policy. Trained in cultural anthropology, her interests include dynamics of sex/gender and exploring diverse political and social realities through personal narratives. She is a founding member of the Sex/Gender Methods Group.

Vivian Welch, PhD, is editor-in-chief of the Campbell Collaboration, director of the Methods Centre at the Bruyère Research Institute, and an associate professor at the School of Epidemiology and Public Health, University of Ottawa. Her research interests include evidence synthesis on health equity and healthy aging.

Index

Printed and bound in Canada by Friesens
Set in Swiss Condensed and Minion by Artegraphica Design Co. Ltd.
Copy editor: Deborah Kerr
Proofreader: Judith Earnshaw
Indexer: Margaret de Boer
Cover designer: David Drummond